A Visit to the City in the Light

A Journey There.......and Back Again with a Message of Hope

Knight's Code Publishing™
5800 NE 34th St., #24, Vancouver, WA   98661

Printed in the United States of America
2nd Edition Printing done by Amazon KDP
First Edition Printing, 2021
First Edition Printing done at Gorham Printing
3718 Mahoney Dr.
Centralia, WA   98531
gorhamprinting.com

ISBN: 978-0-578-88292-5

16 15 14 13 12 11 10 9 8 7 6 5 4 3 2

This book is dedicated to the following people:

To Judi, my greatest joy and my most heart wrenching sorrow, who has always owned a piece of my heart, pain and all, even though she does not want it at all.........

To Rebekah, Mari, Dana, Madisyn, Lyndsay, Shirley, Cara, Melanie, Isla, Anna, Julia, Linda, Kate, Raffey, Josie, Miranda, Catalina, and Mercedes, my angelic muses, whose perfection inspire my heart and fill it with love, hope and joy, even though they do not know me at all.......

To Derreck, Randy, Jeff, and Dan, my brothers from other mothers, who always accepted me, flaws and all.......

To my dad, who taught me how to believe, have a strong faith, be a man, and always stand tall.......

To Clair and Rita, who have always stood beside me and guided me, even when my back was against the wall.......

And of course, to God.......for loving us all.

Table of Contents

Introduction

I remember playing a game with my friends called '*If I could solve a problem, what would I do?*'. It was one of the many *mind* games that we would play with each other. Others were '*If I were in charge of fixing that situation, what would I do?*', and '*If I could solve that issue, what would I do?*'. But my favorite, the one that I would bring up all the time, was always the larger topic of helping our world and our race, the human race, because there are so many things going on in our world that bothers me, including war, disease, hunger, and hate in all forms. We would laugh, tell each other the things that we would do if we had '*unlimited power and influence*', so to speak, and it really gave us the opportunity to speak our minds about what we would do to try and make things better for all of us. My friends would always laugh at me though and tell me that our race would never stop hating and fighting each other because it was too ingrained into our subconscious to hate others that we disagree with, and to fight each other for dominance. As a result, they would tell me that we would never come together to fix all the problems that we face as a race.

Then, one day, something life changing happened to me. You see, I had a heart attack, and where it happened was in a part of my heart called the Left Anterior Descending Artery, or the LAD. Doctors call this type of heart attack the '*Widow Maker*', because almost no one survives this type of heart attack when it happens. I remember the doctors telling me that they did not know how I survived because of how bad the heart attack was, and they told me that I must have had an angel on my shoulder. I have always felt that way, though, because there have been many times when something happened to me that should have killed me, but I always survived against all odds. There was the time that I was hit by a rockslide while driving my car across a mountain pass, and it should have sent me over a cliff that was next to the road, but it did not, and

1

A Visit to the City in the Light

I survived. There was the time that I hit a deer while driving across a mountain pass in a blizzard, and my car went off a 60-foot embankment into the snow. Even the road crew who found me that time said that they did not know why they decided to go down that road in the middle of the night, because they were not supposed to until the next day. They just said that something told them do it, and that was why they found me freezing to death in the snow. There have been many other times when something bad happened to me, but I always survived. As a result, I have always felt that I was meant to do something important, and that I was being saved because there was a plan for me, but I never realized just what that plan was until recently.

You see, the night that I had my heart attack, it was revealed to me. That day I had to go take care of some business downtown where I live. When I returned home, I started having severe chest pain, and I eventually lost consciousness. When I did, I had what I am convinced was a '*Near Death Experience*'. I remember that it felt like my entire body was being pulled apart one nerve ending at a time because the tingling was so intense, and then the next thing I knew I was floating into a bright light. Then, when the light dissipated, I found myself standing on what looked like a piece of solid ground, and I was staring at a gateway which led into what looked like a city in the background. The city was beautiful. It shined intensely, like every building was made of neon blues and whites and golds, and it glowed more brightly than anything that I have ever seen in my life. I remember feeling like I was extremely happy, and then I noticed that I did not feel any pain or sadness, which was strange for me because I am disabled, and I cannot walk without the help of a cane. As a matter of fact, I remember being able to stand on my own, without the cane, and I felt stronger than I have felt in a long time. Then I noticed that, standing in front of me, was a man who had a smile on his face, and the strange thing

2

about that was that I could actually *'feel'* his smile (I never knew that I could feel a smile, but I felt his, and it made me feel happy, warm, and content inside).   His hair was short, wavy, and white, and there was a glowing aura around him.   Then he took my hand, and when he did, I felt even more happy, happier than I have ever felt in my entire life.   He looked at me and said, *"Be careful, don't fall."*, in a very calm and soothing voice, and I believe that he said that because he saw that I was a little unsteady as I did not have my cane, and it surprised me that I did not need it to stand.   Then, after other things happened (which I will mention during this book and detail in the last chapter), I remember looking at him and saying, *"I'm not ready."*.   I do not know why I said that, but I have an idea (which I will explain in the last chapter).   This caused pause in the man, but then he smiled at me, and he said, *"I know you're not ready.   It's not your time."*.   Then he approached me and touched his finger on my forehead.   After he did, everything was enveloped in a blinding light again, and I found myself back on earth.

    After I came back, I felt a very strong urge to spread a message to the world, as if, when the man touched my forehead, he implanted the thought in my mind to do so.   A message of peace, love, and hope.   Intended to bring us all together as one, and more importantly, a plan to make it happen.   It is for that reason that I wrote this book.   A book about a plan of hope for our race, a plan to bring us all together in peace and love.   I call this plan the *"Philosophy of Acceptance"*, because it revolves around bringing us all together so that we can work together to solve the problems that our race faces today.   I was also *'instructed'* to write this book humbly, and that is why I am writing this anonymously, because this book, and the message of hope that it contains, should not be about me, it should be about the message.   I am not looking for fame, I am not looking for recognition.   As a matter of fact, the only reason that I am selling this book is because I was also instructed to take

3

A Visit to the City in the Light

the money from the book and use it to do many things, like helping those who need it by donating money to places like the many children's hospitals around the world, and to different charitable organizations that help people (like homeless shelters do), and of course, to different churches who truly do help those in need. Again, I am not looking for fame, and I am not looking to become rich, I am just looking to do what I was instructed to do by spreading the message that was given to me, and by using a lot of the money from this book to help people who need it during these troubled times while making sure that the focus of this book be about the message that it contains and not me.

To continue, though, it is that one message that I was given, the *"Philosophy of Acceptance"*, that I want to talk to you about. Am I a psychologist, a religious leader, or anyone else in authority? No, I am just an ordinary person who went through an extraordinary event (and, as is evident by the poor sentence structure, etc., I am not an author. As a matter of fact, this is the first and only book that I have ever written. In addition, I am not rich, which is why I could not even hire an editor to proofread this book. Therefore, I beg your forgiveness for the way that I wrote this, because I am sure that there will be those of you out there who will find many mistakes in my writing). I will say this. Among the other things that I am, I am a graduate of the school of life, or as some call it, the *'School of Hard Knocks'*. I feel that the most important degree that I have is the one that I did not go to school to get, because it is the one that I have in *'street smarts'*, with my classroom being the human race. Even though I am not rich, though, I have had the opportunity to travel all over the world, and the opportunity to help many people in my travels, both men and women, while they were in some of the worst and most intensely bad situations imaginable. I have done everything that I could do in order to help them not only solve their own personal problems, but how to handle what was going on in general as well.   I did this because I truly do have love for our race, the human race, and all my brothers and sisters in it, and every time I saw someone in need of help, I did what I could to help them, because that is what you do when you see someone in need of help, at least in my opinion.   You see, the message that I was given to spread, and how it can work to help all of us come together in peace and love and understanding, really applies to all of us no matter where we live, who we are, or what is going on in our lives, because coming together in peace, love, and compassion, is truly a universal practice that can work for all of us.   Again, it makes no difference where we live or who we are.   It can work, and I will explain how as this book goes on.

Again, even though I am not rich, I have been blessed in the fact that I have had the opportunity to travel all over the world.   I have been to many countries, and met many different people, and I have worked with them to make a better life for them, and to make a better person of myself.   I have met and worked with people whose lives were far different from mine.   On the contrary, I have met and worked with people who lives were just like mine.   People in rural areas to people in major cities.   People from all walks of life, and all ages of life.   People whose beliefs are far different from mine.   People whose beliefs are exactly the same as mine.   People who hated the way that I believe, both religiously and personally, as well as the way that I live my life, because they feel that their beliefs, and the way that they live their lives, are the way that everyone should believe and live their personal lives.   As such, they believe that the way I feel, and believe, and lead my life, makes me their *'enemy'* because they feel that my beliefs, and the way that I live my life, threatens them and the way that they want to live their lives.   They believe that my personal beliefs, and those who believe like me, stop them from controlling their world, and changing those around them to the way that they believe.   They spend their time convincing

5

others to change their lives, and the way that they feel, to the way that **they** feel and lead **their** lives, and they do this by using manipulation and other tactics. On the contrary, I have met many people who feel that my beliefs, and the way that I live my life, are exactly the way that the world should be, and they feel that I should join them in an effort to change the world to the way that we believe and lead our lives, through the use of manipulation and other tactics. But therein lies the problem, and it is not what the philosophy of *"Acceptance"* is all about.

I know that what I am doing may seem to be flying in the face of the message that I am trying to relay. I know that this may seem like an attempt to change the world, and the way that individual people live and believe, but that is not the case. What I am trying to do is just the opposite. What I hope to accomplish is to show that the message that I was given to spread to the world means that we do not try to change the world to the way that we believe individually and lead our own personal lives. Instead, the message dictates that we should accept each other no matter how differently we believe and live our lives by accepting the fact that we are all uniquely different, so that we can *'get along'* and stop the hate that exists between us. So that we can, for once in our history, achieve true peace. So that we can all work together to lead our race into the future. Then, by doing that, we can solve many of our race's problems for the benefit of all of us, instead of just fighting each other so much that we never accomplish anything good and world changing for our race. Now, I do recognize that we are accomplishing some things that benefit our race, but can you imagine just how much more we could accomplish for the human race if we stopped all the fighting and hate that currently exists in our world?

In addition, the philosophy of *"Acceptance"* dictates more

than just accepting other people for who they are and how they believe.   It also means that we accept responsibility for our own actions as well and accept the fact that nothing bad in our world (like all the fighting and hate that exists in our world) will change unless we accept the fact that it is our responsibility to change our attitudes towards each other.   So that we can fix our world's, and our race's, problems once and for all.   Once we do that, then we can do what we need to do in order to solve our world's problems, and we do that by effecting change in ourselves and our attitudes of conflict towards others just because of the way that they believe, or how they look, or how they love, or how they lead their lives.   I mean, it is our race, and our world, and if we do not do something to make our world, and our race, a better one, then it might not ever happen.   We need to accept the fact that we are responsible for change, not only individual change concerning our attitudes of hate towards others because they are different than us but change on a much more global scale where our attitudes towards each other are concerned.   Otherwise, if we just sit back and hope that the world changes all by itself and fixes the problems our race faces without our help (like finally fixing the problems of homelessness and world hunger), then it may never happen.

We all need to effect change through accepting responsibility for our actions towards others, so that we can finally work for a better tomorrow.   What is the change that I am talking about? Again, that's the change in our attitudes, the attitudes that cause us to say things like, *"They are my enemy because they believe differently than I do, and/or because they look differently than I do, and/or because they talk differently than I do, and/or because they live their lives differently than I do, and therefore, I need to cause them problems, and I will never accept them or work with them to solve our world's problems because they are different than me."*, and we can change those attitudes that keep us from coming together

A Visit to the City in the Light

by accepting everyone for who they are, and we can do that by practicing the philosophy of *"Acceptance"*. It is simple. It is called mutual respect, and without it, we will never come together in peace and love for the benefit of our race.

I would like to ask you a couple of questions, but first, let me tell you a story. Once upon a time there was a student (who we will call **"Student A"**), and this student was studying a language that was particularly difficult (learning languages have always caused me problems, as well as given those that I have met in different countries literally hours of amusement at my expense). It seems that the more he tried to learn the new language, the more problems he had with it. Then, one day, he saw another student (who we will call **"Student B"**) who was having no problem at all learning the language that he was trying to learn, but student "B", the one who was having no problems with the language, was the *'class pariah'*, so to speak. He was the one student that no one wanted to call their friend. Some thought that he was just *'too weird'*. Others thought that he was *'ugly'*, while others thought that he held religious beliefs that everyone thought was *'different'* than the way they believed. The bottom line was that no one liked student "B", or wanted to talk to him, or spend any time with him, because he was new and he just appeared out of nowhere while talking about things that seem to cause a lot of controversy, things that seemed strange to others. However, student "A" decided to overlook the way that all the other students perceived student "B" to be, and since he really wanted to learn the language that he was having such a problem with, he made the decision to go over and talk to him about learning the language. So, he went over and asked him how he was so easily able to learn the language, and he showed student "A" a method of learning that he used to study, one that he had never even thought of trying before. Student "A" decided to try it, as he had never thought of using such a method to study before, and suddenly, as if by magic, he was able to learn the language very easily. It caused him to get good grades in the language course, raising his GPA in the process. Then, as if it were an answer to a prayer, it caused more good things to happen, things like helping him to cruise through his other courses as well.

So, student "A" decided to help his friends in the same class by teaching them the studying method, and suddenly, the whole class started doing great, in a *'ripple effect'* sort of way. Now, student "A" realized that this same method of studying could apply to any subject matter that students are trying to learn, and wanting to help even more students, he and his friends in the language class started teaching this method of studying to students of other courses as well. Suddenly, as a result, more and more students started using it, and they started seeing their GPA's raise dramatically. Then, because of the excitement that this new method of studying caused, more and more students started sharing it with everyone at the school. Students that they had never seen talking to each other before (because of the different *'cliques'* that they belong to) started coming together and sharing the new way of learning, all because it was new, and exciting, and most importantly, because it actually worked! Then, as a result, everyone who used the studying method graduated with flying colors, and as a result of that, they all became great friends, no matter what *'clique'* they belonged to in the school, and they all went on to do great things in our world.

Some of them invented new and fantastic ways to create energy that did not damage our planet anymore, and the energy itself was plentiful and cheap. Others invented cures for some of the most devastating diseases in our world, like cancer. Even more went on to solve things like new methods of growing food that ended world hunger. Then, one day, they all went to a class reunion, and they reunited with all their former classmates, and they

9

realized that their graduating class did more to help our world than any other ever has. When they all sat down and started talking to each other they realized that, **because** they all took the time to talk to each other and work together back in school and share that new studying method, they were all able to learn even more things beyond school, and it was those things that helped them to achieve all the many world changing things that they accomplished. In the end, it helped all of them to change the world forever. Then they realized that the new method of studying also allowed them to come together in peace, friendship, and harmony, powered by a newfound love in each other, and in the world.

Then, tracing it back, they realized that it was all because of the studying method that student "B" used and taught to them.......the one student that no one wanted to talk to, or even be seen talking to, let alone being seen doing anything that he suggested. Because of that they all realized that the student who taught them the new studying method was a pretty cool person after all, because he ended up helping them all make the world a better place by helping them to come together and work together. To do great things for our race and our world, no matter what the *'clique'* was that they belonged to in school.

So, here are my questions for you. First, who would you want to be? The students who did not want anything to do with student "B"? The one student in the school that no one wanted to be around, all because the other students thought that he was *'weird'* because of who he was, and how he believed and lived his life? Or the student who said, *"I don't care what other students say or think. I will learn from him, because if he has a plan that works, then I want to learn it."*? Second, if you hear of a plan that could work to bring us all together in peace and love, would it matter where the plan came from, or who came up with it? I do not know about you, but I have always been like student "A", the one who said that he wanted to learn the plan, no matter who was teaching it or where it was coming from, so that I could help myself, and more importantly, help others.

This is why I believe that practicing the philosophy of *"Acceptance"* can change our world, if we all just give it a chance. It is the key to bringing our race together.   In addition, not only is it the message that was given to me to spread to the world when I was taken to the City of Light, but it is also a plan that has been around for an exceptionally long time, and was taught to our race, and our world, by an incredibly special student/teacher in our past.   You see, I firmly believe that we, the human race, are at the crossroads of the next step in our evolution, and that if something is not done to stop all the hate and conflict, then we will fail, and vanish into history, just like other *'advanced'* civilizations have done throughout time.   I say that because, as we all know, the human race's potential for the true and meaningful advancement that we could achieve is being stagnated and destroyed through hate and conflict, and this is happening because so many of us feel that everyone should believe and lead their lives exactly the way that we, as individuals, believe and lead our lives.   Many of us are quick to judge, but slow to accept and learn.   So many people have a tendency to hate anyone who believes differently, or leads their lives differently, or even looks differently, than they do, and it is tearing our race apart.   Let me explain.

There are those who say, *"I hate people who have a different skin color than me, so everyone should hate them, and discriminate against them."*, or *"I hate people who live alternative lifestyles, and we need to do something to them so that they start living and loving in the same traditional lifestyle as me."*, or *"I live my life by a certain alternative lifestyle, so everyone should change the way that*

11

they are, and live and love like me, even if they want to live and love with a lifestyle that is traditional, and they should practice the same lifestyle that I do, even if I have to use lies and manipulations to trick them into betraying their traditional beliefs.", or they say *"We were discriminated against for a long time, so now we should discriminate against those who discriminated against us in the past.*", or something things that are even worse. Even our children are getting into the act, and in the place where they should be the safest, our schools, by saying things like *"That kid does not participate in any sports, he just spends his time studying, so we need to pick on him, and make him feel inferior.*", or they say things like *"That kid is overweight (or is ugly, or dresses funny, etc.), and we are so much more beautiful and perfect than them that we need to make fun of them and make their lives miserable.*", or even worse, they say *"Wow, I have been picked on by bullies for years, and I can't take it anymore, so now I'm going to show them. I will make all of them pay.*" (it is this last one that absolutely breaks my heart the most, because no child should ever be bullied, and this instance can lead to very tragic results, but I will go into that in more detail later in this book). My point is this. Every day I see stories of people who are taking extreme, and in some cases, horrific steps to change others into believing and leading their lives to the way that they do, instead of accepting them for who they are, and how they want to live their lives. Terrorism, murder, discrimination, and of course, war. All the tools of those who believe that the only way that the world should be is the way that they want it to be. To change others, through force if necessary, so that everyone will live their lives and believe the way that they want them to, no matter what it takes.

The philosophy of *"Acceptance"* is not about that. *"Acceptance"* dictates that we stop trying to force other people to change into the people that we want them to be, and to accept them as they are, because once we do that, then we can all work together to solve many of the world's problems, instead of just fighting and hating each other. We may not agree with them, as a matter of fact, we may hate the way that they feel and live their lives. But if we, as members of the human race, ever want to try and find true peace for the betterment of our race, then we need to find a way to stop all the hatred, violence, and war, and I feel that the best way to do this is if we all accept everyone's differences so that we can finally work together to bring our race into the next step of our evolution. We can do that by working together to advance ourselves into a better, and much more productive, tomorrow by simply accepting each other, no matter what our differences are, instead of just hating each other like we have done for an exceptionally long time.

Now, am I saying that we should just accept some people no matter how they want to live their lives? Should we just accept people who want to, for example, run their countries in a way that causes their citizens to suffer, or just accept those who want to commit crimes without taking action to solve the problem of criminal activities? Should we just accept bullying because bullying is what the bullies want to do? How about the people who want to harbor extreme hate in their hearts, hate that escalates into violence through acts of terrorism. Should we just accept them? Of course not, and I will explain what I mean where these problems are concerned in later chapters. What I am saying is that, if we are to make positive changes in our world for the betterment of our race, then we need to accept that these problems exist, and why these problems exist, instead of ignoring them in the hope that someone else solves them, or worse yet, ignoring them thinking along the lines of *'out of sight, out of mind'* or *'It is not my problem because it is not happening to me or affecting me, so why should I care?'*. Also, we need to face these problems in order to solve them by accepting the fact that it is our responsibility to come together as a

13

race, and work together as one, so that we can solve these problems, because they will never be solved until we all join together to solve them. Again, we can come together to solve these problems.......but first we need to accept each other without blind hatred, and we can do that by practicing *"Acceptance"*.

One thing that has always bothered me is messages like *'Stop the Bullying!'* and *'Stop the Hate!'*, even though these are really great messages. Why do these messages bother me so much? Because most of the time that is all anyone ever says, *"Let's do it!"*, without ever giving anyone a game plan. No one has ever said *"Let's stop all the bullying, and here's how we are going to do it!"* or *"Let's stop all the hate, and here's how we are going to do it!"*. That is what the philosophy of *"Acceptance"* is all about, and after my life changing experience, it is why I wrote this book.......so that I could spread the message to our world that I was given to spread. The message that gives us all a great game plan to make these goals and messages a reality through utilizing the philosophy of *"Acceptance"*. *"Acceptance"* is an attitude that changes the way that we all think, so that rather than saying *"Yeah, the problem exists, but what can I do about it?"* we say *"Yeah, the problem exists, so let's all accept the fact that it is our responsibility to solve it now by coming together to solve it, and here's how we are going to do it!"*.

Imagine, just for a moment, a world where war no longer exists. Where we all work together to better not only ourselves, but the entire human race as well. A world where we all come together to protect our planet, working together to accomplish goals ranging from curtailing the depletion of our natural resources to protecting our planet from outside threats like asteroids (this may seem like something that is an exaggeration, but I will address this in a later chapter, because this threat is a lot closer than most people think).

A Journey There.......and Back Again with a Message of Hope

A world where we all have common goals, like the eradication of all diseases, so that a lot of them are no longer an instant death sentence, instead of only thinking that *'Well, these diseases aren't happening to me, so why should I worry about it?'*. A world where we all work together to branch out to the stars in order to solve problems like over population by bringing our race to other worlds so that we can colonize them in order to expand our race, and in doing so, possibly finding definitive answers to age old questions like *'Are we alone in the universe?'* (now, I do know that there are people who are already talking about taking us back to the moon, and then to Mars, but can you imagine just how much faster we could achieve this if we all worked together to make it happen?). Imagine a world where the quest for money is secondary to the quest to improve ourselves, and our race, in order to advance us into a better future.

Imagine a world where hunger no longer exists, because we all work together to help us have the basic necessities that we need, like food, and even shelter. Imagine a world where fear no longer exists, from major fears like the fear of war to fears that are closer to home like *'Will I be able to feed and shelter my family tonight?'* because we, as members of the human race, address these fears together in order to solve them by accepting the responsibility to come together in order to work together to solve them as an entire race. Imagine a world where world leaders are truly *'World Leaders'*, as in, leaders of the human race, instead of leaders of individual countries who try and fight each other for dominance through intimidation, violence, and war (and again, I will discuss what I mean when I say this in a later chapter, as I am not proposing a world dictatorship when I say this. Freedom is too important, especially where this endeavor will be concerned, and no one is free in a dictatorship. I believe that *'World Leaders'* should represent us, and therefore, be placed in their leadership positions by us

15

through the use of elections, and if they don't represent us the way that we want them to, then we should be able to replace them with leaders who do represent us the way that we want them to).

Imagine a world where we all work together to improve ourselves, to make a better future for all of us, instead of working against each other because of our irrational hatred towards each other. Imagine, just for a moment, a world where people, no matter how they live their lives, all stand side by side and say, *"Yes, I may not agree with you, and I may even hate you because of who you are and the way that you believe and live your life, but I will not do anything to cause you harm through my actions or my words. Instead, I will accept you as a fellow member of our race, and I will work side by side with you, because it is time that we all worked together to help our race advance into a better future for all of us."*. **That** is what the philosophy of *"Acceptance"* is all about. Bringing us all together so that we **can** take that next step into the future by working together to better our race as a whole.

The change in our attitudes will not be easy, and it will definitely not happen overnight. We, as members of the human race, have had it ingrained into our sub-consciousness to only think about ourselves at times. To do whatever it takes to promote our own agendas, so that we can achieve our own goals as individuals, without consideration of how it affects those around us, or the rest of the human race. We tell ourselves that we care about others, and in some ways we do, but each and every one of us have been taught to *'take care of number one'*, so to speak, and in doing so we have lost track of how our actions affect those around us. I will talk about this in more detail in a later chapter. I will also talk about how the message that I was given to spread to the world, the message of *"Acceptance"*, can be used not only in our own personal lives, but in our dealings with others, and how it can be used to achieve our goals for the betterment of everyone in the human race. Doing this, though, will be a tough process, because there will be those who do not want universal *"Acceptance"*, mainly because it will cause them, in their eyes, to lose everything from their perceived positions of power to being able to manipulate and control those around them, and their individual worlds. In some cases, they will be willing to fight to keep their ability to control everything and everyone around them, and they may even try and go as far as to discredit this philosophy by calling it things like a *'pipe dream'* for example. Again, though, I will talk more about this in later chapters as well.

    "Acceptance", if we truly place it into practice to better our race and our world, will require all of us to change the way that we think about each other, so that rather than hating each other, we will learn how to accept each other for who we are, how we believe, and how we want to live our individual lives. As you will see, though, if we all put *"Acceptance"* into practice, then the change will not be as big as one might think, at least not for all of us. It will require those with power (like the rulers of countries who don't allow their citizens to have things like the freedom that is enjoyed in countries like America, for example) to change their way of thinking as well, but if we are to evolve, and change our race in order to achieve a better and more hopeful tomorrow, then that change needs to happen, because no one should ever live in fear just because of where they live, or who is in charge. We should be able to look up to our leaders and admire them for what they do for us, instead of fearing what they might do to us, which again, I will discuss in more detail in a later chapter.

    As a fan of writings that consider possible ways that we can advance into the future, I have always asked myself, *"Why does it have to be Science Fiction? Why can't we make the worlds where these stories take place Science Fact?"*.   Have you ever noticed that, in a lot of the worlds where Science Fiction stories take place, everyone works together in order to operate as one race, especially when the race in question is the human race?   How they do this to better our race in order to make a better world for all of us?   To take it one step further, have you ever noticed how even races from other worlds work together with our race in these stories to achieve common goals?   Why can't we do that?   Seriously, what is stopping us?   For example, it has been stated in a few of these series that we, the human race, had stopped trying to do things just to satisfy our own selfish needs, and that we are now working together to advance our race into a better tomorrow for all of us.   Again, why can't we do that?   Why does it have to be fiction?   Why can't it be fact?   If I had to state one thing that could make this cooperation happen, it would be the message that I am trying to spread to everyone, because once we accept each other, instead of trying to fight each other, then we can work together to bring our race into a better tomorrow, and a better future for all of us.

One thing is for certain.......you will probably get tired of hearing the word *"Acceptance"* in all its forms while reading this book, but it needs to be heard repeatedly if we are ever going to put it into practice.   You see, it is my hope that, after reading this book, you will ask yourself questions like *'What can I do to be more accepting of myself by accepting responsibility for my own actions, as well as more accepting of those around me in order to help make our race, and our world, a better place to live through peace, love, and cooperation?'* and *'What more can I do to accept responsibility for making myself, and the world in which we live, better?'*, because it is when we start asking ourselves questions like this that *"Acceptance"* truly starts taking effect.   In addition, I strongly feel that once *"Acceptance"* starts taking effect, we will all see our world in a new light, and we will start seeing positive changes, for not only ourselves, but for our race as a whole.

Now, again, this will take time. *"Acceptance"*, if we all truly start practicing this philosophy to stop all the hatred and problems that we face, is just the beginning. The first *'baby steps'* of a much longer journey. But like I have said many times, change for the betterment of our race has to start somewhere, and I truly feel that this philosophy is a great starting point if we are to better our race, and save us from failing and fading into history like so many other civilizations in the past have failed and vanished into time due to rampant hatred and violence.

It is our race. It is our responsibility. If we are to truly advance into a better, and more productive and secure, tomorrow, then we need to be the ones who take responsibility for making that change a reality. If we do not do it, then who will? After all, if we want a better tomorrow, then we need to accept the responsibility to make it happen, because it will not happen on its own.

All I ask from you, the reader, is a couple of things. First, please read this entire book from cover to cover before you make any judgments about the contents, or about the philosophy of *"Acceptance"*. If you do this for me, then I am sure that you will understand why I am asking you do to this, and I honestly believe that you will understand the importance of making the philosophy of *"Acceptance"* a reality for the benefit of our race, the human race. Second, if you know who I am, then please, keep that information to yourself. Again, I am trying to do what I was instructed to do by writing this book humbly. I am not doing it for the fame, or the recognition. I am doing it in order to do what I was instructed to do when I went to the City of Light. I am doing it in order to try and help our world, and our race, come together for the betterment of everyone by spreading the message that I was given, and if people publicize who I am, then the focus of this book may shift from the message of *"Acceptance"* to me, and I do not want that to happen. Let the message be the important thing, not me. Who I am does not matter.......the message contained in this book does.

Speaking of the message, what I want to do at this point is try and illustrate just how the message that I was given can help all of us, and be utilized by all of us, in all aspects of our lives in order to help us in ways that may not be apparent at first glance but will become apparent as you read further. We all have areas in our lives that are universal situations we all have to deal with, things that affect us on a daily basis. What I want to try and do from this point on is to try and show just how we can use *"Acceptance"* to make these areas and situations in our lives not only much easier to deal with, but actually make these areas go better for everyone so that we can all have better lives through the practice of *"Acceptance"*. In addition, I will be doing a couple of other things in this book. The first is that I want to share some of my experiences while on the other side. I will do that by sharing some of the things that were told to me at the start of each chapter so that you can see why I feel that I was told these things while I was there, and how those things apply to different areas of our lives where *"Acceptance"* is concerned (I will detail the entire journey, and everyone that I saw and what they said to me, at the end of this book). Also, there are some quotes from the people that I saw on the other side where they actually say my name. In those instances, I will be censoring my name from the quote. Like I said before, the reason that I am going to do this is because I was instructed to write this book humbly, and that is why I wrote this book anonymously under a pen name. Therefore, if my name is included in the quotes, then I will be identified (even though it is just my first name). That is why I am censoring it, so that I will keep my word, and not identify myself.

A Journey There.......and Back Again with a Message of Hope

Second, I will be sharing my personal suggestions as well, concerning things that I see that are issues to a lot of people and how they could be solved by all of us practicing *"Acceptance"*. I will be doing this because that is what *"Acceptance"* is all about. Bringing us all together to share ideas on how to fix the problems that we face, and then all of us working together to solve these issues through mutual respect for everyone's opinions, ideas, wants and desires. Therefore, concerning my opinions, there will be things that you might agree with in this book, and conversely, there will be things that you may not agree with. However, again, this is a major part of what the philosophy of *"Acceptance"* is all about. Bringing everyone together so that we can start the conversation by talking to each other, sharing ideas, and working together to come up with ideas to solve the problems that we face as a race without hate stopping us, like it has for far too long.

We need to start somewhere to bring us all together without hate stopping us. We need to start somehow to solve all of our race's problems by everyone working together to do it. It is my hope that, once you finish reading this book, you will agree that the best way to start healing our race, and start advancing us into a more productive, and better, tomorrow, is by finding a way for everyone to work together, so that we can build a better tomorrow. It is my hope that, after reading this book, you will agree that the message that I was given to share with the world, the philosophy of *"Acceptance"*, is a great place to start, and a great plan to bring us all together in peace, love, and cooperation for all time.

21

Chapter One
Acceptance and You

"I'm proud of you kid.   You done good." - My Dad, standing
outside of the City.

There is an old saying that goes *'The journey of a thousand miles begins with a single step'* (Chinese Proverb - ascribed to Lao Tzu and Confucius).   That is why I would like to start with this topic, because how can we practice the philosophy of *"Acceptance"* with others if we cannot accept ourselves, and who we are.   This encompasses a whole lot more than just accepting who we are and the way we act.   What it truly encompasses is accepting the fact that we need to accept responsibility for ourselves, and our actions, during our lifetime.   After all, how can we accept the responsibility for bringing our race and world together if we cannot even accept ourselves by accepting responsibility for who we are, the way that we act, and the way that we conduct ourselves?   Most importantly, though, it also encompasses the way that we think and feel about ourselves, which is going to be important as we go through our lives.

I think that this is why my dad said this to me when I was on the other side and we talked outside of the gates to the city.   He always told me that it was important to be a good person, and he would always be sure to tell me that he was proud of me when I would show him my maturity as I was growing up, like when I took responsibility for myself and my actions.   Things like when I got my first job (at 9 years old), and when I would do things to help other people.   The bottom line is this.   I feel that this chapter not only addresses what my dad was saying to me, but more importantly, addresses how we can use *"Acceptance"* to make ourselves a better person and a more contributing member of our race.

I think that the best way to start is by asking ourselves a few questions. Who am I? How does the world see me? What are my flaws (which is usually the toughest question of all)? What are my weaknesses (again, another tough one, because we sometimes let our egos stop us from recognizing the fact that we have weaknesses)? What are my strengths? How can I make myself a better person? What can I do to improve myself in order to be a more productive member of the human race? I think that, if we are to truly start accepting others, and accepting the responsibility for taking care of our race and our world, then we need to learn how to accept ourselves.......and that starts with learning who we are by admitting to ourselves who we truly are. We do that by acknowledging and accepting both our strengths and weaknesses, so that we can recognize who we are, and take responsibility for ourselves, good and bad. That starts with what I call a *"Personal Life Assessment"*.

The first step in this is to figure out who we are right now. I usually tell people to take out a piece of paper and a pen, and then write down everything that they know about themselves. This can be very hard and can take some time. We want the world to see us as a good person, someone to be admired, someone that other people both want to know, and be in their lives, and because we feel that way, we sometimes hide our true selves in order to pretend that we are someone we may not be. I feel, though, that it is especially important that we be brutally honest with ourselves, because if we aren't, then the only person that we are fooling is ourselves. We may think that we hide our problems well, however, others can see more than you think.

So, let's start with a simple exercise. Take out a piece of paper and a pencil and make a list of the following things about yourself.

1) **What are my strengths?** Now, it is important that we be completely honest when asking ourselves this question. For example, we may feel that one of our strengths is that we are a totally honest person, however, we may forget that we were not honest in a certain situation. This could be something like going to a nightclub and telling someone that we are interested in romantically that we work a great job (when we know that we are unemployed) in an attempt to impress someone that we are interested in by lying to them. We might lie on a job application in order to try and impress a future boss, because we want the job very badly. So, remember, be completely honest when writing this list. Another strength could be how we live our lives and treat our bodies. Do we work out every day? Do we eat healthy? Do we try and better ourselves through education (Now, even though I will go into more detail about education in a later chapter, allow me to say here that I firmly believe that education should made as available as possible to everyone, especially to those who have high intelligence levels, by making it as cheap as possible. However, that does not mean that we need to go to school to become more educated. Libraries used to be a great place to educate ourselves, but now that we have access to options and opportunities like the internet, we can take education into our own hands even more, and open our world to more learning than we ever thought possible. I will talk more about this in a later chapter). We could also tell ourselves that we are very loyal and loving to our romantic partner, but then we find ourselves *'checking out'* other people, and even being flirtatious in social situations, and while this may be innocent, this could still be very hurtful to the person who we are romantically involved with (I will discuss this more in a later chapter as well).

25

A Visit to the City in the Light

This is why it is especially important that we be completely honest with ourselves when making this list, because we may feel that we have a lot of strengths, when in reality, we have been lying about this, both to others and to ourselves.   After all, we need to be honest with ourselves, and accept who we truly are, before we can accept others and the way that they believe and live their lives.

2)   <u>What are my weaknesses?</u>   This will probably be the hardest part of making this personal assessment.   No one wants to admit that they have weaknesses, because we do not want others to think badly about us, and our own egos may make us want to ignore any weaknesses.   However, in order to accept ourselves, and improve ourselves, we first need to know what our weaknesses are so that we can turn our weaknesses into strengths.   They could include many things.   We may have addictions to things that harm our health, like drugs, cigarettes, or even eating too many snacks for that matter, because they ultimately harm our own health, and in some cases, they harm those around us.   We may be addicted to gambling, which is a very common addiction, more common that people think.   How educated are we?   We may want others to think that we are experts in certain areas, like when it comes to our job, or history, or math, or astronomy, or cooking, or any one of a number of other areas, when in reality, we are faking it in order to impress others.   I have always told people that, if they want to impress me with their knowledge, then all they have to do is be honest with me about what they know, and most importantly, what they don't know. I will always have more respect for those who tell me that they are not an expert in certain areas, but that they want to learn more so that they can be more knowledgeable about the world around them. Definitely more respect than I have for someone who just fakes like they know everything, or who goes through life as a *'know it all'* who takes pride in acting like they know more than everyone else when, in reality, they don't know that much at all.   I have often said that there is no such thing as a dumb question because every question that someone asks me shows me that who I am speaking to is an honest person, and that while they recognize that they may not be knowledgeable about everything, they are willing to learn in order to grow as a person.   That means more to me than anyone who walks through life pretending to know everything.   Another question to ask ourselves is this.......are we lazy, or unmotivated? Would we rather go through life being a *'couch potato'*, or would we rather lead our life by actually going out and being around others to not only solve problems and achieve goals, but even to just play, which I feel is especially important in order to keep a healthy balance in our lives.   I always say that it is important to be serious when it is time to be serious, but it is also important to make sure that we reserve time for play, because play is one of the best gifts that we can give ourselves to live a more stress free and healthy life, both physically and mentally (and it can really help us where our relationships with others, especially our loved ones, are concerned).

3)   What am I doing to improve myself?   Here is where we can make a huge step in putting *"Acceptance"* into practice in our own lives by being honest with ourselves and truly asking ourselves *"What am I doing to make myself a better person?"*.   It could be things like accepting the fact that we have problems in our lives, like addictions, and then taking steps to improve ourselves by dealing with those addictions in order to make sure that we conquer them and remove them from our lives.   It could be something like taking steps to educate ourselves further.   We are the only ones who are stopping ourselves from learning, especially today when we have options like the internet.   Whenever I decide that I want to learn something, I either go to an expert (or anyone who truly has more experience with what I want to learn), or I go to a school or college (if I can afford it), or I go to the internet.   Now, anything that you learn while on the internet should be taken with a grain of salt, unless you are learning it from a reputable source, because there are sites that allow anyone to post anything about a certain subject, and therefore (as one of my friends told me) I could be learning from a *'maniac'*, and the way to make sure that what you are learning is true is to go to multiple reputable websites to compare what you are learning, so that you get a much fuller, as well as verifiable, picture of the subject that you are studying.   No matter what we are doing to improve ourselves, though, we should list the things that we are trying to do here, even if it is just a simple act that we normally don't do (like showing your partner that you truly do care about their happiness by doing something like working an 8 hour shift and then, even though you are tired, coming home and saying something to the effect of *'Hey, you cooked a great dinner, so let me help by doing the dishes.'*, or by doing something to help a stranger like saying something like *'Hey, I see you having a problem with getting that off of a shelf, so can I get that for you?'* or anything else that shows that we care about others.   These may not seem like big things when talking about improving ourselves, but you would be amazed at the effect that they can have on others, and especially on your romantic partner, because it does show them that you truly do care about them and their happiness).

4)   What more can I do to accept responsibility for my actions, including my strengths and my weaknesses, so that I can be a more productive member of the human race?   It is quite common to pat ourselves on the back when we do something that is good, or that helps us and others, or gives us a good outcome in our lives or the lives of others.   On the other hand, it is common for us to blame other people when we are talking about accepting responsibility for our actions that affect us, or others, negatively.   I feel that truly taking responsibility for ourselves, and our actions, is key to practicing the philosophy of *"Acceptance"* and is at the very heart of putting it into practice.   Here is a good example of what I am talking about when I say *'accepting responsibility for our actions'*. I have seen people, especially those who find themselves in a serious romantic relationship while they are still very young and unprepared for the responsibilities of such a relationship, who want to blame their partner when things start going wrong with the relationship. I remember talking to a very young couple (both of them were 19 years old) who were dealing with the fact that their relationship was falling apart around them. The young man was saying that he felt *'trapped'*, and that all he wanted to do was hang out with his friends like he could when he was still single and living with his parents. The young woman was saying that she wanted to go to college and that she had sacrificed her education in order to be with the young man. The saddest part of this tragedy? They already had a child together.

Now, I will go into this topic further in a later chapter, but I wanted to mention it here just briefly for a reason, and that reason is this. At no time did they stop to recognize the fact that they both needed to accept the responsibility of admitting that they were really too young and unprepared for such a commitment, and if they had only taken the time to just enjoy their love and taken the time to think about what they were doing before jumping into a serious situation, like moving in together, or having a child, then they might still be together, deeply in love, without all of the problems that they were facing at such a young age. Problems like having their love fall apart around them. Problems that had developed because they had moved in together before they were ready to, because let's face facts, in the majority of the cases that I have seen, 19 is incredibly young to be thinking about getting married, moving in together, or anything else serious. I have seen, in more than one instance, where two people who were too young to be serious about a relationship get into one, and then, when reality hits them in the face, they panic, and it ends up destroying a love that could have lasted a lifetime.   If they had only taken the time to let their love grow without taking huge leaps into the permanency and commitment that is required of a couple who make long term commitments, like moving in together or having a child, then their love might have been something that could have made them happy forever.   Also, like I said previously, it was even worse because they already had a child together, and it breaks my heart when I see a child who is born into a broken home.   Does that mean that a child cannot have two parents who love them, and get along, just because they are no longer together as partners?   Absolutely not, because in some instances, it is better for the child to have two parents who love them while having a friendly relationship, but are apart and even with other partners, than two parents who are together, but do not love each other, and as a result, they fight constantly around the child.   This fighting usually causes the parents of the child to not do a very good job of teaching their child about how a loving relationship should look like, which in turn can cause their child to have problems in their relationships later in life, because they did not have the best example to learn from when they were growing up.

   The point that I am trying to make is this.   Young people should take the time to think about what they are doing before they *'do it'*, so to speak, because if they did, then they would realize that it is much better to take their time and think about what they are doing before they *'do it'* in order to make sure that they are ready for the responsibility of loving someone for a lifetime, and the responsibility of raising a child.   If they did that, and they waited and took precautions (like birth control, or even practicing abstinence) until they were ready, and they actually took the time to let their love grow into something more permanent over time, then in a lot of instances, not only would their child have two parents who loved each other and were ready to commit to each other for a lifetime, but their child would also have two parents who were together and with them 24/7 during their entire childhood, which is what every child deserves. They would have two parents who would be able to show them, through example, what a loving, permanent relationship truly looks like, setting the example so that their child would have a basis to go by for when they grow up and look for a love that lasts a lifetime. I was blessed in the fact that, while I did grow up in an extremely poor household (I had my first job when I was 9 years old - not much of a childhood, but I definitely learned, at an early age, all about responsibility, and that nothing genuinely good in life ever comes easy), I did have both my parents with me during my entire childhood. Parents who loved each other for that entire time (over 50 years before my dad passed away), and it was because they had taken the time, before they were married, to truly prepare themselves for the big step of marriage by accepting the responsibility to get to know each other before they made the long-term commitment of getting married.

This is why I always try and advise young people to think *'7 moves ahead'* (as if they were playing chess) when planning their lives, because it can cause their lives to be so much better when they accept the responsibility to take the time to think about what they are planning to do before they do it, rather than just jumping into a serious situation (like marriage and even just moving in together) without thinking about the possible consequences of their actions beforehand. This also includes thinking about how they share intimacy, because which is more important to you? A few seconds of pleasure (without taking precautions like a condom) or taking the time to build a great loving relationship with the person you love by making sure that both them, and you for that matter, are truly ready for the serious commitment that is required when making a permanent commitment to another person, and/or raising a child together. You see, once you make a permanent commitment to

31

someone (like getting married and/or having a child together), then the days of having fun like a single person, and partying, and running around with your friends, end (unless you are one of those people who are so selfish and self-centered that you truly do not care about anyone but yourself, and therefore, you do not care what happens to the person you had a child with, or your child for that matter. Even if you are one of these people, though, you will still be facing the very real court issue of child support, so your life will still be changed).

Raising a child is a real responsibility, whether you have your child living with you 24/7 or you are responsible for supporting your child financially. It can, and will, change your life forever. Children deserve to have parents who are deeply committed to each other, and who genuinely love each other, if for no other reason than to learn from their parents what a truly loving and permanent relationship should look like. This is just one instance where accepting the responsibility for our actions can help us to lead a happier life, but there are many more, and I am sure that you will think of many other instances while you are asking yourself this question.

Another example of recognizing and accepting our weaknesses would be when people come up with excuses, sort of emotional crutches, for their actions versus actually accepting responsibility for them. This can demonstrate itself in many ways. One way is when we tell ourselves that we drink to excess because we do not like what we do for a living. Another would be to say that we are drinking because we are unhappy with our romantic partner, or worst of all, because we are depressed about a lost love, like when a partner leaves us, or someone passes away that we loved. Still another could be that we saw one of our parents drink too much and, as a result, we came from a broken or abusive home.

The bottom line here, though, is that we would rather blame someone else, or something else, for our problems and addictions, and it gives us an excuse to continue doing something that is not only harming ourselves, but those around us who care about us as well.   We can change our bad habits, no matter what they are, but first we need to accept the fact that we have these bad habits and accept the fact that they are harming us.   Then we need to accept the fact that it is truly our responsibility to change what we are doing in order to help ourselves overcome them in order to thrive.   I am not saying that it will be an easy thing to do in order to achieve this, nothing really good in our lives ever comes easy.   However, if we just take that first step of truly admitting to ourselves that we have a problem in order to change our lives for the better, so that we can defeat the things that are harming us, then we can beat anything. The human spirit is a powerful ally, especially where beating addictions is concerned.   We just need to take that first step where we admit to ourselves that we have a problem.   Then we need to accept the responsibility to get help overcoming the problem that we have in order to beat it, because once we accept the fact that we will, in a lot of cases, need help to beat an addiction, then we have an excellent chance of beating the problem.   Then, once we beat it, it will open up a whole new, and better, world for us.   One that we probably never thought would be possible for us to have.

5)   What more can I do to help others?   While this is important, this is usually not a very long topic to cover in a personal life assessment, because most of us are so wrapped up in our own personal lives and relationships that we sometimes do not do much to help others until we take the time to honestly think about if we could do more.   I do think that it is important, though, to at least start thinking about what we could do to help others more, especially where implementing the philosophy of *"Acceptance"* is concerned.   We may be doing some things, from being there for someone when they need us, to volunteering at a hospital, and everything in-between, but I am sure that we could do more if we think about it. I will say this. Once we accept responsibility for our actions, our problems, and our lives, then we will realize that we are in more control of our lives, and it could open up our lives by giving us more time to help others. Start small, even if it is just offering someone help who needs it, like getting an item off a shelf at a store for someone who has their hands full, especially with a child, or who is disabled. Lots of times people will decline the offer, but it is important to offer help anyway, especially if we are ever going to come together as a race, because compassion for our fellow human beings is going to be **especially important** in this endeavor. On the other hand, though, it is important for us to realize that it is ok to accept help from someone when **we** may need it. It is not a weakness to need help and accept it, because we all need it at one time or another. Now, I am not saying that we should invite a total stranger into our homes to help us, oh say, carry in an item, because we also need to accept the fact that, in today's world, there are a lot of really bad people out there who want to cause us harm, and it is that fact that causes me even more sadness.

What I am trying to say is that, in a lot of cases, it is ok to accept help from someone from time to time. I try and offer help to others whenever I can. I call it committing a *'Random Act of Kindness'*, and it is something that I personally try to do on a daily basis. Just the other day I saw a person who was having trouble with pumping their own gas because they were elderly, and they were having trouble getting the nozzle into their vehicle. So, I asked them if I could help. The reason that they felt ok about me helping them is because I have been committing random acts of kindness in my area for a long time now, and I am known in my town for doing things like this, and it was in a public area, with people around us. In addition, I started the conversation with me saying *"Hi, my name is _____."*, and this made them feel comfortable.   It is a sad time we live in, because usually people are very wary about accepting help from others.   Unfortunately, many people in today's world are afraid that they could be receiving help from a bad person who wants to cause them harm, but I still offer anyway.   If the person that I am offering my help to says that they do not want my help, then I tell them *"Ok, have a great day!"*, and then I go about my way.   I do not try and push the issue, because to me, when someone does try to push the issue, it raises a red flag about the intentions of the person offering the help, because then it stops being about helping the other person and it becomes more about you gaining something from helping them, and helping someone else should be about helping them, not you.   I want to show people that what is important to me is helping others, and not trying to force anyone to accept my help, because I do not have a hidden agenda, I just have a kind heart.   You would be amazed, though, that if you lead your life with a kind heart, just how quickly people recognize that you are not a bad person, and then how willing they will be to accept your help in the future.

Now, I am sure that there are many other things that we could ask in order to learn more about ourselves, but for now, I think that what we have asked so far is plenty to get us started, and we could always broach those other things later as we advance into putting *"Acceptance"* into practice in our lives.

Now that we are getting to know ourselves better, I want to suggest the following exercise.   Start each day by reciting the following mantra, which I call the ***"Rules of Acceptance"***.   These are rules that I try to live by every day, and I feel that these rules, or guidelines, encompass the true meaning of *"Acceptance"*, and that they are a mantra to help us be a better person, and in turn, a better and more contributing member of our race.   They are as follows:

35

A Visit to the City in the Light

Rule #1 - I **will** accept myself, including my strengths and weaknesses, and I will try to do something, every day, to improve my strengths by working on them, and to correct my weaknesses by accepting the fact that I have weaknesses, and then by getting help to deal with them if I need help to overcome them.

Rule #2 - I **will** accept responsibility for my actions, and the way that I lead my life.

Rule #3 - I **will** be more accepting of others, to include the way that they believe and want to live their lives, in order to work together so that we might bring our race together in peace, compassion, and love, as long as their actions do not cause harm to anyone else, and their beliefs do not believe in causing harm to anyone else.

Rule #4 - I **will** try, every day, to do something to help someone, or at least to offer help to someone, even if it is just with a small thing.

Rule #5 - I **will** try, every day, to learn something new.

Rule #6 - I **will** try to think of one thing that I can do or think of one plan that I could come up with, that would change our world for the better, or that would fix a problem that exists in our world today, no matter how small that thing is.

Rule #7 - If I need help in any area of my life, then I **will** seek out and accept that help, without ever thinking that it makes me a weak person because I needed the help, and I **will not** let my ego get in the way.

I know that there are many more things that could be added to this list, but I feel that this short list of general rules is a great starting point where *"Acceptance"* is concerned. If you think of more things to add, then by all means, add them, because that is a huge part of what *"Acceptance"* is all about. All of us taking responsibility for making *"Acceptance"* work in order to bring our world, and our race together in peace, compassion, and love. Make sure that you do more than just read these and then forget about them. Make them visible to yourself so that you can see them every day. I hang a copy of these on both my refrigerator, and on my bathroom mirror, so that I can see them every day. In addition, during the day, I read them each time I see them. By doing this I am reinforcing them in my mind, and after a while, I do not even need to think about them, because they are stuck in my mind. Then, as I go about my day, I try and see where I can apply them in everyday situations.

Like when I go to the grocery store. If I see someone that could use my help, then I offer it. When I meet someone new, I see if I could talk to them, to see if they would like a new friend, and by doing so, finding out how they feel and believe (without judging them for how they believe and lead their lives, because not judging others is going to be particularly important if we are ever going to come together as a race). You would be absolutely amazed at how many people feel totally alone in today's world, and who would love to have a new friend, or just someone to talk to every once in a while. One of my favorite places to do this is at a nursing home. There are so many wonderful people in retirement homes who feel all alone because not that many people come to visit them. Maybe their children are too busy with their own lives, or maybe they never had any children, but the bottom line is this. Nothing makes a person feel sadder, or more alone, than feeling like no one cares about them anymore, and nothing makes them feel better than learning that someone cares enough to actually come to visit them, even if it is a stranger. Many of these people have amazing stories to tell as well, and a whole lifetime of wisdom to share.

A Visit to the City in the Light

Another place to go where a little TLC goes a long way is at any of the children's hospitals that exist, where our littlest wonders are fighting for the life that they have yet to live, all because they are fighting deadly illnesses. Just remember one more thing, though. Never try and force yourself into someone's life or force your help where it is not wanted at the time. The best way to help somewhere like a hospital or a retirement home, whether it is for senior citizens or children, is to report to the welcome desk, and ask if it is ok to be there and either volunteer or just visit people who are there, because I am sure that, if you do it this way, then they will be able to guide you to where you could do the most good, and to the right people to visit with. The people who need your random act of kindness the most. Also, if you do this, then cooperate with them if they ask you about your background, credentials, etc. (they should do this), because they are not trying to make things hard on you, they are making sure that you are ok, and not someone who is there to cause anyone harm, especially to a child. You would want to make sure that everyone around your loved one, like your child, was ok, right? Then show them the same respect by being completely honest and cooperative with them when they want to check you out before you are allowed to volunteer at the hospital or visit with anyone who is in a facility like this. Cooperating with them is just the right thing to do, especially if you are volunteering your time because of your kind heart, and not because you have a hidden agenda.

Let us talk about another area on the list that we can cover during our day, and that is taking further responsibility for our actions to make our personal lives, and more specifically our health, better. I want to break these down so that we can approach them individually. That way we can take them on one step at a time. Now, I am sure that there are other things that could be added to this list, and if you can think of other things to add, then do it, because each of our lives is different, and by adding things that are personal to your life you are taking an important step in recognizing how you, as an individual, can improve your life.

1) Accepting responsibility for what we eat.   This is an area where each and every one of us is different.   We all have our favorite foods, and we may already be eating healthy, but if you are like me (or as I refer to myself, the original *'junk food junkie'*), then this is a great starting point, because when we eat healthy, it makes us feel better, and that alone can help us in other areas like dealing with addictions and/or just being emotionally happy with our lives in general.   It starts with what we eat, and how we get our food. For example, when I go shopping, I try and get things that are going to be healthy for me, instead of just getting snacks and junk food. Now, I am not saying that I am better than anyone else, because I have my weaknesses, but I accept them for what they are, and I accept responsibility for them, which in turn helps me to accept responsibility for correcting them whenever I can.   Though it is a struggle for me at times, I do try and do what's right for my body, even if it drives me nuts (and, believe me, it does, especially when burgers and fries come into the conversation), and what we do to help our bodies now will pay huge dividends in the future (the whole *'golden years'* thing).   In addition, there are situations where junk food is the order of the day, like during major sporting events, or during the holidays, when overeating is almost expected.   But when I can, I do try and eat healthy, if for no other reason than to set the example when I am around children, and to try and make sure that I am still around in the future.   Now, I am not saying that we should never indulge ourselves, like eating chocolate during the holidays or on Valentine's Day.   After all, chocolate can be very therapeutic because, as some things do, it releases Endorphins into our system, which can help our emotional selves in a noticeably big way.   They make us happy, and happiness is very key when it comes to taking care of our emotional selves (not to mention the fact that, if you are in a romantic relationship, it can make your loved one incredibly happy as well if they receive a surprise gift of chocolate, which is one way to take responsibility for making sure that our romantic relationships are better and thriving as well).

So, one thing that I would like to suggest is that you take the time to educate yourself on what healthy foods you might like to try in order to lead a healthier life.   One thing that I did was to talk to my doctor (now, I understand that, in today's world, not everyone has a doctor, which makes me extremely sad.   I really feel that proper medical care should be made as available as possible to everyone by making it as cheap as possible for everyone, especially children, and that this is something that we need to fix after we all come together as a race.   I, myself, went many years without having proper medical care, and it cost me dearly, but if you do have a doctor that you can go to for this type of advice, then this is one thing that you can do to really help yourself in the future).   She helped me by recommending foods that could help me lead a more healthy and productive life (as what we eat really can help us in areas such as having more energy to do the things that we want to do).   Another thing we could do is online research on reputable web sites (again, try and avoid the *'anyone can post here'* websites for important research, because you do not want to be accepting advice on what to eat from the maniac that I mentioned earlier).   However, wherever you decide to go, the most important thing is that you are taking the time to do the research, because just by taking that step, you are already on your way to accepting responsibility for how you eat and accepting personal responsibility for your health is the important thing.

2)   Accepting responsibility for how we sleep.   This is another area where we can really help ourselves.   I used to be really bad about this.   I would tell myself *'I can always catch up on sleep* *tomorrow.* ', but the only problem is that I would just tell myself the same thing the next day, and in the end, I missed out on getting proper rest, which caused me to miss out on enjoying a lot of my life to the fullest. It could be for a number of reasons that we lose sleep. Maybe we have an important project that we are working on for our job, and we could have a deadline that has to be met. It could be the fact that we want to go out and have fun, and we do not want the evening to end. It could be the fact that we have an important test coming up in school, and we need to cram in order to make sure that we are prepared. It could also be the fact that we are losing sleep because we have fears (like how I will pay my bills, or feed my family, which makes me incredibly sad that these fears even exist at all). Whatever the reason is, it can be very detrimental to our overall health, and it can actually defeat the reason that we are losing our sleep (because if we can't sleep, then for one, we can't even concentrate enough to solve the problems that are causing us to lose sleep).

Take that project that we are working on. We could push ourselves to the point where we make a mistake, and that could cause the project to fail. Take that important test that is coming up. If we are losing sleep because we need to stay awake and study, then we will not be able to concentrate properly when we are actually taking the test, and it could cause us to fail miserably, even though we completely covered the material that we were studying. Or if we are losing sleep because we want to keep partying as long as we can, then it could affect us to the point where our judgment is impaired, and that could cause us to make some awfully bad decisions. What if that causes us to fall asleep at the wheel on the way home and it causes us to have a terrible accident (it can happen, even if we think that we are in control. All it takes is one time, and it could cause the loss of either our life, or worse yet, someone else's life. Is that really worth pushing ourselves past our limit?). I know that these may seem like *'scare tactics'*, but sometimes we need to look at the worst-case scenario in order to plan our lives so that we can make sure that they never happen.

Now, I am not saying that we should never lose sleep, because there are times where losing sleep is a part of our lives. Like when we send our children to bed so that we can stay up late to assemble Christmas presents. What I am trying to say is that we can plan in advance so that we don't lose sleep at times when we shouldn't have to, and we should keep that promise to ourselves when we say, *'I will make up for the lost sleep later.'*, because it will help us to accept responsibility for our overall health. Take that project for example. A lot of us (me included) procrastinate at times and put things off, thinking that we can always finish it at the last minute, but if we know that we have something important coming up that we need to do, then we should plan the best way to do it, which means that, instead of waiting until the last minute, we should try and manage our time so that we are not trying to do it at the last minute.

3)   Accepting responsibility for our emotional health. We can do this in a number of areas. Let us take having fun for example. I am not going to go into great detail on this topic here, because I will mention more about this in a later chapter, but we should remember this. It is important to have a healthy balance in our lives, like when it is time to be serious and when it is time to have fun.

This involves more than just playing so that we can have fun, though. It also involves areas such as our love life, our personal friendships, our relationships with our children, and just making sure that **we** are happy with ourselves and our life. I will cover all of this in later chapters as well, but I just wanted to mention it here because we need to accept responsibility for ourselves, and that includes taking care of our emotional health as well, because if we do not, then we could fall prey to things like depression, and that can actually cause our physical health to deteriorate as quickly as our emotional health.   Depression can cause us to give up on even trying to do anything, and that can be disastrous.   We could fall into depression for a number of reasons.   It could be because we do not feel important to the overall scheme of things, because we do not feel that we are loved, or maybe because we are lonely, or because we are not happy with what we do in life as far as our job is concerned.   I, myself, have dealt with depression in my life, and it was after I accepted the fact that I was depressed, and then accepted the responsibility of identifying just why I was depressed, and then accepted the responsibility of asking someone for help with my depression, and then accepted the fact that I needed to fix those areas in my life that were causing my depression, that I finally came out of my depression and started living a more well-balanced life with a happy mind.

So, that is it where our personal selves and the philosophy of *"Acceptance"* are concerned.   Now, I am sure that you will probably think of other things that you could add to this topic and chapter, especially where your own personal lives are concerned (because, after all, we are all individuals, with our own unique lives), and when you do, be sure to write them down so that you do not forget them.   So that you can continue to take steps to improve yourself in the best ways possible.   After all, if you genuinely want to practice the philosophy of *"Acceptance"*, then always remember this.   If you want to do it, and you are going to do it, then you will need to accept the responsibility of making sure that you are truly ready to practice *"Acceptance"* with others by accepting the responsibility of being able to accept yourself.   You will also need to accept the responsibility of taking care of yourself, and we all do that by being honest with ourselves where our personal lives are concerned.   Just remember, life is a balance, and it is up to us to maintain that balance in our own lives in order to have a healthy and happy life, emotionally **and** physically.   It is important that we keep that healthy balance in our lives, because when we do that, then we have taken the first step towards practicing *"Acceptance"*, and that is especially important if we are to lead a life that is fulfilling. Always remember this.   Before we can make our world a better place, and before we can make ourselves a better race, we need to take care of ourselves so that we will be ready to change the world, as well as ready to lead ourselves into a better tomorrow.

Chapter Two
Acceptance and Relationships

"She's a good one (name).   You're a good one too." - My
Grandma, when we were driving in my truck.

Now that we have talked about accepting ourselves in order
to take responsibility for ourselves and our actions, let's talk about
"Acceptance" where our relationships are concerned.   Now, I am
not just talking about romantic relationships.   I am talking about all
of our interpersonal relationships.   Everything from the
relationships that we have with our co-workers, with our friends,
with our family and loved ones, and everything in-between.

I believe that this is why my grandma said this to me when
we were in my truck and I was driving down the country road.   She
used to tell me not to worry, that one day I would find the girl who
was meant to be with me.   She also used to tell me to not just jump
at the first one who came to me, because I needed to take my time in
order to make sure that she was right for me.   My grandma really
cared about me, and my happiness, and she used to let me know this
whenever I saw her.   Also, while my grandma was referring to my
romantic relationships, I believe that *"Acceptance"* can really help
us in all of our relationships, and that is why I would like to talk
about that now, in an attempt to show just how it can help us in
these areas.

I think that one of the hardest things to do where
"Acceptance" is concerned is accepting the fact that everyone
should have the right to live their lives in the way that they choose
to, as long as the way that they choose to does not violate anyone
else's right to do the same thing, and as long as they do not harm
another person through their actions or their words that call for

A Visit to the City in the Light

violence against anyone.   I want to be truly clear about this.   This does not mean that we should be tolerant and accepting of someone who, for example, wants to live their life in a way that harms another person, like someone who wants to commit crimes against other people, or someone who abuses the most precious people in our lives, our loved ones and our children.   We should never, ever, be tolerant of someone who wants to harm another member of our race, because that is one of the problems that we, as a race, need to fix in order to advance us into a better tomorrow, but I will cover this more in a later chapter.

Let us talk about one of the most obvious topics when we are talking about relationships and *"Acceptance"*.   Let us talk about how we can apply this to our romantic partners.   One of the biggest reasons (at least in my mind) that relationships fail is because we do not take the time to honestly care enough about our partner get to know them completely before we make a serious commitment to them.   More and more in today's world, we see someone that instantly captures our heart, and then we are *'off and running'*, so to speak.   Pursuing the person who has captured our love and our heart with everything that we have got inside us.   We want to have them love us, because they are perfect in our minds, and instead of taking the time to *'court'* them, and get to know them, we just want to jump into a serious commitment with them.   This could involve instantly moving in with them, or even getting married to them, before we really know them, and this could happen, and be our stance, for a number of reasons.   It could be the fact that we are afraid that if we do not *'claim our territory'*, so to speak, then we will lose them to someone else.   It could be the fact that our feelings for our love interest are so intense that we cannot wait to be with them 24/7, and we feel that we need to do or say whatever it takes to be with them all the time, without taking the time to get to know them completely as a person.   Whatever the reason is that we use to rationalize our motives for just jumping into a serious relationship before getting to know the person that we have fallen in love with, it can very easily spell doom for the relationship before it ever gets the chance to evolve into something incredibly special and permanent.

Now, am I saying that we should not believe in *'love at first sight'*? No, not at all. As a hopeless romantic, I really do believe in love at first sight, and that it can lead to a lifelong relationship that is an incredibly beautiful thing. However, if we fall in love with someone, then we should see if the feeling is mutual first. Then, if we decide that it is mutual, it can evolve into something that is great and permanent as long as we are then willing to take the time to get to know each other completely. We should not confuse love at first sight with *'lust'* at first sight, though. When we first fall in love with someone, there is that intense *'Wow, this feels great!'* period where we are head over heels in love, and we are willing to treat the person who has captured our heart like they are the most important person in the world. Someone who we want to make happy, whatever it takes, and if they feel the same way, then it can be a very magical period in our *'love story'*. Just remember, though, that a true *'love story'* does not just involve that first intense period. If it is a true *'love story'*, then it should be a *'love story'* where both partners feel that they can take the time to work together in order to truly get to know each other. So they can bring each other together, through both embracing their similarities **and** making compromises where their differences are concerned (and yes, every *'love story'* includes things that we need to compromise on in order to bring us both together forever). This is important in any romantic relationship in order to make sure that it is a true *'love story'*, and not just a *'short story'* full of intense feelings.

It is during this first magical period, though, when we need to decide if this is the person that we could see ourselves spending

A Visit to the City in the Light

the rest of our lives with, because in the end, that is what we all want, a love that is both intense and that lasts a lifetime. The best way to do that is to spend this initial time with our love interest truly getting to know them, and figuring out if we could still love them even after the initial wave of *'wow'* feelings start to fall off and the building of a permanent relationship becomes more imperative. That is why I advise people not to jump into a serious commitment in this initial phase no matter how intense these feelings are. We should accept the responsibility to use this time to show each other that we care enough about each other to actually get to know each other, to see if we can accept each other, which includes accepting each other's strengths and weaknesses, so that we can decide if we are truly meant to be together forever.

Now, we can still be together during this time, and we can even love each other intensely as well. But we should take precautions. One precaution that I always advise people, especially young couples, to take is this. Do not bring children into a world where we, as a couple, are not even sure if we are going to be able to love each other forever, because children deserve better than that. Yes, making love feels a lot better when we do not have to take precautions like using birth control devices, but this is where we need to accept the responsibility for our actions by asking ourselves a question. Is that few seconds of pleasure (sans condom for example) worth a lifetime of responsibility, especially when we, ourselves, are probably not ready to start a family by being a parent to a child? Something to always remember is this. A relationship that will last a lifetime is not based on sex alone. Love should be based on compassion, trust, communication, and caring, not just sex. If you can love each other, and want to be with each other, without sex being involved, then you have the start of a relationship that could last a lifetime. This is one of the biggest reasons why people, once upon a time and even now, will wait until they go through a courtship phase before starting a sexual relationship with the person that they love, because they want to develop a deep and meaningful love before they start the physical part of a relationship.

Now, I know that this attitude may seem antiquated, especially in today's world where people are more concerned about having sex than they are about developing a meaningful relationship with someone, and especially in today's world where sex with our new love carries so much importance (the misguided attitude of *'If you love me, then you would have sex with me'*), because it can really cloud our judgment at the start of a relationship.   There is a lot of wisdom in waiting to start having sex with our romantic partner, especially if we want a love that lasts a lifetime.   Now, I am not saying that children are not a blessing, because they can be the most wonderful thing to happen to us in our lives, as long as we are truly ready to accept the responsibility of being a parent.   There are a lot of young people who are in love with the image of being a parent, and with the thought of *'playing house'*, so to speak, until they realize the tremendous responsibility that comes along with being a parent.   There are also a lot of people who feel that they need to *'lock down'* someone that they want to be with, and they think that, by having a child, then the person who they love will never leave them, but in the majority of instances that is just simply not the case.

Children are not pawns to be used in a relationship, and especially not to be used to try and keep someone with another person.   They are **human beings**, and they deserve to be brought into a world, and a family, that not only genuinely wants them, but wants them because both parents are ready for the lifetime of responsibility that comes with being a parent.   Then again, there are a lot of people who just want to have sex with as many people as they can, because, as a lot of them say, they are *"only _____* *years old"*, and they can *"do what they want to do"*, and as such, they don't care if they have a child or not, because they are too selfish and wrapped up in themselves to care about who they affect with their actions, including how they affect the child that they have with someone. They just want to have a good time, which includes having sex, and in their minds, if they have a child, then *'who cares'*, because they *'got what they wanted'*, which was just having sex with someone.

The problem with this attitude is that there are a lot of women who are attracted to the bad boy attitude of *'Hey, I'm just out for a good time!'*, and they end up having children with these boys who lead their lives this way (and I call them *'boys'* because a real man, at least in my mind, does care about women, especially the one that they claim to love, and as such, they take the necessary precautions to make sure that they don't have children if they do decide to have sex with their partner. They **do** mean it when they say that they love their partner, and with love comes a definite level of caring about the woman that they claim to love. This means, in my mind, that they care enough to make sure that they are ready to have a real relationship based on love, not sex, and they are ready to make the lifelong commitment to their partner that the child they create deserves to grow up in). The women who want to love these boys feel that they can change them into good men and husbands, but it rarely works, and in the end, many of those women end up with children but no fathers, or only part-time fathers, because these boys who were never serious about settling down with the women that they had unprotected sex with either end up running off with other women, or worse yet, they use the woman that they claim to love to satisfy their own selfish needs (for example, either they like the fact that the women are supporting them financially, or they love the fact that, no matter how many affairs that they have on the woman they claim to love, they know that the woman will always forgive them and take them back, because they want to keep their family together).   The sad reality is that they do not love their partners enough to be good husbands and fathers (because if they genuinely loved their partners then they would genuinely care about them as well) and then they end up just having multiple affairs on them because they don't care about them completely, which not only hurts their children emotionally, but also sets a horrible example for their children to learn from.

Children are not dolls that we can just toss aside because we do not care about anything but our own selfish needs where having sex is concerned.   Again, they are human beings who are entitled to have loving parents who are with them 24/7.   Not people who are either just in love with the idea of being a parent without considering (or being ready for) what it means to be a parent, or who just want to have unprotected sex without caring about the consequences, even if that means that their children grow up in a broken home.   A lot of times I have heard these same parents (mainly boys.......again, not men), who were never serious about the person that they had sex with, and who didn't care if they had a child or not as a result, say *'No one will ever treat my daughter like that!'*, without even considering the fact that, because of the example that they set for their daughter, their daughter will grow up thinking that this is the way that things should be.   Then, because of that, they end up getting into relationships with boys who treat them the same way, because they grow up thinking that this type of treatment is normal for them to receive when they have romantic relationships in the future.

We, as adults, need to realize that the example that we set for our children is how they are going to grow up thinking that things should be for them.   So, if we really care about what happens to our children in the future, then we need to accept the responsibility to set

51

the right example for them to see while they are growing up. If they see their parents having multiple affairs, or they see their parents doing drugs, or they see their parents being violent with each other, or they see one of their parents just walk out of their lives, or they see one of their parents using the other without really loving them, then they are going to grow up thinking that this is the way that things should be for them as well. So, again, if we really care about what happens to our children in the future, then we need to accept the responsibility to set the right example for them while they are young. Otherwise, it does not matter if we say, *'That will never happen to my child!'*, because the chances are incredibly good that this is exactly what will happen to them, and the only person that we will have to blame for what happens to them is us as their parents. So, if we really care about our children, then we, as parents, truly need to accept the responsibility to set a good example for our children by teaching them through example.

People often say that they wish that they could meet someone who would love them forever, just like what they saw people do in the past, but right there they are not taking the time to ask themselves just why those relationships lasted so long in the *'old days'*. If people would take the time to study just how those relationships came to be and lasted for so long, they would see that people would actually take the time to get to know each other, in a *'courtship'* phase. So that they truly knew the other person that they were in a relationship with before they took the next step and made the relationship final, and definitely before they had any children. They realized that, in order to truly know a person, and see if they could be together with that person for the long haul, then they needed to take their time until that initial *'wow'* period was over so that they could see who the real person was that they were in love with. I have always told young people that *"People can only put on a fake face for so long. Eventually, if we are patient, they*

A Journey There.......and Back Again with a Message of Hope

will show their true colors, and when they do, then and only then can we decide if they are someone that we can genuinely love for a lifetime.". They accepted the fact that the person who they were interested in had their own lives, their own likes and dislikes, their own hopes and dreams, and everything else that made them an individual person. They recognized the fact that people, especially the person who had won their heart, had their own sets of morals and values. As such, they accepted the fact that, if they wanted to love them and have that love returned to them, then they needed to accept the responsibility of truly getting to know the person who had captured their heart. Therefore, they waited to see if they could accept them for who they were, especially if they wanted their love interest to accept and respect them and the way that they wanted to lead their lives.

Now, again, am I saying that I am against *'love at first sight'*? Absolutely not. As a matter of fact, I truly do believe in instantly falling in love with someone. What I am saying is that, if love at first sight does happen, then while we are just starting our romantic relationship and we are in that wonderful first phase of it, we need to accept the fact that, before we just jump into something as serious as marriage, and definitely before we start having children, we need to take the time to get to know the person who has captured our hearts in order to try and see if we can build a permanent relationship with them. Does it work all the time? No, it does not, but as I have said before, nothing really good in our lives ever comes easy, and I believe that fact is for certain. However, if we do take the time to get to know the person that we want to have a permanent relationship with, and accept the responsibility to get to know them and take the time to see if we can accept them for who they are, then we stand a much better chance of having the happy type of permanent relationship that we want to have with the person that we love. It could keep a relationship that we have with

53

someone from failing, because which would you rather have?   A love that lasts a lifetime with a person who is perfect for you because you both took the time, and made the necessary compromises, to make sure that you were perfect for each other? Or the heartache of a failed relationship because you find out that, after making a permanent commitment to your love interest, you cannot accept them for who they are, and how they believe. Always remember, in order to have a permanent, loving relationship with someone, then we need to really care about them, and that includes caring about them enough to find out who they truly are. Then, after finding this information out, we need to take the time to ask ourselves this question - *'Can I love this person forever?'*. After all, isn't that what we all want?   A true, passionate, and caring love that lasts a lifetime?

Now, am I saying that we should just force ourselves into accepting someone that we want to love, no matter how they believe and who they are?   Or should we only look for someone who is just like us?   No on both counts, because if we say that *"The only person for me is someone who is just like me."*, or if we say, *"I can change this person, no matter who they are and how they believe."*, then we may never find someone to have a permanent loving relationship with, and we will definitely be in for a lot of heartbreak, because finding two people who are exactly alike, and who want to love each other forever, is rare indeed.   On the other hand, trying to change someone into what we want them to be may not work as well, because they will come to resent us for trying to control them, and because we are trying to change them into who we want our partner to be, we may miss out on someone who truly is someone that we could love forever, and who could be perfect for us.   What I am trying to say is this.   In any relationship, there should be some level of compromise.   We should take the time to figure out who the person truly is that we want to love, to figure out what compromises need to be made in order to have a lasting relationship. Then we need to ask ourselves, *"Can I make the compromises necessary to have a permanent, lasting love with the person that I want to love?"* and *"Can I be happy making these compromises to my life in order to make my partner happy?"*.

We should never enter into a relationship with the mindset of *"I want this person, and I don't care what it takes, I am going to force this person to love me by forcing this person to be the person that I want them to be."*, because once we start thinking that we can force a person to love us, and force a person to make changes to who they are no matter how drastic those changes are, then we are dooming the relationship that we want with that person right from the start. Also, we could be missing out on another person who would be perfect for us and who we could be genuinely happy with if we think that the way to gain everlasting love is to take away a person's identity through control in order to make them love us. We need to accept the fact that, in order to have a lasting, loving relationship with someone, we need to find out if they can love us without forcing them to or forcing them to change drastically into the person that we want them to be (now, I am not talking about compromises, because every relationship takes some compromise. What I am talking about are very drastic changes which basically tries to change another person entirely, like they have no choice in who they want to be and how they want to live their lives at all), because forcing someone to love us, and trying to change them by taking away their identity entirely, is not love, it is control, and we should never control the person that we say we love. We should want to see if the person that we love truly does want to love us and is willing to accept us without being told to do so, or without being controlled or coerced into loving us, because the person that gives us love without it being forced or coerced from them is the type of love that we want and that truly can last a lifetime. It is the type of love that will make us happy for a lifetime. To me, I would much rather have someone love me who truly does want to love me (instead of someone that I have to force to love me through control). That is the type of love that feels the best because it is **true**.

There is one situation, though, that screams the fact that it is anything but love, and that is the situation where someone is saying that *'You will love me, or you will pay'*. We see it all the time now. People look for something to hold over a person's head, and then they try and use it to force the other person to love them and never leave them. Here is a prime example of what I am talking about. We find ourselves in a relationship, and then, for example, one of the partners says *'Hey, let's make a sex tape!'*. They may give you all sorts of excuses as to why they want to do it. They may say *'I want to have something with me to remind me of you when you are not with me'*, or they may say that *'It will spice up our sex lives'*, but nothing good ever comes of it. What usually happens, and the most common reason that someone wants to make a sex tape of them and their partner (unless they are in the sex industry), is so that they can have leverage to use against the person that they claim to love. So that they can always have that *'If you leave me, then I will show you what you get for leaving me'* evidence that they want to use against the person that they claimed to love, to *'punish'* the person who might want to leave the relationship.

You should never need leverage to keep a person loving you, and you should never want to cause hurt to the person that you claim to love (or you claimed to love, for that matter), because if you truly do love someone, or you did love them at all, then you should love them enough to say *"If you want to leave, and it will make you happy to leave and start another relationship with someone else, then even though it may hurt me immensely, I will let you go so that you can be happy"*. Putting someone else's happiness before your own.......**that** is what true love is all about, and it is a quality that both partners need to share completely if they truly want to have a permanent relationship (it is also why lots of people wait to get to know a person in a courtship phase before making a permanent commitment to them, in order to make sure that it is a relationship that can last for the long haul). Let's face facts, it hurts to lose someone that we love, to the point where we do start thinking along the lines of *'How can I make my ex-partner hurt as much as I am hurting right now'*, but if we start thinking along those lines, then that is not love that we had for our ex-partner. It may feel like the right thing to do at that time, but if we ever loved the person that had our heart, then we should not want to hurt them, even if we are hurting. Now, I do realize that this is easier to say than to do but hear me out.

Sometimes, if we know that the love that we had for someone was true, to the point where it is displayed in the fact that we are willing to let them go without causing them any hurt, then the person that we loved will, in some instances, see that the love we had for them was true and real, and sometimes when they realize that fact, it will cause them to return someday. There used to be a saying that went something like this, *'If you love someone, then set them free if they choose to be. If the love you shared was true, then they may return to you, and if they do, then it is because the love that you shared was true, and it will be stronger as a result of the separation. If the love, however, was not true, then they will not return, and you will be free to find the true love that you always wanted, one that will make you happy forever'* (variation on a quote from Richard Bach). There is a lot of wisdom in that statement. The worst type of pain that we can face is the pain of a lost love because love is so important to us, and because it is not a type of hurt that can be healed the way that physical pain can be healed. Whether it is the lost love of someone who passed away, or the lost

A Visit to the City in the Light

love of a precious pet, or the lost love of a romantic partner. Losing love is one of the worst types of pain that we can experience. We spend a lot of our time just looking for the love that we can get from a romantic partner, thinking about it, wanting it, and when we find it, we never want to lose it, because if we do, then it is an emotional pain that actually hurts more than any physical pain ever could. The reason that it hurts so much is because, while a doctor can fix a physical pain, only time can fix an emotional pain. Time to heal our hearts, time to learn how to be happy with ourselves again, and time to let our sorrow take its course. All so that we can try to be happy with ourselves again, and then, be happy with a new partner. We have to heal ourselves, and our heart, before we can give our heart and love to someone else completely, like they deserve.

Now I would like to, just briefly, talk about how accepting responsibility for our actions during a relationship can stop a lot of hurt feelings, hurt feelings that can permanently destroy a relationship that had a chance of being great and lasting. There are times when, during a relationship and the time when we are having problems like arguments, we may make the fateful decision to stray to another person because we are looking for those intense feelings that we had when we first started the relationship, instead of accepting the fact that we should be going to our partner and seeing if the relationship can be worked on so that those feelings can be rekindled. As a result, we might actually go outside of our relationship to seek those feelings again with someone else, and that's the worst decision we can make. Then, to make matters even worse, after we are done going outside of our relationship, we feel bad because we did not go to our partner to rekindle those intense feelings, and it is because we feel guilty about seeing someone else to share our love with. So, instead of accepting responsibility for our actions, and accepting the fact that we made the worst decision ever, one that could permanently destroy our love story, we try and justify our actions by blaming anyone but ourselves.

One classic example of this is when we tell our partner something like *'Yes, I had an affair, but it was your fault!'*. Now, I never fully understood that statement, because your significant other was not there when you had the affair, they did not take off your clothes, they did not force you to have sex with the other person, and the last thing that they would want you to do is have the affair in the first place, which is the main reason why the person who was cheated on gets terribly upset and hurt. True, they may have had a very bad argument with you, and they may have called you names, and they may have even gone to their mom's house to spend the night (or had you sleep on the couch) until they cooled down, but do you really think that they wanted you to betray them in the worst, and most intimate, way possible? You might have had problems for a while. Arguments, fights, calling each other names.......but if you truly have love in your heart for each other, then it is important to understand that it is that love that should make you want to talk to each other instead of straying to someone else.

A true lasting love takes work, and that includes lots of open and honest communication with each other. You have to be willing to work to keep your love alive, instead of just giving up and running to someone else when you start having problems. That is what it means to be *'truly committed'* to each other, because a real commitment dictates that we take steps to keep our love fresh and alive, instead of taking steps out the door towards someone else. That means that we talk to each other when things start to feel stale, or when we have arguments and problems in our relationships, so that we can figure out what is going on, and then take steps to figure out how we can keep our love alive. We need to care enough about each other, and our love for each other, to communicate with each other instead of running away.

59

A Visit to the City in the Light

Communication is key to having a love that will last a lifetime. It is more important than most people think. If you cannot communicate with each other, then that can be a huge problem, because it is so important to be able to talk to each other. People sometimes do not understand what it truly means to *'fight for your relationship'*. It does not mean actually pulling out the gloves and physically fighting or being violent with your partner over problems that you have in your relationship (and believe me, there will be times when you will have problems, and get into arguments, with the person that you love).   What it means is that you are willing to do what it takes to keep your love alive (other than being violent or trying to force someone to stay with you through control or the use of things such as *'sex tapes'*) and talking with each other is one of the best ways to *'fight'* for your love (other ways include having fun with your partner and showing them that you truly do care about them and their feelings by being spontaneous. Everything from surprising them with small gifts to helping them around the house even though you just finished an 8+ hour shift, and everything in-between).   It lets your partner know that you really do care about them, and their feelings, because you are willing to take their happiness into consideration.   It shows your partner that you truly do care about them, enough to take the necessary step of talking with them from your heart, because if you really do care about the person that you love, then you really do care about their feelings, and about making them happy always.

Now, let me be clear about something by repeating it here. Forcing someone to love you, through manipulation, and worse yet, through violence, is not love.   It would infuriate you if someone else tried to force your partner to love them, or worse yet, tried to take advantage of them by doing the most abhorrent act that one person can do to another person by assaulting them sexually.   So why, if you truly love your partner, would you try and force them to love you using the same tactics. It took a long time for us, as a race, to realize and accept the fact that, even if you are in a relationship, you can be sexually assaulted by the person who should be loving you, and defending you, and making sure that rape, or any violence for that matter, never happens to you. Let's be clear, rape is a very violent and horrific act. We all want to make sure that it never happens to the person that we love at the hands of someone else. Why then, if we never want to see the person that we love taken advantage of by someone else through the use of force, would we ever want to do it to the person that we love ourselves? Love cannot, and should not, be forced upon anyone.

Would you tolerate anyone hurting the one that you love? Would you tolerate, even for a moment, someone calling your loved one a hurtful name, or worse yet, physically hurting them? Then why would you ever want to be the person who hurts the one that you love through hateful words or violent actions? I want to be very clear about this. Love, and I mean true love, dictates that we are never hurtful or violent towards our partner. That is hate, so how can you hate the person that you claim to love? It absolutely kills me to see someone that I love in tears, or in pain in any way, and I am sure that it would infuriate anyone else as well. So why would anyone want to cause the person that they purport to love pain in any way? I always tell people that, if they feel the need to harm the person that they love through using hurtful words or physical actions, then they need to accept the fact that they may not love their partner completely, and that they probably have a problem with anger as well. Then they need to accept the responsibility of evaluating the love that they have for their partner in order to determine what they need to do in order to give their partner the love that they deserve, and also possibly seeking help for their anger if they need it, and definitely before they cause the person that they love pain in any way, and this goes for both partners.

61

A Visit to the City in the Light

Now, am I saying that, if you do get into an argument with the person you love, and you get so mad that you say something hurtful to them because you are hurting due to what they said to you, then you are a bad person? Not necessarily (even though we should strive to never hurt the person we love), because arguments with our loved ones do hurt us, and to hear them say hurtful things towards us does hurt, and as a result, we may want them to hurt as much as we are hurting. What makes us a bad person is if we go through our relationship calling our loved ones names for no reason, just because we want to belittle them, and exert some type of control over them by destroying their self-worth, making them feel like they are worthless and beneath us. What I am saying is that, if we do get into an argument, and it escalates to the point where we start wanting to say hurtful things to the person we love, then we should step back, catch our breath, and take a break before we start saying hurtful things. One way that I have seen this work in the past is to say to our loved one that what they said was hurtful, and that we do not want to start saying hurtful things to them because of the hurt that we are feeling. Then we should tell them that we do love them, and that we do not want to hurt them by saying something that we will regret saying, because they are important to us, and we really do love them and care about them with all of our hearts.

Sometimes (by just saying to our loved one during an argument that we do not want to say something that is hurtful) it can cause our loved one to step back themselves and realize that whatever the argument was about, it is not worth hurting each other over, and it can cause an argument to even end at times. This can happen mainly because it gives us a moment to think about what we are arguing about, and most of the time, if we just think about it, it can cause us to realize that it was not even that important to begin with, and it can stop us from permanently hurting the person that we love the most. One thing to always remember is this. Once you say something hurtful to the person you love, you can never just '*suck it back into your mouth*', because once it is out there, it is truly '*out there*'.   Sure, we might be able to say, '*I'm sorry that I said that*', and sometimes what you said can be forgiven, but once you say it, it cannot be unsaid.   So, remember that fact, because sometimes we can say things in the heat of the moment that can really hurt the one we love, and it can leave an emotional scar that might never heal, no matter what we say to try to be forgiven for it. Always remember, arguments are going to happen in any relationship, but if we establish early on that we want to have good communication with each other, then it will help us get through those times when arguments happen, because our loved one will remember and realize that we really do love them, and that we would much rather talk to them in order to solve the argument than just fighting and saying hurtful things to each other.

Also, never just walk away from an argument forever, because it will fester into something much bigger later on, and our loved one could have hurt feelings that get much worse over time.   I always advise young people to tell their loved one, early in the relationship when the '*ground rules*' are still be negotiated, that they would much rather talk with their partner to solve any situation that would cause an argument, instead of just letting it fester into something that could explode later on.   Tell your loved one that you want to be able to care about them, so much so that you would rather settle an argument before too much time passes.   There is an old saying that goes '*never go to bed angry*', and there is a lot of wisdom in that.   Always care enough about your partner to let them know that you don't want to fight with them, and that if an argument does happen (and they will), then you want to be able to solve it by loving them enough to talk to them about it because you really do care about them, and you want to solve it as soon as possible so that you can both get back to the '*hugs and kisses*' that you both want, because that's what we all want from a romantic relationship. We want to know that our partner does care enough about us to want to love us instead of fighting with us. Sometimes, by letting them know this, we will see the love from our partner that we want from them in return for caring about them that much.

This, again, is especially true when we start thinking that we need to control the person that we say we love in order to force them to love us, because we should show our partner that we care about them, and their feelings, by not doing things to control them. If we do love them, then we need to show them that we love them by caring about them, and not by controlling them. Again, let me be truly clear about this. If you need to control the person that you say you love, through playing mind games, or worse yet, through physical violence, then that is not love, ever. Let me ask you a question. Wouldn't you rather have someone love you because they want to? Forcing someone to love us, through control or other deceitful tactics, is not love, and I cannot stress that, or repeat it, enough. We may want the person that we love to love us no matter what, but if we have to force them to love us, then it is not love, and all we are doing is destroying the fantastic love that might have been there if we had never tried to force them to love us. In addition, to repeat, by trying to force someone to love us, we could miss out on receiving the love from another person who truly does want to love us with all of their heart, and which would you rather have? The love that you have to force out of someone, or the love from someone who genuinely wants to love you?

I know that I keep talking about love in this chapter, but I am doing it for three reasons. One is the fact that love is one of the most basic of our needs as human beings, and it is extremely important to us. Another reason is because, especially in today's world, there seems to be a huge problem with people breaking up and getting divorced, and this can be prevented if we just take the time to develop our love and genuinely care about the person who we say we love.   The third reason is the fact that I have seen just how bad actually doing something to hurt our partners (like using a sex tape to hurt our partner) can destroy someone's life, and I will detail that later in this book.

To continue, though, I feel that the love that comes to us freely and willingly because it wants to is the type of love that can last a lifetime, and at least for me, it is the type of love that feels the best.   We can all have that kind of love if we just show our partner that we truly do care about them and their feelings right from the start.   It is because of this that, again, I regularly recommend to people, especially young people, to wait before they just jump into something as serious as marriage or moving in together, because these are serious commitments, and they should be taken seriously if we want them to work out.   In a lot of instances, children result from these relationships, and then they end up in broken homes because their parents did not take their wedding vows or their relationship seriously.   Or worse yet, people think that the first 'wow' period is what true love is all about, and then when it wears off, they think that the love is gone, when in reality that is when true love begins because it is driven by our hearts, and caring for each other, and not just by our initial intense feelings.   The bottom line is that they were not ready for marriage, or even taking their personal romantic relationship to the next level by moving in together, because they did not get to know each other well enough in the beginning to make a serious commitment, which affects their children more than you could possibly imagine.

What I tell young people, when it comes to them wanting to start a serious commitment, is to accept the responsibility to take a good look at themselves, and then ask themselves this question....... *'What is most important to me?'*.   Is it playing video games, or going out with friends, or other things that single people get to do?   Or is it things like spending time with the person that they love, and doing things with them, and helping them (with things like housework, etc.) because the person that they love makes them happier than doing the things that they did when they were single?   If it is more important to you to play than it is to work so that you can provide for yourself and the person that you love, and it is more important to you to spend time with other people, and it is more important to you to *'goof off'* than it is to plan for a wonderful future with the person that you love, then maybe you are not ready for a serious commitment.   Does that mean that you cannot have a relationship with the person that you love while you are getting everything that you want to do, that you can do as a single person, *'out of your system'*, so to speak?   No, not at all.   However, if you truly do want to have a relationship with the person that you love, one that will last a lifetime, and you truly do care about your partner and their feelings, and you want nothing but happiness for yourself and your partner, then you need to accept the responsibility to make sure that you are ready to be in a committed long-term relationship before you make a serious commitment to someone.   You should see your partner as your true *'partner in crime'*, to coin a phrase, and you should want to spend time with them, and you should genuinely care about them and their feelings.   You should be excited about seeing them, and about spending time with them, and about planning your future with them, instead of just viewing them as someone that you are with for now, or worse yet, until *'something better comes along'*.   Just remember to ask yourself this question before you decide to take the next step in a relationship.   *'Do I love the person that I want to have a relationship with, and do I truly care about them, and their feelings, as much as I care about my own?'*.

A Journey There.......and Back Again with a Message of Hope

This is why we should never need leverage to keep someone with us, doing something like talking our partner into making a *'sex tape'* so that we have something to hold over their head in order to force them to stay with us. Would you want someone to hold something over your head to force you to love them? Then why would you ever do it to someone else? It all goes back to caring about their feelings as much as you care about yours. Again, let me just state here, for the record, that I truly feel that anyone who does this (forcing someone to love them by threatening them with a sex tape) should be prosecuted, just like someone who commits rape, because if someone putting a video of you (with such personal details in it) on the internet for the whole world to see (without you wanting them to) is not a form of a personal violation, then I do not know what is. The bottom line is this. Everyone should be able to be in control of their own body, and who sees it. It should not be the choice of just the person who made the tape. Sure, one of the partners may have agreed to make the *'sex tape'* with the person who later posts it online, but that does not mean that they wanted it to be shared with the whole world.

Look at it in another way. Again, let us say that you willingly make a sex tape with your partner. I do not know why anyone would do this, because only bad can come from it in the end, but let's say you do this willingly. I know that some people have told me that they did it because they wanted to let their partner have something to *'remember them by'* when they are apart, or they wanted to remind their partner of what was waiting for them when they got back home. Let's be honest here though. The main reason that a lot of people say they want their partner to do this for them is because they want something to hold over their partner's head by having some type of way to hurt the person that they claim to love if they ever split up. Let's face facts. When we end a relationship, there are going to be hurt feelings, and the person who loses their love partner usually wants their ex to feel the same pain that they are experiencing.   Then, just when they are feeling this way, they remember that they have a *'sex tape'* that they made, and they decide that the best way to hurt the one who left them is to post it online for everyone to see (there are whole web sites that are devoted to displaying these sex tapes, some of them even advertise that they are entirely made up of videos of people's ex-partners having sex with them).   They do not care if it hurts their ex because they just want to hurt their ex at any cost after a breakup, and they want their ex to feel the same pain that they are feeling.   So, they decide to post it online for everyone to see in an attempt to hurt them emotionally.......and usually it does hurt them in extreme ways. People care about how the world sees them, and their reputations, and when this happens it can damage a person emotionally by destroying their reputation, which is what most people who post these videos of their ex-partner want to happen to them.

Again, if you think that this does not happen, just do a search of pornography sites online.   There are entire sites that devote themselves to videos that are sex tapes of someone's ex having sex with them, and they are being posted in an attempt to make the person's ex look like a bad person or to humiliate them.   It works too, and that is the bad thing, because all their ex did was break up with them because they were not in love with them anymore, or they decided that the person that they broke up with was not the person who they could commit to for a lifetime after they truly got to know them and who they were as a person.   People's lives and reputations are being harmed permanently by this type of behavior, and no one should be harmed in this way, **ever**.   In my mind, this is the same as if someone got drunk, and then they were taken advantage of while they were not in their right mind by having a sex tape made of them. It might be them in the video, and they might have even agreed to have sex with the person who was taking advantage of them by making the sex tape, but did they agree to have that intimate moment shared with the entire world? Considering that, then how can it be ok to post a video online of someone engaged in a sex act when one of the people in the video did not give consent for the video to be shared with the whole world? Both partners may have said it was ok to have the video made, but that does not mean that both partners wanted it to be shared with the world once they broke up. In my opinion, if both partners do not agree to have the video shared with the whole world once the relationship is over, then the video should not be shared with everyone on the internet. Again, I believe strongly that this should be a crime. It should be simple. If both parties do not agree to have the video shared with everyone, then it should be a crime if the video is shared. At a minimum, the person who did not agree to have the video shared should also be able to sue the person who shared the video against their wishes.

My whole point is this. We need to accept the fact that, in today's world, not all relationships work out, and when we accept that, then we need to accept the fact that, if we ever loved our ex at all, then we should not want to do anything to cause any pain, or harm, or humiliation, to the one that we claimed to love. It is all part of accepting the responsibility to be a good person, and when we do that, we help the world be a better place to live in by being the 'hero' instead of the 'villain', and isn't that what practicing the philosophy of "Acceptance" is all about? Making our world a better place for all of us by being a good person, especially to our partners? I will say this. I have seen, on more than one occasion, people who have broken up get back together at a later date, and end up having wonderful permanent relationships, and when I have seen this happen it was because the person who left told me that they remembered how loving and understanding the other person was, even during the breakup, and that was important to them in wanting to return to the person that they left. It showed them that the person

69

A Visit to the City in the Light

that they left really was a good person, with a good, loving heart, and that they really did love them because they genuinely cared about their feelings, even when they were breaking up.

Another reason that we should accept the responsibility to be a good person, even during the most difficult time in our lives (like when we lose love) is, again, because we may lose a future chance at starting a really good relationship with someone new, and this is more important than a lot of people may think. You see, there is a good chance that future potential partners will see how we treated the last person that we were in a relationship with, and how we tried to hurt them after the breakup (like trying to humiliate them by posting a sex tape online), and they could have second thoughts about wanting to start a relationship with someone who does something that hateful to someone that they proclaimed to love. However, the most important reason that we should accept the responsibility to be a good person where relationships are concerned, at least in my mind, is this. Being a good person towards others that we have any type of relationship with is just the right thing to do. If we want others to be good to us, especially our love partners, then we should give them a reason to treat us the way that we want to be treated by treating them the same way. Isn't that what everyone wants? To be treated with respect, love, and care in our relationships? How can we expect others to treat us good if we go around treating everyone else like we do not care about them, or their feelings, and we get the reputation of being the type of person that no one wants to have a relationship with because we treat everyone else like garbage? Once again, isn't that what the philosophy of *"Acceptance"* is all about? Bringing us all together by being good to each other and respecting each other? That starts with how we treat those who are closest to us, because if we cannot treat them good, then how are we ever going to have enough care and respect for anyone else when talking about coming together as a race?

In addition, we need to accept the responsibility of showing the future leaders of our world, our children, how to have healthy relationships with others, no matter if it is a friendship, or a romantic relationship, or even a relationship with other family members. We do that by setting the example for them to see and follow, and we do that by accepting the responsibility to be good to all of the people in our lives by treating everyone else the way that **we** want to be treated. This can be shown, and applied, in many areas where our relationships are concerned. One of the best areas we can show this is by showing others that our word actually means something, especially when we give it to those who we love.

Let me explain. At one time the most important thing to everyone was our word. When we gave someone our word, whether through a promise or a vow, we kept it above all else, because to put it bluntly, our word was *'our bond'*. It proved that, even though we might falter in some areas, we never faltered where keeping our word, and our promises and vows, were concerned. This was especially true where keeping our word to our loved one was concerned. You see, in everyone's minds, keeping our word was the most important thing in the world, because it showed that we could be trusted and counted on, especially in the most difficult of times and situations. It proved that we really were good people, and it showed true strength of character, which showed that we could be relied upon to all of those around us.

In today's society there are those who feel that, in order to show their strength, then they need to *'prove their prowess'* by hooking up with as many people as possible, even if that means that they have many children with many different partners, because in their minds, the more partners that they have, then the stronger

71

person they are, but that is just simply not true. True, they may have many romantic partners in their lives, and they may have many children, but is that what really proves that they are strong? To me, it does not prove that they are strong, what it proves is that they are weak where their character is concerned because they are incapable of keeping their word to anyone, especially the person who they claim to love. Rather than meaning it when they say *'I love you, and only you, and I will be faithful to you'*, they only prove that they don't mean it, and that the word that they gave to their loved one was meaningless, even more so when they told the person that they were having a child with that they would not only be a good, loving, and caring partner, but that they would also be a good role model to their children by setting the right example for them to see while they were growing up.

Let me ask you a question. Who do you think is stronger? Someone who goes around using women for sex, always giving in to temptation and never keeping their word to their partner when they tell them that they love them? Or someone who means it when they say *'I love you'* to their partner, and then proves that love by being loyal to them and only them? I look at it like this. It takes more strength to resist the temptation of having multiple sexual partners in order to keep your word to your partner than it does to give in to temptation and have sex with multiple partners, thereby having many children with many partners, at least in my opinion (also, I am the only one who determines who I have sex with, not anyone else, no matter how sexy they dress or what they tell me they want to do to me in the bedroom. I tell women all the time that they do not get to determine if we are going to be intimate, because I am in control of me, not them, and keeping my word to my partner is more important than anything that they could do for me or to me. It is all about strength of character and keeping my word). It's real easy to give in to the temptation of having sex with multiple partners, but it takes real strength to say *'Yeah, you look real sexy, and you are making me feel like having sex with you because of the way that you are acting towards me, etc., but I am the only one who decides who I have sex with, and having the will and the strength to keep my word to my partner is more important to me than proving that I am so weak where my character is concerned that I cannot even keep my word to my partner when I tell them that I love only them'.*

Now, am I saying that we should just stay with someone forever when we learn that they are not the person that we can commit to? No. What I am saying is that we should be completely honest when we first start a relationship with someone. That includes telling them that, while you do love them, and you do want to see if they are the one that you could spend a lifetime with, you need time to make sure before doing something like having a child. All the time I hear people saying things like *'Well, I just said whatever the other person wanted to hear in order to have sex with them'*, but again, let me ask you a question. Is this the way that you want people to treat you, or more importantly, your daughter? Then why treat them like that in any situation, especially where romantic relationships are concerned? Mean it when you say that you love your partner, but also be completely honest with them right from the start by telling them that you need to make sure that you can love them enough to be with them forever by getting to know them completely. Honesty and communication go hand in hand in any relationship, but especially where our intimate relationships are concerned, and being completely honest with your partner, right from the start, shows your partner that you not only care about them, but that you respect them completely. Show them that you are someone that they can rely on, instead of someone that they should be wary of.

To go back to our relationship with our children, this is

another definite situation where we can accept that it is our responsibility to shape the future of our race by teaching our kids the right way to live their lives, and we do that by fostering a good relationship with them by showing them how to live their lives through caring and love. Things like teaching them to be responsible for how they live their lives, and for the decisions that they make, in order to help them by teaching them the right way to do things, and also teaching them the wrong way to do things so that they don't make bad decisions when they are adults. Kids are this wonderful sponge, full of promise and hope, and they absorb everything that they see their parents, and other adults, do and say. We, as adults, need to accept the responsibility of setting the right example for both our children, and other people's children. We need to show them how to live a good life, and how to be good people, through the examples that we set every day, because kids watch and hear everything that we do and say. Since they want nothing more than to make their mom and dad happy and proud of them, they will want to be just like their mom and dad so that they will be proud of them. They learn how the world operates, and how people act and behave, by watching and listening to everyone around them. So, what example do you want to set for your children? What type of people do you want your children to grow up to be?

Think about it. If they see mom and dad fighting all the time, then they will think that this is what they need to do in order be just like them when they are old enough to have a romantic relationship. Worst of all, if they see their parents being violent towards each other, then they will grow up thinking that they should be violent towards the person that they end up loving as well (in other words, their son will grow up being violent towards women, which is horrible, or their daughter will grow up thinking that it is ok for a man to hit them, or to leave them and have multiple affairs on them, and that is never ok under any circumstances). However, if they see their mom and dad being loving and respectful towards each other, and they see them using communication instead of yelling and fighting with each other when they are faced with problems during their relationship, and they see that their parents actually care about each other and that they are truly committed to each other for the long haul, and they see their parents keeping their word to each other when they tell each other that they love *'only them'*, then they will learn how to behave and act when they are in a relationship. It will be the start of a wonderful life for them where love is concerned. Always remember, in order to teach our children what a real, loving, and caring relationship looks like, then we need to show them what it looks like by being that way towards the person that we love.

If they see mom and dad working hard every day in order to make the necessary money to provide for them, and to make their dreams come true, then they will want to work hard to provide for their family, and to achieve their dreams when they are married and have kids. If they see their mom and dad talking to them when they misbehave in order to make them see why what they did that was wrong, instead of just immediately punishing them with no explanation as far as why what they did was wrong, then they will want to raise their kids without being violent towards them as well. They will learn the value of communicating with others instead of just losing their temper. Another area where showing our children that violence is not the answer is when they see us interacting with others. We should teach them, by showing them and communicating with them, that if we have problems in our lives, then we deal with it by not being violent towards others, and by utilizing the right methods to solve our problems.

Now, I would like to touch on something here that I will

mention in more detail in a later chapter. However, the reason that I want to mention this here is because I feel that what I am going to talk about now is also important to discuss when talking about communicating with our children in order to teach them the right way and the wrong way to deal with issues that are occurring, not only in their lives, but in our world as well. Let's face facts, children are sponges, and they see a lot more than we think. There are a lot of issues in today's world that are really sad, at least to me. We have people who do not like the way that a lot of our individual governments are being run, for example, and they are resorting to violence to express their frustration, and while this may not be happening around our children, they can see this going on because of the internet, the news on television, and from other sources.

This is an incredible opportunity for parents though, and I say that because it gives us the opportunity to talk to our children about these topics in order to try and explain to them how these issues should be handled, especially where *"Acceptance"* is concerned. You see, I truly feel that, if we are ever going to come together in peace and love without violence being involved, then we need to explain to our children how these situations should be handled. Here is the way that I would do it, see if you agree. First, I would tell children that we should never resort to violence to solve anything, because it does not change what we are angry about, especially where our governments are concerned. Then I would explain to them the fact that, the best way to solve an issue with our government, especially if we are upset about who is in charge of our government and what they are doing, is to let our dissatisfaction be shown when we exercise our right to vote, because that is the way that true change can happen. I would also tell them that, if they are worried that not enough people will vote for the change that they want (whether we are talking about changing a law or changing who is in charge of our government), then they should get involved in

76

drumming up support for the candidate/law that they want, even if that means that they take the time to campaign for what they want. When we vote is when we effect real change in our government, and it is change that our governments cannot ignore. If our elected officials see that we are doing what it takes to have them removed from office by voting them out of office, then they will listen to us, because they know that we can replace them with elected officials who will listen to us. The only thing that violence will do is cause chaos, and it will never effect real change (at least not in major countries like America), and therefore, if we want real change, then we need to let our voices be heard at the polls. Also, if we are worried that not enough people will vote in favor of our candidate or law, then that is where we need to make sure that everyone who agrees with us gets out and votes. Therefore, while we are campaigning, we should also be talking to people about whether or not they need help getting to the polls to vote.

Voting gives us the power to do a lot more than just replace a major politician though, it also gives us the power to do other things. Everything from deciding who will run our country all the way down to who runs our children's schools, because believe me when I say that what goes on in schools is something that is on our children's minds every day. Let's face facts, that is where they spend a lot of their young lives. Lately, for example, there has been a lot of controversy in America concerning some of the topics that are being taught in their schools. Let me give you one example. Let us talk about the trend lately concerning teachers teaching children topics that all parents do not agree that their children should be taught (to be specific, teaching children sexual issues). Now, I am not saying which side of the fence I sit on where this subject is concerned, however, what I am trying to say is how we can accept the responsibility to talk to our children about these topics in order to teach them how these situations should be handled. How to deal

77

A Visit to the City in the Light

with them so that they will know what to do when they are adults, and their children are in school. Now, the first thing that I think that parents should do is talk to their children constantly in order to see precisely what is bothering them about the schools that they attend, and to keep track of exactly what is going on in their schools and what they are being taught. Again, communicating with our children is key, not just to show them that we care about them, but to also learn what is going on in places like the schools that they attend. Then, armed with that information, parents should take action if they feel that their children are being taught things that they don't agree with, or if they feel that their children are not being taught things that parents feel they should be learning, and they do that by voting, because the people who run the schools in America, for example, are there because the voters voted them into their school board positions, and they can be voted out of their positions as well if they are allowing things to be taught in the schools that parents don't agree with, or if they are not allowing things to be taught that parents want their children to be taught. Parents should, and more importantly, can control what their children are being taught at school, because they should be in control of what their children are learning while they are growing up.

Now, having said that, I would tell children that, when they are adults and they see things going on in schools that they may not agree with, then that is where the power of their vote comes into play again. You see, in America for example, the school boards are the ones who control what goes on in the schools, and they also control who is teaching the children in those schools and what those children are being taught. Therefore, if parents do not agree with what is being taught in the schools that their children attend, then they should do more than just complain about it, because complaining will not solve anything or change anything. What they should do is let their displeasure be known at the next election by

voting to remove the school board members who are allowing things
to be taught that parents do not agree with so that they can be
replaced by school board members who will listen to the parents and
change what is going on in the schools that they do not agree with.
This is why I feel strongly that accepting the responsibility to
communicate with our children is so important, because they are the
ones who are going to be running our world one day, and we need to
teach them that we do have the power to control everything by doing
one simple thing, and that thing is exercising the power to vote (in
countries that allow voting that is, because unfortunately, there are
still countries that really don't allow their citizens to control things
by voting, and that is something that I feel we should address when
we do come together through *"Acceptance"*. Citizens are the ones
who should have the power over their governments, and the power
to control how their governments are run, not those in power). We,
as adults, should be the ones who control how things are done, and
who is in charge, of our individual countries, and we do that by
voting. We need to make sure that our children are taught this
lesson because it is so important.

Now, to continue with the topic of disciplining our children,
am I saying that children should never be punished? No, not at all,
because there are times when some type of punishment is necessary,
even if that is just a little swat on the butt. Children need to learn
that there are consequences for their actions. Bad consequences
when they do something wrong in order to teach them that they
should not do bad things, and good consequences when they do
something that is right. Always remember this because it is critical
when raising children. Children are very fragile, and it is extremely
easy to overdo it when we are punishing our kids. In order to
properly teach our children about right and wrong, we need to
explain to them why what they did was wrong before we just punish
them with no real explanation as to why what they did was wrong.

A Visit to the City in the Light

On the other hand, we need to explain to them why they should always try to do good things and how good actions can have good consequences as well, like helping them to achieve their goals. Goals like being successful and finding a love that will last a lifetime. The bottom line is that we need to talk to our children, and not just respond to them with intense emotions that have no reasoning what-so-ever. You would be amazed just how much of a difference that communicating with our children can make in their lives while they are growing up.

It is very easy for adults to get angry with their children (especially if they have had a bad day) when they are cranky and upset, and as a result they are misbehaving. A lot of adults might take their frustration out on their children when they should take a deep breath, step back, and determine calmly just why their children are upset so that they can help their children solve their problems without violence being involved. Remember this because it is important when raising children. Whatever the reason was that we had a bad day, say at work for example, it is not our children's fault. So, we should not take our adult frustrations out on them. They were not the ones who caused your boss to get mad at you, they were not the ones who gave you a speeding ticket, they were not the ones who *flipped you off* in traffic.......so we should not take these (or any other) adult frustrations out on them. Children cannot always express what is wrong with them. It could be the fact that they are hungry, or they are sleepy, or they are frustrated with something in their own little worlds. That is why we need to remember that they sometimes *'act out'* in order to get our attention. That is also why we need to remember this important fact.......they are innocent bystanders to our problems, so we should never treat them like they are the cause of our problems.

The key is this. Accept the responsibility to start showing

your children, when they are young, that you do care about them, and that you want to spend time with them and talk to them.   Show them that you want to spend quality time with them, that you want to teach them, and that how they feel is important to you.   If you do those things and spend time with them when they are first learning, then there is a good chance that they will grow up wanting to have the both of you, as their parents, in their life.   They will listen to you, and they will want to keep you in their lives, instead of trying to shut you out as they grow up.   This can be especially important as they get older and they are exposed to peer pressure.   Then, when other young people their age start doing things like illegal drugs, or committing crimes, they will definitely be more willing to talk to you about these problems than if you never spent any time with them and then just started to *'lay down the law'* in order to keep them out of trouble when they are older.

Now, does that mean that, if we did not spend the quality time with our children when they were young, we should just give up on them because we feel that it is too late at that point? Absolutely not.   We should never give up on trying to help our children, or on showing them that we truly do care about them. What I am saying is that we, as adults, need to accept the responsibility to set the example for our children early on by teaching them how to care, how to communicate, and everything else that sets the right example for them.   The earlier we do this, the easier it will be to help guide them through their lives.   Never think, though, that it is too late, because we should always try and be there for them, to teach them right from wrong.   Again, isn't that another big part of practicing the philosophy of *"Acceptance"*?   After all, if we want to have a world where everyone is good to each other, and respects each other, and accepts each other enough to get along and work together, then doesn't that also include teaching our children the right way to do this (and other things) so that they will be able to

81

continue teaching *"Acceptance"* to their children when they are running our world? Like I said, *"Acceptance"* is not going to happen overnight, but it will eventually happen if we teach our children the proper way to do things and how to be good to and respect others. Like ripples in a pond, if we teach our children the philosophy of *"Acceptance"* by showing them how to respect and care about other people, then they will teach their children, and eventually, it will spread until the goal of *"Acceptance"* is a universal practice that brings us all together in love, care, and peace.

For example, I have friends who never rose a hand towards their children (other than to give them a little swat on their behinds when they were young), and instead of them being spoiled brats who never listen to them, they are both caring children who actually talk to, and listen to, their parents. Why? Because their parents always raised them with strictness blended with kindness, compassion, and most importantly, by talking to them, and now they are more concerned with their parents being pleased with them, and making them happy, than they are with doing wrong. As a matter of fact, the only times that I have seen their children upset is when they thought that they did something to make their mom and dad upset, or they thought that they may have disappointed their parents through their actions, because that is the last thing that they want to do. When their parents have had to ask them for help with anything, they are more than willing to help, even if it is doing chores around the house, and the reason is because their parents actually took the time to let them know, through communication, that they are very important to them, and that they actually care about them, and how their day, and life, is going. If they ever see their children having problems with anything, they always try and let them know that they really do care about them, and that they are sincere when they tell them that they want to help them solve their problems.

A Journey There,.......and Back Again with a Message of Hope

My point is this.   The relationship that we have with our children is one of the most important relationships that we can foster with anyone else in our lives, because our children are our future, and if we want it to be a bright future, then we need to make sure that we set a good example when we are raising them, instead of teaching them the wrong lessons.   We should teach them that hard work will bring them what they want in life, because of the value of money in today's society, and that hard work will bring them that money and possibly huge success.   It will also teach them responsibility, as well as taking responsibility for their actions in their life.   We should be showing our children how a loving, caring relationship looks like by making sure that we actually care about our significant other so that they can see what true love should look like through example.   We should be showing them that a good education is key to getting what they want in life, and the multiple ways that we can educate ourselves.   We need to teach them how to be successful, through setting goals and developing plans to make those goals a reality.

The bottom line is that we should be taking responsibility for fostering a good relationship with our children by taking the time to show them that they are especially important to us, and we do that by actually spending time with them, talking to them, and teaching them ourselves, instead of just adopting the attitude of *'Well, that is what school is for'*.   If we show them that we do not care about them, then they will grow up not caring about us or anyone else, or what anyone has to say to them, and that can cause them problems throughout their lives.   On the other hand, if we show them that we do care about them, and we teach them the right way to do things in order to be a success in life, and we communicate with them, they will care about how they live their lives and how they interact with others.

A Visit to the City in the Light

There are some especially important areas where we should show them that we really do care about them, and what is going on in their lives. One of the areas where it is important to teach them the value of communicating with us is where bullying is concerned. Even though I will talk more about this in a later chapter, I would like to say here that, if we just take the time to find out how their day went each and every day by talking to them and showing them that we not only truly care, but that we want to help them with their problems no matter what they are, then it can make a world of difference in their lives, especially in the areas of peer pressure and where bullying is concerned. If children think that we don't care, then they will start adopting the attitude of *'Well, no one cares, so I need to do something about this myself'*, and that can be a dangerous attitude for a child to have, because they may feel that they need to take drastic steps in order to solve the problem of bullying in their lives, and as we have seen in such tragedy's as the rash of school shootings, their solutions could have devastating results.

That is why, again, I advise parents that it is especially important that they foster a good relationship with their children early in life by communicating with them to show them that they care about them, and that they also want to help them whenever they can. If we do these things, then they will carry on that tradition by doing the same things with their children, which is a really good cycle to foster. It is also important to know our children, which includes how they act and behave normally, because it can stop a tragedy from happening if we see a change in our children's attitudes, and we address it before it gets out of hand. It could be the difference between stopping something bad from happening because our children may feel that they have no one that they can turn to for help and having something really bad happen because no one was there for them when they needed us the most. The bottom line is that we need to always try and be a part of our children's lives.   If it is early on, then they will understand, and if it is later in life, they may hate us for trying to intrude into their lives, but in the end, they will understand, and it could help them turn their lives around if they are headed into trouble.

Speaking of fostering relationships where *"Acceptance"* is concerned, let us talk a bit about relationships with others around us, even if they are strangers.   It is sad to me just how wary people are of accepting help from others, especially total strangers.   There are so many people who have caused others harm (through crime and other despicable actions) that our trust in our fellow humans has been diminished to the point where *'good samaritans'* are an endangered species.   As such, it has caused us to not want to accept others into our lives when they are offering us help, even though they may have the best of intentions in mind, or even when they just want to meet us and possibly be our friend.   It is one of the biggest reasons that we will have a very hard time coming together as a race to help each other into a better future.   We are all so afraid that, if we do accept someone new into our lives, even if they are just offering to help us for a brief moment, that we could be harmed in some way, and that, in my mind, is one of the saddest things in the world.   It is important, though, to at least offer people help, because helping others, and even just meeting others to see if they want to be our friend, is another important part of practicing *"Acceptance"*. You see, by doing so, we are accepting the responsibility to be a good person, and to be there for others, and this can have such a positive effect in people's lives.   I've said it before and I'll say it again, *'random acts of kindness'* are some of the best acts of kindness just because of the positive effect that it can have on a person.   It is also why I feel that it is especially important to take the time to meet people, because once we get to know a person, and know that they are a good person (once they have earned our trust), then we can trust them more when they want to offer us their help in

85

A Visit to the City in the Light

the future.

Now, should we just trust someone completely that we just met? No, not in today's world, because there are so many people who do have hidden agendas that could cause us harm. I honestly believe that trust is not something that should be given to anyone immediately. Trust is something that should be earned over time. However, if people do earn our trust, then we should be more accepting of them. If they violate our trust though, then those are the people who we should be wary of. I'm not saying that people can't make mistakes, but I do feel that there is a difference between someone who violates our trust by telling a *'little white lie'* in order to plan a birthday party for us and someone who tells us that they are a loving partner and then they become violent with their partner, or who commits another type of crime against us like robbing our house after telling us that they would never commit a crime in order to gain our trust.

Criminal activity should never be tolerated, especially when it is a violent crime being committed by someone against the person who they should love and protect the most, their romantic partner. I absolutely abhor people who abuse their partners, because I strongly feel that, if you really do understand what love is, and you truly do have love in your heart for someone, then the last thing that you should ever want to do is harm them through hateful words or violent actions. Again, would you want your partner committing violent crimes against you? Then why do it to them? It is the same thing when meeting someone for the first time in today's world. Do we just give someone our complete trust when first meeting them, or when they are offering us their help and we do not know them that well, or do we allow them to earn our trust by taking *'baby steps'* with them until they have shown us that we can trust them?

A Journey There.......and Back Again with a Message of Hope

Unfortunately, in today's world there are people out there who want to cause us harm, however, there are also people out there who are good people, and who do want to earn our trust and be our friend. Therefore, I do believe that we should allow people who do want to be our friend and who do want to help us the opportunity to earn our trust. Take it slow, though, and truly give them the time to earn your trust. If they are good people, and they do not have a hidden agenda (like trying to take advantage of you in some way), then they will understand, and in the end, you stand a good chance of bringing another good friend into your life, and again, isn't that also what *"Acceptance"* is all about? Bringing us together for the benefit of all of us?

Look at it like this. Let's say that you meet someone one day, and you decide to just give them your trust immediately, without giving them time to earn it, and then, because you invited them over to your house right away, and they had a chance to see everything that you owned, they robbed you while you were at work one day. Is that something that you would want to happen all because you gave them your complete trust too quickly? Or worse yet, would you want to find out that someone that you love, say your wife or daughter, was raped by someone that you just met, all because you did not wait long enough to see if the person that you just met could be trusted and you invited them into your personal life too quickly? It is sad, but this is the world that we live in today, and because of that, we need to truly get to know someone before we can fully trust them. However, I believe that if we do take the time and get to know someone who is a stranger, and give them the time to earn our trust, then we can become friends with others.......but we must have them earn our trust before we just let them into our personal lives too quickly. I truly wish that things were different, but that is the world that we live in today. We can change things, though, if we just accept the responsibility to do so by learning to trust each other, and we do that by taking the time to earn each other's trust.

Now, does that mean we cannot work with them, or join them at a social gathering, or watch a game with them at a local pub? Does that mean that we cannot have lunch with them, or do anything else with them in a public social setting? Does that mean that we cannot be friends with them while they are earning our trust? Absolutely not, because that is how they will earn our trust, and we need to accept the responsibility to give people the chance to earn our trust before just writing them off, especially if they want to be our friend. There is a lot of evil in the world today, and we have to be careful of strangers as a result, but does that mean that we should not try to make friends, and be friends to others who may need a friend? Look, if we are ever going to come together, then we need to try and actually bring everyone together, and that involves making friends, and being a friend to those who need it, because there are a lot of people, right now, who are sitting at home alone wondering if they will ever have a good friend that they can trust. Again, if we are ever going to bring our race together through the practice of *"Acceptance"*, then we need to start trying to come together to get the things that we need to get done accomplished, and there is no better way to do it than by making friends. If I have learned anything in life, it is that we can accomplish things faster, and get more done, if we are doing it with our friends.

To sum this chapter up when talking about how to apply the philosophy of *"Acceptance"* where relationships are concerned, consider this. How do you want to be treated? How do you want to be loved? How do you want your co-workers to treat you? For that matter, how do you want everyone to treat you? With respect? With courtesy? With true caring and compassion? Then do this. Accept the responsibility to treat everyone the way that you want them to treat you.   Can you imagine how much better our world would be if everyone had compassion for everyone else?   Always be careful though, because unfortunately there are those who will try and take advantage of you, and may even want to commit crimes against you, but that is why we need to have strangers earn our trust by giving them the opportunity and the time to earn it.   If they are good people, and they do not have any hidden agendas, then they will understand.

Also, accept the responsibility to take the time to give your love for your partner a chance to grow, because true love that lasts a lifetime takes time to develop.   In addition, our children need to know that their parents will be together for life, because they deserve to have that level of security in their lives.   This will all take time as it will not happen overnight, but if we all pull together and start bringing our race together with love, care, and compassion, and start building trust in each other, then we will finally be able to start the healing process that our race desperately needs.   When that starts to happen, then our world will become an incredibly beautiful place in live in indeed.   Accept the responsibility to be the type of person that others want in their lives, the type of person that a partner wants to love, and the type of parent that a child wants to have.   If we do that, then we can finally come together.......and that is what the philosophy of *"Acceptance"* is all about.

Chapter Three
Acceptance and Work

"She sounds happy." - Me, in my truck.
"She is." - My Uncle Albert, in my truck.

Here is another area where we can really help ourselves and our lives through practicing *"Acceptance"*. We need to ask ourselves this question, *"Where am I now with the job that I am doing to make a living, and is this truly what I want to do, and am I truly happy with what I am doing?"*. Now, I want to state here that I really do believe that there is no job that is unimportant, especially when it comes to helping our world operate, and especially where our own happiness is concerned. We need to accept that fact, and once we do, then we will realize that our job, no matter how menial it may seem to others, is important. It is so important to be happy with our lives and accepting the responsibility to be happy where our job is concerned is critical to that. I think that this is what my uncle Albert was trying to convey to me, because the girl that he was talking about was tending to some flowers, and he wanted me to know that she is happy with what she is doing. Being happy with what we do is important to our life.

Ask yourself this question, *"Am I happy with what I do to make a living?"*. People sometimes think that they are not important because their job may be seen as menial or what people perceive to be not that important to the general scheme of things but believe me when I say that every job is important. I have tremendous respect for anyone who works any legitimate job (and I say *'legitimate'* because, at least in my mind, being a thief, or drug dealer, or any other type of criminal is not legitimate employment. Sure, they may get money when they commit their crime, but are they contributing to helping our race operate, or evolve for that matter?   All they are doing is hurting our race, not helping it) because they are contributing to making our world work, and to me, that is just as important as the person who does a job that people perceive as *'important'* to society.   The people who I worry about are the ones who make the conscious decision not to work at all, and they just stay at home in order to do nothing but play, or sleep, or basically say *"The world owes me a living, so I'm not going to do anything to contribute to our race."*, because they contribute nothing to society in my mind, or making our world a better place (unless, of course, their job is to do something like operate a home business, or they are a stay at home parent, which is incredibly important, but those type of situations are different than people who stay at home and do nothing to help our race operate and evolve).

Now, don't get me wrong, because again, in my mind, being a stay-at-home parent in order to raise your children properly is just as important as being a doctor.   Why?   Because our children are our future, and if we take the time to raise them properly, then our future will be bright.   They will be running our world one day and taking care of us in our *'golden years'*, so to speak, and if we take the time to better our children through raising them with the right ideals, and a kind heart, then they, in turn, will run our world better, which is especially important where the future of our race and practicing *"Acceptance"* is concerned.

Again, in my mind, there is no job that is unimportant, because every job out there is necessary in one way or another, and if you truly try and do it to the best of your ability, then you are a success.   I have more respect for someone who is doing a job and trying to do it to the best of their ability, than someone who just goes to work and does a poor job in order to just make a paycheck, all because they do not care about what they do, or how well they may do it.   The person who truly tries to do a good job in order to make our world work and be a better place truly does understand that work is what we all need to do in order to improve and evolve our race, because the people who work really do help our world operate in order to take us into a better tomorrow. *'Taking pride in your work'* is more than just a saying, it is a mental attitude that makes anyone who adopts it a better person, and a more productive member of socicty and our race.

A lot of people may think that something like working at a fast-food restaurant is not an important job but consider this. Is it important to the single mother who has just worked a full shift at her job, and she wants to feed her children, but she does not have the time to cook a full meal after work? Is it important to a single person who is ill, and they are just returning from the doctor or the hospital, and they need to eat some food with their medicine, but they do not have the energy to even make a sandwich? Is it important to the person who needs to eat something fast in order to get back to their job before their lunch break is over so that they will have the energy in order to do a good job at work? My point is this. If we would all just accept the responsibility to take a good look at the need of a job that some people think is unimportant before judging someone who works that job, then I truly feel that we would see that all jobs are important in order to make our world operate efficiently. Now again, let me be clear about something. I am talking about legitimate jobs, because something like robbing houses may be the way that someone makes money, however, it is not a legitimate job because it is a crime, period.

Fast food jobs are not the only jobs that some people consider unimportant jobs. Take janitorial work for example. If you think that this type of work is unimportant, then consider this. Just how much work would a medical company get done if they had to stop working and start cleaning the building they work in every

A Visit to the City in the Light

day?   They need to have a very clean workspace because of the type of work that they do in order to help our race, and they would not get much done if it weren't for the hard-working janitors who make sure that they have an immaculately clean workspace because they would be spending a lot of valuable time cleaning, time that could be used to do their medical jobs.   Or imagine any company or business for that matter, having to stop what they are doing just so that they can spend hours cleaning to make sure that they can run their company and get their work done.   Or how about cooks, like in a retirement home.   How would the nurses and doctors be able to take care of our loved ones properly if they had to stop what they were doing so that they could cook for them?   Wouldn't you feel better about where your loved ones lived in their golden years if you knew that the doctors and nurses could spend all of their time taking care of them, instead of spending the many hours that it takes to do the support jobs that are needed to care for them, like preparing all the meals?

My point is this.   In the overall scheme of things, there are no unimportant jobs.   Every job is critical to helping our race operate at maximum efficiency in order to advance into tomorrow, and that means that everyone who does one of these jobs is absolutely deserving of our respect.   That also means that everyone who does one of these jobs should be proud of the job that they do, because like I said, they are critical to making sure that our world keeps *'spinning'*, so to speak.   We need to accept that fact, because when we do, we can stop spending so much time and effort on feeling like we are unimportant just because we do one of these jobs, and we can be proud of ourselves for helping our race operate and get the things done that we need to get done in order to advance and evolve as the human race.

Let's try an exercise.   Tomorrow, when you leave home to

go to work (or even if you are not working tomorrow), take a look around and see how many people that you can see who are doing the support jobs that keep our world operating. Then, at some point, I want you to go up to someone who is doing one of those jobs and just say something to the effect of *"Thank you for doing a great job!"* or *"I really appreciate the hard work that you do!"* or *"You are really doing a great job and I really do appreciate it!"*, and then see the effect that it has on them. I do it every single day. When I go to get a burger (like I said, I am a *'junk food junkie'*), I always say *"Please"*, *"Thank you"*, *"Have a great day!"*, or something else to let them know that I really do appreciate them and the job that they do, and when I do, it always amazes me just how much better it makes them feel, and how much they appreciate it. Remember, *'random acts of kindness'* don't always have to be a physical gift like money, or even a hug. They can just be a few kind words that can really make someone's day special, and you would be amazed at just how much it can mean to someone who does a support job like being a janitor, or a landscaper, or a fast-food worker, or a gas station attendant, or any number of other jobs that some people consider to be unimportant. Like I said, I try every single day to let people know that there are no unimportant jobs to me, and that I do appreciate the hard work that they do, and the happiness that I see in their faces gives me happiness as well, because sometimes something as small as a kind word really can make a person's day special.

Now, once we accept, in our hearts, that there are no unimportant jobs, next we need to accept the fact that we need to do our jobs to the best of our ability, and the best way to do that is to first take a good look at our job performance. Then we need to accept the responsibility to make improvements to our performance (if needed) by doing things like accepting help from others in order to do our jobs better. However, if we are doing a good job at what

95

we do, then we should accept the responsibility of helping others who work with us in order to help them perform their jobs better (if they need help). It is always easy to see if someone needs help, because they struggle with things like getting their work done on time. Also, we need to accept the fact that there are times when we all need some kind of help where our job is concerned, no matter what our egos may tell us. We should ask others for advice, even if we do our jobs well, because another employee may know something that could be a trick to helping us perform our job better, something that we may not have even thought of doing before that could really help us to do our job easier or quicker. All we need to do is set aside our egos and simply ask someone for advice on how to do something better. It does not make us weak or a bad employee. What it does is shows everyone that we really do care about our job performance. Like I have said many times, the only time that the words *'stupid'* and *'question'* should ever be used in the same sentence is when we make the *'stupid'* decision not to ask a *'question'* because we let our *'stupid'* egos get in the way of asking a *'question'*, especially when the answer might really help us.

Now, as we all know, it is much easier to ask someone for help if we need it, because when we do, it shows others that we care about our job performance. We are not stepping on anyone's toes, so to speak, because we are the ones who are asking for help. However, when we do something like trying to help someone else with their job performance, it can be trickier. It is always important to remember that everyone has some level of pride, and as such, we need to approach this effort with some tact. We do not want them to feel like we are attacking them personally, or that we feel that we are better than them. So, we need to really think about how to do this before we just charge in with suggestions.

Here is how I would do it. See if it helps you the next time you attempt to help someone at your work.   First, when you see someone who is either new at your job, or who may need help, start out by befriending them first.   Introduce yourself if they are new or talk to them in a friendly way if they have been there for a while.   Let them know that you want to be their friend first.   Then, if they are approached by a supervisor and/or reprimanded, or if you see them struggling, more than likely they will be much more open to you trying to help them with their performance because they will see you as a friend who is trying to help them, instead of someone who is just trying to attack them or criticize them further.

Next, if you see that they need help, rather than saying something like *'Hey, you look like you are having problems, so let me tell you how to do it better'* (because they could see that as a personal attack), say something like *'Hey, can I show you a trick that I use to do that better (or faster)?'* or *'Hey, I found a way to do that easier.   Can I show you?'*.   When you approach people at work in this fashion, the chances are much better that they will not see it as a personal attack, instead, they will see it as a friend who wants to help them do their job easier.   We all have friends, whether at work or in our personal lives, and we are always open to our friends helping us, no matter what it is that we are doing, because we know and accept the fact that they are our friends, and as such, we accept the fact that they are not trying to attack us.   Instead, we see that they are trying to help us because they are our friend.   Always remember that we can get a lot more accomplished if we are all friends who are working together.   A lot more done than if we feel like we are all competitors who are trying to outdo each other.   So, remember, accept the responsibility to be friendly with your co-workers, especially if they are new employees.   It can make everyone's day go easier if we feel like we are working with our friends.

A Visit to the City in the Light

In addition, when someone approaches you with a suggestion, do not feel like they are trying to degrade you, or that they are *'after you'*, so to speak. Instead, look at it as a chance to learn how to do something better, or faster, or easier, and accept it as it is coming from a friend who cares about you. Do not let your ego get in the way, just listen to what they have to say, and then see if it does help you. You do not have to follow their advice, but you should at least listen to them in case it is something that can help you at your job. In this way, you could also be learning who you can trust at your job, because if the person who is offering you advice really wants to help you, then they will give you advice that really can help you, which goes back to earning trust. In the end you might actually pick up tips that could help you be a better employee and help you to do your job a lot faster or easier, which in turn can help your day go much better.

Now, does that mean that we have to invite our work friends to our homes, or maybe have them date our daughter, or name our first born after them? No, not at all, but we should, at least, try to befriend them when we are at work in order to work with our fellow employees better. I have always advised people to keep work separated from home if at all possible, because our work deserves our full attention, and just as importantly, our home and family deserve all of our attention when we are there with them. If we take our work home, then it will affect us and our relationships with our loved ones, because we may have worries at work for example, and if we bring those worries home, then they could cause problems at home with our loved ones. Now, am I saying that we can never have friends at work who are our friends outside of work as well? No, I am not saying that either, because we can have the same friends in both arenas. What I am saying is that we should not feel that we need to have the same friends at work that we have at home.

A Journey There.......and Back Again with a Message of Hope

While our work friends could be great friends to have fun with after work, we should never feel like we have to be friends with our fellow employees after work. It is ok to say that we want to keep our work separated from our home, and that can be especially important when we are talking about co-workers who are the opposite sex, as recent tragic events have shown us. One example would be when someone at work decides that they want to have a romantic relationship with another employee who does not want to have one with any co-worker, especially when one of the co-workers is the other one's supervisor. It can cause one of the employees to feel like they either have to have a romantic relationship with the other employee or else, which should never be the case. No one should ever try and take advantage of someone that they work with by making them feel like they either have to have a relationship with them or they could lose their job. I absolutely abhor people who try and force others into romantic relationships with threats, or even veiled threats, and the ones who do it at the places we work are some of the worst, at least in my opinion.

Let me explain. It is very easy to be manipulated into thinking that we have to be more than friends with our co-workers of the opposite sex both at work and when we are away from work, especially when they are our supervisor, because we could be lead to believe and feel that our jobs may depend on being more than friends with them on a romantic level, and that is a problem, because it could lead to our co-workers treating us inappropriately, and cause them to take advantage of us in ways that should never happen. Let me repeat that because it is too important. Co-workers trying to force other co-workers to have a romantic relationship with them, just because they work together, is wrong. It should never, ever happen to any woman or man just because they work with someone else.

A Visit to the City in the Light

We need to accept the fact that it is ok to be friendly with our co-workers, but it should stop there. No one should ever feel like they have to be *'more than just friends'* with a co-worker. We need to accept the fact that, just because someone is friendly with us at work, it does not mean that they want a romantic relationship with us. It is called *'Being Professional'*. Be professional with co-workers, be friendly with co-workers, but never think that our place of work is a singles bar, and someplace where we go to meet someone to be intimate with. Our co-workers are just that, our co-workers, and they should be treated as such, with dignity, respect, friendliness, kindness, and nothing more. You would not want to find out that someone you care about, say your daughter, or son, or wife, or even your husband, was suffering sexual harassment at their place of work. So why would you ever treat anyone at your place of work like that?

Now, am I saying that romance never blossoms between co-workers? No, not at all, because I know a wonderful couple who worked at the same job as their significant other, and they still have a great relationship together. It happened, though, because they met outside of work before they realized that they were working in the same company (in this case because they attended the same church) and they had the chance to get to know each other and develop their relationship outside of their job. Also, they were both on the same level, meaning that neither was the other's supervisor, so there was no threat of *'You are going to lose your job if you don't go out with me'*. As a matter of fact, when this happened, one of them actually left their job and found another one so that there would never be any problems at their place of employment (like arguments that started at home and continued at work). In other words, they met each other before they realized that they were working together at the same company, and they got to know each other because they attended the same church. Then, once they realized that they were

100

working for the same company, they accepted the responsibility to continue to develop their relationship outside of their work, because they realized that they should keep their work and home life separate so that there would not be problems at their work, or with their relationship, and they are still incredibly happy and in love because of that.

Now, be careful here, and I say that because of this reason. If you start working with someone, and they show an interest with you, and then suddenly they start showing up at your church, or the night club you hang out at with your friends, etc., then that is a sign that maybe they may be stalking you, and stalking is never ok, under any circumstances, for any reason. It is sad, but unfortunately, it is a fact of life in today's world. There are people out there who do not have the best intentions in mind, and they can be extremely dangerous. That is why I want to state the following. Anytime you go out for the evening, make sure that you are not alone, make sure that you are with friends, because it can keep you safe. Also, if you think, for any reason, that someone might be stalking you, especially if it is someone that you work with, then tell people about it so that they are aware of what might be going on as well. In other words, do not keep things inside of you just because you are afraid of causing someone trouble, or because you think that you might be over-reacting.

If you think that someone might be stalking you, then tell your friends, your family, your church, even the police. Then always be with someone when you go out. I know this sounds like a very paranoid stance to take, but which would you rather be? The person who is wrong and safe, or the person who suffers through a sexual assault or even gets murdered at the hands of a lunatic? I know which person I hope my friends decide to be. Also, if you do get harassed at work, and you report it, and/or you tell the person who is being *'too friendly'* with you that you do not like what they are doing and that they need to stop, and then they do not stop.......then that is when you definitely need to take further action. Don't just *'suck it up'* because you think that you need your job too badly, and/or because you are afraid of being fired.   Tell people what is going on, both inside your job and outside your job as well. In other words, be safe at all costs, and do not put up with it.

Just remember this.   Treat your co-workers like they are your co-workers, and not like they are *'on the menu'* where your intimate social life is concerned.   Also, if you are a supervisor, always remember that your subordinates are **people**.   People who are there because they need to be able to survive, and so that they can contribute to your company and to making our world and race operate, and they should be treated with respect, the way that you would want others to treat, oh say, your wife, husband, daughter, or son.   The people who are being harassed know that they need their job, and it is actually scary for them to think of how they would survive, and pay their bills, without it.   So, do not use your position of authority to try and take advantage of them.   Treat them with respect and dignity.   Help them to do a great job by putting them at ease, and the way to do that is by not trying to be too friendly with them at work.   If you let them know that you view them as an employee and nothing more, then they will be happy working for you, and a happy employee is a productive employee, and as a boss, isn't that what you really want in the end?

As a matter of fact, I would recommend to any supervisor that they never date a subordinate at their work, even if they approach **you** in an intimate manner.   Again, let me explain.   Let's say that you are a supervisor at a company.   Then suddenly, one day, a single (or married) subordinate comes to you and starts flirting with you, to the point where they actually ask you out on a date.   So, you go, and then later on, everything goes wrong.   It could be the fact that the other employees at your company start saying that you are showing favoritism towards the employee that you are dating, and they start doing things like filing grievances, which can cause you big problems.   Or maybe the subordinate that you start dating starts coming to you and saying that you had better promote them, or give them the best shifts at work, or they will claim that you harassed them, even though you never harassed anyone.

There are those who feel that they need to do whatever it takes to get ahead in their career, even if that means making false claims against you as their supervisor.   They could even be thinking that, if they get rid of you by setting you up with a false claim of harassment, then they could take your job.   Once upon a time they called it a form of *sleeping your way to the top*, and unfortunately, it still goes on today.   Now, again, do not get me wrong, because I do know that there are supervisors who are harassing employees, but there are also subordinates who are doing what I just said as well. So, how do you protect yourself at work, whether you are a supervisor or an employee?   It is really simple.   If you are a supervisor, then accept the responsibility to be a supervisor, and nothing more.   Be a good person.   Do not put yourself in a situation that could be misconstrued as something bad, because when you do, either you are up to no good because you are harassing an employee, or you are setting yourself up to be falsely accused as someone who is harassing an employee, and in either case, it will end up bad for you.

Accept the responsibility to do things a certain way, a professional way, and that includes doing things the right way when you are looking for love.   There are many web sites now that are for single, professional people.   People who are supervisors at their

103

places of work, or who hold professional degrees and specialized jobs, and who want to meet others like themselves for dating and romance. That is one place where I would recommend that supervisors or other professionals meet their partners for dating. Another place is where the couple that I mentioned earlier met, which was at their church, or at any outside organization where people can meet each other in a social setting.

The bottom line is this. If you are a professional person, or you are a supervisor, then the worst place, at least in my mind, to look for love is at your place of work because of all the potential problems that it could cause. Problems that include the stress that is caused to the subordinate that you are harassing, or problems that could include claims against you if you decide to date a subordinate who approaches you romantically. Keep your work and your love life separate, because worrying about how good of a job someone does while they are working is stressful enough. Adding the stress of having someone try to make advances towards them, or take advantage of them in an intimate way, or making them feel uncomfortable in any way that does not have to do with their job performance, should never be a part of anyone's job. People, especially employees, deserve to be treated with respect and dignity at all times, so accept the responsibility to treat all of your employees like that. By treating your employees with dignity and respect, you will get the respect that you deserve as well. Accept the responsibility to be the example, not the problem.

Ok, in the spirit of *"Acceptance"*, I am going to suggest something here. If you can think of a better way to do it, then please, write it down, because we need to accept the responsibility to make workplace sexual harassment a thing of the past, and we are the ones who can make it a thing of the past. To me, it's really simple, and it comes down to a few steps.

A Journey There.......and Back Again with a Message of Hope

Step #1: Accept the responsibility to accept the fact that if you are a supervisor, then all you will do is be a supervisor, and nothing more. Supervise your employees job performance, and give them instructions concerning what is expected from them where their job is concerned, and monitor their job performance in a professional manner. Make sure that they do a good job, because after all, their job performance directly affects your overall job performance. It is not your responsibility to touch your employees, you can supervise them without doing that. It is not your job to do things like make questionable comments or tell jokes that may be offensive to some of your employees (unless you are a comedian, I suppose, but even then, keep it on the stage and not in the face of your employees) and supervise all of your employees to make sure that they are doing their jobs without doing anything to harass or offend their fellow employees as well. It is not your job to invite your subordinates (or even fellow supervisors) out on a date, or to even contact them after work at all (unless they are expected to work from home, but even then, you could email them, or give them their instructions while they are at work. There are ways to communicate with employees who work at home without being inappropriate with them). If you want to find love, then do it properly by going to places outside of work to meet people. You place of employment is not your *'hunting grounds'* where your love life is concerned. Bottom line? Just be a supervisor, and nothing more. Treat your employees the way that you would want to be treated, and the way that you would want others to treat the people that you care about at their job. Like I said, accept the responsibility to be the example, not the problem.

Step #2: If you are an employee, then be an employee, and nothing more. Let your job performance speak for you as an employee. Do not tell questionable jokes that may offend other employees or touch other employees inappropriately or in a questionable manner (you can be friendly with you fellow co-workers without offending them).   Do not harass fellow employees in any manner.   Do not look for love at work, again, go outside of work to seek a partner.   If you are one of those employees who think that you need to *'sleep with your boss to get to the top'*, then maybe you either need to improve your job performance so that it can get you to the top, or you need to find another type of employment that you can do well enough to be a success at without having to sleep with anyone.   Again, accept the responsibility to be the example, not the problem, and treat other employees the way that you want to be treated.

Step #3:   (This is the one that is going to cause most people to raise their eyebrows, because of the *'Big Brother'* thing, but if you can think of a better way to combat workplace harassment then suggest it, or better yet, put it into practice, because we have to stop this type of behavior once and for all)   If you own a business (or you are the one who can make this happen, like the Chairman or CEO of a company), then here is what you do.   You put up security cameras throughout your entire business (except in places like the bathroom, of course, I mean, come on, we have to have some privacy), and then you let everyone know that they are there in order to protect employees and stop workplace harassment by catching the bad employees in action.   As history has shown us, trusting people just has not worked, and we need to take action at this point to stop this type of behavior once and for all.   I can tell you this.   Just the thought of being caught on camera while being inappropriate at work will stop a lot of people from doing things that they should not do at work, and anything that can stop this type of behavior is a good thing.   In addition, there are already some businesses and companies that are doing this, so this is not as controversial as some might think.   As a matter of fact, in my opinion, the people that this would bother the most are either the people who are already harassing employees and they want to continue doing it without being caught, or those who are wanting people to believe that they have been harassed when they know that they were not harassed (because they would want to make the claim that they were harassed without any proof to the contrary, and the cameras would provide proof that they were not harassed).   Let me ask you a question.   If you were ever harassed at work, wouldn't you want to video proof that it happened?   Also, if you are a supervisor, or an employee, and you are falsely accused of workplace harassment, wouldn't you want to have the same type of proof that it never happened?   Again, the attitude of *'We are just going to trust people'* has not worked, and at this point, this type of behavior has gone on long enough.   To coin a phrase, *'Desperate times call for desperate measures'*.   We need to put a stop to this, and we need to do it now.   No one should ever be harassed at work, and no one should ever be falsely accused of harassing someone at work as well.

Now that we have talked about one of the ugly sides of work, let's go back to examining what type of job we do, and if we are happy doing what we are doing.   Let's try another exercise.   First, I want you to take a piece of paper and a pencil, and I want you to write down 5 different jobs that would be your *'5 dream jobs'*. Then, next to each one, I want you to write down why each one would be your dream job.   For example, let us say that you write down *'Doctor'* as one of your dream jobs.   First of all, what type of doctor would you want to be (because there are all sorts of specialties where the field of medicine is concerned)?   Then, write down why you would want to be that type of specialist.   Now, I know that most everyone who writes down *'Doctor'* as one of their dream jobs is going to say that, among other reasons, they want to be one because of the money.   Now, while being a doctor would bring you good money, you should not list that as the only reason that you want to be a doctor, and I say that because of this.

A Visit to the City in the Light

If money is your only goal, then you will never be happy with your work. Oh true, money can rent happiness for a while, but in the end, it never truly brings you happiness at your work, and as such, you will never be able to truly enjoy your job, because if your only focus is the money, then you will be so busy worrying about the money that you are making (over things like taxes, and bills, and investments, to name a few) that you will miss out on the many wonderful things that being a doctor can bring you. Things like helping people live a healthy life, being the person who saves someone's loved one, curing diseases that people get, and the like. You see, we should accept the fact that it takes more than money to make someone genuinely happy with their job, and I can sum it up with these words.......**personal satisfaction** and **true inner happiness**.

I am not talking about fame, I am not talking about conceitedness, bragging rights, or even having an over inflated ego. What I am talking about is the satisfaction of knowing that you were responsible for helping the human race operate better by doing a great job at what you do, no matter what you do for a living. It could be the satisfaction of knowing that, as a doctor, you helped a small child by giving them hope for a better, and healthier, tomorrow. It could be the satisfaction of knowing that it was you who helped the single person get the fast food that they needed in order to feed their children after work. It could be the satisfaction of knowing that you did a good job at making sure that the medical company you work for would have a very immaculate space to work in when they come in tomorrow (so they could concentrate on doing things like curing diseases, all because of the great job that you did). Or maybe the satisfaction of knowing that it was you, as a fireman, who saved a family by putting out the fire in their building. Or maybe the satisfaction of knowing that it was you who made sure that all the filing and correspondence was done correctly so that the doctor that you work for could concentrate all of their attention and efforts on saving the small child that I mentioned earlier. I am talking about the personal satisfaction of knowing that you helped make sure that our race was able to operate at maximum efficiency so that we could get everything done that we need to do in order to advance into a better tomorrow. When you can come home and feel good about yourself because of the job that you did at work and be happy with yourself without bragging or receiving any praise for what you did that day, then that is what personal satisfaction is all about. That is when you know that you are happy with the job that you are doing. In addition, when you achieve that level of personal satisfaction, it will bring you the inner happiness that makes you feel good about what you did.

Now, let's talk just briefly about another concern where working a job is concerned.......and that is making enough money to survive and pay our bills. I understand that a lot of people who work jobs like fast food preparation, janitorial, and the like, would like to make enough money to pay their bills on a one-person income each month, but unfortunately, it rarely happens in today's world, especially if we are married and have a family. Now, I always advise people that, if they are single and working a job that does not pay much, then they need to do what it takes to make sure that the bills are paid. If that means that they need to move in with a roommate if they are single, then they should do it (of course, be cautious about it. Select a friend that you have known for a while, someone who you know is responsible and who is working so that they can help you pay the bills. In other words, someone that you know you can trust. Never move in with a total stranger unless you have absolutely no choice, and then check them out thoroughly, including getting references and performing extensive background checks, so that you know that you are not moving in with a 'maniac', so to speak).

A Visit to the City in the Light

We cannot expect the world to just give us a living, and no one owes us a living, so if we want to be able to make it on a smaller income, then we need to be proactive in making sure that enough money is coming in to pay the bills. This is what is meant by the saying *'make a plan to reach your goals'*, because that plan should include how the bills are going to be paid until you reach your personal goals for success.

Again, if that means that you need to move in with someone, then do it (again, get references and do your homework). If that means that you need to get a second job, then do it. The bottom line is this. Until you can get a better job that pays more, or a higher position where you presently work, then you need to do what it takes to survive, achieve financial security, and thrive (without committing any crimes, of course), and only sitting at home worrying about how to pay the bills is not the answer. There are a lot of people who do work two jobs, even when they are in school trying to get a better education in order to get a better paying job, and while it is hard at times, it often pays off in the end. If you are doing that, then the chances are good that the school counselor or advisor can lead you to places at the school you are attending where you can find lists of jobs for students as well as lists of students who are looking for roommates (again, check them out thoroughly). There are also a lot of couples who both have to work in order to survive. Sometimes we need to do what we need to do in order to make it until we are a success and achieve our goals, however, I do have a suggestion that can help people who are struggling to bring in enough money to survive, and I will go into that in more detail later.

The bottom line is this. We all want to be a success. We all want to have financial security. We all want to work a job that does more than pay the bills. We want a job that makes us happy while giving us financial security. We want to be able to provide for our family so that they can have everything that they want and need. We want to be able to go out and buy the nice things that we want in life, like new cars, nice furniture, electronics, and whatever else we may want to make us, and our loved ones, happy. We want to be able to take nice vacations whenever we want, like to amusement parks or maybe the beach. Now, in a perfect world, we would be able to work any job and be able to afford to do all of that. Unfortunately, we do not live in a perfect world. What that means is that, in order to provide ourselves with the financial security and success that it would take to do all of that, then we do have some choices, ones that could make all of this happen (again, I am not going to list committing crimes as a choice. Look at it like this.......would you want to come home and find everything that you had earned through hard work stolen from you? Then why, as a good person who loves and respects their fellow humans, would you do it to someone else?). Some choices that are realistic, and others that are more, well, out of reach to most of us.

Like I said, there are some realistic options that we have available to us, options that could give us more financial security (if you can come up with more, then write them down, and then pursue them if you are able to). One is to work more than one job, or to have both partners in a relationship working so that you can bring home enough money to buy the things that you want, and to do the things that you want to do. Another one would be to go back to school and get a degree so that you can get a better paying job and afford the life that you want (and please, do not let *'I didn't graduate from High School'* stop you, because there are options to take care of that).

Now, there are some unrealistic options as well. One would be to become *'famous'*, or to get *'discovered'* by a talent scout or a celebrity, and then get rich doing that (good luck, even with the

111

internet helping you.   Most people who become famous enough to make a fortune have two things.   Some kind of talent that everyone wants to see, and the people connections who will help them get ahead of everyone else by giving them the *'breaks'* that they need). Another one would be to become a famous athlete, and then sign a multi-million-dollar contract to play for some team (long shot at best, because of all the competition).   One more would be to invent something that no one can live without, and then make a fortune selling it (but in this case, you would still need to make the money necessary to live and pay the bills until you come up with an idea for something that no one can live without, and then you would need to come up with the money to buy the materials to build a prototype, and then you would need to pay to have it patented, and then you would need to get the money together to manufacture the product, and then you would need the money to advertise your product, and then.......well, you get the idea).   It takes a lot of money to be an inventor, because you still need to survive while you are producing and selling your invention, which is not as easy as it sounds, unless, of course, you get investors to help you with your product, but there again, good luck.   Still another one would be to win the lottery, but even the lottery knows that this is an exceptionally long shot (when they tell you, in their own ads, that the lottery should be played for entertainment purposes only, and not investment purposes, then that should tell you something.   I know people who have played the lottery all of their lives without winning much of anything, so consider that before you run down and spend all of your money on lottery tickets instead of saving it up to do the things that you want to do).

I guess what I am trying to say is this.   Sitting around wishing that you were rich (while not doing anything to actually make it happen) will never work.   It takes hard work to make your dreams come true, but if you are willing to put in that hard work, then it can pay off for you, no matter what your dream is. I know people who started out working in the landscaping business, and now, because of hard work and saving their money, they own their own landscaping company. I know other people who started out working for other companies, like fast food restaurants, and through hard work and saving their money, they now own their own franchise businesses. How did these people achieve their dreams? By making a long-term plan to make their dreams come true, and then by making it happen through hard work and saving their money.

These successful people saw what they wanted to be, and then they came up with a plan to make it happen, and then they put in the hard work to make it happen. They did not sit around hoping that it would happen for them, and they did not just wait for someone else to give them their dreams. They got up, made a plan, and then they made it happen. Just remember, though, that no matter what your dream is, it will take hard work and sacrifice. Nothing good in this life ever comes easy, and no one owes you a living, so it is truly up to you to make it happen. You have to accept the fact that you will need to survive until you achieve your goals and dreams. If you do what it takes, however, then you will have a chance to make your dreams come true. It can really help you if you are in a relationship, because now you have someone to help you make both of your dreams a reality. There is an old saying that goes *'Two heads are better than one'*, and this is especially true if you have a partner who wants to help both of you succeed.

So, just remember these few things where your job is concerned. First, accept the responsibility to find a job that makes you happy, no matter what it is, because there are no unimportant jobs when it comes to helping our world and our race operate and advance into the future. So never let anyone tell you that there are.

113

A Visit to the City in the Light

Second, if you have a dream where your job is concerned, then accept the responsibility to make a plan and then go for it, just always remember that it will take hard work to achieve your dreams (because the bills will still have to be paid).   If you are willing to accept the responsibility to put in that hard work, though, then you have a good chance to succeed.   Third, do not just consider yourself where your, and other people's, job is concerned.   Accept the responsibility to always be willing to take the time to let others know that you appreciate them and the job that they are doing.

Also, do not harass anyone at your place of work.   If you are a supervisor, then be a supervisor and nothing more.   If you are an employee, then be the employee that does not make others that you work with uncomfortable by harassing anyone either through physical actions, questionable words, or offensive jokes. Remember, treat your co-workers the way that you would want to be treated, and the way that you would want others to treat the ones that you care about and love.   Accept the responsibility to be the example, not the problem.   Fourth, accept the responsibility to give your partner the respect that they and their dreams deserve, especially if they are a stay-at-home parent, because being a stay-at-home parent is incredibly important to helping our race succeed, and they are worthy of our respect at all times.   Finally, accept the responsibility to do a job that gives you personal satisfaction and true inner happiness.   I am not talking about doing a job just for bragging rights or doing a job because you want praise or the money.   Do it because it makes you feel proud of doing it.

After all, at the end of the day, if you are proud of the job you are doing to help our race operate and advance into tomorrow, even without praise, then you are happy, and being happy with the job that you do will make you happier with your life in general, and isn't that the most important thing of all?   Being happy with your life, and helping our race advance and evolve into tomorrow, the way that *"Acceptance"* dictates we should all be working together to do?

Chapter Four
Acceptance and Fun

"Yeah, let's have some fun." - My Uncle Albert, outside of the City.

Now, let's stop being serious for a bit, because in order to make ourselves a better person, and a more productive member of the human race, we need to take care of ourselves in other ways as well. We need to take care of ourselves both physically, and just as importantly, emotionally in order to be a more well-rounded person and lead a more balanced life. This is why I believe that my Uncle Albert said this to me outside of the city before we went anywhere together. He always asked me if I was having fun when I was growing up and tell me that it was good to have fun. Therefore, let us talk about accepting the responsibility to take better care of a part of our emotional selves for a bit. Let us talk about how important it is for us to take the time, as often as possible, in order to play and have fun. After all, if we are going to put *"Acceptance"* in to practice by caring about others, then isn't it also important to care about ourselves as well?

Now, I can just hear a lot of people out there telling their partners *'See, I told you that I need to play these video games, because if I don't, then I am going to get sick and die, and you don't want to see that do you?'*. Now, allow me to state here, for the record, that I am not saying that we should only play and not get anything else done, like work. If we do not work to bring in money to pay the bills and to achieve our dreams of financial security, then we will not have much of a way to play video games while being homeless. What I am saying is that we need to have that healthy balance for the sake of our emotional selves, and the best way to do that is by making time for fun.

117

A Visit to the City in the Light

Now, there are some who may say that there is no room for play past a certain age, but I have always believed that, if we are to take better care of ourselves, then we definitely need to take care of our emotional selves, and one of the best ways to do that is to always make time for play. Play can be one of the best gifts that we can give ourselves. I have always said that laughter is medicine, and there is a lot of truth to that, and one of the best ways to produce a good laugh is through play. I have always told people that the day we start ignoring the kid inside us and start being serious all the time is the day that we start to die emotionally. Remember what it was like to be a kid? Remember what it was like to play? If you cannot remember what it was like to play just to make yourself happy, then there is a problem, because you are not taking care of your emotional self as good as you could be. When people say that laughter is medicine, they truly do mean medicine. Medicine for your emotional self.

Try this. Find something humorous, like a joke. Go on, I'll wait. Now, ask yourself this question. Didn't that make you feel better, just by laughing? We all feel better from a good laugh because of what it causes to happen within our bodies when we do laugh. Hormones that are activated and released within our brain called Endorphins. They are released into our bodies anytime we do something like laughing, and they can really do a lot to take care of our emotional self. Why? Because Endorphins are *'feel good'* chemicals that reduce stress and are said to activate opiate receptors in our bodies causing an analgesic effect. They trigger a positive feeling in the body, similar to that of drugs such as morphine. In other words, they make us feel happy, because they cause feelings of euphoria and general well-being to be released into our bodies. The best part? They do this without us having to take any drugs to get the same effect. This is one of the biggest reasons that it is enjoyable to play games, because when we do, it makes us feel better due to the endorphins.   Playing games also do other things for us that help us cope with life in general, things like fulfilling our innate competitive need to win or to be good at something.   There are other activities that release endorphins into our system as well (like when we make love), but for now, let us stick to our need for play.

What was your favorite game when you were a kid?   Was it a board game, or maybe a video game?   Was it something as simple as *'Hide and Seek'* or *'Tag'*?   Whatever it was, try this.   The next time you get a chance to, get some friends together and play a game like *'Hide and Seek'* or *'Tag'*, and definitely involve your kids if you are blessed enough to have them.   When you do things like this with your children, you are not only accepting the responsibility of taking care of your emotional self, but you are also accepting the responsibility of fostering a great relationship with your children and of teaching them how to take care of their emotional selves as well. I know lots of adults who play these (and other) games all the time, and they are some of the happiest people that I know because they are not afraid to have fun no matter what their age is.

Now, there are a lot of people who might think along the lines of *'Well, that's just silly, playing games like that as an adult'*, however, those are the people that I truly feel sorry for, because they have forgotten how to have fun like a kid.   So, find some good friends, schedule a time that works for everyone, and just play for the sake of playing.   Now, I am not saying that you should only play either *'Hide and Seek'* or *'Tag'*, because there are a lot of other games that are fun, especially when you are outdoors.   Games like *'Cornhole'*, *'Croquet'*, or *'Badminton'*, for example.   They are all fun outdoor games that we can play.   We can also play different sports if we have enough people to play with, like Basketball, Baseball, or Football.   The point that I want to make here is this.

A Visit to the City in the Light

When you get the chance, accept the responsibility to go play and have fun. You will be amazed at just how good it can make you feel.

We all have the need for play. A lot of us, though, tell ourselves that we are either too busy, or too serious, to play for the sake of playing. I know people who are so serious that they literally work themselves into an early grave. I say that because I am a firm believer that all work and no play can literally cause us physical harm, and cause us to not only suffer certain illnesses, but also make some illnesses worse in our bodies. We can get physically sick because of worry, or stress, and what is one good way to fight this harm? Play, pure and simple. This is especially true when it comes to people who are in a relationship with someone. I have seen many relationships grow stronger just because both partners play together. If you are in a relationship, show your partner that you care about them and their happiness as much as you care about your own. It can really make love grow stronger if both partners accept the responsibility to show each other how much they care about each other, and that includes caring about their happiness in all ways possible.

Doctors say that stress can exacerbate many health conditions, to include increasing the risk of worsening conditions that already exist. Conditions like obesity (after all, a lot of us eat to make ourselves feel better when we are stressed), heart disease, gastrointestinal problems, depression, and high blood pressure, just to name a few. Take my word for it, because I had a heart attack, like I mentioned earlier, and my doctors told me that the problem that I had with my heart was exacerbated by the stress in my life. It was then that I decided that I would make sure that I reduced the stress in my life by playing every chance I got, and since I made that life altering decision, I have actually felt so much better that I now advise all my friends to play as often as possible. So, believe me when I say that stress can be a killer, because it almost killed me.

Now, I am not saying that we should only play by ourselves, ignoring everyone else around us (especially our partners), because play is also a great way to improve our personal relationships, whether they are new or established ones. Take going out on a first date with someone, for example. Which date sounds more fun to you? Going out to a restaurant, having a few drinks at a local pub, and then heading home, or going out to a play spot, like a miniature golf course, or an amusement park, or a carnival, and having a lot of fun and laughs with that special person that you want to impress? I do not know about you, but when I have spoken to people, especially women, they always tell me that they love a person who can *make them laugh*, and what better way to make a person laugh than by taking them to a play spot on a first (or second, or third, or whatever number) date? It can go a long way to making a relationship start off on the right foot by showing the person that we want to impress that we truly do care about their feelings and whether or not they are happy, and it can also help to keep an established relationship stay on the right foot by keeping the love alive, no matter how long people have been together. Keeping love alive in a long-term relationship can be hard at times, but I can say this with certainty. It is a lot easier if both partners have a lot of fun together during their lives. I have spoken with a lot of people who have been married for many years, and they all told me that one of the best ways to keep love alive and happy in a long-term relationship is by keeping the spontaneity and fun alive in their relationships, and one of the best ways to do that is by playing together.

But playing should not be something that we do just for ourselves, or for our romantic partners. As I stated earlier, playing

A Visit to the City in the Light

can be extremely important in helping us foster good in all sorts of relationships. Take our relationship with our children, for example. I have spoken with many people who have told me that some of their fondest memories from their childhood was when their mom or dad (or a relative) took the time to sit down and play a game with them. Or when their mom and dad took them to an amusement park, or to a carnival, or to a sporting event. Some told me that their fondest memory was when they went to have a picnic in the park with a family member and they played a game there, or when they went camping or fishing with a family member. The bottom line is this. Their fondest memory involved having fun with the adults in their life, and when an adult takes the time to show a child the importance of having fun, then that is something that they will take into adulthood with them, and this healthy cycle will be passed on to their children when they take the time to have fun with them.

Now, I am not saying that we are all blessed enough to have adults in our lives that took the time to have fun with us when we were young, but this should not be an excuse to not have fun with our children. Neither should the fact that some people grew up in poor households, and as such, their parents did not have any money to do things that were fun with them when they were children. Take my childhood for example. I got my first job when I was 9 years old, because I came from a poor home. It was not because my dad did not try, because I saw him work himself to death at times. It was because I saw that I needed to do something to help, and since I grew up in a rural area, I made the decision one day to walk the few miles away from my home to our nearest neighbor and ask them if I could work in their fields to make some money, and I continued to work every day after school, and on weekends, the whole time I was in school.

Even though we were poor, though, and even though my dad

worked himself to death just trying to make sure that we had enough money to survive, he still took the time to try and make sure that we had some kind of fun together.   No matter how tired he was, he would take me to see the baseball team in our town, or he would take me fishing, or do something else with me that was fun. Whatever he did, though, he always wanted me to know that having fun was just as important as working hard, and now I try and foster this in the children who are in my life as well.   That is why I believe that everyone should foster a good relationship with their children that includes fun, no matter what the circumstances of their own childhood was.   It is just too important because our children are our future.

I know, of course, that not everyone grows up in areas where it is easy to find ways and places to play.   There are some people who grow up in neighborhoods where it is a struggle just to survive, thanks to situations like crime and poverty.   This, though, is where we need to find ways to fix this so that everyone, especially children, can have a place to play and a chance to do so safely.   I will discuss this more later, as every child should have a place that is safe to play in, but for now, let me just say this.   It is our responsibility, as adults, to accept the responsibility of ensuring that all children have a safe place to play in, no matter where they live. It really does upset me to think that any child should ever lose their childhood chance to play just because of where they are growing up, and because of what is going on around them.   Every child should be allowed to be a child and play, and every adult should have the opportunity to play as well, either with their children or with their friends and loved ones, no matter what is going on around them. The bottom line is that it is up to us to make sure that it happens by accepting the responsibility to make it happen.

Now I realize that this is going to be a challenge, especially

123

in some cities and neighborhoods where poverty and crime has taken its toll on the area, but if we all accept the responsibility to work together and make this happen, then it will. It may not be overnight, as a matter of fact, it may take a while, but it will never happen if we do not accept responsibility to start the process of making it happen. Again, *"Acceptance"* is what will do it. Accepting the responsibility to make it happen, accepting the responsibility to see it through, and accepting the fact that it will never happen if we do not come together and work together. If we do this, however, and we see it through, then the end result will be glorious, because nothing is more glorious than seeing a child with a happy heart because we made it possible for them to be a child by helping them to be able to play in a safe environment.

I see some people already trying to make this happen. Every day I hear about people who have made a success of their lives, doing things like playing professional sports, and then returning to the neighborhoods where they grew up to do something to improve the area, and in some instances, to improve other places as well. All in an effort to fix the problems in poorer areas so that the children who live there have an opportunity to play, the way that every child should have the opportunity to play, safely and securely. That is great for people who have lots of money, but what about the rest of us? Shouldn't we be pitching in too? Again, it is up to us to make our race better, not only for ourselves, but especially for our children as well, so that they will continue the good work that we started when they are adults, and we can do that by adopting the philosophy of *"Acceptance"*.

Now that we have talked about playing in general in order to take better care of our emotional selves, let's talk about other ways that we can accomplish that same goal. Question.......when was the last time that you watched a good comedy? For that matter, when was the last time that you watched a good cartoon? I am not just talking about something like a cartoon movie. I am talking about even a cartoon short, one that only runs for a few minutes, that is short and made to make us laugh. Now, I know that these cartoons are sometimes hard to find, especially in today's world, but they do exist. Just look online (now, I do realize that, even in today's highly technological world, there are still those who do not have internet access, which I think is sad, especially if you have children. Now, if I had a magic wand, then I would make sure that everyone had reliable internet access. Just another problem that we can all solve when we come together finally). Go ahead, I'll wait. Now, didn't that make you feel better, just watching a cartoon with no real story line, made to make us laugh, even for a few minutes.

Ask yourself this one question. What was your favorite cartoon short from your childhood? Who was your favorite character? Try this. Sit down and remember what cartoon character has made you laugh in the past, and then go online and find one of their cartoons (or two, or three for that matter) and just watch them. Nobody ever said that watching cartoons was bad for an adult to do (unless they are rapidly aging themselves by denying their inner child, or they do not want anyone else to have the type of fun that they are afraid to have), and it can have an amazing effect on our day, because it, like other fun activities, can release those Endorphins that make us feel good.

Want another reason to have some fun, or to watch something funny, just for the sake of laughing? How about this. There are so many people who live with regret where their childhood is concerned. Take me for example. For many years I lamented my childhood. Having to work since I was 9 years old, never being able to spend time watching cartoons, or playing games as often as other children did. Most of the time I was either

125

working or studying.   Almost never having the time to be a child in any way (unless my dad came up with the time to do something fun with me).   That regret really started getting to me after a while, and it affected both my emotional health and my physical health.   It also affected my personal relationships with those I loved.   I was actually finding myself becoming jealous of those around me because they would tell me about the fun things that they did as a child, and I found myself becoming bitter and resentful.   Then one day I realized that I should not be jealous of those around me who had a fun childhood, and I should not be bitter towards anyone just because my childhood was rough.   So, I decided to do something about it.

What did I do?   I took responsibility for my own happiness and accepted the responsibility to do something about it.   So, I decided to start doing the things in my adult life that I was not able to do as a child.   The first thing I did was that I started watching cartoons.   As a matter of fact, I actually started collecting cartoons, and now I have copies of many of the cartoons that was not able to watch as a child.   Another thing that I have started to do is take the time, whenever possible, to play video games and even board games (not all the time, though, because all play and no work makes us unable to pay the bills).   Not just the new ones, though.   I have made a point of playing games that are considered *'retro'*, just so that I can, in my own mind, catch up on everything that I missed out on when I was a child.   You would be amazed at how much it has helped me out psychologically, because now rather than saying *"I really missed out on a lot of things."* I am saying *"So this is what I missed out on!"*, and in my mind, it has helped me convince myself that I really did not miss out, because I am getting to do those things now as an adult.

I know this is kind of a different approach on *'making up for lost time'*, but if you do lament on missing out on something when you were growing up, then try this. Pick out something that you wish you had gotten the chance to do either when you were a child or when you were a young adult. Then, find the time to do it now that you are an adult. Then ask yourself this question. *'Don't I feel better now that I have had the chance to do what I missed out on when I was younger?'*. One thing that I have learned is this. Once we have the chance to do the things that we wanted to do, but never had the time or opportunity to do when we were younger, it really can help us feel better about ourselves because it can really help our emotional well-being.

You see, it is these type of *'I hate the fact that I never had much of a chance to do this'* laments that can really weigh on us when we are adults, and they can really burden our minds and affect our adult interpersonal relationships with others, like it did to me by making me actually bitter towards others because they got the chance to do the things that I never got much of a chance to do when I was young. Like I said, my regrets consisted of not getting the chance to play much and not being able to watch cartoons. What are your laments? If you could do something now that you missed out on doing when you were younger, what would it be? Whatever it is, and no matter what people may tell you, it is really never too late. I knew one guy who decided to take his wife on a vacation to a place where dancing was allowed so that they could dress up and he could get the chance to take her to the Prom that they never got to go to. Then there was the girl who got together with her friends and they held a bachelorette party for her at their home because she had been married at the courthouse years ago and she never got the chance to have one with her friends. There is also a guy that I know who never misses a single carnival when it is in town, because he never got to go as a child.

A Visit to the City in the Light

I could go on, but the bottom line is this. Accept the responsibility of taking care of your emotional self by not only doing things now that are fun and make you happy, but by also taking care of any *'emotional laments'* from the past that may be bothering you and weighing on your mind. Accept the responsibility of first identifying them, and then doing them now, if at all possible, so that they do not affect your emotional health. You will be surprised at just how much better you will feel emotionally when you make up for lost time in this way, and the only person who is stopping you is.......well, you. Yes, you may not have much time to do these things, and you may not have much money to do them either, but you do not have to start big. Start small if you need to. Like the old saying goes, *'The journey of a thousand miles begins with a single step'* (Lao-Tzu), or in this case, *'The journey of a thousand smiles begins with a single activity'*.

You do not need a lot of money to have fun or a good laugh. It is not expensive to watch a cartoon online. Board games are pretty cheap. You may not have the money to go on a vacation to a major amusement park, but most people spend way more money on their cable bill each month than it would cost to go to a carnival. There are restaurants that have video games as part of their draw, and if you go out to eat every once in a while anyway, why not go out to a restaurant that has video games you can play. Like I said earlier, if you really want to impress your date, or make your present partner happy, and you are not looking for just another *'dark and candle lit'* corner like many people do, then show them that you really do care about their emotional health and them having a lot of fun by taking them to a place where you can actually have fun with them. As I said before, most people (especially women) have told me that they love someone who can make them laugh, and what better way to make them laugh than by taking them somewhere where they can have fun. Not only will you be showing them that you do care about them having a good time, but you will also be taking care of your emotional self as well.   A true win/win situation, especially where love is concerned.

Now, there are other things that many people do in order to take care of their emotional health, and some of these activities do not involve playing a game at all.   Let's take having a *'Movie Night'* with your friends, watching movies with them that have topics you are all interested in.   There are a lot of people who even go as far as dressing up as their favorite characters from these movies/television shows, and as a result, they all have fun while participating in an activity that they all share a common interest in. Speaking of this, there are many people who hold entire conventions concerning certain types of movie and television shows, like the Sci-Fi and Comic Book conventions that are held all over where people *'Cosplay'* as their favorite characters from these shows.   They may dress up as *'Anime'* characters, or *'Sci-Fi'* characters, or even as their favorite superheroes, but the bottom line is that they have a lot of fun doing these activities.   They are keeping their inner child alive by escaping their normal selves in order to become someone that they consider special and fun, even if it is just for one day.

Speaking of dressing up, whatever happened to having costume parties where everyone comes in a costume just for the fun of it?   At one time it did not matter if it was Halloween or not, people would hold these parties just for the sake of having fun, and they were definitely fun.   I mean, who does not like going out on Halloween in a costume and having fun (other than the person I mentioned earlier who is dying emotionally because they are denying their inner child)?   So why not do it just for the sake of having some fun with our friends, no matter what the occasion is? For that matter, why not have any kind of get together/party with friends that has a theme?   Use your imagination.   Just do it for the

A Visit to the City in the Light

sake of fun.   There doesn't need to be a special occasion, not if having fun and fostering relationships is the goal.   Have fun just for the sake of having fun.

Here is an idea that some of my friends do, and they always have a great time doing it.   Have a *'Script Night'* where you invite some friends over and then come up with your own movie or television show.   Here is how they do it.   They invite their friends over, and then they start by voting on what type of movie or television show that they want to write.   Horror, drama, comedy, or whatever.   Then they pick a person or couple to start the script, and whoever was chosen starts by writing a few pages of the movie or show.   Then, at a chosen time, those people hand the script to the next person or couple, who then proceeds to write the next few pages of the script.   This continues until it is the last person's or couple's turn, and then they are tasked with writing the *'Big Finale'* to the script.   Then, at the evenings end, the host takes the script and reads it to everyone.   You would be surprised just how much fun this is, and just how crazy some of these scripts get.

Another thing that my friends do is have what they call a *'Comedy Night'*.   What they do is they invite their friends over, and then they have each of their friends do a *'Stand Up Routine'* where they tell jokes and put on a comedy show.   Then, at the end of the night, they see who got the biggest laughs, and the person who did is crowned the *'King of Comedy'* for the night, and they even have a trophy that is awarded to the person who won.   Then that person gets to keep the trophy until the next *'Comedy Night'*, at which point the person who wins next is crowned the *'King of Comedy'* for that night, and the trophy is passed to them until the next *'Comedy Night'*, and so on and so forth.   Again, you would be amazed at just how much fun these get-togethers are for everyone, and how much this strengthens all of their relationships as a result.

A Journey There.......and Back Again with a Message of Hope

Now, I want to touch base, just briefly, on another topic where humor and having fun is extremely important. You see, feeling like no one cares about us is one of the things that we, as the human race, needs to deal with in order to bring us together, because it can destroy us. Now, I am not just talking about having fun for our benefit alone, to keep ourselves from becoming sad due to loneliness. What I am talking about is helping others who may be living with feelings like they are alone and that nobody cares about them, and that no one wants to do something with them, like having fun with them, or spending any time with them for that matter. They may feel like the world has forgotten about them, because no one cares enough to play a game with them, or to watch a movie with them, or even just listening to them share their stories about their life, because they may have no one in their life, for example. You see, there is nothing more depressing than thinking that the world has forgotten about us, and that no one cares about us, and this is the situation that a lot of people are facing each and every day, and not just because they may be alone with no one to love. I am talking about other situations as well, like people who do not have many friends, or those who never had a family or a partner, and they are truly alone. This is where we, as caring humans, should use humor and fun to help others, even if that means that we just spend time with them. Like I have said before, it is my hope that this book helps our race come together so that we can advance into a better tomorrow through *"Acceptance"*, and here is one area where we can help our race come together.

I want you to sit back and think about this for a few minutes. Let's say that you have led your life doing good things for other people, even if they were strangers. You may have always been a good person, putting others wants and needs ahead of your own, but then, when you are in your *'Golden Years'*, you suddenly find yourself alone, with no one coming to visit you, feeling like the world has forgotten about you and doesn't care. It could be a situation where you are living in a nursing home with no one coming to visit because you never took the time to find that someone special, or worse yet, you did find that special someone, and you even had a family, but they never visit you because they are always too busy to take the time to come and visit. It could be a situation where you spent your life in the military, but now you are a disabled veteran, living in a nursing home, or worse yet, living alone at your own home, with no one coming to visit. It could be the fact that, as I mentioned a few minutes ago, you never found that special someone, and you find yourself alone, day after day, running out of hope because most people view you as being too old to start a relationship with someone, and you feel that time is running out.

Now, I know that there are more and more options for older people to find that special someone, with dating options online specifically for older people, but once those sad feelings start kicking in, it can be very hard to pull yourself out of it, even if you do have options. You do not even need to be an older person, because there are many people out there, right now, who should be living their life to the fullest because they are in their prime of life, and yet, each and every day they find themselves alone, wondering if they will ever find someone special for them. Now, while this is also a situation that we need to pay attention to as well, for right now, I would like to concentrate on older people, because they are some of the most vulnerable members of our race, and unfortunately, they are the ones who are forgotten about the most.

To continue, though, this is where we can all come together, and start helping those who find themselves feeling hopeless with the help of humor and having a little fun. We can do all sorts of things to help others by making their day a little happier. We could go to a nursing home and offer to help them by volunteering there in an effort to make the residents day a little bit better and happier, even if that is by just spending time with them to let them know that they are not alone and forgotten (as I've said before, though, make sure that you do it right.   Check in at the reception desk and be sure to get permission from the staff to visit with people there and cooperate with them when they want to check you out.   They will be able to direct you to who could use your kindness the most).   You would be amazed at just how much happier it can make someone just because you are interested in listening to them tell you stories of their life, or because you want to do something fun with them, like watching a movie or playing a game with them.   Making a difference in people's lives can be a quite easy thing to do if we are willing to just take the time and do it.   Do not do it for the praise, do not do it for the recognition.   Do it to make our world a better place by actually caring about someone who may need it the most.

There are other places where we can make someone's day a little brighter, like in a children's hospital.   True, there are nurses and caregivers who are there to spend time with them, and of course, they also have family members who spend time with them, but these caring people can't be with them all the time, and even if they are, there is just something special about having someone that the child doesn't even know come in and say *"Hey, how are you doing?"* or something like *"Hey, my name is _____.   Do you want to play a game with me?"*.   It breaks my heart every time I even think about the youngest members of our race having to fight diseases just so that they can live a normal life.   Why is it so hard to take some time out of our day (even if it is just for one day) to try and let them know that there are people out there, people who they don't even know, who care about them enough to let them know that they care about them and their happiness.   People who care enough to come in and try to make their day a little bit happier (now, as I have said before, if you ever do this at a children's hospital, be sure to get permission from not only the hospital in advance, but also from the parents of the child, so that they know that you are not there to cause any problems, and so that they are on board with the kindness that you are trying to do).   If you need motivation, then think about it this way.   Close your eyes, put yourself in their shoes, and think about how much better it would make you feel to know that there are people out there who care about you and your child.   People who care enough to try and make your child's day a little bit better and happier.   I mean, think about it, it could be you and your child in their place one day.   I hope that it never is you and your child in that position, but life is funny in the fact that we never know what is coming next, even though we like to convince ourselves that we do.

Now, here is another area where I think that our ability to make someone's day a little bit better and pull them out of depression by caring about their happiness, is especially important, and that is with our friends.   Here is what I mean.   You can usually tell when someone is struggling, especially if you have known them for a while.   They may start acting differently, or they may start to close off from the world.   When you notice something like this, offer to talk to them.   Tell them that you are their friend, or that you noticed that they seem like something is bothering them, and that you care.   Ask them if they want to talk to you.   Most importantly, do not just ignore the warning signs that something is wrong, or think that *'Well, they are just in a slump, and they will get out of it on their own'*, because it is this attitude that can really cause things to go horribly wrong.

Again, we need to actually care, not only about ourselves, but for others as well, and the best way to do that is by being observant, and caring enough about others to actually step in and show others that we care if we think that something bad is

134

happening to them emotionally, and one of the best weapons that we can use to help someone who may be suffering from depression is our ability to make others happy by actually showing them that we care as a friend. Ask them if they want to talk. Try to see if they are willing to open up to you. One method that I always use is to approach them as if I am having a problem, and that I would like to talk to them, because sometimes if they see that I am being vulnerable to them, then a lot of times they will open up to me as well. The bottom line is that we need to show them that they are not as alone as they think, and that there are people who care, because if they see that we care about them enough to talk to them, then there is a good chance that they will see that they truly are not as alone as they think, and that could open up the door to helping them.

Look, the bottom line is this where our need for having fun in our lives, both for our own benefit and the benefit of others, is concerned. We need to have happiness in our lives, because we need a healthy balance where our emotional selves is concerned, and to have that we need to balance our serious side with our happy side. So, if we want to be happy, and we want others to care about our happiness, then there are many things that we can do to achieve that goal. Use fun, and have fun, where fostering relationships are concerned. If you want to impress a date, then show them that you actually care about them by caring about them having fun and being happy. You know how good it feels when others (especially those who we love, and we are in a relationship with) show us that they genuinely care about our feelings by doing things to make us happy. Then why not show them that their happiness is important to you as well by doing things to make them happy? Make others happy whenever possible, especially if they are in their *'Golden Years'*, or in a hospital, like too many children currently are in today's world. Spend time with them, even if it is just to let them know that they have not been forgotten, and to let them know that there are a lot of us who truly do care about them.

Use fun when fostering good relationships with your children. Have fun with them, give them happy memories of having fun together with you, and then they will continue to foster that good cycle with their children. Have fun with your friends in order to foster good relationships with them, which will strengthen your friendships, and don't we all want to have strong relationships with our friends? Strong relationships with our friends can really help them, especially if they are showing signs of depression. Help them by letting them know that you are there for them, and that you truly do care about their happiness, and that they are not alone no matter what is going on in their lives (also, if you are worried that your friend will see your caring about them as a sign that you want to have an intimate relationship with them, then try something like this. When you go to speak with them, do something like bringing a friend (or multiple friends) with you, and make it clear, if necessary, that all of you care about them because you are all friends, and all of you want to help them with whatever is bothering them or making them sad).

Do not forget to do things to make yourself happy as well. If you have any regrets because you missed out on something when you were young, then make the time to do these things as an adult whenever possible, because the last thing that you want to do is live with regrets. Make time, as often as possible, to do things that make yourself happy. Watch a cartoon, go to a sporting event, or attend (or throw) a party. Just be sure to make yourself happy by having fun whenever possible, because fun is one of the greatest gifts that we can not only give ourselves, but to others as well. After all, if we are going to practice *"Acceptance"* in order to bring us all of us together, then we will need to actually care about each other, and having fun with each other is a great way to do just that.

Chapter Five
Acceptance and Education

"You done what I told you to do." - My dad, outside of the City.

I really feel that, when my dad said this to me, he was referring to what he told me to do when he was on his death bed. You see, my dad was always there for me, but he knew that he was dying and that, after he was gone, I would need to be able to take care of myself. My dad always worried about people taking advantage of me legally, and so, one of the things that he told me to do was to obtain some sort of law degree so that I could protect myself should I ever find myself in need of an attorney without being able to afford one. So I did. It literally cost me a fortune in student loans, but I did get a degree in law, and even though I am not a licensed attorney, it has come in handy. I will say this. If you ever need an attorney, then do everything in your power to hire one. However, it is just a fact of life that not everyone can afford an attorney, and as a result, more and more people are finding themselves in a place like Family Court, for example, without an attorney. That is why I feel that he told me this, because he wanted me to know that he was proud of me for following his advice on the importance of going to school to obtain a degree in law.

This brings me to another sad point of today's world, though, and that is the fact that it is getting harder and harder to obtain a college education, and it is because going to college is getting more expensive. Now, I know that there is a reason that it costs so much to go to college, but I just think that there has to be something that we can do about that. There has to be a way that we can make college cheaper so that more people can attend. It is just too important.

A Visit to the City in the Light

You see, I have always felt that education makes us a better person, and more importantly, that education should be a right for everyone, and not just a privilege for those who can afford it. Let's face facts, education is going to be key in practicing *"Acceptance"*, because in order for us to come together to solve all of our race's problems, then one of the things that will help us solve them is finding those in our race that have the high intelligence levels. After all, you cannot have too many scientists, doctors, etc., working on all of our problems, especially if we want to solve them as quickly as possible. Therefore, without education, and more importantly, access to it, there could be people out there, right now, who have the high intelligence levels to help us solve all of our problems, but because a lot of them can't access higher education (due to the costs), they will never have the opportunity to get the education that they need in order to help us solve all the problems that our race faces today. We need *'all hands-on deck'* where solving the problems that we need to solve are concerned, which is what *"Acceptance"* is all about. Without education for all, however, all we are doing is delaying our advancement as a race. Oh sure, we have some people getting the education that is needed to solve the problems that we face, but can you imagine just how many more problems we could solve if we had more people working on them due to everyone (regardless of income level) having the chance to access higher education, and how much faster we could solve those
problems?

Can you imagine how things would be for our race in today's world if, from the beginning of time, education was not made available for everyone? Where would we be today? For example, let's say that, when we invented fire, the secret was never shared, and those who did not know how to make fire were never taught how to do it. How much longer would it have taken for us to progress forward?   Or how about the secret to making metals, like iron and steel, and transforming those elements into making items that were used to advance us as a race.   How much longer would it have taken us to advance and evolve?   If the only people who had access to education were just a few people, instead of everyone, then can you imagine how much longer it would have taken us to get to where we are today?   We need to make sure that education is available to as many people as possible, because when we do that, then we advance ourselves as a race instead of stagnating and delaying our evolution further.

Somewhere along the way we were taught that, if we do not have a piece of paper that says that we have learned something, which was issued to us from a college or trade school, then we should not have the same opportunity as someone who does have that piece of paper, even though we may have the same knowledge as someone who does.   Why is that?   Is it because some people decided that, if we are not willing to pay for that piece of paper, then we should be treated like we are not as good as them, and that we are not as smart as them?   Why is it that we are not considered smart if we do not have a degree?   Why is it that people think that we do not know how to do something unless we have a degree in that field from a college that charges such outrageous costs that only certain people can afford to go there?

Take a trade like being a mechanic, for example.   I know some people who are great mechanics, who can fix almost anything on wheels, and yet, they have never gone to a school to learn how to be a mechanic.   Why is that?   Why are they great mechanics when they have never attended a trade school?   The reason is because they were taught by other mechanics while working on actual vehicles.   Another example would be welders.   I know some really talented welders who never attended a trade school, and it is because

141

they learned how to do it from other welders. Even one more example would be people who learned carpentry (or anything else that it takes to build a building, like electrical wiring or hanging sheet rock) from other contractors by actually doing it side by side with them.

My point is this. Why is it that, in today's world, these talented workers are being told that suddenly they are less talented or inferior to other people who have attended a trade school, and therefore, they are not being hired, or they are being paid less money than someone who has attended a trade school? Now, I do understand what that piece of paper means, and what it represents, and in some cases I do feel that we need to have that piece of paper, because it does prove that we did learn how to do something that we need to have an incredibly good education to do. Take a medical degree for example. We need to have a really good education in order to be a doctor, because let's face facts, being a doctor is not something that just anyone can do. Doctors have our lives in their hands, and as such, they need to have a very structured education in order to practice medicine so that they can take care of us properly.

Again, though, my point is this. Why should certain people be the only ones who have the opportunity to obtain this degree? I can guarantee you that there are some incredibly smart people out there who could obtain a medical degree, and be great doctors, if they were just given the opportunity to get the degree necessary to be a doctor. I just think that it is a shame that only certain people get the opportunity to go to medical school, and that, if you do not have the money, then you do not get the opportunity to be a doctor. Now, I do know that there are ways to get the money, like loans, but what if we go to school using a student loan and then, because we did not make it all the way through college, we find ourselves working a job that does not pay nearly as much as a doctor gets paid.

A Journey There.......and Back Again with a Message of Hope

Then, to make matters even worse, we find ourselves being forced to pay back the enormous debt that we have acquired because of all the loans that we had to take out just to try and go to a medical school. I have seen many good people find themselves in big trouble because of this, and I just feel that there has to be a better way of doing this.

My point is this. Why should only a few people be allowed the opportunity to obtain certain educations? Why shouldn't everyone who has the ambition, the drive, and the intelligence level, be allowed to, at least, have the opportunity to do so? Oh sure, like I said, we could get a degree if we are willing to go into incredible debt to do so, or if we come from a rich family and can afford to pay for the education in advance, or if we get a scholarship (good luck), but what if we do not succeed in our attempt, and we had to take out enormous loans just to try? What's next? I will tell you what is next. The person who tried will not only have failed in their attempt, but then they will also have a huge debt just for trying, one that could ruin them financially, all because they wanted to try and get the education to do a certain job.

Ok, as far as I know, the following is how things are done now (or, at least, a *'down and dirty'* explanation of how it is done now). I know that this flies in the face of *'affordable education for all'*, but it is how things have to be done at the present time, because let's face facts, it costs a lot of money to run a college. First, we need to take tests to see if we have the aptitude to attend certain colleges in order to get certain degrees. Now, I understand why these are necessary, because it shows whether or not we have the intelligence to obtain certain degrees, which is why a lot of colleges state that, if we don't have high enough test scores, as well as the necessary GPAs to attend, then we don't get to go to their college. Then, we need to determine where we are going to get the money to

143

attend college, because again, it costs a lot of money just to operate a college, and that money needs to come from somewhere.   Then, once we get the money to go to college, we have to get the necessary grades as we go to college, otherwise we don't graduate, and each semester that we attend costs more and more money.   Then, if you do all of that, and you get the degree that you wanted to get, you have to pay back all of the money that you borrowed in order to go to the college in the first place (unless you are rich, and you can pay for college as you go along, or you get a scholarship, but that is not the case for the majority of people who attend college).

Now, as far as I know, the reason that it presently costs so much in tuition fees to go to college is because of how much it costs to operate a college.   I mean, someone has to pay the salaries for the professors who teach the courses, as well as the salaries of the assistants, the Dean's salary, and the others who run the college. Then the people who take care of maintaining the college have to have their salaries paid as well.   People like the janitorial employees, the landscapers, the maintenance crews, and everyone else who handles the general upkeep of the college and it's buildings.   Also, there are the costs for things like campus security, and other support jobs that are needed.   Then there are the costs of things like the books, the computers, the papers, and everything else that a college needs in order to operate the classes, as well as teach and test the students.   There is more, but as you can see, it costs a lot to operate a college.   So, how do we make it more affordable so that everyone has the chance to attend a college and get a degree?   I mean, do we make college more affordable by cutting the operating expenses?   If so, then how do we do that?   Do we turn the maintenance of the college over to the students?   If so, who gets to tell everyone who is depending on those jobs to support themselves and their families that they will all lose their jobs?   Is that fair to them?   Or how about the teachers at the college?   Without them, who do we learn from?   You see, it really does cost a lot to operate a college.   So, how do we make college more affordable for everyone?

If I had my way, this is how I would run things, see if you agree.   After all, *"Acceptance"* is all about having us come together and figure out ways to do things for the benefit of everyone, so here is my suggestion.   First, I would give (and I mean literally give, as in, for free) anyone who wanted to try and be something that they wanted to be (like a doctor) a chance to see if they could make it by letting them take a test to see if they have the aptitude and intelligence level to proceed into the first four years of school, even if their high school GPAs were not the best (I mean, there are a lot of people who have been called "geniuses" in our history who did not have the best grades when they were in school, mainly because they were actually bored with what they were being taught in Grades 1 - 12, and that happened because they were intellectually far above what they were being taught).   Then I would allow them to attend the college for, at least, the first four years of education.   Now, in order to make these first four years free (or as cheap as possible), I would work with politicians to figure out a way to have the college paid for, either through tax dollars or donations (especially donations.   I will explain what I mean by this in a bit).

Then, if students made it through the first four years of college, I would give them the opportunity to advance their degree further by allowing them the financial backing to finish their education, provided that, if they did get the career that they wanted, they would agree to pay back the money for everything past the first four years of college, like the way that student loans are handled now.   However, if they did not make it the rest of the way to get the major career field degree that they were trying for, like being a doctor, then I would give them credit for the first four years of

145

education so that they could try and go into another field (while still being in the medical field like they wanted to be, but maybe in another role, like being a Physician's Assistant, which takes a six year degree), but I would not ruin them by making them pay back the money that it took to get as far as they did in huge monthly payments (for example, let's say that they made it for six years, but then, they did not make it any further towards being a doctor. What I would do is say that they could have college credit for those six years, but I would only have them pay back the money for the two additional years that was beyond the first four years). Instead, I would tell them that they could pay back the money at a rate that would be proportionate to whatever career that they ended up in, calculated using a sliding scale, instead of treating them like they had become a doctor (or something else) and making them pay the money back in amounts that they cannot afford.

In other words, I would really try and give a student every opportunity to fulfill their dreams, no matter what they are, without destroying them with enormous loan payments that they cannot afford. Also, for those who became a doctor (or whatever else) utilizing this plan (first 4 years free due to things like donations), I would have them agree that they would have to donate a certain percentage of their income each year (for a period of time) to the college that they attended so that it would make it possible for other students to utilize the same plan to get their first 4 years free. In other words, they would have to *pay it forward* to future students so that they could have the same opportunity that the person who got their degree received. Is it a perfect solution? Probably not, but at least it is a suggestion, and that is a key component where practicing *"Acceptance"* is concerned. Having us all come together so that we can solve all of our problems, including the problem of making education as affordable as possible for everyone. I do know that we can figure this out if we all just pull together to come up with a solution to this and practicing *"Acceptance"* will help us do just that.

So, does that mean that I think that everyone should be given endless opportunities to obtain the major degree that they want? No, and here is where *"Acceptance"* comes into play again. We need to accept the fact that not all of us has the aptitude and intelligence to be a doctor, or lawyer, or dentist, or scientist, or astrophysicist, or whatever else your dream may be, because we would never get any work done if we all just stood around taking an endless stream of classes for degrees that we do not have the intelligence for. Does that mean that we should just give up on our dreams and goals? No, not at all. What I am saying is that, in order to play our part in helping our race succeed and advance into tomorrow, then we need to accept the responsibility to accept the fact that while we may not have what it takes to do certain jobs, we may definitely have what it takes to obtain another line of work, one that we can be successful in and that makes us a productive member of our race. This might be a hard thing to accept, but like I said in a previous chapter, don't feel bad, because there are no unimportant jobs in my mind, and everyone who contributes to making our world operate, no matter what their job is, **is** an important person doing an important job. Besides, you might have the aptitude and intelligence to do another job that you would consider your *'dream job'*, like being a game programmer/developer, a photographer, an artist, a historian, a teacher, or something else.

It is ok to have more than one dream and goal, and there is absolutely nothing wrong with pursuing our dreams, as long as we accept the responsibility to accept the following things. The first is the fact, like I said, that we may not have what it takes to be a doctor, lawyer, astronaut, etc., but we might be able to do something else in the field that we want to work in, and that there is nothing wrong with doing that if we fail at being a doctor, etc., and second, that we still need to work while we pursue our dreams so that we can pay the bills and contribute to helping our race advance and evolve into the future.

To continue, though, another way that I would change college would be to give someone a chance to be pursue their dreams if they studied and learned on their own. Let me explain. Let's say that someone who has an incredibly high intelligence level studied on their own, and they were able to learn everything that a doctor, who went to a prestigious college, learned. If I were in charge, what I would do is give them the opportunity, after they felt that they were ready, to take all the tests necessary to prove that they have the book knowledge to be, for example, a doctor. If they proved, in this way, that they had amassed the knowledge to be a doctor, then I would fast track them into things that allowed them to prove that they could be a doctor. Things like what doctors do, like actually performing an internship for a few years, under the supervision of regular doctors, of course. If they were able to do all of this, then I would allow them to receive the degree to be a doctor, because in my mind, they would have proven that they have not only learned what they needed to learn, but they would have proved it to the college and the *'powers that be'* that they have what it takes to be a doctor.

Now, I do understand that there are ways to challenge a college in order to obtain a bachelor's degree by taking the tests to prove that you have the knowledge through self-learning, but I just have to wonder. Why don't more people challenge for degrees in this way, and why can we only challenge for a bachelor's degree in this fashion? Why can't we pursue higher degrees by doing this? I know that this may not be a popular way to do it (especially from the college's standpoint, due to the loss of income for one), but sometimes we need to do what it takes to pursue our dreams, and that is why I stated what I did as far as how I would run things, to start the dialogue where low-cost education is concerned. You see, when we all start talking about how to accomplish something good, we can come up with a plan to make it happen. Like I said previously, that is another part of putting *"Acceptance"* into practice. Having us all come together to come up with ideas to make good things happen.

I think that what bothers me is the fact that there are people out there who have incredibly high intelligence levels, but they are being held back by the fact that they do not have the money to obtain the necessary degrees to share that knowledge with the world, and to do great things to help our race. Imagine, just for a moment, that there is someone out there who has such a high intelligence level that they could develop a cure for diseases like cancer. Now imagine all the lives that will be lost to that horrible disease because that person was never allowed to obtain the degree necessary to get the opportunity to become a scientist and find a way to cure that disease, all because of money. It is one of the most tragic things that I can think of. I am sure that there are many people out there who could help our race by curing all sorts of diseases, or they may have the intelligence to do many other things, like come up with a method of travel that could take us to other worlds. It makes me sick to think that the only thing that is holding these wonderfully intelligent people back is having the money to obtain the degrees necessary so that they can have access to the resources to develop these gifts into reality.

Here is where it bothers me the most. Every day I think about all the sick children who are out there fighting for their lives because they have terrible illnesses. Now imagine that there may be someone out there who could help them, and quite possibly save them, if they only had the money to obtain the degrees necessary to become a scientist and develop the cures to save those children. Every child should be allowed to live a long and healthy life. No child should spend their entire life just fighting to live. Now, I know that we can donate to hospitals and organizations to help these sick children, and a lot of people do that, including me. But how can we, as caring members of the human race, justify not allowing people with incredible intelligence levels to have the opportunity to save these children just because they are poor, or they live in poor areas, and they cannot afford to obtain the necessary degrees by paying for college?

My point is this. We need to accept the responsibility to figure out a way to help people who have high intelligence levels pay for college so that they can have the chance to accomplish all sorts of wonderful things, like saving these children. We need to accept the responsibility of bringing us all together so that we can first, identify those who have high intelligence levels no matter if they live in upper class or poor neighborhoods, and then second, accept the responsibility to make sure that they do have the opportunity to obtain the necessary degrees so that they can help us all by figuring out ways to save these children, or so that they can come up with ways to end the energy crisis, or so that they can figure out ways to bring us to other worlds, or.......well, you get the idea.

It goes back to when humans first came up with fire. How much longer would it have taken us to advance and evolve as a race if the only a few people were given this knowledge? To equate this to modern times, how much longer will it take us to come up with the knowledge to cure certain diseases if the only ones who are allowed to learn are the people who can afford the education (and, again, I know that we can get scholarships, but even those are hard

to get.   Also, we can take out loans, but so many people are afraid
to do this because they worry about how to pay them back if they
fail that they actually talk themselves out of taking out the loans so
that they can go to college.   Also, a lot of people find out that they
do not even qualify for taking out a student loan, even if they do
want to take out the loans, because their credit is not the best, so
they end up being held back as a result of that, no matter how
intelligent they are).   Not to be blunt with such a delicate and
emotional subject, but how many more children will die because we
only allow certain people to get the degrees to come up with the
cures?   If you think that this is extreme, and not a critical subject,
then ask a parent of a sick child just how important this is.

Again, it all comes down to *"Acceptance"*.   Accepting the
fact that we need to identify everyone (whether they come from high
class, middle class, or poor communities) with high intelligence
levels, accepting the fact that we need to make education as
affordable as possible for everyone so that those who have high
intelligence levels can obtain the necessary degrees to help us no
matter if they are rich or poor, and accepting the fact that, if we do
not figure out a way to do this, then it all comes down to one simple,
yet tragic, question.   How much longer will it take for us to come
up with these cures, and how many more will die in the meantime?
For that matter, just how much longer will it take for us to do all the
things that we need to do in order to solve all of the problems that
we face as a race?

Let's look at another area where affordable education for all
could help us.   Let's talk, just briefly (because I will be discussing
this in the next chapter), about just how much education could help
us all to obtain equal justice.   Having a law degree, or at least a
general knowledge about the law, is absolutely critical in today's
world.   Every single day someone is finding themselves in court.

A Visit to the City in the Light

It could be because they are getting a divorce.   It could be because they have been accused of a crime.   It could be for a number of reasons but let me ask you a question.   What will someone do if they cannot afford an attorney and they find themselves in court? Now I do know that, in some countries, if someone is charged with a criminal offense, then they are supposed to be allowed to have representation, but therein lies the problem.   Each and every day there are more and more people who are being accused of crimes, and unfortunately, while a lot of those people are guilty of committing those crimes, there are a lot of people who are being falsely accused as well, and that is a very big problem that needs to be dealt with and fixed as
quickly as possible.

While we are allowed, in a lot of countries, to have representation during these trying times, a lot of the time that representation is overburdened at best.[1]   Because of the enormous number of cases that are being tried in the courts every day, the attorneys that are appointed by the courts normally have more cases than they can handle properly, and this is a situation that could cause many problems for these attorney's clients.   As a result of that burden, a lot of good people who are innocent may be assigned an attorney whose only care is to fast track these cases by recommending that his clients accept a plea bargain to a lesser charge, even if they are innocent.   Or worse yet, the attorney might miss something that could prove his client innocent, and his client could go to jail for an awfully long time as a result of that, all because their attorney had so many clients that they ended up needing to finish these cases as quickly as possible so that they could move on to the next case.   As a result, they cannot give any one case the proper time that it needs in order to make sure that their client is represented properly, like they are supposed to be.

A Journey There.......and Back Again with a Message of Hope

Is this the fault of these court appointed attorneys? I would like to think that this is not the case, because I would like to think that every attorney actually cares about each and every one of their clients, and spends actual time making sure that everyone gets the representation that they deserve, but you know what they say, *'life imitates art'*. Let me explain. There is a very good movie (*"A Few Good Men"*. Directed by Rob Reiner. Performances by Tom Cruise, Jack Nicholson, and Demi Moore. Castle Rock Entertainment, 1992) about a couple of soldiers who find themselves in trouble. I won't go into much detail here about the movie (other than to say that it is a must see), but at least allow me to say this. The court appointed attorney who was assigned to the case in the movie made a point of bragging about the fact that he had disposed of many cases in a truly short amount of time. Meaning that, rather than trying each case in court, and rather than taking the time to evaluate each case to see just how it could be best defended in court and at trial, he had just approached each case with the frame of mind of just seeing how fast he could get rid of each one through the use of plea bargains (although he finally does give the two soldiers mentioned above the defense that they deserve. Again, a must see). Now, this may seem like it is pure fantasy, but the scary thing is this. This movie was based on a real case involving real soldiers.

Now, I am not going to go into any more detail about overburdened attorneys until the next chapter, but the reason that I brought it up here is this. How much better would it have been for the soldiers who were accused if they had, at least, some working knowledge of the law? Wouldn't it be better if they knew something about the law, if for no other reason than to help their defense attorney prepare their case so that their attorney had more to work with when preparing their case and defending them? Let me explain. Let's say that you were accused of a crime, and let's say that the attorney representing you had an extremely full plate of clients already.   If you had a working knowledge of, at least, how cases are prepared for trial, you could help yourself by preparing your case in such a manner so that your attorney would already have everything ready to go for trial, with everything laid out so that he could present it without much trouble.   Now, this might be hard for someone who has no knowledge of how cases are prepared for trial (like knowing what important evidence to look for, etc.), but if you had the knowledge of how Paralegals prepare cases, all because you had obtained something like an Associate's Degree in Paralegal Studies, then you could really help yourself by helping your overburdened attorney prepare your case.   This does not just apply to criminal cases though.   It can apply to someone who is facing a civil situation as well and let me show you how by telling you a fictional story that illustrates how important education can be.

Let me tell you a story that illustrates how having a working knowledge of the law can really help someone save themselves in a court case that they may have to go through in family court by helping them prepare their case for trial.   You see, once upon a time, there was a guy who was facing a nasty family court case against his ex-wife who would stop at nothing to make him appear like he was a bad father, and the worst part was that he could not afford an attorney.   You see, this man was not an attorney himself, but he did take the time to learn how to be a Paralegal (by getting an Associate's Degree in Paralegal Studies), which included learning how to prepare cases for trial, and how to present them in a clear and concise manner.   He learned things like how to make objections during a trial and where to research the law to help him uncover case precedents.   He also learned what evidence to look for, evidence that would best help him present his side at a trial in a clear and concise manner, because in order to win a case in a family court proceeding, he learned that he needed to prove his case with a *preponderance of the evidence'*, which is the standard in a civil family court case (unlike the standard in a criminal court, which is *'guilty beyond a reasonable doubt'*).

You see, what happened was that his son had gotten sick at his ex-wife's house, however, she went to court and said that their son must have gotten into something that made him sick while at his dad's house when he was visiting him the day before. She claimed that their son must have gotten into a household poison while visiting his dad, and she said that it was the household poison that had made his son get sick.

The judge ordered that the man would only get supervised visitation until the case went to trial. What happened? Well, because the man had learned how to be a Paralegal, he actually set about gathering the evidence that would help him to prove his side of the case at trial so that he could present all of the evidence in an orderly fashion, like a good Paralegal would do. Then, after gathering all of the evidence proving his side of the case, he proceeded to represent himself at the trial. The result? He won. He showed the court, with the evidence that he had collected, that his son could not have gotten sick at his house. He showed that, if it had been a household poison, then there would have been other symptoms, like damage to his son's esophagus. He discovered this information because he knew that it would be important to talk to the doctors (who treated his son when his son arrived at the hospital) in order to collect the evidence that he would need to show his side of the case.

Then, because he knew that he would need as much evidence as possible to prove his side of the case with a preponderance of the evidence, he decided to do more research by examining the medical records at the hospital where his son was treated. By doing this, he found even more evidence that helped his side of the case.

155

A Visit to the City in the Light

Evidence that included the fact that the doctors who treated his son were not aware of all the medications that his son was taking at the time he got sick and was taken to the hospital. This was due to his ex-wife not telling the doctors at the hospital about all of the medications that his son was taking at the time he got sick. Then, he did some more research into the side effects of all the medicines that his son was taking, and by doing that, he discovered that, if the medications his son was taking were taken at the same time, then his son would have suffered the problems that he was suffering from when he arrived at the hospital. By gathering all of this evidence, and then presenting it in court in an orderly fashion, he was successful in showing that, based on the evidence, it was much more likely that his son had gotten sick because of the medications that his son was taking.

The bottom line is this. If the man did not have a working knowledge of how to prepare a case for trial, and how to do research on things like what evidence to look for, case precedent, objections, and the like, then he could have very well never been able to see his son ever again. In addition, he could have been sent to jail, because his ex-wife was trying to accuse him of *'Endangerment'* by claiming that his son had gotten into a poison at his house. My point is this. If he had never accepted the responsibility to educate himself concerning the law, then he would not have known how to prepare to, and defend, himself at trial. In addition, he could have been sent to jail as an innocent man.

True, a fictional story, but that is not important. What is important is this. This illustrates the importance of obtaining an education like a working knowledge of the law, because not everyone can afford an attorney. We have to accept the responsibility to make education as affordable as possible for everyone, because without it, we could find ourselves as the one who is *'alone in the cave without fire'*, and it could cost us dearly. Also, we need to accept the responsibility of making sure that our children understand the importance of education. There are many ways that we can do this, and thanks to the internet, we can now succeed in this important endeavor (which is another reason that I feel strongly that we all need to come together so that we can ensure that everyone has access to the internet, no matter where they live or how little money they have).

Let me explain. Currently there are many web sites that offer early learning opportunities to our children if we, as parents, are willing to accept the responsibility of making sure that they can access these sites, with our help and tutelage. Just look online. They are out there, and they offer many opportunities for our children to get a head start on their education. There are also sites that can help our children learn while they are in school as well, in order to help them advance beyond the curriculums that they are being taught. We can also take our children to other sites on the internet to come up with our own curriculums in order to teach our children about things that they want to learn more about (but be careful if we take this approach because, like I said before, we do not want to take our children to a site that anyone can post information on, because we could be teaching our children what a *'maniac'* posted. We want to make sure that what we teach our children is clear, and more importantly, accurate information).

Now, the internet can be a very useful source of information for those of us who have access to it, but how do we do this if we can't afford to pay web sites to help our children learn, or if we don't have access to the internet at all? Well, there are options for that too, but it will take creativity on our part. You see, a lot of people in today's world say *'close the libraries'*, because they claim that we all have the internet to learn from, but that is just not the case.   There are too many families out there who still do not have access to the internet, because they live in poverty and they cannot afford what most people take for granted, like a computer, a tablet, or a smart phone.   There are even more families who live in very rural areas, and they cannot get internet access because of the poor area coverage from any service provider (I know of one area where they cannot get any cable access because there are no providers in the area, and the WiFi coverage is so bad that they are basically paying for nothing because of all the signal interruptions).   So, what do we do about this?   Let the children who live in these areas, and the ones who don't have computers, just get left behind, no matter what their intelligence level is?

This is why I feel strongly that we need to make sure that every child has a chance to learn, and to grow through learning, because there could be a child out there who has the genius to do something like cure cancer when they grow up, but they might never get the chance to expand on their genius by having access to learning tools like the internet all because they are poor or they don't have the access to the internet that a lot of us take for granted. So, how do we do this?   We do this by accepting the responsibility to make sure that every child has a computer and access to the internet in order to help them learn.   So, again, how do we do that? Well, I see some people, and companies, with the resources trying to do something about it now.   They are doing things like providing computer access to students at schools where there were not that many computers before by giving these schools computer labs so that they can use them to learn.   They are doing other things as well, like donating money to programs that help students have access to learning options.   What about the rest of us, though? What are we doing to help our children learn?

Look, if we are ever going to make sure that all children

have access to the internet so that they can have learning options, then we are going to need to make sacrifices. If you have children, then take the money that you were going to use for your own entertainment purposes and save it up so that your children can have a chance to learn. If you have a computer, but you are looking to upgrade, then take your old computer and donate it to a family that does not have one for their children (now, if someone with a kind heart does donate a computer to you so that your child can have one to learn on, then have it checked out first, because you want to make sure that it is safe for your child to use. You do not want to have your child use a used computer that might have bad things on it, like pornography on the hard drive, and you definitely don't want to accept a computer that might be stolen). I am sure you can come up with many more ways to make sure that all children can have access to the internet and learning options, so let's work together to come up with them. It comes down to all of us accepting the responsibility to make sure that all children have access to learning options like computers and the internet. We can do it, but it will never happen if we do not make it happen. I do know this. The absolute worst thing that we can do is to tell a child, any child, that because they are poor, or because of where they live (or for any other reason for that matter), they will never have access to learning options like the internet, because to tell a child that they will never have a chance to be great and succeed will do nothing but kill the genius that may be living inside them and kill the hope that all children are born with.

I guess the point that I am trying to make here is this. First, we need to accept the responsibility to make sure that everyone has the opportunity to learn, because it is through learning that we advance and evolve as a race. In order to do that, we need to make sure that everyone has the opportunity to go to school and college, no matter if they are rich or poor, because it is in those arenas that we advance ourselves. Also, if people cannot attend a college because it costs so much, then we need to make sure that we figure out a way to make it as affordable as possible. Second, we need to accept the responsibility to make sure that all of our children have that same opportunity by giving them access to learning options like computers and the internet. The earlier that we start helping them learn the better, because they are literally sponges when they are young, and you would be amazed at just how much they can learn if we start them out as early as we can, no matter what sacrifice that we, as parents, have to make in order to give them the learning opportunities that all children should have. Like I said, one way that we can make sure that all children have the opportunity to learn on the internet is by making obtaining a computer for your child a top priority, and this can be cheaper than most people think. There are places that sell used computers, and while they may not have the fastest processor or the most memory, they can be good enough to allow your children to have access to early learning sites. Also, if you already have a computer, but you are looking to upgrade, then take your old computer and donate it to a family with children that does not have a computer (but again, as a parent, be sure to have any computer donated to you checked out).

Now, I would like to say something here about giving our children access to the internet, something incredibly important. If you do make it possible for your children to learn by accessing the internet, then be careful by being involved. There are a lot of unbelievably bad people out there, and they will try to take advantage of your children if you allow them the opportunity to. Don't give them the chance to hurt your children by saying something like *'Well, my child is learning, so I don't care what site they are on. I will just leave them alone, because I have better/other things to do than help them while they are learning'*, because that is the exact scenario that a lot of bad people hope they will find your children in.   Care enough about your children to get involved, because the last thing that you want to do is find out that your children were hurt because you did not care enough to help them learn by being involved.   One method that I have seen work is telling your children that you want to learn as well, and that is why you want to be involved while they are learning on the internet.   It goes back to what I said concerning your children in the *"Relationship"* chapter of this book.   If you show your children early on that you are not just trying to rule or control their lives, but that you are trying to have a good relationship with them because you truly do care about them, then they will be more open to you spending time with them while they are learning on the internet, especially if you convince them that they are actually teaching you while they are learning.

It is this simple.   If we are to advance into a better tomorrow, then education is going to be key to making that happen. We can do many things to make this goal a reality.   We can do things like figuring out a way to make education as affordable as possible so that everyone can have the opportunity to learn, because again, it is in those arenas where we obtain the knowledge to advance as a race.   We need to find everyone who has high intelligence levels, whether they come from upper class, middle class, or poor neighborhoods, and we can do that by actually testing everyone, especially children, because the fact that people come from poor neighborhoods is absolutely no indicator of their intelligence level (I can guarantee you that there are some incredibly smart children who live in poor neighborhoods.   We just need to find them).   We can make sure that everyone has access to the internet, especially children, because the internet can really facilitate the advancing of a child's intelligence level.   We can also make sure that we find a way to put a computer in the hands of families with children, so that children can begin learning as early as possible

A Visit to the City in the Light

(after all, they are the future of our race).

      So, let us all accept the responsibility to make it happen for adults and children alike, because it will never happen if we do not accept the responsibility to make it happen.   It will take work, it will take sacrifice, it will take ingenuity.......but if we do it, then it can make our future a wonderful place to live in, and in the end, isn't that another key component to practicing *"Acceptance"*? Helping our race by identifying those with high intelligence levels and then making sure that they receive the education necessary in order to solve all the problems that we face?

Chapter Six
Acceptance and the Law

"Got to have rules.   Got to follow them." - My Uncle Albert, at the
top of the Dam.

As you will find out in the last chapter, we were at the top of
a small Dam when Uncle Albert said this to me, staring at the scene
that was occurring at the bottom of the Dam where the water should
have been.   I believe that, based on what we were witnessing, he
was trying to tell me was the fact that we need to have laws, and
more importantly, we need to follow them.   Otherwise, our world
can turn into a literal nightmare of chaos and violence.   That is why
I would like to talk about the law in this chapter, because it is
important that we understand the need for laws, and how they will
be needed when putting *"Acceptance"* into practice.

A wise man once said that, in order to have a structured
society instead of chaos and anarchy, then there has to be rules that
we all accept and agree to follow.   Our ancestors understood this,
and that is why, in their wisdom, they created the first set of laws,
because structure is particularly important in order to ensure that we
all can, and have the right to, live our lives in peace, security, and
tranquility.   Without these laws, all we are doing is hurting
ourselves, instead of helping us to live more happy and secure lives.
This is because all that will happen without the structure that laws
provide is total and uncontrollable chaos that will destroy our lives
instead of helping us to advance into the future and succeed.   In
addition, this topic is also the one area of our lives that can literally
destroy someone's life as well.   Therefore, I feel that this topic is
one that deserves as much attention as we can give it.   After all, if
we are living in a world controlled by chaos, then how are we ever
going to come together to make *"Acceptance"* a reality?

A Visit to the City in the Light

I have to say, before we delve any further into this topic, two especially important things.   First, I want to be clear that **I am not trying to give anyone legal advice.......period**.   What I am trying to impart in this chapter is really common-sense things.   However, I cannot stress the point enough that, if you find yourself in need of an attorney, then hire an attorney, or have one appointed to you by the court if you are facing criminal charges (like many countries will do for someone who is facing criminal charges).   The bottom line is that you should try and do everything possible to make sure that you are represented by proper legal counsel anytime you are in court (unless, of course, you find yourself in something like the *'Small Claims Court'* that they have in America, because in no other arena does the phrase *'us versus them'* apply more appropriately than in that type of court). There is a tremendous amount of truth in the old saying that goes *'A man who represents himself has a fool for a client'* (Abraham Lincoln, although similar sayings have been around for years before this) because most people do not have the knowledge to represent themselves in court (which is another reason that we need to make sure that we make education as affordable as possible so that, if you do find yourself in a situation like the man I spoke of in the last chapter did, you can, at least, have a fighting chance to win).   So please, if you do find yourself in a situation where you are going to be in court, then do everything that you can to have an attorney represent you.

Second, I have to say that this will probably be the most important chapter in this book.   Why?   Because this topic is one of the most important topics that the philosophy of *"Acceptance"* will tackle.   Unfortunately, this is not a good thing if you think about it, and that is because of the following reasons.   The first one is that we need to accept the fact that there are laws that should be changed, mainly because many of them are so antiquated that they really do not apply in today's world.   The second one is the fact that the law itself truly needs to catch up with modern technology.   With new technology the law is way behind in keeping up with the way we lead our lives now, and as a result, there are many criminal acts that are being perpetrated without any real laws in place to punish the criminals who are perpetrating these crimes.   Crimes like identity theft, cyber bullying, fraud, and others just to name a few.   The third one is the fact that, more and more, there are innocent people, **good people**, who are being falsely accused of different crimes every day, and it is destroying their lives.   And the reason is because, in my opinion, we are in the midst of a *'witch hunt'* where the standard of *'proven guilty beyond a reasonable doubt'* (that criminal courts are supposed to be held to) is not being adhered to the way that it should be, mainly because, just like the *"Salem Witch Hunts"* of old, all it is taking, in a lot of cases, is someone pointing their *'magic finger'* at someone else and saying that they *'did it'*. As a result, more and more people are being convicted of crimes that they did not commit.

There are many other reasons that this chapter will be long, but the bottom line is this.   We need to accept the fact that the legal system, in most countries, needs to be updated, with some laws changed entirely, in order for us to truly have *'Equal Justice for All'*, like we should have.   Then we need to accept the fact that it is truly up to us to make these changes happen, and to make sure that they are enforced.   Otherwise, we will have no one but ourselves to blame when things go wrong, like they have for way too many innocent people already.   People like the ones who have had their lives ruined because of false allegations, and by cyber criminals, and *'Cyber Bullies'*, just to name a few.

To continue, though, we need to really put an attitude of *"Acceptance"* into this, because we need to accept the fact that we need laws in order to have a structured society, and then we need to

A Visit to the City in the Light

accept the fact that we need to obey these laws if we are ever going to come together in order to fix the problems of our race. There, I said it. We need to be *'law abiding citizens'* if we are ever going to come together as a race and fix our problems. Now, does that mean that we should obey every law on the books no matter what they are? Well, yes, for now, but that does not mean that we cannot question a law, and it does not mean that we cannot change a law if we feel that it is a bad law.......but we do need to accept the fact that, until a law is changed or revoked, then we need to follow it. That is what separates us from other species on our earth, because we have laws to help us live better and more secure lives, and we have the capability to enforce those laws. More importantly, we also have the ability (in a lot of countries) to change the laws that we deem to be wrong or questionable. However, we also need to accept the fact that there are proper ways to do this.

Our ancestors understood this, and that is why they gave us the opportunity to hold elections in a lot of countries, and included with that is the opportunity to introduce Bills that could change laws that we feel are bad, like citizens can do in a lot of countries, because these elections allow us the opportunity to challenge laws that we feel are wrong, or change them, or completely replace them with better laws. Like in America, for example, where they can even change the Constitution of the United States.......sort of. Americans can do that by proposing that Amendments be added to their Constitution. So even the oldest of laws can be changed or amended, but we need to do it properly. Like I said, elections allow us the opportunity to change or replace laws, and this has been vividly demonstrated in recent years with a couple of the states in America that have voted to remove certain laws so that it is now legal to possess, buy, and smoke marijuana, just like the way that marijuana is already legal in some countries around the world.

A Journey There.......and Back Again with a Message of Hope

This is an excellent example of what I am talking about concerning changing laws that are currently on the books. For many years marijuana had been illegal in all of America, and all that the government said was that *'All legalizing marijuana will do is cause rampant crime, and it will cause everyone to become 'drug addicts', and it will really hurt any state that legalizes it'*. What has happened since it was legalized in the few states in America that have now made it legal? Well, the states themselves are making tons of money from the sales taxes, and snack makers are also making tons of money.......but I have yet to see any of the catastrophic problems that many said would happen if marijuana was legalized anywhere in America. So, the bottom line is that those state's citizens saw a law that they thought should be changed, and as a result, they wrote the change to the law, and then they put it on the ballot as a new law, and then they changed it, thanks to the people of those states (where marijuana is now legal) voting for the change. Now, am I saying that we should legalize all drugs? No, not at all, because there are some drugs that can have very devastating effects on us, and that can really ruin our lives, at least in my opinion.

Here is my point. Laws can be changed, but they need to be changed in a proper manner. We need to accept the fact that first, we should follow the laws that are on the books, because they were voted to be the prevailing and governing laws by the people. Second, we need to accept the responsibility of changing any laws that we feel need to be changed. Third, and this is the most important part. We need to accept the fact that, if we want to change a law, then it needs to be done the right way by making sure that the change is approved by the people through the voting process. We cannot change anything just by refusing to obey the law. True, we might be able to break a law, but if we do that, then all that will happen is that we will go to jail, and the law will still be on the books. It is possible to change a law, but it needs to be done right, and it should always be up to the people, no matter what country they live in. We should first identify a law that we feel should be changed, and then we should either write a better law and then put it on the ballot, or we should just vote to remove it entirely. Then, as I said, after having a law removed from the books entirely, we can replace it by voting in a better, and fairer, law that will benefit us all in a way that we can all live with.

The bottom line is this. Do we all want to have a safe place to live? Do we all want to be treated fairly? Do we all want to have our children grow up in a world where we do not have to worry about them being harmed in any way? Do we want to be able to do anything that is considered legal, either alone or with our family, while being protected? Of course we do. On the other hand, do we want to live in a world where, from the moment that we leave our front door, we are confronted with complete anarchy, with everyone doing whatever they want, with no consequences at all? Of course not, because we would never get anything done to advance our race if we had complete anarchy, so therefore, we need to have laws, and we all need to accept the responsibility to follow them.

Now, having said all of that, the way that I want to do this chapter is by splitting it up into sections, because of the different areas that laws cover. So that we can better deal with each one. I want to make sure that I cover how *"Acceptance"* can really help us understand how it can help us where the law is concerned, and how it can help us deal with the law in order to cope with it in our daily lives, because the law can be a very frustrating topic to deal with. However, with understanding of how *"Acceptance"* can help us deal with this topic, and how, if we are going to practice *"Acceptance"*, then it will rely on a proper legal system in order to succeed, this topic will be much easier to deal with.

Criminal Laws

Let's talk about this area of the law first, because it is this topic that can really affect our lives the most.   It can ruin our lives if we are not careful, even if we do not break a law.   I will explain what I mean about that last statement in a bit, but for now, let me say this.   Every single day, in every country around the world, there are people who break the law.   Some of those people actually get away with breaking the law, and that is a very distressing part of this, because no one should ever get away with breaking the law, at least in my opinion.

Consider this.   Let's say that you have spent your whole life doing the right thing.   You have worked hard at your job your whole adult life, and you have done so because you wanted to make sure that your family and loved ones could have everything that you could give them, and so that they could have everything that you did not have when you were growing up.   You wanted your family to have a good home to live in, and so you bought it for them.   You wanted to give your children the things that you did not have when you were growing up, like electronics and movies for example, and so you worked overtime just so they could have those things to make them happy.   You wanted to give your wife expensive and unique jewelry to wear so that she could feel like the most special woman in the world, and so you bought her those things, items that were maybe even especially made just for her.   You wanted to have a new car, or at least one that looks good, and so you worked even more overtime in order to ensure that both you and your wife had one.

Then, one day, you decide that you want to do something

169

A Visit to the City in the Light

special for your family, because they stood by you through all of the long days that you put in working, even though you lost precious time with them. After all, you know that they know you did it just so that you could give them all of the things that you wanted them to have, and so now you wanted to thank them for all of their understanding by doing something extra special with them, to make up for lost time. So, you decide to take your family on a long overdue vacation, let's say to an amusement park, or to the beach, or maybe even to another country. So, you pack up your family and you fly them somewhere to enjoy some much-needed time and relaxation together. However, shortly after arriving at your destination, you get a call that delivers bad news, and because of that, you need to return home immediately, canceling the chance that you finally had to spend some much-needed quality time with them.

The news? Someone broke into your home, so you rush back. Then, when you arrive, you realize just how bad it is. The thieves stole everything that you had worked so hard all of those years to give to your family, including the jewelry, the electronics, and maybe even your cars. Everything that was not nailed down, anything that could bring a quick buck from a *'fence'*, on the black market, at a swap meet, online, or anywhere else where stolen items can be sold quickly, is gone. All that sacrifice, all that time you lost with your family because you had worked so hard all those years to give them good things, is wiped out in one night. To make matters even worse, your wife, and especially your kids, are upset because not only did they lose everything that they were proud to have, but they are also scared that the thieves might return while they are there. If you think that it is a shock to you when you are robbed, you should see how much it affects children, because to them, the *'boogeyman'* is real, and it can affect them for the rest of their lives in some cases, especially if they think that the real life *'boogeyman'*

A Journey There.......and Back Again with a Message of Hope

may come back to take something else, or to harm them.   No child should ever live in fear.

So, you go to the police and tell them what happened.   Can you imagine how much worse you would feel if the police looked at you and said, *"Well, there's no law against theft, so I guess that you are just out of luck."*.   Think about it for a minute, because my point is this.   Sure, we may have insurance, but anyone who has ever had to deal with filing a claim with an insurance company knows for a fact that they never compensate us fully for our losses.   Also, if they do, then it is because we had to hire an attorney in order to get them to compensate us correctly, and if we do, then we are losing money again because attorneys want to get paid as well.   It is not just about the money though, because money cannot replace our true losses when we are robbed.

Like the loss of all those years that we worked, sacrificing time with our loved ones just so that we could provide them with the life that we wanted them to have.   Can that be replaced by an insurance company?   How about the loss of our children's innocence, because now they are afraid to sleep at night, scared that the boogeyman will return and hurt them?   Can an attorney get anyone to erase that fear with compensation?   How about the special things that were one of a kind, things that we bought for our family, like the specially made, one of a kind jewelry that we bought for our wife, or whoever our love interest is?   Maybe it was things that we bought that represented a special time in our lives, like when we went on our honeymoon and we found a one-of-a-kind necklace made of gold or silver.   Or maybe even things that were family heirlooms, things that were passed down to you from many generations ago.   Can anyone ever replace these things once they are stolen?   No, of course not.   Not to say that jewelry cannot be replaced, but how do you replace a memory?

171

A Visit to the City in the Light

Again, my point is this. Without criminal laws in place, we would live in a world where chaos would reign, and it would literally be everyone for themselves. Let's take that one step further. Let's say that there were no criminal laws where stealing anything is concerned, and that thieves could take whatever they wanted, if they could get away with it, that is. I say that because, if there were no criminal laws, then killing people, like thieves, would be legal, and since everyone would want to stop a thief from stealing from them and their family, everyone would be armed to the teeth. A lot of thieves would be killed just trying to break in and steal something. Conversely, this would also mean that those same thieves could come into our homes and kill us without any recourse. How could we, as a caring human race, live with all of that death?

Speaking of killing, if there were no criminal laws, then murder would be legal as well. So, let's say that you neighbor coveted more than just what you owned, let's say that they also coveted your wife or daughter as well. How would you feel about the knowledge that they could come over and just open fire on you in order to kidnap your wife and make her his wife? Or worse yet, how would you feel about them doing this to your children, because there are some really sick people out there who would do this to our children if we let them.

The bottom line is this. I am not trying to use scare tactics on anyone, and I know that these examples are extreme to say the least. What I am trying to do is illustrate just how much chaos would be created without criminal laws, and what that chaos would really look like. Kidnapping, murder, rape, theft, assault, arson, and other crimes. They would all be the *'order of the day'* if we did not have criminal laws. As horrible as this all sounds, though, there is something that is just as bad as having these crimes committed. It is the horrible truth that, every single day, there are people out there

172

who are being accused, and jailed, for these crimes.......even though they are completely innocent.

Let's examine that thought for just a moment. In today's world, we are all supposed to be *'Innocent Until Proven Guilty'*, right? Everyone is supposed to have their day in court, right? Then why is it that every single day there are more and more people who are being convicted of crimes that they did not commit? With new forensic science, including DNA testing, this should not be happening.......but it is happening. In some cases, there are innocent people who are losing everything, including their freedom, and in the cases of crimes such as murder, maybe even their lives as well, all because they were accused of a crime and convicted even though they did not commit the crime in question. You see, even though we do have a way to test DNA evidence, there are times when crimes are committed and there is no DNA evidence to test, or the DNA evidence was corrupted or lost due to mishandling. As a result, there are innocent people being convicted of crimes that they did not commit, all because the judge (or jury) just decided to believe the person who was pointing their *'magic finger'* at the accused. It happens all the time, and it needs to stop. We need to accept the responsibility to first, accept the fact that this is happening, and second, accept the fact that we need to do something about it, because even though you might be the most law-abiding citizen in the world, it could happen to you.

Here is one of the biggest problems where this type of tragedy is concerned. There are so many people out there who say *'Well, that's sad, but it doesn't concern me, because it is not happening to me or my family, so why should I worry about it?'*. It is that type of attitude that facilitates these tragedies, because if they are being ignored, then they will continue to flourish, and if we are ever going to come together as a race, then we need to address these

173

issues so that you do not find yourself one day saying *'I am innocent'* in a court of law while no one listens to, or believes, you.

Here is one of the reasons that I feel this happens. Like I have said many times before, we are all born with the innate need to *'hunt the monster'*, and this is an extremely dangerous attitude for a court and/or jury to have, because not only do they have this innate need, but suddenly they find themselves in charge of deciding if the person sitting at the defense table is *'the monster'* that they want to hunt. This can have very devastating consequences for an innocent person who has been accused of a crime, because some of those times the innocent person is being accused of a crime that is very bad, to include murder, rape, and other vicious crimes, and when they are accused of these types of crimes, the judge and/or jury goes into these trials subconsciously thinking that they need to *'hunt the monster'* and *'punish the monster'*, even if they don't want to admit it.

Now, am I saying that everyone who is accused of these types of crimes is innocent? Absolutely not, because there are some awfully bad people out there, and they do unbelievably bad things to people. What I am saying is that we need to make sure that the person who is being accused of a crime is actually guilty before we convict them, and even though, in a perfect world, that is the way things should be, things do not always happen like that. The standard in a criminal court is supposed to be *'Innocent Until* **Proven** *Guilty'* and *'Proven to be Guilty* **Beyond** *a Reasonable Doubt'*, and it is supposed to be up to the prosecution to actually prove, beyond a reasonable doubt, that a person committed a crime before they are convicted, but more and more this is not happening. It is like this for a number of reasons, at least in my opinion.

A Journey There.......and Back Again with a Message of Hope

The first reason is this.   Like I said previously, juries can be swayed by their subconscious need to *'hunt the monster'*, even if they do not want to admit it.   They see that a horrible crime has been committed, they see the victim and the victim's family that has suffered because of the crime, and in some cases, without any proof at all, they are swayed to convict a person based solely on someone saying that the person who is being accused did it.   You do not think that this happens?   Why don't you look at the many convictions that are being overturned now because DNA evidence has cleared the person who was first, accused by someone's *'magic finger'*, and then second, convicted by a jury, and then third, sentenced to spend many years in jail by a judge.   Also, if you do not think that this can destroy an innocent person's life, then look at all the cases of innocent people who were accused of crimes but now they are being exonerated of those crimes, even though they spent many years in jail, and in some cases, many years on death row.   Not only did they lose many years of their life, but then, they also lost their reputations as well, because people still look at them, after they are released, as if they are someone who cannot be trusted.

This is especially true for certain crimes because some crimes are so distasteful and dastardly that we are very ready to convict a person who is accused of one of these crimes without any proof at all, other than someone saying that they committed the crime.   Let's talk about the worst of the worst crime that someone can be accused of, and actually convicted of, without any proof at all that the accused person actually did it.   Why do this?   Because I really want to drive the point home that there are some crimes that people can be accused and convicted of without any proof at all, and these crimes are literal prime examples of how an accusation can virtually destroy the life of the person who is accused of it.   All that needs to happen, especially where these crimes are concerned, is to have someone point their *'magic finger'* at a person, and without

175

any proof at all, the accused can have their life completely destroyed by these allegations, even if they eventually do prove that they are innocent in court.

What crimes are the prime examples of this? *'Child Molestation'* and *'Sexual Assault'*. Now, let me be clear about what I am saying here. Anyone who molests a child, or sexually assaults someone, should get every punishment that the law can give them, because these are extremely horrible and horrendous crimes. No one should ever hurt someone like this, and I mean ever. Now that I have made myself truly clear about the way that I feel concerning this, allow me to say this. More and more, there are innocent people who are being accused of these crimes, and they are having their lives destroyed by these accusations, because no matter what people may say to the contrary, the *'stink'* that permeates around a person who has been falsely accused of these crimes never really goes away, even if the accused person proves their innocence.

Why are there more and more people being falsely accused of these crimes in today's society? Well, in the case of child molestation, it is happening more often because of these two words....... *"Divorce Proceeding"*. Nothing, and I mean nothing, gets a divorce judge's attention faster than one parent accusing the other parent of molesting their child in order to win custody of their children. Then, without any proof, other than the parent who has the child saying that *'My child said that it happened'*, or maybe even the child themselves saying that they were molested, people are actually being punished for this crime by losing custody of their children, or worse, by being put in prison.

Now do not get me wrong, because I know that there are parents (and other people) who do commit this heinous crime against children, and they should be punished for committing this

crime to the full extent of the law, but the bottom line is this.   More
and more parents are being accused of this, even if they did not do
it.[2]   These types of allegations are so prevalent now that it is even in
the mainstream media.   What people do not realize is the fact that,
once someone accuses a person of this crime, then it does not matter
if they are innocent, because everyone who hears that they were
accused will always look at the person like they actually did it, or
like they are someone that everyone should be wary of.   Also, the
person who was accused will bear the stigma of being accused for
the rest of their lives.   Another troubling thing about this is the fact
that, if it is proven that the accused person is innocent, then the
person who made the false allegation (or coached their child to make
the false allegation) normally suffers no punishment for filing the
false allegation, like it is ok for a person to tell this lie about another
person (or to coach their children to tell this lie about another
person).   It is not just happening where child molestation is
concerned, though.   It is also happening in today's world when
almost any woman files a criminal sexual allegation against
someone that is later proven to be false.[3]   Now, I do know that there
are many women, both past and present, who are being abused
sexually, and I hate the fact that it is happening to them, but there
are also many women who are making false criminal allegations
concerning a sex crime as well, and that is a real problem, because it
takes some of the credibility away from all the women who were
actually abused or raped by making people wonder if they are lying,
at least in my opinion.

It makes no sense to me and let me explain why.   I have
always said that everything should be run according to this
equation....... *'equal = equal'* (if we are ever going to have true
equality in our world that is), and if that is the truth, then why
doesn't everyone who files a false criminal charge against someone
face the same type of punishment, regardless of sex?   I mean, are

we saying that it is ok to make false criminal allegations against someone else if they are sexual in nature?   Again, we all need to realize the fact that once a person has been falsely accused of a crime (especially rape or molestation) then the *'stink'* of being accused of that type of crime will never go away from the falsely accused, even if that person proves, in a court of law, that they are innocent.   It will affect them for the rest of their lives.   I mean, are we really saying *'Hey, it's ok with me if a person destroys the life of another person with a false allegation of child molestation or sexual abuse or rape of a woman'* because we are not willing to punish everyone who was proven to have made false allegations against someone?   I mean, we do know that these false allegations can ruin a person's life even though they proved their innocence, right?   Or are we not willing to punish someone for making a false criminal sexual allegation because we honestly think that it is ok for someone to falsely accuse another person of a sex crime?   How is that anything even remotely resembling *'equal = equal'*, especially when there are crimes on the books that make it illegal to file false criminal allegations against someone?

Also, before anyone says it, yes, a child can lie about this. You see, children love their parents, and if one of their parents is telling them to say this, then they will say it, because they want to make their parent happy, and they want their approval.   In some cases, they could be promised all sorts of things if they are willing to say what one of their parents wants them to say about the other parent.   This type of *'parental pressure'* has caused many false allegations to be made.   My point is this, though.   Even after the allegation is made, and the other parent (or anyone else for that matter) **proves** that they did not do this, it will never end, because the parent who was falsely accused can, and in almost all instances still does, suffer the stigma of being accused in the first place.   This is especially true if the parent who has custody of the child refuses to let it go and decides to spread rumors in the community where they live in order to make the person who was accused seem like they actually did it. This does happen, especially in contentious divorce cases. Now, children can make this type of allegation for other reasons as well.

You see, again, children really do look for approval, and they look for it from anyone that they can get it from. Clergy members, counselors, relatives, and the police. All people who will, naturally, feel sympathy for any child that molestation happens to (like they should). Then, these children find themselves at the center of a contentious divorce between the two people who are the most important to them, their parents. Then, because one parent tells their child to tell this lie about the other parent, suddenly they are getting all of this attention from everyone around them. Question. Why do Hollywood celebrities have such a hard time when their career starts failing? It is because they crave the attention, and it is the same with a child. When they see that they are getting this from people for making allegations against someone, and then the attention goes away once the divorce ends, they miss it, and it can cause a child to make another allegation so that they can get that attention again. Now, again, just to be clear, I do know that there are many monstrous people out there who really do molest their (and other people's) children, but what I am talking about here are the allegations that are made when the accused person does prove their innocence in court. Here is my question, though. When an accused person does prove their innocence, then why aren't people trying to find out just why the child made the false allegation by having the child go to counseling? I mean, if they were not abused, and there is any chance that they did it for the attention or for some other reason, counseling could really help to determine just why they made the false allegation in the first place.

A Visit to the City in the Light

So, as I said before, are we saying, as a society, that it is ok to lie about people as long as the allegations are sexual in nature? Are we saying that only some people should face punishment for making false criminal allegations against another person, while saying that other people who are making a false allegation should get a pat on the back for telling lies that absolutely ruin people's lives? If we are saying that, then we, as a structured society, are in serious trouble because we are setting a dangerous precedent, one that could cause many more problems that it could ever solve. Does the name *"Salem Witch Trials"* ring any bells?

Now, I can guarantee you that there are definitely many men as well who are telling lies about women in order to get them into trouble. I mean, it is despicable to me when men tell lies about women in order to get them into trouble, but my point is this. How is it equal justice when there are some women who are making false sexual criminal allegations against others while getting no punishment for doing it, and there are other women (and men) who are doing it while being punished (now, I do know that, recently, more people are being punished for this, but not all of them, and that is wrong. Also, I am not suggesting that children should be punished under the law for lying about people hurting them, but they should, at least, receive counseling so that people can determine just why they made the false allegation)?

I mean, whether people want to admit it or not, we, as a society, have it pre-programmed into our subconscious to protect women, even if that means that we are more forgiving towards women if they do something wrong, but is it right? Is it equal justice? Now, I do not agree with anyone (regardless of sex) filing false criminal accusations against someone else, because of how much it can affect anyone's life if they do have false charges made against them, but I can guarantee you that, if a man files a false criminal allegation against a woman, then she will not suffer the consequences to her life and reputation that will happen to a man if he has a false sexual criminal allegation made against him by a woman. So, how can we try and stop the spreading of false criminal allegations? There is a solution to this, but it will only work if we are brave enough to place it into practice, and I will talk about that in a bit.

Also, when speaking of how everything should be *"equal = equal"*, how is it that we have people of both sexes committing crimes that are sexual in nature against children, and yet some of those people are put away in prison (for life in some instances, which I agree with, because they should never have any chance to do it to any other child), and yet, we have others who are receiving almost no prison time (or only probation) when they commit sexual crimes against children? This happens most often when the adult is a teacher, and the child is a student.[4] Now, I am not going to go into much detail about this here, as I will cover how everything should be equal later, but allow me to say this. It is absolutely wrong for this reason. Like I have said before, everyone who sexually assaults a child, and is found guilty of taking advantage of a child sexually, should face the same punishment, period. It should not matter if they were a teacher when they committed this type of crime, or if they were a *'cloaked in the dark'* molester.

Again, the way that I feel is this. Everyone who commits this type of crime should face the same severe punishment, regardless of who they are, or what sex they are, or what they do for a living. As a matter of fact, I feel very strongly that anyone who is in a position of authority over a child (and then that child ends up being molested by that person) should be punished very severely, because our children look up to these teachers, etc., and they look to these people for protection. To me that betrayal is unforgivable.

181

A Visit to the City in the Light

So why go into this one crime so much? One, because of the fact that it is (in my opinion) the most heinous of crimes, the one that everyone reacts to the most, and it is one of the only crimes where the *'stink'* of just being accused of it never really goes away, even if the person who was falsely accused proves their innocence in a court of law. Two, and most importantly, is this. This type of false accusation dictates (if we are ever going to halt the spread of these and other types of false allegations) that we accept the responsibility, and have the courage, to seek the facts for ourselves when we hear that someone has been accused of a sex crime and we are forming an opinion about that person. I talked about child molestation and sexual abuse/rape so much because it is the one type of crime that makes everyone want to *'hunt the monster'* (especially me), but we need to make sure that the person who is being accused of being the *'monster'* truly is the *'monster'* before we decide to ruin them, and I do mean ruin them.

Case in point.......when a person is accused of this type of crime, they are normally put in jail while they are awaiting trial, and it is in jail where a lot of the people who are accused of this crime get attacked, and even murdered, all because they were just accused of this crime (not convicted, just accused), and if that is not ruining someone, then I do not know what is. This is why we have a criminal justice system. To determine if people are guilty or innocent of a crime, and everyone, even someone who is accused of a crime like this, should have their day in court, instead of just being convicted in the court of public opinion because someone is saying that they did it. Most importantly, once they have had their day in court, and if the court determines that they are innocent, then we need to accept the fact that they proved their innocence and let them continue on with their lives without punishing them on our own by treating them like they did it.

182

A Journey There.......and Back Again with a Message of Hope

Now, I am not trying to be a bleeding heart for the worst of the worst here, but I will say this. I know for a fact that more and more innocent people are being accused of this, and many other, crimes falsely, and it is causing many good people, with good reputations, to be destroyed, even if the case has been in a courtroom and a judgment has proven them to be innocent. It is not just this type of accusation that causes people's lives to be ruined just by being accused, it is true about other crimes as well. Murder, theft, arson, and others. These accusations also make people want to distrust the people who have been accused. These, and others, are crimes that make people say *"Wow, they were accused of what?"* and *"Wow, I can't trust that person!"* and *"Wow, we need to keep an eye on them!"*.......but do these innocent people, who were falsely accused of these crimes, deserve to be treated like this?

If we are ever going to come together and work as one to better our race, then we need to stop those who use lies and manipulation in order to destroy the lives of good people with false allegations, because it is those people who will always keep us apart. Like I said, one way to do that is to accept the responsibility to ask ourselves *"Ok, I heard what this person was accused of, but did they really do it?"* and *"If they went to trial for this awful crime that this other person is telling me about, then what happened? Did they have their day in court? Were they convicted or exonerated?"* before we just let what someone is telling us about another person make us think that the person who is being accused actually did it, without any proof other than the rumors that are being spread saying that they did it.

This is especially true if the person who was accused never goes to jail. We need to ask ourselves *"Why did this person not go to jail?"*, instead of just taking someone's word for it that the accused person did it, because the answer may just be that the accused person proved their innocence in court. Then we also need to take a look at the person who is spreading the rumor and ask ourselves *"Why does this person want us to believe that the accused person did it? What do they have to benefit by trying to ruin the reputation of the other person?"*. You see, sometimes when we do that, we may learn that the person making the false criminal allegation has something to gain by ruining the other person, like custody of their children, or getting things that they want (like money or attention), or even just something as simple as the fact that they are mad at the accused person because they had a bad breakup and they want to take revenge on the other person by making a false criminal allegation against them (and yes, I have heard of cases where this was the exact reason that people wanted to ruin another person's reputation and life. In their mind, if they could not have the person that they wanted, or they were mad at their ex for what happened during a breakup, or they wanted custody of their children during a divorce, then they would make sure that no one would ever want to be with or around the falsely accused person by making everyone think that the other person is a *'monster'*).

However, if the person who was accused of a crime is convicted in a court of law, then we have to accept the responsibility to make sure that they actually did it by making sure that it was proven *'beyond a reasonable doubt'*, like the court standard is supposed to be, because there are way too many innocent people in jail already, and innocent people going to jail has to stop. Now, I am not saying that everyone who was accused of a vicious crime (and was not convicted of it) is innocent, because unfortunately, there are way too many cases where lack of evidence, or a technicality has set more than one accused person free. What I am saying is that there are too many innocent people who are being falsely accused of crimes, and we need to all work together to stop the *'witch hunts'* (where someone is accused with no evidence other than someone saying that they did it) before it is too late, and before more innocent people are sent to jail. But like I said, more and more there are many guilty people who are getting away with crimes because of lack of evidence, and now I would like to suggest how, in my opinion, we can catch the people who are committing these, and other, heinous crimes.

Like I said, another reason that I mentioned child molestation when tackling this topic is because this is an extremely hard thing to prove after the fact, unless the poor child was actually raped and there is physical evidence. That is why we need to accept the responsibility to watch our children especially close, and if they make an allegation, then we need accept the responsibility to take the child to a hospital and checked out immediately, as well as contacting the police immediately. Another thing that I have always said is that (and please, I can already hear everyone out there screaming *'big brother'*, but hear me out), to protect our children, and ourselves for that matter, maybe we need to take the extra step of installing something as simple as a *'nanny cam'*, or even an internal home security system, for our protection. Having said that, and since I am not offering legal advice to anyone (again, when in doubt, contact an attorney about any situation that might evolve into a legal issue), I feel that we need to do something about catching the guilty people, and proving the innocent people to be innocent, so here is what I have done.

I installed a home security system, but instead of having the cameras facing outside, I faced the cameras inside, so that I have a recording of everything that happens in my home, especially when I am not there. It provides me with proof that I did not commit any crimes in my home, or when I need proof that I was at home in case someone accuses me of robbing a store or killing someone outside of my home, or.......well, you get the idea. You might think that

185

this is an extreme step to take but let me ask you a simple question. Which would you rather do? Place cameras in your home in order to prove that you did not commit a crime in your home, or to a child in your home? Or would you rather be falsely accused of a heinous crime? For that matter, would you rather have your children molested, maybe for years, without you knowing anything about it because you did not want to take the step of placing cameras in your home in order to catch anyone molesting your children. Or would you like to be able to prove that someone molested your child? Also, wouldn't you like proof that you were at home when a crime was being committed elsewhere, especially if you live alone and you are your only alibi?

Another thing. If you think that any type of false allegation cannot happen to you, then you are dangerously naïve, because you can be accused of crimes that you did not commit, just like many other good people have been for many years. So, if you ever do find yourself accused of a crime falsely, which would you like to be able to say? Either *"I am innocent, your honor!"* or *"I am innocent, your honor, and I can prove it!"*. These cameras didn't cost me much money, they were easy to install, and after recording a day's worth of video, I drop the video to a zip stick. At which point I placed the stick in a home safe, and there it is, proof that I am a good person in case I ever find myself being falsely accused of a crime (again, I am not offering legal advice, but allow me to say that I always make sure that I tell people, when they come into my home, that they are on camera, and I even point out the cameras so that they can actually look at them, which shows that they are aware of the cameras from the first moment that they enter my home. That way I know that I cannot be accused of capturing people on video without their permission, because I can prove that they were completely aware that they were being recorded. Like I said earlier, though, get the advice of an attorney if you decide to do this to be sure that you are obeying the laws where you live concerning this).

Now, I know that this may seem to fly into the face of what I said earlier when I talked about not making sex tapes, but I handle it like this. I take the time to court a potential partner, which means that I do not have sex with them until I, and my partner, are absolutely sure that no one is being forced to do anything of a sexual nature if we do take it to the next level. Also, I practice "Acceptance", which means that I accept the responsibility to be a good person. This means that I never, ever, share anything that goes on in my home and bedroom with anyone or online, because I really do care about my partner and their feelings as much as I care about my own (remember what I said when I talked about caring about your partner more than you care about yourself, or your needs, and that it is a quality that both partners need to share?). It goes back to what I said concerning the fact that love should be based on caring and trust, not sex. Afterwards, I lock the tape in a safe, and I give the key to my partner. That way I have the safe, they have the key, and we can destroy the tape when we are ready to.

To continue, though, I know that I spent a lot of time just now talking about being falsely accused of a crime, but I did that for an important reason, and that is the fact that nothing can ruin someone's life faster than being falsely accused of a crime. False criminal accusations need to stop if we are ever going to have a criminal justice system that we can completely trust and depend on, and we really do need to have a criminal justice system that we can trust, because without that we are in big trouble. We need to take the necessary steps to stop the *'witch hunts'* that are going on right now (and believe me, when good people can be falsely accused and convicted of a crime just with someone pointing their *'magic finger'* at them, then it is a *'witch hunt'*, just like what happened during the

187

A Visit to the City in the Light

"Salem Witch Trials" many years ago).

I know that many people are worried that camera systems will mean that *'big brother'* will have access to your personal lives but consider this.   The government will only have access to your recordings if you give them to the authorities, otherwise only you will have access to these tapes, because of the laws that protect us in some countries against illegal *'search and seizures'*, like the protection that is afforded to Americans thanks to their Constitution. Also, if you are worried about this, then consider introducing a Bill for a law that would make it clear that no one, except yourself, would ever have access to these tapes (unless, of course, you decide to turn them over to the authorities).   It is going to take sacrifice in order to stop having innocent people go to jail, and like I said, this is a step that I take myself.   I do more than this, though, and this is another area where *"Acceptance"* comes into play.

You see, I am not trying to say that I am better than anyone else, because believe me, I have my flaws, but one thing that I always do is accept the responsibility to be a good person, and to never commit a crime.   I also accept the responsibility (and this is important) to never put myself into a situation where I could be falsely accused of committing a crime, especially where being accused of sexually abusing someone is concerned.   The reason that I say that here is because, especially lately, there have been a rash of accusations where people, especially men, are being accused of harming someone else sexually, and in a lot of instances, the allegations are completely true.   However, there have been instances where men have been falsely accused of sexually abusing someone as well.   Don't believe me?   Just do an internet search. There was the woman who accused several men of raping her when it was not true, and she did it because she liked getting all the money that she was getting from victim's funds after each and every

188

accusation that she made against someone.[5]   There was another case
(and this one really proves my point when I say that women can, and
do, accuse men falsely for a variety of reasons) where a girl accused
a couple of young men of raping her and then, when she admitted
that they had consensual sex (she said she lied about the rape
because she did not want another man that she was interested in to
know that she had agreed to have sex with other the young men),
she then said that she was interested in the other man romantically,
and she felt that, if she said that she had been raped by the young
men, then the man she was interested in would feel sorry for her,
and then she could finally start a relationship with him.[6]   So, again,
we need to protect ourselves in order to make sure that innocent
people stop going to jail for crimes that they did not commit, and if
that means that we have to take extra steps to prove that we did not
commit a crime, then we have to do it, because again, there are
already way too many innocent people in jail, and even one person
accused, or convicted, of a crime when they are innocent is one
person too many.

        So, to wrap this section up, I guess that the bottom line is
this.   One, we need to accept the fact that we need criminal laws,
because their purpose is to make sure that we are safe by making
sure that we have order instead of chaos, and to make sure that
criminals are punished for committing crimes.   Two, we need to
accept the responsibility to follow those laws, and if we feel that a
criminal law needs to be changed, then we need to accept the
responsibility to change those laws in a proper manner.   We need to
either reword or revoke them and then approve the changes through
the voting process or write entirely new laws that we do not have
presently and then putting them up to a vote, especially laws that
bring the criminal statutes up to date with the new technology that is
being developed every day.   Like laws that cover internet crimes
more effectively.   Three, we need to come up with ways to protect

A Visit to the City in the Light

ourselves so that we can prove that we did not commit a crime if we
are being falsely accused, and so that we can protect our loved ones
(like our children) from having crimes committed against them
when we are not able to be there to protect them ourselves.   If that
means that we need to take the step of installing something like an
internal security system or a *'nanny cam'* like I did (again, I am not
offering legal advice, I am just saying what I did) then so be it,
because something needs to be done to protect ourselves from false
allegations, and to protect our loved ones from being the victims of
crimes.

So be smart, be safe, follow the law, protect yourself and
your family, and your life will be much more secure, happy, and
special for both you and the ones that you love.   We all need to
obey the law by not committing crimes, after all, if we are all going
to come together through the practice of *"Acceptance"*, then we are
going to need to be able to trust each other enough to be able to
work together.   I mean, if we cannot trust each other, and we cannot
trust in the fact that the people that we are working with will not try
to harm us by committing a crime against us, then how are we ever
going to be able to trust each other enough to come together through
"Acceptance" in order to solve our race's, and our world's,
problems?

Civil Law and Torts

Ok, let's talk about another area of law that affects all of us,
that being, Civil Law, and how *"Acceptance"* can really help us in
this arena.   This section will be much shorter than the previous
section, but it is just as important as Criminal Law, because these
laws can affect us deeply as well.   Now, this is going to be an
extremely basic explanation of Civil Law, and again, I am not
offering legal advice, I am just trying to explain how *"Acceptance"*

can help us here as well. So, even though Civil Law covers a lot, I am really going to concentrate on the areas that would affect us the most often, that being, Tort Law and Family Court Proceedings. You could say that these laws cover almost everything else that needs to be solved in a court of law to, well, bring order to what occurs between all of us that is not necessarily criminal in nature, and also where our interactions between us and government agencies are concerned.

These are the types of laws that, again, are not necessarily criminal in nature, but they can be tied into criminal laws as well. To put it plainly, these laws and procedures can be summed up in a few thoughts, at least in my opinion.......do not be a jerk, do what is right, follow the rules, do not take advantage of people, and when someone does try and take advantage of you or cause you harm, these laws can protect you by giving you a type of recourse. We all need to accept the responsibility to follow these laws as well, because included in these laws are things that you would not want other people to do to you, so why would you do these things to anyone else? Accept the responsibility to be a good person, and treat everyone else with respect and dignity, especially if you find yourself in a divorce proceeding, because these laws do cover Family Court proceedings as well (now, there are instances where a family court proceeding can involve some type of criminal accusation, like child molestation or neglect, at which point the proceedings can spill over to criminal court, but for now let's just approach this as if there are no criminal accusations in the proceedings). Follow the rules of normal society. Treat others the way that you want to be treated. It is basic decency, so why do we have so much trouble with this?

Now again, let me be clear about the fact that I am **not** offering any type of legal advice here. If you need an attorney, or

191

you even think that you might need an attorney, then seek the advice of an attorney. Having said that, let me explain what I was just talking about. Let's say that someone who takes care of your investments suddenly disappears with all your money. Now, this is covered in the Criminal Theft Statutes, like the Embezzlement Statutes, but where does this leave you? With a lot less money for one. Now, let us say that you are lucky enough to have the person who did this to you caught and arrested, and now they are in jail for theft. Is that it? Is it over? Not necessarily. You see, you may have had a crime committed against you, and you may have the person arrested and punished for it, but not only will you be able to have the person who committed the crime arrested and prosecuted, you may also be able to sue them and/or their company to get back, at least, some of the money that they stole from you. How? Through the utilization of Civil Tort Law, which gives you the power to sue someone who has wronged you.

Ok, I am about to repeat something that I said earlier, but we need to accept the responsibility to hear it until it really sinks in, and that is that fact that we need to accept the responsibility to be good people by not taking advantage of people, and by following the law. There, I said it again, we all need to be *'law abiding citizens'*, especially if we want to be treated fairly by others, and these laws give us rights that help to ensure that we are all treated fairly by giving us a type of recourse, especially when someone tries to take advantage of us, and it ends up harming us. We need to accept the fact that there are people out there who will try and take advantage of others in all sorts of ways, because of their need to *'take care of number one'*, but in this way they will be *'taking care of number one'* by taking advantage of you. So, we all need to accept the responsibility to watch out for these people, and to hold them accountable for their bad actions by utilizing these laws as well as the Criminal Statutes if necessary.

192

A Journey There.......and Back Again with a Message of Hope

Does that mean that we should be wary of everyone, and never give anyone our trust? No, not at all. We just need to accept the fact that greed is a very corrupting influence in a lot of people's lives, and as long as people's greed causes them to try and take advantage of us, then people will try and do it. I have often said that *"I wish that there were a way to remove greed so that it would not corrupt so many good people."*, but obviously the only way that we could do that is if we figured out a way to reward us for our contributions to our race and society without money being involved, and as much as I would like to see our race figure out a way to make our driving force be the advancement of our race instead of accumulation of money, then we may never see this goal. I know that I still have not been able to figure out a way to do it, or at least, a way that everyone would agree on. How about you? Can you figure out a way to make our world run without greed? Can you imagine just how much better our world would be, and how much better we would all get along, if money was no longer what determined how good of a life we have, and instead, our contributions to society determined our success?

These laws cover a lot more than just someone stealing your money, though, and your possible recourse if they do. They can cover many more things, and they do in our daily lives. Let's say, for example, that something happens to you, like an accident in a car, or maybe getting injured (like suffering a *'slip and fall'*) while at a business. If it was not for Civil Tort Law, then we would not have much in the way of recourse to help us recover from these incidents. Instead, we might lose a lot, especially if we have a family that we are trying to provide for. Sure, there are insurance companies that will pay us compensation if we lose time from work due to something happening like an accident, and they can be great, but not everyone can afford these policies (in addition to affording other policies like car insurance, medical insurance, etc.). So, if we

193

cannot pay for them to protect us, then what?   Well, again, this is where Civil Tort Law comes into play, because it allows us to take people to court and sue them.   Now, am I trying to promote and endless stream of lawsuits?   No, not at all.   What I am trying to do is illustrate the importance of having Civil Tort Law and how it can protect us, as long as we are willing to do what's right (as well as follow the Criminal Law Statutes) and try to not take advantage of people (there I go again, the whole *'law abiding citizen'* thing).

I think that what distresses me the most, especially where Tort Law is concerned, is the many people who look to take advantage of it for their own benefit, causing harm to other people. Let me explain.   Recently, for example, there was a scam that was happening where the people who were performing the scam would pull their car in front of another person and then, without warning, they would slam on their brakes, causing the car that they just pulled in front of to hit them from behind.   Because the car that hit them was behind them, the person in the second car was held to be at fault for the accident, and the person who actually caused the accident would end up getting a free payday from the insurance company after suing them.

So, the people who did not want this to happen to them would make sure that they kept a safe distance from a car that had just pulled in front of them.   How did the scammers respond to this? They actually started doing this when they stopped at stop lights, and then, when both their car and the car behind them (their target) was stopped, the car in front would actually put their car into reverse and then they would hit the car behind them, making it appear like the car behind them ran into them, and once again they would collect their free payday from the insurance company.   So, how do we protect ourselves from this type of scam?   Well, again, I am not offering legal advice, but here is what I did to protect myself.   I

194

saved up the money to have a dash camera installed in my car. That way, if someone does this to me, then I have actual video proof of what happened. They are not too expensive, and they can really protect you.

Ok, another area where Civil Law comes into play is in the arena of Family Court. Now, I am not talking about things like Juvenile Proceedings that involve crimes, because those instances are covered in the Criminal Law Statutes. What I am talking about is the area that affects a lot of us, that being, when we find ourselves in a Divorce Proceeding (How sad is this? There was a time when getting a divorce was almost unheard of, but unfortunately in today's world it seems that getting a divorce is almost expected in a lot of marriages. This is why I talked about romantic relationships at length in an earlier chapter, because not only do we deserve to find a love that lasts a lifetime, but our children deserve to have both parents with them 24/7 while they are growing up as well). Now, there are times that Divorce Proceedings do involve some type of criminal accusation (like I mentioned earlier when I was talking about the rash of accusations lately concerning child abuse), but since I touched on this earlier, let's just approach this as if there are no criminal accusations being tossed back and forth. This is another area where the proceeding would be handled in a Civil Family Court because these proceedings do not involve criminal charges per se, but they do have rules that we must follow when we are pursuing a divorce.

Like I said earlier, these two types of proceedings (Tort and Family Court) are the ones that we will probably have to face the most where Civil Law is concerned, and that is why I wanted to just touch on them, because if we are ever going to all come together through *"Acceptance"*, then we need to be able to trust each other and take care of each other better than ever before. In order to do that, then I genuinely believe that this includes taking better care of all of our relationships so that we don't find ourselves in a Divorce Proceeding or a lawsuit. However, if we do, then at least we will be kind of familiar with the laws that govern these court proceedings.

Now, like I have said, there are many other areas that are covered by the Civil Law statutes, but how do they apply to the philosophy of *"Acceptance"*? Well, if we are all going to come together, and work together, to solve all of our problems by accepting each other, then we are going to need to follow these laws and rules so that we can trust each other enough to work together. As I said, for one, Civil Tort Laws make it so that we can sue people if we are injured, which is a good thing because it affords us some type of protection when bad things happen to us as long as people don't try to take advantage of these Civil Tort Law Statutes and rules. We need to accept the responsibility to follow all laws without trying to use them to take advantage of others, or to take advantage of the *'System'*, because we would not like it if some people tried to take advantage of us, right? Then why should we try to take advantage of others by violating these laws, especially if we are all going to come together through universal *"Acceptance"*? It is all going to come down to trust. If we cannot trust each other, then how are we ever going to work together?

So, to put it bluntly, Civil Law Statutes give us the protection that we all need (whether we are in a lawsuit or a divorce) as long as we all follow the rules, do what's right, and don't try to take advantage of them for our own personal gain. Also, just like any other law, these laws and rules can be changed, as long as we all accept the responsibility to do it the right way. I hear people all the time say *"Well, we can't fight city hall"*, but that is not the case. We can change laws as long as we do it the right way. There are ways to do this, and this next section will explain that better.

A Journey There.......and Back Again with a Message of Hope

Time to Get to Work

Ok, it is time to place *"Acceptance"* into action where the laws that govern us are concerned, because if we ever want to change any law then we truly need to accept the fact that it is our responsibility to do it the right way. Now, again, I am not offering legal advice, and this is a very *'down and dirty'* basic explanation of what to do if we want to change things for the better, but it works. So, let us talk about changing laws that we think are either bad, or antiquated, or that need to be updated or amended for the better. Now, this is done differently depending on which country you live in. For example, in many countries, the proposal for a new law (a Bill) must first be drafted, and then it must get sponsored, and then it must be approved by both the House and the Senate in order to be presented for final signature (by the President in America, for example) so that it can become a law (there are more steps but check your individual country to see how it is done exactly). However, if the elected representative that you go to with your Bill refuses to sponsor it, then there are things that we can do about that as well.

This is the importance of having elections, because if the elected representatives are not representing the people the way that they want them to, then the people need to vote those politicians out of office and replace them with politicians who will do what the people want them to do. Is it a lot of work? Yes, it is. Is it worth it? Why don't you ask the citizens in the countries where they have done this and changed laws, and politicians, for the better. The bottom line is this. Our elected representatives work for us. We are the ones who put them into office when we elected them, and therefore, we are their bosses. As such, we can elect them out of office if they refuse to represent us the way that we want them to. This is why I tell everyone that one of the most important things that we can do is register to vote, and then actually go out and vote

197

during each and every election, because we have the power, and we use that power when we vote. If politicians want their jobs, then they need to represent us, not their own selfish wants and needs. Just remember this one thing. If they will not work to represent us the way that we want them to, then that will be something to remember when the next election comes up.

Look, it is really simple, and it's where the philosophy of *"Acceptance"* really comes into play where laws are concerned. We need to accept the responsibility to either follow the laws on the books, or to change them if we think that they need to be changed. We can do it, but the problem is that most of us would rather just complain than actually take action to change anything where our government is concerned, and especially where laws are concerned. Complaining about how unfair things are will not do anything. Actually doing something about it will, as long as what we do about it is done correctly. Now, let me be truly clear about what I am going to say here. There are those who feel that the only way to be heard, or to change anything, is to use violence to effect change, and violence is never, ever the answer to anything. All we do when we commit acts of violence, especially against the government, is make it impossible for positive change to happen. Oh sure, the government reacts, and normally in an awfully bad way, but is that what we want to happen?

Violence is how change will not happen. We need to beat the system by using the system to effect change. If we show everyone that we know how to effect change by using the system the way that it is set up for us to use, then real change will happen. We need to accept the responsibility to do things right, with the help of our elected officials, and if they will not help, then we need to accept the responsibility to go out, on election day, and have them elected out of office by casting our vote, thereby replacing them with new elected officials who will fight for us and our rights. This is also true if we feel that a government office has not followed its own rules, and as a result, they have treated us unfairly. Our elected officials are there for us where this is concerned too, because we can file complaints in some countries so that the government office who wronged us can be investigated.

The bottom line is that we need to vote for politicians who truly do care about us, and want to work for us, instead of just *'following the sheep'* and voting for whoever everyone else is voting for without doing any research on how, or what, they have been doing while in office. All we have to do is stand up for ourselves, and we do that by accepting the responsibility to take the necessary steps to either vote out laws that we want changed, or by voting out elected officials who won't represent us the way that we want to be represented. It is really simple. We have the power to do it, so what is stopping us from beating the politicians at their own game by voting?

Now, I will say this. When you, or your group, decides that you want to propose a Bill to try and make it into a law, then make sure that you follow the entire procedure as it goes along so that your Bill is not just buried because no one in the process thinks that you are not watching things closely. Now, I am not suggesting that politicians are bad people, because I do know of elected officials who are really good people, and who really do care about their citizens. What I am trying to say is that, if the politicians in the process think that you and/or your group are pushing a Bill that no one really cares about, because no one in your group is following the progress of your Bill closely, then the politicians might put it aside in order to concentrate their efforts on a Bill that they think carries more weight because they think that more people are concentrating on it.

A Visit to the City in the Light

Think of it as just like a project at your work. If your boss hands you two projects, and then only follows the progress of one of the projects because he is showing you that he really cares about getting that project done, then you will naturally concentrate all of your efforts on it, and you will bury the other project until another time, which could delay its completion for a long time. It is the same way with elected officials. They really do have a lot to try and do to represent us at times, and so, if they feel that there is a Bill that more people care about because those citizens are following the progress of it more closely, then they will concentrate almost all of their efforts on it, while putting less effort on your proposal. So, if you want to make sure that they concentrate as much of their efforts on your Bill as they are on other Bills, then let them know that you, and your group, are following it very closely.

This is especially important, and I will tell you why. You need to make sure that, with your Bill proposal, you include a petition with the signatures of as many registered voters as you can get on it and be sure to present this petition to your elected representative when you present your Bill to them. Nothing, and I mean nothing, gets an elected official's attention faster than the knowledge that all of those signatures are registered voters. The same voters that put that elected official into office in the first place, and more importantly, the same voters that can vote to have them removed from office at the next election. If your elected representative knows that there are a lot of registered voters who are genuinely concerned about the new Bill that you and your group are proposing, then they will pay attention to it. They will work hard to have your Bill presented and approved, which is what you want your elected officials to do.

The bottom line is this. If we take the responsibility to change laws properly, or even lawmakers if necessary, then we can

200

take control of our governments, and have our governments work and do things for us instead of doing things to us. All it will take is for us to accept the responsibility to take charge and utilize the power that we have to control our governments. We do that by utilizing the power to vote. Why is that so hard? During elections in America for example (especially the Presidential Elections), there are so many people who get upset because the candidate that they want to have elected does not win. Why? It is because so many people do not even go out and vote for their candidate?

This is exactly what I am talking about. What do people expect to happen if they cannot even be bothered to go out and vote. I have talked to people who were so upset that their candidates did not win that many of them were actually in tears. What good does that do? Sure, it causes people to gain sympathy from other people, but does it do anything else? No, it does not. To prove my point, when I talked to a lot of people, they all gave me the same answer, and that was *"No, I did not go out and vote"*. Why are they getting so upset if they did nothing to help get their candidate elected? If they really wanted to effect the change that they wanted, then they should have registered to vote, and then they should have actually gone to the polls and voted. It is extremely hard (at least for me) to have any sympathy for anyone who is upset about the results of an election when they could not even be bothered to do something about it by actually exercising their right to vote. I know that I go out and vote, because I know the power that a vote holds and what it can cause to happen.

I know that I have been talking about this for a bit, but I have to say again that I just do not understand why there are people who complain all the time about the results of an election, or about a law that they think is unfair and that they feel needs to be changed, and then they refuse to go out and do something to change the law that

201

A Visit to the City in the Light

they feel is unfair by proposing a Bill and then putting it on the ballot to be voted on, or by voting for who they want to win an election. It just does not make any sense to me at all. What makes even less sense to me is the fact that, after an election that did not go the way that some people wanted it to, they always want to blame anyone and everyone for the results, instead of blaming themselves for not exercising their right to vote so that their voice could be heard.

Now, I could continue this chapter with other areas of law, like administrative types, agency rules, and the like, but I think that you get the idea where the law, protecting ourselves concerning the law, and changing laws are concerned, so let me just close this chapter by saying this. It truly is up to us. If we want to have the law protect us, if we want to have our voices heard, if we want our choices to succeed, if we want our countries, and our world, to be the way that we want it to be, then there is only one way that it will ever happen where the law is concerned. It is really easy, and it falls directly into line with the philosophy of *"Acceptance"*. We need to accept the responsibility to do the right thing and be *'law abiding citizens'* so that we never find ourselves in trouble with the law. In addition, we need to accept the responsibility to protect ourselves in order to make sure that we are never falsely accused of a crime.

We also need to accept the responsibility to take steps to protect the ones we love so that they never have crimes committed against them, especially when it comes to protecting our children. If we see a law that needs to be changed or updated, then we need to accept the responsibility to change it by following the right procedures to do so, and if our elected representatives will not help us, then we need to accept the responsibility to vote them out of office so that we can elect representatives who will represent us the

A Visit to the City in the Light

they feel is unfair by proposing a Bill and then putting it on the ballot to be voted on, or by voting for who they want to win an election. It just does not make any sense to me at all. What makes even less sense to me is the fact that, after an election that did not go the way that some people wanted it to, they always want to blame anyone and everyone for the results, instead of blaming themselves for not exercising their right to vote so that their voice could be heard.

Now, I could continue this chapter with other areas of law, like administrative types, agency rules, and the like, but I think that you get the idea where the law, protecting ourselves concerning the law, and changing laws are concerned, so let me just close this chapter by saying this. It truly is up to us. If we want to have the law protect us, if we want to have our voices heard, if we want our choices to succeed, if we want our countries, and our world, to be the way that we want it to be, then there is only one way that it will ever happen where the law is concerned. It is really easy, and it falls directly into line with the philosophy of *"Acceptance"*. We need to accept the responsibility to do the right thing and be *'law abiding citizens'* so that we never find ourselves in trouble with the law. In addition, we need to accept the responsibility to protect ourselves in order to make sure that we are never falsely accused of a crime.

We also need to accept the responsibility to take steps to protect the ones we love so that they never have crimes committed against them, especially when it comes to protecting our children. If we see a law that needs to be changed or updated, then we need to accept the responsibility to change it by following the right procedures to do so, and if our elected representatives will not help us, then we need to accept the responsibility to vote them out of office so that we can elect representatives who will represent us the

202

way that we want them to. The bottom line is this. If we do not follow the law, and we do not do things the right way, and we do not protect ourselves and the ones that we love, then we will have to accept the responsibility of looking in the mirror when we want to find someone to blame for things not happening the way that we want them to happen. To put it bluntly.......if we do not follow the law, then we will only have ourselves to blame when things go wrong, and if things do go wrong, then exactly how are we ever going to trust each other enough to work together to solve all of our problems by practicing *"Acceptance"*?

<u>Chapter Seven</u>
<u>Acceptance and Religion</u>

"I'm thinking about changing churches." - Me, in my truck.
"Well, you got to do what you think is best." - My dad, in my truck.
"Look for the one with her in it." - My Grandma, in my truck.

      I am convinced that the reason that this conversation happened was because I have become very disillusioned with the church that I belong to. Not because of the entire leadership of my church, or it's beliefs, or even the individual people who attend, but because of the leader of the individual meeting house that I attend. As my dad was a Roman Catholic, he always wanted me to stay with his church when I was young. However, I became disillusioned with what was happening to me in his church, and as a result, I left it. At the time that I left my dad's church he agreed with my decision, and he told me that he wanted me to find a new church, but to always look for one that practices what it preaches. I think that this is why my grandma said what she did, because I genuinely believe that she wanted to help me look for the right church so that I can finally be happy with the one that I attend. Since the time that I left my dad's church I have gone to many different ones, looking for one that truly practices what it preaches. I thought that I had finally found the church that I was looking for, but because of recent events, I am not sure now. The one thing that I am sure of is the fact that I am strong in my beliefs, and I will defend them always. Having said that, I would now like to talk about how *"Acceptance"* can help us where religion is concerned, because we are going to need to accept each other in all areas, and religion is one of the areas where we are going to run into a lot of conflict where accepting each other is concerned.

      So, let's talk about religion, something that everyone has a

A Visit to the City in the Light

strong opinion of. Let's talk about our personal beliefs where religion is concerned, and how *"Acceptance"* can help us in this area. We all, whether we want to admit it or not, have an opinion on this, and we all feel very strongly about our opinion. So, let's tread softly here and see how things go, because while I want to show how the philosophy of *"Acceptance"* can help us all come together no matter how we may feel concerning religion, I do not want to disrespect anyone concerning their beliefs, or disrespect their religion either.

Like I said, whether we want to admit it or not, we all have some sort of opinion on this, and we all hold beliefs that are near and dear to us, near and dear enough to fight, and unfortunately, kill over. There are those who feel strongly that there is a higher power, and that he watches over all of us. Then again, there are those who feel just as strongly that there is no higher power at all, and that when we die, we are all nothing but, to coin a phrase, *'food for the worms'*. Then again, there are those who feel that there is more than one higher power, like many civilizations believed in the past, and that we should worship them all. There are also those who feel that, when we die, we are reincarnated in another form, whether that be as another human or as an animal. There are also those who feel that the higher power that people believe in was a member of a race of aliens who visited us a long time ago, and that they still visit us from time to time. Then there are those who feel that the person who we should be worshipping is a darker power, and that this darker power can give us whatever we want, as long as we dedicate our lives, and our worship, to that darker power. There are many other beliefs as well, but no matter how we feel or believe, one thing is for certain, and that is the fact that we all feel that we are absolutely right where our beliefs are concerned, and that anyone who feels differently than us is wrong.

A Journey There.......and Back Again with a Message of Hope

This is an area where we need to practice *"Acceptance"* in many ways. I mean, if we cannot get along because we are fighting over our religious beliefs, then how are we ever going to be able to come together to solve all of the problems that we face as a race? One of the first things that we should accept is the fact that there are many different beliefs, with many followers for each one. Also, while we may not agree with other's beliefs where this topic is concerned, we need to accept the fact that everyone should have the right to believe any way that they want to, no matter how much others may disagree with them. Most importantly, we need to accept the fact that no one should ever stop us from believing the way that we want to believe individually (either through ridicule or by physical force) just because they feel and believe differently than we do. We need to accept this fact if we are to ever stop fighting each other over our beliefs and believe me when I say that we do need to stop fighting each other over our religious beliefs, because no one topic causes more fighting than this one.

Here is the important thing. There are some people who may be upset about what I am about to say, but it needs to be said, and we need to follow what I am about to say if we, as the human race, are ever going to come together and get along so that we can all work together to advance ourselves into a better tomorrow. It is this. We should all have the right to believe any way that we want to believe concerning religion, as long as we do not try and force other people into believing the way that we do, and as long as (and you will get tired of me stating this, but this is too important, and it needs to be stated very clearly) we never, ever, cause any harm to anyone else in the name of our beliefs. This means that we need to stop condemning and persecuting others for the way that they believe, and we need to start respecting their right to believe the way that they want to. It is all about mutual respect, and if we are ever going to come together as a race through *"Acceptance"*, then we

207

need to have mutual respect for each other. Otherwise, we will never come together, and we will never be able to work together no matter how bad the problems are that we need to solve for our race.

This includes not discriminating against others because of the way that they believe, not being confrontational with them about the way that they believe, and not ridiculing them for the way that they believe. In short, we need to allow people to practice their beliefs without being afraid of persecution in any way, shape or form. I'm not just talking about *'We're coming over to physically stop you from practicing your beliefs'*. I am talking about allowing people to believe the way that they want to completely and accepting them completely by respecting them for the way that they want to believe, no matter how they believe, so that we can all stop fighting each other in the name of our beliefs. We need to allow people to believe the way that they want to without ridiculing them, either publicly or through the gossip circles that exist in our social lives, neighborhoods, work circles, and the like. If we are ever going to be able to come together completely and get along so that we can work together and accomplish all of our goals for the betterment of our race, then we need to have the freedom to believe the way that we want to believe, again, as long as our beliefs do not cause harm to anyone at all.

Now, here is another area where we need to implement the philosophy of *"Acceptance"* where religion is concerned. To repeat, we need to accept the fact that, no matter how much we may disagree with another's beliefs, we should never try and stop them from believing the way that they want to. Also, we should never try and cause others harm for believing the way that they do, especially (and here is the important part of this) if the person who is being caused harm is being caused harm by members of their own religion.

A Journey There.......and Back Again with a Message of Hope

Let me explain. Let's say that someone is a worshipper of a darker power. Let's say that they are hard core on this belief, and that they do things like wearing pentagrams and holding ceremonies to practice their belief. Here is where it becomes a problem, and where we need to accept the responsibility to say, *"That is not acceptable!"*. Let's say that, for whatever reason, the people who worship a darker power decide that they need to perform a human sacrifice, and they decide that they want to murder someone in order to perform their ceremony. As I stated before, murder should never be allowed in a civilized society, ever. It goes back to what I was saying in the chapter concerning the law. We should all strive to obey the law, and as we all know, murder is illegal and should never be allowed or tolerated no matter what the reason. Again, if someone feels that they want to worship a darker power, then, per the philosophy of *"Acceptance"*, they should be allowed to, as long as their beliefs do not cause anyone harm (I know, I keep saying this, but it is important that this is understood very clearly, because no religion should ever include harming someone).

Now, let me add to this by stating the following again using another set of beliefs as an example, and let me be truly clear about what I am going to say here. Like I said, we need to accept the fact that we should not harm people for believing the way that they want to believe about religion, but does that mean that we should allow people to harm others using their beliefs as an excuse for causing that harm to others, like some cults do? Absolutely not. I have heard of so many cults that have ended badly. Some end in mass suicides, others end in mass murders of members of the cult or others who the cult set their sights on. No matter how they end, though, they usually end very badly, harming not only their members, but others as well. Nothing is worse than getting the news that your loved one was killed in a mass murder/suicide because they belonged to a cult. It hurts even worse when there was no way that you could stop your loved one from dying in a cult because the cult had shut everyone out so that their loved ones could not do anything to save their loved ones from either committing suicide or being murdered (to see this for yourself, just research *"Heaven's Gate"* or *"Jonestown"*).

I am not sure what the technical term is for what the survivors go through when something like this happens. In layman's terms, it is basically something akin to *'Survivor's Remorse'*, because the relatives of those who died in the cult all get the feeling like they could have done **something** that could have saved their loved one from dying, and they feel bad because they lived, and their loved one died. My heart truly does go out to those people who have lost a loved one due to that person belonging to a cult that ended their life. It leaves the family irreparably broken. That is why I say that we need to accept the fact that everyone should be allowed to believe what they want to believe, as long as their beliefs not cause harm to anyone, because then their beliefs go from being just a personal belief to being something ugly. So ugly that it causes harm to other people. No one should ever be harmed because of the way that they, or others, believe. Ever.

Harming their own members is not the only way that cults can cause harm to people, because there have been cults where the members have set their sights on harming people who are not even members of the cult. There was a cult in America at one time that was led by a leader who wanted to try and take over the neighboring town politically, and they felt that the way that they needed to do it was to harm the people in the town that they wanted to take over so that they would not be able to vote in the upcoming election, which would allow the cult to take over the town.[7] So, they actually used a biological weapon to poison the people who lived in that town. They sprayed the agent on ten different salad bars in the area

210

(according to reports) and a total of 751 people who lived in the town were poisoned. This is a prime example of what I am talking about when I say that we should allow people to believe the way that they want to believe concerning religion as long as the believers of that religion do not cause harm to anyone.

To continue, another area where we need to practice *"Acceptance"* where religion is concerned is in the area of people wanting to see if others want to join their religion, as in, people going from door to door wanting to talk to people. Now, I know that this bothers a lot of people, because no one likes to be bothered at their home, but at no time should we get so upset about this that we get confrontational and rude with the people who are going from door to door asking if we want to learn more about their religion. In a lot of religions there are many people who feel like they want to share how they believe. In a lot of cases, they are actually sent on *'missions'* by their church to see if there are people who want to learn about their religion and join their church. They do this because it is part of the way that they practice their religion. But is this really causing harm to anyone? Is it really something that should cause us to get so upset that we yell at these people, and try to make them feel like they are our enemy, or actually threaten them? I mean, they find people each and every day who do want to learn more about their religion, and in a lot of cases, the people that get the visitors end up going to the church that sent their members to their door. However, if you do not want to learn more about their church because you are happy with the way that you believe religiously, then there are better ways to handle the situation that just getting upset at the visitors. After all, if we are going to try and bring everyone together through *"Acceptance"*, then we need to find a way to handle the situation without getting upset or treating people rudely.

211

A Visit to the City in the Light

Let me tell you how I handle this. Anytime someone comes to my door, and they want to talk to me about religion and their church, I always tell them, in a very polite way, that I already belong to a church, and then I thank them for coming by and I tell them to have a nice day. Then, if they continue to try and talk to me, I tell them that they are catching me at a bad time, and that I need to go. I then remind them that I already belong to a church, and that they should try someone else's home in the future because I am happy believing the way that I do and going to the church that I belong to. Then, once again, I tell them that I hope that they have a good day, and I close the door. I am not rude to them, and because of the way that I spoke to them they normally never come back, and everyone parts happy. They are happy because they tried to talk to me about their church, even though they were unsuccessful, and I am happy because I did not have to be mean to them in order to have them to leave. Everyone wins in a peaceful, respectful, and caring way, without any harm coming to anyone.

Now, if that does not work, or you do not want to talk to them at all, then another way to handle this situation would be to simply post a sign on your door saying something like *'No Solicitation'*. They sell these signs at a lot of stores, they are not expensive, and it lets everyone know that you do not want people coming to your door to try and sell you something, including those who are trying to sell you on their religion. If you do not want to buy a sign, then make one and put it on your door (have fun with it, like my neighbors do. They have a sign on their door that says *'We are too broke to buy anything. We know who we are voting for. We have found Jesus. Please go away and have a nice day!'*). Then, if people still come to your door, all you have to say is that you are not interested, like the sign says, and then very politely wish them a *'good day'*. After a while, word will spread among the local churches that you are not interested, and the visitors will stop

212

coming by.

The bottom line is this.   There is no reason to get upset at people who are just trying to come by and talk to you about how they believe, or to try and invite you to come to their church to worship.   If we are ever going to come together as a race and get along, then we truly need to stop being confrontational and angry at each other, especially over things like how we believe individually.   Instead, we should be respectful towards each other, because if we want to be respected, then we need to respect others.   Again, it all comes down to mutual respect.   If the fighting continues, then it will be impossible for us to ever come together.   I mean, wouldn't you rather live in a world where there is no anger and fighting just because of the way that we want to believe?   Wouldn't you rather live in a world where we all have many friends, no matter how they believe, instead of just a few who believe exactly the way that we do?

Now, I am not saying that we are required to invite someone over to our house who holds religious beliefs that are quite different from ours, or to start some type of intimate relationship with them.   What I am trying to say is that we need to accept the responsibility to figure out ways for all of our race to get along so that we can work together to advance into a better tomorrow, and if we continue to fight over things like how we believe individually, then it will never happen.   Why get angry over how a person believes?   True, it is a bother to have strangers come by your home at unexpected times, but is that really a reason to make enemies out of people that you just met?   We need to accept the responsibility to figure out ways for us to all get along and work together, so let's truly accept the responsibility to do that.

Let me ask you a question.   Do you like it when people

make fun of you because of something that you like or something that you like to do, no matter what it is? Doesn't that make you feel bad, or even angry? It is the same way with how we believe religiously. Why condemn someone just because of how they want to believe? Let's take that a step further. Let's say that your religious beliefs include the belief that you need to wear certain clothing every day, like a school uniform for example, no matter what day it is. How would it make you feel if people around you made fun of you openly and ridiculed you in public for practicing your beliefs? Wouldn't that make you feel bad, or upset? It all goes back to this. If you want people to respect you and the way that you believe religiously, without ridiculing you, then set the example by respecting them and not ridiculing them.

It all goes back to accepting the responsibility of respecting others for their beliefs just the same way that you want to be respected for your beliefs. We all want to be respected, accepted, and treated fairly. So, if you want to be treated that way, and you want the respect of those around you, then show others that you want that by respecting them no matter how they believe, unless they want to harm others in the name of their beliefs. I don't think that I can state this enough, because there will be those who will try to say *'My beliefs state that me, and my followers, should commit suicide in order to follow our religion'*, or they will try and say *'See, this book says that you need to respect me for believing that my religion gives me permission to kill others, because they don't believe the same way that I do'*, but that is not what I am saying. No religion, or any other belief for that matter, should give anyone the right to cause harm to others. The philosophy of *"Acceptance"* dictates that we accept and respect others no matter how they want to believe, but we should never respect anyone who wishes to harm someone else in the name of their religious beliefs, no matter what they are.

214

A Journey There.......and Back Again with a Message of Hope

Let me take this one step further. Now, this is where things may get a little confusing (I mean, I was confused when writing this section, but please, stick with me, because this is especially important where religious freedom for all of us is concerned), but let's discuss how we should approach religious freedom when we move to another country. Ok, it is just a fact of life that there are countries where their strict religious beliefs basically run the way that their country operates. We may not like their beliefs, and we may not agree with their beliefs, but does that give us the right to move into their countries and say that, because we moved there, then everyone in the country that we moved to should stop believing the way that they have been believing in order to start believing the way that we believe, and even try to change the way that their country's government operates so that they stop operating their government according to their strict religious beliefs? On the other hand, should people who move **from** countries (that are operated by strict religious beliefs) **to** countries that have religious freedom try and change how those governments are operated so that they stop allowing **their** citizens to have religious freedom and so they start operating their countries according to their (the people who moved to the new country) strict religious beliefs? No, not at all.

If anyone moves to a new country to live, then they should accept the fact that they have moved to a country that has its own set of beliefs and/or religious freedoms, **especially** if the government where they have moved to is run according to strict religious beliefs. We should not try and stop them from believing the way that they believe and run their governments just to try and force them to believe the way that we believe. Now, does that mean that we should stop believing the way that we want to believe just because we moved to a country that believes in strict religious beliefs, and who operates their government according to those strict religious beliefs? No, not at all. We should all be able to believe the way

215

that we want to believe, as long as (again, let me be clear on what I am about to say) no one harms another person in the name of their beliefs, and as long as we respect other people's religious beliefs. This is just as important as never harming anyone, or causing harm to come to anyone, just because of the way that they want to believe. There are some religions that are very sacred to their believers, and that are extremely strict religions, and as such, we should always be respectful to not only those people whose beliefs are strict, but also to their religion itself.

It all goes back to treating other people the same way that you want to be treated. You would not want other people to make fun of your religion, so why make fun of their religion? You would not want other people to disrespect your religion, so why would you ever disrespect their religion? If we are ever going to get along and work together for the betterment and advancement of our race, then we need to be respectful to everyone, and that includes being respectful to their religion. Now, does that mean that we need to change the way that we believe because someone is claiming that the way that we believe is disrespectful to their religion, all because we believe differently than they do? No, because again, we should all be allowed to believe the way that we want to (again, as long as we never cause harm to anyone in the name of our religious beliefs), and no one should claim that the way that we believe individually is disrespectful to their religion, especially if we are ever going to have true universal religious freedom for all. Again, it all goes back to the meaning of *"Acceptance"*. We truly need to have mutual respect for everyone if we are ever going to come together as a race and solve all of the problems that we face, and that is what *"Acceptance"* is all about. Bringing us all together for the benefit of all of us through mutual respect, peace, love, and care for each other.

A Journey There.......and Back Again with a Message of Hope

Now, let me take that even one step further.   Let's say that you move to a country where their religious beliefs truly do control the way that their country and government operates, and that they are very strict in the way that they believe, run their government, and most importantly, write and enforce their government's laws (because there are governments that have laws that state that, if you practice a religion that is different than the strict religion that operates their government, then you can be charged with breaking the law in their country if you practice a different religion in public, and you can be punished in their country for doing so.   This is incredibly sad to me, but it is a fact of life in those countries).   If is the case, then I do not mean to sound harsh, but here is the way that I think things need to be in today's world in order to make sure that we all get to believe the way that we want to believe while living where we want to live, at least until we have true religious freedom worldwide and we can move anywhere while practicing any religious beliefs that we want to.

Knowing that some countries run their governments in a strict religious way, then I don't mean to be harsh or sound uncaring, but if anyone moves to a country that operates their government according to their strict religious beliefs, **and** if the person who is moving into that country knows that their new country operates their governments and their laws according to their strict religious beliefs (which happens to be different from the way that the person moving there believes), then the person who is moving there can't expect to be treated in any way except the way that their new country's government operates and enforces their laws, even if it is quite different from the way that the person who is moving there believes.

In other words, there is an old saying that goes *'You made your bed, now lie in it'* (variation of a fifteenth century French proverb), and unfortunately, it is absolutely true in today's world because we still don't have religious freedom worldwide. Therefore, if you move to a country that operates its government, and enforces its laws, according to their strict religious beliefs, then do not expect to be welcomed with open arms if you move there believing in a way that is quite different from the way that they believe, especially if the way that you believe, and most importantly your actions in public, are disrespectful to their religion and their laws (which are enforced according to their strict religious beliefs). You moved there fully informed of the way that they believe and the way that they operate their government, and so you cannot expect them to change the way that they operate their government just because you believe differently. That means that you should never go into their country disrespecting the way that they believe or disrespecting their religion by breaking their religious laws.

Now, does that mean that I agree with the way that some governments run their countries when they run them according to strict religious beliefs? No, I am not saying that at all. What I am saying is this. If I know that there is a country that operates their government according to very strict religious beliefs in today's world, and I know that those beliefs are very different from the way that I believe, and I know that they expect their citizens to conduct themselves according to their strict religious beliefs, then I am going to accept the responsibility of making the decision to not move to that country unless they change their government and laws so that all of their citizens can believe and worship in any way that they choose to in public without fear of retribution in any way. I know that it could cause me harm if I move there because my beliefs are different than theirs, so I am definitely not going to move to their country and disrespect the way that they believe or disrespect their religion all because my beliefs and my actions are different than theirs, and how they expect their citizens to behave in public.

A Journey There.......and Back Again with a Message of Hope

Now, herein lies the problem, and it is one that I wish I had the solution for, but unfortunately, I don't. However, it is a problem that we all need to address once we come together and work together for the betterment of our race. You see, I truly feel that no one's religious beliefs should ever cause them harm. Unfortunately, though, there are countries in our world who do enforce their laws by strict religious beliefs, and a lot of them cause harm to anyone who believes differently than they do while in their country, because they feel that the visitor's religious conduct in public disrespects their religious beliefs. So, what do we do about it? Do we respect the way that they believe, and operate their government, when they believe that anyone who believes differently than they do should be jailed or even executed while in their country?

This is why I say that, as someone who believes in true religious freedom, and as someone who believes differently than they do, I will make the conscious decision to not move to their country until they change the way that they operate their government, and they start allowing their citizens to have true religious freedom without any persecution. I think that another thing that makes me really sad about this whole thing is the fact that I love to travel, and as a lover of history, I do love to see the truly wondrous things in our world, and I know that, even though there are incredibly beautiful and marvelous sites in our world to see, I won't be able to see all of them because of the way that I believe religiously. I believe that this is why a lot of governments believe in separating church from state. I just wish that all governments would do this.

To continue, though, I want people to respect me for believing the way that I want to believe, and I do not want anyone to disrespect my religion, so therefore I am going to respect anyone

219

else's right to believe the way that they want to believe, and I am never going to disrespect their religion, as long as their religious beliefs do not harm anyone else. You see, if you think about it, it is not their religious beliefs that are harming those who believe differently than they do, it is their governmental laws that causes harm to happen to others who believe differently. Therefore, until things change, and all countries allow true religious freedom, then we all need to accept the responsibility to think before we act, and that is especially true when we are getting ready to move to another country who operates it's government in a way that could cause us harm just because of the way that we believe religiously.

Now, does that mean that I hate everyone in that country just because of the way that their government operates (according to strict religious beliefs)? No, I am not saying that either, because as I stated earlier, everyone should be able to believe the way that they want to believe, and everyone should be respected for believing the way that they want to believe. Look, if we are ever going to come together as one race, then we need to stop hating each other, especially where our religious beliefs are concerned. There are people who live in those countries that are happy with living their lives according to their strict religious beliefs, and we aren't going to change the way that their government operates by hating everyone who lives there. We need to set the example by not hating others if we genuinely want to bring us all together through *"Acceptance"*, no matter how different their beliefs are than ours. It is peace, caring, and most importantly, mutual respect for each other that will change our world, and I honestly believe that is what *"Acceptance"* will do, if we all just give it a chance.

Ok, now, does that mean that I believe that the people living in those countries should never be allowed to move to another country if they want to believe differently than their government does, especially when their government runs their country and enforces their laws according to strict religious beliefs? No, not at all. I believe that everyone should have the opportunity, and the right, to believe and lead their lives in any way that they choose, as long as those religious beliefs do not cause harm to anyone else or causes disrespect to anyone's religion. If that means that the citizens who live there want to move away from the country that they live in (that operates its government according to strict religious beliefs) and move to another country that allows them to believe any way that they want to believe without being harmed, then they should be allowed to do so without being harmed for wanting to move to another country that allows them to practice their beliefs with religious freedom.

So, does that mean that I think that these other countries (who operate their countries according to their strict religious beliefs) should be forced to stop running their countries according to those strict religious beliefs? No, I do not. That may sound like I am not sympathetic to people living in those countries and who are having to live their lives in a strict religious manner, a manner that may be causing their citizens to have to live their lives in a way that we would consider harsh and unfair but hear me out. This is why I said that we all should be allowed to move from those countries if we want to live our lives with religious freedom, instead of being forced to live our lives without religious freedom, or any freedom in general. Like I said before, we should all be able to live our lives while being able to believe the way that we want to believe, and that includes allowing other countries to run their governments the way that they want to, as long as they allow people who believe differently than them to move from those countries if they wish to.

Now, if they are harming people for believing differently than they do, and they are not allowing their citizens to move from

221

their countries so that they can have religious freedom, then what do we do about that?   Well, once again, I wish I had all the answers, but I don't.   However, this is another thing that we need to address when we all come together, and we can come together through *"Acceptance"* to solve these, and other, problems that we face, because as I have said, I believe very strongly that everyone should have freedom, which includes religious freedom.

To continue, though, we may not agree with the way that they operate their government based on their strict religious beliefs, but we should respect their right to believe the way that they want to believe and respect their right to operate their government according to their strict religious beliefs, because if we do not, then we are no better than those who want to stop us from believing the way that we want to believe when they move into our countries.   I know that I have said this before, but it bears repeating.   I truly do wish that our entire world embraced religious freedom, but until it does, then we need to remember that it does not when we are deciding where we want to live and worship in today's world.   Something else to consider is this.   There are people who are happy living in the countries that are run according to strict religious beliefs, but if there is anyone living in one of those countries who is not happy living their lives according to those strict beliefs, then they should be allowed to leave those countries and move to another country where they can have religious freedom, even if we need to take certain action to help them do so.

Please allow me to explain.   I believe that, if people want to leave the country that they live in so that they can have religious freedom, then they should be allowed to, even if that means that we need to help them move.   I know that I have said this before in this chapter, but it is especially important, important enough to repeat. No one should ever be harmed because of their religious beliefs, and just as important, no one should be forced to live in a country that does not allow them to have religious freedom.   In addition, we should also help people who live in countries that are run by strict religious beliefs if they also hold those same strict religious beliefs, but they are **still** being harmed.   This goes on a lot more than many people think, and it needs to stop.   No religion should harm its own members, ever.

Therefore, if people want to leave the country that they live in so that they can have religious freedom or because they are being harmed by members of their own religion, then we should, if we can, help them by helping them move to a new country if they want to so that they can practice the religious beliefs that they want to practice freely and openly, without fear of any harm.   Now, I will be the first to say that I am not sure just how we are going to be able to help people leave countries that will not allow them religious freedom or that are harming them in the name of the same strict religious beliefs that they also hold.   I will say, however, with all certainty, that if I ever find myself in the position to help someone move to a new country so that they can have true religious freedom or so that they will not be harmed in the name of religious beliefs, even their own beliefs, then I will do whatever I can in order to make it happen, within the law of course.

Now, I know that this may seem impossible in some ways, because some countries may not want to let their citizens leave, but this is where something that I spoke of earlier needs to come into play.   This is where our world leaders (for the betterment of our entire race) need to step up and be true world leaders and speak for those people who want to leave their country but are not being allowed to, because no one should ever be a prisoner in their native country, especially if their religious beliefs could cause them to come to harm.   Now, I am not saying that we should go to war with another country over this, because war is the worst thing that can happen to any country, and it should never be declared lightly. We should help people where and when we can though, and that includes helping people to move if they want to in order to have true religious freedom without any persecution.

Again though, I am not sure just how we can help these people move to a new country where they can have religious freedom. Maybe this is a topic that we can all talk about in order to work together to come up with solutions to this problem, like what the philosophy of *"Acceptance"* is all about. Like I said, there are many people who are happy living their lives in countries that are operated according to strict religious beliefs, and they, themselves, hold those strict religious beliefs near and dear to their hearts, and they are happy leading their lives according to those beliefs. However, if there is anyone who is not happy, and who wants to leave their native country so that they are not harmed because of their beliefs, then they should be allowed to do so. Religious freedom without any persecution is important, and it should be afforded to everyone who wants it.

Now, another part of this is the obvious fact that, once these people move to another country, we should accept the responsibility to welcome them into whatever country they want to move to and not discriminate against them. This also means that, if someone moves from a country that holds strict religious beliefs, and they do so while still believing in those strict religious beliefs, then we should accept the responsibility to welcome them as well, without trying to force them to change the way that they believe. Now, does that mean that, once they move to another country while they are practicing their strict religious beliefs, they should be allowed to try and change the country that they just moved to (and change the laws that govern their new home) to the way that they believe?

Absolutely not.   It goes back to what I said earlier, when I said that
we need to accept the fact that we *'made our bed'* when we moved
to a new country, and therefore, we should accept how our new
home is governed, and we should accept the way that the people
believe in our new home country, without trying to change it or the
way that the people there believe religiously, because religious
freedom should be afforded to all.

Now, what I am about to say will probably upset a lot of
people, but it needs to be said and addressed because unfortunately,
in today's world, there are those who feel that they want to commit
crimes, or worse yet, acts of terrorism, and they want to make any
excuse that they can in order to move to new countries where they
can do this.   Now, I stand by what I said when I said that we should
help people move to countries where they can practice religious
freedom, but we also need to make sure that the people who are
coming into new countries are doing so because they want to
practice religious freedom, and not because they are trying to come
into a new country to commit things like acts of terrorism.   So, how
do we do that?   Now, I could go into an entire section about
immigration here, but I do not want to deflect our attention away
from the core subject of this chapter, which is how do we ensure
religious freedom for all utilizing the philosophy of *"Acceptance"*.
So, let me say this.   Once again, I wish that I had all the answers,
but I don't.   However, this is where the philosophy of
"Acceptance" comes into play again, because it is truly about all of
us coming together, without conflict and with true *"Acceptance"* in
our heart for all of our differences in order to solve our world's
problems, and that includes solving this problem as a caring,
compassionate, and loving human race.

So, to sum up this chapter, I would like to say this.   First,
everyone should have religious freedom.   We should all have the

right to believe the way that we want to without being persecuted, without being ridiculed, and most importantly, without being threatened with harm or discrimination for the way that we want to believe. We should not be hostile towards others who want to share their religious beliefs with us, even if they do come to our homes to do so. Instead, we should either invite them into our homes, or tell them that we believe differently, or that we are not interested, but always in a caring and polite manner (like you would want someone to treat someone that you care about. How can we expect people to be polite and respectful towards us where our religious beliefs are concerned if we do not treat them in the same manner?).

We truly need to come together and work together to come up with solutions for those people who live in countries where they do not have religious freedom, because no one should be jailed, or have things even worse happen to them, all because of their religious beliefs. Now, those solutions should include helping them to immigrate into a new country so that they can have religious freedom (as long as we help them to immigrate legally, because we don't want people trying to immigrate to a new country in the name of religious freedom if their real goal is to harm the citizens who already live there by committing crimes against them, and the only way that we can be sure is if they immigrate legally by being vetted properly). The bottom line is this. No one should ever be afraid of being harmed just because of the way that they believe religiously. We truly need to come together, utilizing the philosophy of *"Acceptance"*, to ensure that everyone can worship in any way that they choose to with true religious freedom. After all, if we cannot learn to get along with each other because of our religious beliefs, then how are we ever going to come together in *"Acceptance"* and solve our race's problems once and for all?

Chapter Eight
Acceptance and the Human Race

"Too much hating." - My Dad, at the top of the Dam.

When we had this conversation, we were looking at absolute chaos. There were scenes of ever shifting violence surrounded by flames, which made the entire vision more horrifying. There were people fighting each other, women and children being attacked, homes on fire, shootings, stabbings, and every other type of violence. The one thing that caught my eye, though, was the fact that it was all people attacking other people (and in particular, there was one scene that I saw that will haunt me to my grave. All I will say here is that the scream I heard will live in my memory, and my nightmares, for as long as I live). There were no demons, or any other sight that would signify that what I was watching was a vision of Hell. No, it was more a sight of what is happening here, on Earth, and how we are treating each other now. Which is why I think that my dad said this to me, because I am convinced that what I was witnessing were visions of how bad things are for us, and how much worse they can get if we do not stop all the hate that exists in our race. It is for that reason that I want to talk about our race in this chapter, and how *"Acceptance"* can really help us to come together so we can stop the rampant violence that our world suffers from.

Ok, while I really could have included this topic in other chapters, and even though I did mention parts of this before, I think that this is important enough to have its own chapter. So, let's start by talking about racism. One thing that I have learned in my travels is that racism is usually based on our differences (where we are from, what the color of our skin is, what language we use, etc.) instead of being truly based on race, like the horrible word *'racism'* implies.   I say this because, as I stated earlier, we may come from many different nations, and we may look differently, or talk differently, but we are all a part of the same race, the human race, and the sooner that we accept this fact in our hearts the faster that *"Acceptance"* can take effect.   Then we can really start to make our world a better place for all of us.   Like I said, practicing *"Acceptance"* in our personal life, especially where this topic is concerned, will be the fastest way to end racism.   After all, how can anyone be a *'racist'* after they accept the fact, in their heart, that we are all brothers and sisters of the same race?

Does this mean that we should not be proud of things like where we come from, or the color of our skin?   Absolutely not, because everyone should be proud of themselves, but does that mean that we should treat others like they are inferior to us just because of these differences?   No, not in my mind, or anyone else's mind who has truly put *"Acceptance"* into practice in their person lives and in their heart.   We truly need to accept the fact that we are all the same race, and as such, no one is better than anyone else where we are concerned.   Sure, some people may have a different job than others, like they may have the spotlight because they are known in Hollywood, or they may be a janitor, or maybe a field worker, or a sanitation worker, or a doctor, or a lawyer, or a judge, or a scientist, or an astrophysicist, or an astronaut, or something else that distinguishes them from everyone else, but does that mean that anyone should be discriminated against, or hated, all because of what they do for a living, or because of what language they use, or what the color of their skin is, or because of something else equally as shallow?   Look, as far as we should be concerned, and especially where practicing the philosophy of *"Acceptance"* is concerned, it should not matter what the color of our skin is, or what the language is that we use, or where we come from.   We may look differently, and we may talk differently, and we may eat different foods, and there may be a dozen other differences that distinguishes us from other people, but the bottom line is that we are all born **human**.   That makes us all the same race, and this fact should be the most important thing to all of us.

I know that I covered this in an earlier chapter but let me touch on this again.   Does being a doctor, a CEO, a lawyer, or anything else that is specialized, make someone a better human being than anyone else?   Yes, maybe some people do critical jobs in order to make sure that we are taken care of properly, like a surgeon does, but does that truly make them a better human being than the rest of us?   I don't think so, because they are still the same as the rest of us when it comes to our race.   They all have a heart, and a brain, and lungs, and other things that make us all human.   So again, while they may do something that is different than what we do, does that really make them a better person than the rest of us?

What I honestly think is the deciding factor, when determining if one person is better than another person, is who the person is and how they lead their life.   Let me explain.   Let's say we have two different people.   **Person "A"** is someone who lives their life being a genuinely nice, generous, loving, caring, and giving person.   They always have a good word to say when they meet another person.   They are kind and giving, and they truly do care about other people.   They are a loyal and loving partner to the person that they love, and they are never violent to them in any way. They try, every day, to be a good role model to their children (if they are blessed enough to have children that is), and to other people's children, by leading their life in a way that sets a good example for all children.   They take other people's feelings into consideration when they are dealing with them.   They always follow the law, because they know that they do not want anyone to commit a crime against them, and they want themselves, and their family, to live safe lives in a safe neighborhood, and so they have made the conscious decision not to commit crimes and cause harm to others, because they want others to treat them the way that they treat others. They try to help other people who may need it, even if that means just helping someone get something off of a shelf in a grocery store. In other words, they are what people call a good person, and someone that we would all like to be our friend and be in our lives.

Now, let's look at **Person "B"**. This person hates anyone who is not the same as they are. They hate people who have a different skin color than them, or speak a different language, and as such, they are what a lot of people call a classic racist. They do not care about anyone else but themselves and what they want, and as such, they do not care about making any contributions at all to helping the human race operate, advance, and evolve into the future. They feel that the world owes them a living, and anyone who does not give them what they want for free is their enemy, and they are not afraid to make their enemies pay for not giving them what they want, even if that means that they are going to use physical violence to obtain their goals. As such, they are willing to lie, cheat, and steal to get what they want as long as they do not have to work for it, because they do not care about causing harm to anyone. They feel that their partner is their *'property'*, and they want to control them no matter what. If that means that they have to hurt them, either through hateful words or physical violence, in order to maintain control over them, then so be it, as long as their partner does what they say at all times. They do not care about the example that they set for our children, because they truly do not care about the future of our race, they only care about themselves and today. As such, hurting a child, or setting a bad example for them, means absolutely

230

nothing to them.

So, which person would you want to be your friend, or would you want to have a relationship with, and be in your children's lives? You see, the reason that I said all of this is because I want to point out the fact that being a better human being should not be a decision that is made based on the way that we look, or what language we speak, or anything else superficial. I feel strongly that what it should be based on is how we lead our lives and based on our actions. We should all want to be person "A", because that person cares about everyone in our race, and as such, they genuinely care about the world that we live in. They want us to succeed as a race, and they want to make sure that our children are taught the correct way to live their lives so that we can advance and evolve as a race. They are willing to lead their lives in a certain way in order to make us successful. Person "B" is the person that we should not want to be, at least in my point of view, because they care nothing about us, or our future. They only care about themselves. Therefore, I feel that person "A" is a much better human being than person "B" is. Who we are, how we act, and how we lead our lives is far more important than how we look, or what language we use, at least to me, and to anyone else who has truly put the philosophy of *"Acceptance"* into practice in their daily lives.

When I say that we should all strive to be like person "A", it encompasses a lot more than just being a good person to those in our own personal lives. It should also encompass being a good person to everyone around us as well, even if they are complete strangers. You know, I have always said that *"Random acts of kindness are some of the best acts of kindness."* and let me give you a real-life example of what I am talking about where being a kind, caring person comes into play. The other day I was at a local mini mart,

231

A Visit to the City in the Light

and behind me in line was a woman who would make most men's jaws drop to the floor.   Model looks, long blond hair, perfect makeup, just gorgeous.   I had never seen her before in my life, she was a complete stranger to me.   She was the type of girl that most men would do anything for, just to make her happy and have a relationship with (now, I am not saying that a girl should be judged based on looks alone, because it takes a lot more than just looks to make someone pretty.   I, myself, am most attracted to intelligence, because I love it when a girl can stand beside me and defend me when I am right, and I also love it when a girl can stand face to face with me while explaining to me why I am wrong by simply explaining it to me using facts, without yelling at me or fighting with me.   I also find it incredibly attractive when a woman is eager to learn and broaden her horizons and has goals for her life.   A girl who can teach me about things that I do not know about, and who has a great knowledge about our world in general).   She was also the type of girl that most people would consider aloof, the type of girl that would not lift a finger to help anyone if it did not benefit her in some way.   Sadly, this is what most people would assume, just because of the way that she looked, but that assessment could not have been farther from the truth.

Anyway, when it came to my turn to pay, I was fumbling with my crushed ice drink trying to get the lid on it when, sure enough, the cup slipped, and I spilled some of it on myself and on the floor.   I was completely embarrassed, and I wished that I could just hide.   The girl behind the counter knew me, and she gave me some napkins so that I could clean up my mess.   Then, as I was trying to clean up the counter (and my shoes) the next thing that I knew there she was, the pretty blond, on her knees wiping up what I had spilled on the floor.   I did not even have the chance to ask anyone for help, let alone her, and yet, there she was, helping me clean up my mess as if we had known each other all of our lives.

232

A Journey There.......and Back Again with a Message of Hope

After I cleaned up the mess on the counter, I looked down to thank her, and she looked at me and said *"It's ok"* in a truly kind and caring tone.   So then, as I went to get more napkins so that I could continue to clean up my mess, I decided to offer to pay for her snacks for her being so kind, but by the time that I returned to the counter she was gone, having already paid.   I have not seen her since.

This is what I am talking about when I say that we should not judge each other for superficial reasons.   As I said, most people would have looked at her and said to themselves *"Well, she is the type of person who only cares about themselves"*, but they would have been completely wrong, and her actions on that day proved it. Anyone can be a good, caring person, if they just take the time to be that person.   We should never judge people just because of the way that they look, because when we do, we are a part of the problem instead of being part of the solution.

It is the same when assuming that people are a certain way, and do certain things, all because of the color of their skin, or because of the language that they speak, or any other reason that would cause some people to say that *'They are all alike'*.   Skin color is no indicator of the person inside, neither is what they wear, or how they speak.   Some people say things like *'Well, they are all criminals'* just because of the color of their skin, or *'Well, they are all white supremacists'* just because they have a historic flag on their vehicle, or *'Well, they are all terrorists'* just because of their religion.   Unfortunately, people tend to lump people together like this, and we all need to accept the responsibility to stop thinking like this, because if we don't, then *"Acceptance"*, and bringing our race together, will never happen.

Let me give you an example of what I am talking about.

A Visit to the City in the Light

Recently I heard of a music group that was facing discrimination in
America, all because the name of their band referenced the Southern
States of America back in the days of the Civil War.[8] Does this
mean that they are white supremacists? Does this mean that they
are actively hurting anyone with that name (and I will explain what I
mean when I say *'actively hurting anyone'* in the next chapter)?
True, their name references a time when the South tried to secede
from America, and a lot of people in the South believed in slavery at
that time, but other than that, is the name of that band really causing
harm to anyone now? I don't think so, and later I will explain in
more detail why I say the following. Don't the people in this band
deserve the same respect that we want, without people saying *'Well,
they must be bad people, I mean, look at their name'*? Isn't that
unfair to the members of this band? That is what I am talking about
when I say we all need to accept the responsibility to stop profiling
people just because of the way that they look, or the way that they
talk, or even what they want to call their band. Like I said, it is
true, the name of their band does reference a time when, in the
Southern States of America, slavery was the order of the day, but
does that mean that they like slavery, or that they support it, or
believe in it at all? How can people say that when they haven't
even taken the time to get to know them as individual people, and
how they believe?

It is just like saying that a person of a certain skin color must
be a criminal. Why, just because of the color of their skin? True,
they may live in an area where criminal activity is predominate, or
they may have grown up in an area that is rampant with crime, but
does that mean that they are criminals? They may be the best
person that you could ever meet, but we would never know unless
we accept the responsibility to get to know them before we judge
them. Also, the last time I checked, people of every skin color are
committing crimes. Again, we need to accept the responsibility of

getting to know a person before we judge them, otherwise we will never come together and stop all the hate.

Or how about the notion that all people from a certain country must be wife beating, whiskey drinking alcoholics? Or the notion that all people from a certain country must be illegal aliens? Or the notion that all people who dress a certain way must be drug dealing criminals? Or the notion that all people who have an alternative lifestyle are child molesting perverts? You would be absolutely amazed at just how many people feel like this all because, instead of accepting the responsibility of getting to know who these people are as individuals, too many people just assume that *'they are all like that'*.

We need to accept the responsibility to actually get to know people, instead of just assuming that they are all the same. When we do that, then we will finally be able to take that first step into the future, and by doing so, we will finally be able to bring all of us together to stop all the hate and prejudice, and truly work together for the betterment of everyone in our race. This is also what I am talking about when I say that the best way to do that is by practicing the philosophy of *"Acceptance"*, because when we accept the responsibility to get to know each other and accept each other for who we are as individuals and the way that we want to live our lives, without hate and prejudice, then we will be able to come together and work together with peace and love and understanding for everyone. We need to do this, because we face many problems that threaten our world today, and without coming together to address them and solve them now, we could be in trouble.

Let me explain. Right now, because of all the differences that are presently stopping us from coming together, we cannot get anything done. Here is a prime example of what I am talking about.

A Visit to the City in the Light

Let's say that we just continue fighting each other and then, one day, we learn that there is an asteroid heading straight for us.   This may seem extreme, but it is not as extreme as you might think.   On July 25th of 2019 for example, it was announced that an asteroid the size of a football field just missed Earth.[9]   The scientists named it **Asteroid 2019OK,** and they called it a *'City Killer'*.   The scientists said that it passed within approximately 45,000 miles of earth, and it was traveling at a speed of nearly 54,000 mph.   To put that into perspective, and to show you just how close to us that asteroid was, the moon is 238,900 miles from Earth.   Think about it.   They said that, if the asteroid would have struck our planet, it would have had the blast force of approximately 10 megatons of TNT.   The reason that the scientists did not see it coming until just days before it passed by us was because of factors like the asteroid's orbit and speed.   Now consider this.   If we just continue to fight amongst ourselves because we still have not accepted the responsibility to work together for the betterment of our race, then what would we do about this if it happens again?   Trust me, it will happen again, and next time, we may not be so lucky.   So, what are we going to do?   Continue to fight amongst ourselves, or come together as one race to take steps to stop such a tragedy?

Let me say this.   Do you really think that the space agencies (of each country on our planet) would be able to come up with a plan that would avert a possible tragedy like this in such a short amount of time?   They didn't this time, so what about the next time?   Now, let's face facts.   There are a lot of people out there who are saying to themselves *"Oh sure, the many different government's space agencies must have **some** type of game plan for such an emergency"*, but do they?   We haven't even made it back to the moon for crying out loud, so what type of game plan could they possibly have to save our planet from a killer asteroid?   Let me tell you what I have seen concerning dealing with this type of tragedy by asking you a question. Have we seen any space projects that are being built in our solar system to divert an asteroid? The International Space Station sure isn't going to stop anything as powerful as an asteroid.

Let me tell you what I have seen. What I have seen are agencies building spaceships to transport people. So, what does that tell you? I will tell you what it tells me. It tells me that, more than likely, the game plan is for the governments to decide who they think are the most valuable people on Earth to save, or the wealthiest, and then to get them off our planet until the worst is over. Now, I can't say that this **is** the game plan for definite, but based on the fact that there are no defense systems in orbit around our planet, and the fact that the concentration of the efforts, so to speak, are on building ships instead of defense systems, then it would definitely appear that the game plan is to run instead of defending our planet, and what worries me is this.......**who** gets to decide who to save, and who dies?

Even private corporations are building spaceships to transport people. Don't believe me? Just do an internet search. As we speak, spaceships are being built to transport people back to the moon, and then later to Mars, to establish colonies (at least that is the *'official'* story). Now, that is great for those who have a lot of money, or for those who are in positions of power, but what about the rest of us? Are we just expected to stay here and enjoy nuclear winter after an asteroid smashes into our planet (if we survive the initial impact, that is)? I think that it is great that there are plans to colonize the moon, and later Mars, but shouldn't we also be making plans to try and stop an asteroid from destroying our planet as well? Isn't our planet worth saving?

So, how do we do that? Well, I can tell you this. We will

never be able to do it if we can't even come together as one race and come up with plans to defend our own planet, and that will never happen until we accept the fact that we are one race, the human race, and then accept the responsibility to all work together in order to come up with outer space defense systems that can defend us against threats. Right now, we have nothing, either out in space or even in the works, because if we did, then the story would have been *'Our defense systems destroyed a rogue asteroid'* instead of what the official story was, which was *'We got lucky because an asteroid just missed Earth'*.

This is what I am talking about when I say that we really need to come together as one instead of continuing to be just individual countries who fight against each other, and if we are going to do that, then a great starting point would be the philosophy of *"Acceptance"*. It will allow us to accept our differences while working together to come up with the plans that we need to have in order to ensure that we survive into the future. It is a lot more than just saving our planet from outside threats, though. We have inner threats as well, and they are very real. I am talking about the depletion of our natural resources, for one. I am also talking about everything from war to homelessness. Now, I can just hear people out there saying things like *"Oh boy, is the person writing this book a liberal wacko or what?"* and *"Here we go again, more tree hugging crying for the planet."*, but they could not be farther from the truth. You see, I view myself as a defender of all of my brothers and sisters in the human race, and of our planet. How is that different? Well, because I view myself as a defender of our race and our planet, which includes being a defender of those who utilize and develop our natural resources so that we can get things done, because they help our race operate presently. I am also a defender of those who are developing other ways for us to get things done so that we do not use up all of our natural resources. Most importantly, though, I consider myself a defender of all of my brothers and sisters in our race, no matter if they agree with me or not (again, as long as they don't want to cause anyone harm). Which brings me to my next point where *"Acceptance"* is concerned.

Let me ask you a question. Why is it that we prey on each other so much? Now, I can just hear people out there saying things like *"They have money, and I am broke, so I want to steal it."* or *"They own something that is expensive, and I want it, so I am going to steal it."*, or worst of all, *"She is beautiful, and I want her no matter what I have to do to get her, even if that means kidnapping her and raping her."*.......but would you want others to view what you own, and especially the people that you love, like your wife or daughter, like that? Think about it. Especially lately, there have been more and more instances of people coming forward with stories of being preyed upon by other people, and in a way that no one should ever be preyed upon because it was in a sexual manner. Why is it that these people have spent many years getting away with preying upon others? Why didn't anyone help these people who were being preyed upon? Now, I know that a lot of these people were preyed upon by people in positions of power, and their victims were afraid of saying anything because they did not want to lose their job, etc., but why is it that people are still being preyed upon, especially when we now know what has been going on (and I'm not just talking about women, because there are stories of men who have been preyed upon in this way as well). I am not just talking about sexual harassment when I am talking about people preying on other people, though.

You see, one of the biggest problems that we have today, where people preying on other people is concerned, is the problem that we have with bullying. I am not just talking about children

A Visit to the City in the Light

bullying other children when I say this, because there are adults who go through their lives bullying other people as well, even people in their own family. This is a lot bigger problem than most people think, and in some instances, it can cause very tragic results. How do we deal with this, though? I mean, I know that I touched on this earlier, but how do we truly deal with this? Now, I have seen many ad campaigns that convey messages like *'Let's Stop Bullying!'*. My question is this. How do we do that? Messages like this are great, but they never take that next step and tell us how we are going to do it. Well, I have an idea, as long as everyone is willing to work together to make it happen. As long as we are all willing to be **'super'**.

Let me explain. If you ask most children (and many adults for that matter) who their favorite superhero is, they will be more than happy to not only tell you that they love (insert name of superhero here), but they will also tell you why. In addition, they will also almost always say *"I wish that I could be (name of superhero)"*. Why do you think that almost all children (and lots of adults) want to be a superhero? As far as I can see, it is because they want to be able to go out and do great things to help people, and to fight bad guys, and of course, to have *'Special Powers'* in order to do those things. I have a question for you. Why is it necessary to have superpowers in order to be a *'Superhero'*? I heard someone say one time that real heroes do not wear capes, they wear regular clothes, and in some instances, they have beer guts, and while I do not think that every real hero looks like that one uncle we all have on football Sunday (you know, torn shirt with his favorite team logo on it, beer in hand), the point is that we do not need to have special powers, or a cool uniform, in order to be a hero. In my mind, you only need two things to be a hero. A love for your fellow human beings, and of course, the courage to help someone when they need it. It does not have to be something big, like saving someone who is in trouble.   It could be something small, such as helping someone get something done (like helping a disabled person at a store).   All it takes is the heart of a hero, and I am sure that everyone who has a caring heart has that.

I will tell you what really bothers me.   In today's world, it seems that there are more and more video games (and movies and television shows for that matter) that glorify war and killing.   At what point did war and killing people become something to glorify? Real war and murder are absolutely horrible.   While they may make an exciting video game, the real thing is not something that should be glorified, ever.   You know, just once, I would like to see a video game where the object of the game is to become a normal, everyday hero, with no magical superpowers at all (at least I have never heard of a game like this before).   Think about it.   You start out the video game as a normal person, working a job and earning money to pay your bills.   Then, as the game progresses, the object is for you to first decide what type of hero you want to be (uniform, etc.), and then earn the money to devise your *'gadgets'* and *'uniform'* so that you can go out and be a hero for those who need help.   Then, dressed as your own original Superhero, you go out into the city and help people, even with something small, to earn coins.   Then, in the finale, you get to fight a bad guy boss in order to win the game by saving the city.   Would that be such a bad game to play?   Would that be such a bad thing to glorify, being an everyday hero?

To continue with what I was talking about a bit ago, let me ask you a question.   Why, if children (and some adults) love superheroes so much, and would love being a superhero, are there not more children and adults actually being real life heroes?   Like I said earlier, you do not need superpowers to be a hero, you just need to step up and be a hero for someone who needs one.   Let's take bullying for example.   Why don't children (who see a child

241

A Visit to the City in the Light

bullying another child) step in and help the child who is being bullied? Sounds like the actions of a real-life hero to me. Now, as I stated earlier, I have always been bothered by the *"Stop the Bullying!"* messages, because while it is the goal, no one ever says *"Stop the Bullying, and here's how we are going to do it!"*. Well, I have a suggestion, a way that we can all stop the bullying, if we are willing to be a real-life superhero. I know that it can work because I have actually seen it work in real life.

You see, one of the things that I have always noticed about a bully is the fact that they like to prey on someone who they perceive to be weaker than they are because they need to be superior to whoever they are targeting. So, let me ask you a question. What would a bully do if (when they were bullying someone) they were suddenly confronted by an entire group of real-life heroes who wanted to protect the person who was being bullied? I actually saw this happen years ago when I was in school. A child was being bullied when, out of nowhere, a group of other children who were on the scene confronted the bully and told them to leave the bullied child alone. What happened? The bully stopped what he was doing and left. The real-life heroes won. In addition, they actually befriended the child who was being bullied, and they are friends to this day. This is what real-life heroes do. They step up when they see something wrong happening, and they do what they can to stop it (while staying safe, of course, because if you see something happening like someone with a gun robbing a store, then the best way to be the hero in that situation would be to become *'Cell Phone Man/Woman'*, the hero with the *'Super Smart Phone'*, and call the police immediately).

Again though, concerning bullying, I look at it like this. I have said many times that *"There are a lot more of us than there are of them"*, and when bullies see that, and they realize that they can no longer get away with their bad actions, in a lot of cases it ends the bullying. You see, another thing that I have noticed about bullies is the fact that they want to prove their superiority, they want to be the *'Alpha'* of the group, whether the group consists of a single classroom or an entire school. In their minds, this makes them better than anyone else, and they think that it makes others admire them, especially those who the bully may want to impress, like members of the opposite sex. In the example that I just mentioned, for example, the bully wanted to impress the girls in the school. The great thing about the situation above was the fact that most of the group of students who confronted the bully were the very same girls that he wanted to impress, and it really caught him off guard. It affected him to the point where he never bullied anyone again. Now, this is not always the case where bullies are concerned. Sadly, some of them do it because of the way that they were raised, and so it is all that they know unfortunately. So, what do we do when that is the case, or in the case of an adult bully? Again, I truly wish that I had all the answers, but I do not. All I know is this. If we all just stand up to the bullies in order to help someone and be the hero in their life, then it can make a difference, and who does not want to be a real-life hero to someone?

Now, let me talk about a different situation where we can help our brothers and sisters in the human race through a simple act of kindness. I know that I already talked about the fact that no job is unimportant, and I honestly believe that, but let me ask you this. How can we make their day a little brighter by actually helping them in a way that they need to be helped, other than just giving them a kind comment like I mentioned earlier? What is the most important thing to them? Well, I think that I can answer that by saying this. Just like all of us who work a job, we are doing it so that we can pay our bills and take care of our loved ones. So, as I mentioned at the beginning of this book, if I had the ability to fix this, I think that this

A Visit to the City in the Light

is what I would do, see if you agree.

First, I would draft a Bill that I think I would call the *"Fountain Initiative"*. What I mean by that is this. What does a standard fountain look like? It has a base that is filled with water, it has a tower that usually has steps that goes up to the top of the tower that hold small amounts of water as well, and of course, it has the top that sprays water up into the air, causing the water that it is spraying to go down into the smaller steps, and then into the base. Now, why would I call the Bill the *"Fountain Initiative"*? Well, think of it like this. What is a major problem for people who work jobs like fast food production, and other jobs that do not pay much? Well, I just said it. They do not pay much. It is hard to earn enough money to survive if people are working one of these jobs, and it is especially difficult if those hard-working people who are trying to raise children. So, how can we help? Well, that is where the *"Fountain Initiative"* would come into play. Imagine, just for a moment, if there was a way to help these people get more money. Well, how about this. Like a fountain, and the water that sprays down from the top, we propose a Bill that gives corporations, and the people who are at the top of the corporation (like the CEO), things like tax breaks as long as they do something to help their employees get extra money in order to make it financially. How? By saying that they have to do more than just *'Profit Sharing'* to help their employees, and that is by having the Bill say that, like a fountain, they have to take a portion of their own personal profits/pay (as well as upper management doing the same thing), and then have it travel down to the employees below them, sort of like the higher ups giving those employees below them tips for doing a good job.

Think about this as an example. Let's say that a corporation makes, for example, $1,000,000.00 in profits for a particular month, and that the CEO gets paid $10,000.00 (1% of the total profits) a month for doing his job (which could fluctuate depending on how much profit the corporation did for that month). So, if this were the case, then the corporation and the CEO would be required (if they wanted things like the additional tax breaks) to take a portion of the CEO's profits (maybe 10% of the CEO's salary each month in addition to the corporation's *'Profit Sharing'* program) and then have that portion travel down the chain, or *'Fountain'*, to the employees below them, in the form of extra bonuses. Sort of like tips from the CEO that would be given to the employees underneath him/her. Now, I know that this sounds like *'Profit Sharing'*, but I really think that this should be an amount above a Profit-Sharing Program, sort of like an extra *'tip'* that lower-level employees could get in order to help them survive on a smaller paycheck.

After all, if it were not for the employees below the CEO doing a great job, then the CEO would not be able to get paid what they are being paid (if their salary is based on the profits), because it is truly the employees further down the *'food chain'* that are responsible for the corporation getting great profits. So why wouldn't they want to reward the employees below them by helping them to survive in a way that makes them happy and more productive employees? After all, wouldn't that give the CEO more money each month if their salary is dependent on the company doing a great job, and on a percentage of the profits? For that matter, even if the CEO is on a fixed salary, then if the company is doing great it would mean that the CEO gets paid better through raises, etc., and that would still be as a result of the lower-level employees doing their job great. So why not share a portion of what the CEO (and management in general) is making with the lower-level employees in order to help them get more money to survive on? I mean, if they do not want to just give their employees raises, then something needs to be done, right?

A Visit to the City in the Light

Also, speaking of tips and the Bill that I would be proposing, why is it that a lot of companies tell their lower-level employees that they are not allowed to receive tips from their customers? I was just at a fast-food restaurant (see, I told you that I am a *'junk food junkie'*), and I wanted to let the girl behind the counter know that I really appreciated the way that she went out of her way to make sure that my order was correct. So, I told her that I wanted to let her keep the change after the transaction was over. Sure enough, she told me that she was not allowed to accept tips. Why? All people who work jobs that have lower pay scales should be allowed to receive tips. The only deciding factor should be whether or not we, the consumers, are willing to give them a tip for the job that they are doing.......period. It should not be the decision of the company that they are working for, and for that matter, it should make the company that they are working for actually happy for their employees because it would help them to have extra money coming in so that they can survive, and happy employees are more productive employees. That is why I would put this in the *"Fountain Initiative"* as well. I would add it on the proposed Bill to say that all employees would be entitled to receive tips, no matter who they work for or what job they are doing. I mean, it just makes sense. The companies, CEOs (and general management) in charge would be getting things like tax break incentives, and the employees would be getting more money in order to survive. Sounds like a *'win-win'* situation to me.

You know, I could go on with more ways that we can be more caring for all of our brothers and sisters in our race, but I think that you get the point. So, I think that I would like to close this chapter with a challenge. Call it a mission that I am challenging you with. Starting tomorrow, see if you can come up with a way to help someone else, or to show them that you care about them. Maybe it could be doing something to help them out, to be a hero to them (like I said, we do not have to save someone from danger in order to be a hero to someone, like saving someone from a bully, although I think that saving someone from a bully would be important if we are ever going to put an end to bullying). It could be something small, like visiting someone in a nursing home (again, get permission from the facility if you do this), or helping someone to get something done that they are having a problem with. Or maybe it could be a kind word to let someone know that you really do appreciate the job that they are doing. It could be a *'Random act of kindness'*, like what the girl did for me when I spilled my drink. It could even be tipping someone so that they can have more money to survive on.

I look at it like this. If we are ever going to change our race for the better, then we need to start caring about each other more, and that includes caring for each other by doing things that show that we really do care about one another. Also, what makes us a good person should not be determined by how we look, or how we talk, or anything else that is superficial. What should matter is this. How we conduct ourselves, and our actions. We should genuinely care about each other, to the point where we do things, no matter how small, to make someone's day a little bit better. After all, wouldn't you like to live in a world based on caring, compassion, and love? A world where love and compassion are the order of the day? I know I would. Besides, wouldn't you like future generations to look back at us one day and say *"They were the generation that had the courage to start bringing us all together, with love, and compassion, and caring"*? We can do it. We can change our world, as long as we have the courage to accept each other with love and compassion by utilizing the philosophy of *"Acceptance"*. After all, isn't that another part of what *"Acceptance"* is about? Bringing us all together so that we can solve the problems that we face without hate stopping us?

Chapter Nine
"Equal" Means "Equal", Right?

"No favorites here." - My Uncle Albert, outside of the City.
"We're all the same." - My Grandma, outside of the City.

When my uncle and grandma said this to me, it was in response to me asking them if they were angels. You see, I was always told that when we die, we can become angels in Heaven. However, I believe that what they were trying to tell me was that the majority of people are all on the same level when we get to Heaven. We are all equal souls who are allowed to live in the city once we are judged. Now, I am not saying that there are no angels in Heaven, because I do believe that there are angels. However, I believe that what they were telling me was that the majority of us are equal souls when we get there. I believe that the angels were there from the beginning, and that our souls are the residents in the City that are watched over by the angels. The way that I view it is like this. If we are to ever going to achieve true peace, then we will need to have true equality (like our souls do in the City in the Light), otherwise we will never come together in freedom in order to advance our race into the future.

So, what I would like to talk about now is how equality is so important to us as a race. Now, having said that, please allow me to say that this is the chapter that will probably cause controversy, but it needs to be discussed because this topic deals with issues that cause a lot of chaos between us in today's world, and in order for *"Acceptance"* to succeed, then we need to stop all the chaos that exists so that we can work together without conflict. So, here goes. Let's talk about the meaning of the word *'Equal'*, and how everyone says that they want everything to be equal when, in reality, almost nothing in our lives is equal, because most of the time the people who are screaming that they want things to be equal don't really want things to be that way.   What they really want, in the majority of instances, is for things to go their way alone, even if that means that equality for others is sacrificed in the process.

Let's face facts.   Everyone wants to be accepted and treated equally.   We all want to have the same rights as everyone else.   We want to be respected for the way that we choose to live our lives, for the way we feel, and for our beliefs.   Most importantly, we do not want anyone to discriminate against us and make us feel bad for the way that we want to live our lives and for our beliefs.   We want the right to live our lives the way that we want to.   To believe the way that we want to, to love who we want to love, to live where we want to live, to have the same opportunities as everyone else for success, and to have the freedom to make our own choices.   Unfortunately, as history has shown, this type of equality did not exist for a very long time.

For many years, a lot of people did not have the same rights as everyone else and they were openly discriminated against, all because of things like the color of their skin, or their religious beliefs, or because they led alternative lifestyles, etc., but then times changed, and with that change came more equality than had ever existed before.   Today, a lot of those discriminatory acts have disappeared.   So why is it that the *'scales of equality'* are still not even?   Why is it that the people who were discriminated against for so long are now discriminating against others by not showing them the same amount of respect that **they** want in today's world? Respect for things like the way that they want to live their lives, who they want to love, and how they want to believe, for example? How is this equal?

A Journey There.......and Back Again with a Message of Hope

Let's take a look at a few examples of what I am talking about, and let's start by discussing the most obvious example of where equality is needed the most. Let's start where the color of our skin is concerned (again, I do not want to use the word *'race'*, because as far as I am concerned, we are all the same race, the human race, and the sooner that we accept that fact in our heart, the sooner that we can advance as a race by finally working together without bigotry, hatred, or discrimination getting in the way). For many years Caucasian people did a host of things to discriminate against people who they considered inferior to them, all because of the color of their skin or because they were from a different area of our planet (like in the days of the *'Old West'* and after the Civil War in America when it was acceptable to discriminate against others, even against people who were Caucasian themselves, like people of Irish descent). It was normal for some informal groups to exist in areas and towns in America at that time whose only function was to make sure that people (who were not Caucasian) were not given the same opportunities and rights that Caucasian people enjoyed. Some groups did a lot more than just discriminate against people who were not Caucasian, like the KKK, who committed many acts of violence against people who had a different skin color than they did.

Today we consider these groups to be completely wrong because of the way that they discriminated against other people, and we would not want to let these groups operate at all because of the way that they hurt people through acts of discrimination and violence against them, but here is the thing. If we ignore the fact that these organizations existed, and we try and erase them from our minds, then we are in trouble. It is when we forget the lessons that history has taught us that history can repeat itself, and when that happens, we have no one to blame but ourselves for wanting to erase the memory of what happened in the past.

A Visit to the City in the Light

Let me explain using what happened in America for example. One of the most tragic periods in the history of America is the time period of the Civil War. The official number (according to historians) of Americans who lost their lives during this war is 618,000 people. More Americans than have died in any other conflict (the official statistics state that, to date, 1,264,000 Americans have died in all conflicts that Americans have been involved in - 618,000 in the Civil War, and 644,000 in all the other conflicts. Obviously, those numbers are rounded, but you see the point).[10] The reason that I point that out is this. This war was largely fought because of slavery and how it needed to be abolished in order for America to advance in a more equal way. That being the case, then why are people trying to erase the memory of this war, and the two sides that were involved in it, from existence? If anything, we should be fighting to keep the memory of this tragedy alive for all to see instead of trying to erase any signs of it.

Here is what I am talking about. As we all know, there are many monuments that still exist in the Southern States of America. Everything from statues to the names of schools, all made to memorialize some of the influential leaders of the South during the Civil War. Lately, as we know, there has been a push to remove these monuments in the South, because as some people say, they are offensive because of who they represent. Now, I understand just why these monuments are offensive to some people, but should we remove them completely? I do not think so, and here is why I say that.

First of all, let's take a look at what these monuments represent, and how we should view them, at least in my opinion. In my mind, these monuments represent the people who were in charge of the American South during the Civil War, and who wanted to make sure that slavery not only existed but continued to exist for all time. So, why do I think that they should be kept where they are? Well, let me use this as an example. As we all know, World War II was horrendous, thanks to the Nazi government and the horrors that they caused. Yet even though it was a very tragic time period in the history of the human race, the citizens of Germany actually built things like billboards showing pictures of what some cities looked like after WWII, and they have kept some of the monuments that the Nazi government built to remind them of what happened. They even kept some of the concentration camps that were in operation back then so that people today can actually visit them (I have gone myself. It was one of the only times that I have ever cried in public, especially when viewing things firsthand, like the places where so many people were executed). Why did they do this? Well, as I was told by the German citizens that I asked about this, they did this so that they would never forget the horrors that were caused by the Nazi's leaders who ruled their country at that time, and the destruction that those leaders caused to happen to their beautiful country.

When I was in Germany, I noticed that there was a billboard in one of the cities, and it showed what that area looked like after WWII was over and that city lay in ruins, and the only words on the billboard were *"Nie Wieder"*, which in German means *"Never Again"*. You can also find these words in other areas as well, and they are there (according to the German citizens that I spoke to) so that the German people will never forget the horrors that the Nazi government caused, and what their actions caused to happen to their country. Now, these billboards, monuments, etc., are definitely offensive to a lot of people because they represent a time when the Nazi government controlled Germany, but the German people make sure that these buildings, etc., stay up and where they are, because they never want to forget what happened in WWII, and most importantly, who was responsible for the destruction that happened

A Visit to the City in the Light

to their beautiful country (and if you ever get the chance to visit, you will agree, Germany is a beautiful country full of wonderful people that I am happy to have met).

Now, let us take a look at the monuments in the American South that people are trying to have removed. Based on what I saw in Germany, and based on the philosophy of *"Acceptance"*, I can think of two good reasons to make sure that the monuments in the American South stay where they are. The first is most obvious. They need to stay there because they are a part of American history, and as such, Americans need to keep them there so that they, just like the German people, will never forget what happened by keeping the monuments, etc., of who was in charge of the American South during the Civil War. The day that we forget the history of our planet (especially the bad things that happened in our history) is the day that we are doomed to repeat it.

The second reason is another area where the philosophy of *"Acceptance"* comes into play, and most importantly, where the practice of bringing true equality to all of us comes into play as well. Yes, these monuments are offensive to some people, but to other people they represent their state's history, and they are proud of their state's history. Now, just consider this, especially if it is true equality that we all want. Aren't the feelings of those people, who live in these states and who want the history of their state remembered (and most importantly, who are not physically hurting anyone by keeping these monuments, etc., where they are) just as important as everyone else's? Isn't what they want as important as what the people who are on the other side of the fence want? Don't they deserve the same respect as others who want those monuments taken down? Again, equal has to mean equal if we ever want true equality. Otherwise, we will never achieve true equality, and isn't that what we all want? We have to accept the fact that everyone's

254

feelings should be respected if we ever want to achieve true
equality.

Now, when practicing the philosophy of *"Acceptance"*, let
me tell you how I handle it when I see or hear something that is
offensive to me (and believe me, I see things that I consider
offensive to me on a daily basis. Now, I am not saying that these
monuments are offensive to me, because I do not want to make this
book about me or how I feel as an individual concerning this topic.
I want this book to be about the philosophy of *"Acceptance"*). I
look at it, or hear it, and I think to myself *'It's really sad to me that
some people feel the way that they do, and it's really sad to me that
there are those who consider this something to be proud of, but I
will respect the right of those who do want to feel this way, because
their rights are just as important as mine. While I do not agree
with what I am looking at (or what I just heard), I will respect the
right of those (who do agree with it) to display it or say it, as long as
what they are saying or doing does not call for, or cause to happen,
physical harm to anyone.'* Now, am I talking about monuments
that exist in the American Southern States, or am I talking about
hate speech videos that do not call for violence on the internet? Am
I talking about the monuments and structures that exist in Germany
that display not only what the Nazi's built, but also the destruction
that they caused to happen to Germany, or I am talking about the
Hollywood director who stated publicly that he could not see
himself casting a person of a certain skin color as a lead in one of his
movies (and yes, this happened, but the director was not a white
man, he was a black man, and it saddens me to say that, when he
said this, he actually received a standing ovation from the people in
the audience there. I see examples of what I call *'Reverse
Discrimination'* on almost a daily basis, but I will talk about that in
more detail later)?[11] I will never say, because again, I do not want
this book to be too much about me, even though I do offer some

personal suggestions.   I want it to be about the message of
"Acceptance", and how it can bring us all together.

I do want to state something again, though.   Something that
I have said throughout this book, and I feel that it is something that
should be stated again here.   I respect the right for everyone to feel
the way that they want to, and to lead the lives that they want to
lead, as long as what they want never ever causes actual physical
harm to another person.   When that happens, then we need to stop
respecting the right of the people who want to do it, and we need to
take action to put a stop to it so that the people who are being hurt
are saved from being hurt, and I feel that what I say next is the best,
prime example of what I am talking about.

What am I talking about?   Two words, *'Child
Pornography'*, and more specifically, *'Child Pornographers'*.
Now, I know that I talked about this topic in an earlier chapter, but it
definitely needs to be mentioned here again, because this is **the**
prime example of people who don't deserve to be respected for the
way that they feel, and for what they want, because they are
definitely, actively, and constantly hurting people, the most
vulnerable people of our race, our children.   Now, do those statues
that a lot of people want to have taken down physically hurt people
just because of what they represent, or do they just hurt people's
feelings?   True, they represent a time in America's history when
many people were hurt, but are they physically hurting anyone now,
or are they just reminding us of what happened a long time ago in
America's history?

Also, are the people who want to keep the statues where they
are physically hurting anyone, or are they just trying to keep the
memory of their state's history alive for future generations to see so
that they know what happened once upon a time?   You see, this is

what I am talking about when I say the following. As long as people today are not being physically hurt by someone's wants (or their wants are not calling for harm to happen to anyone) then everyone's wants should be respected, otherwise we will never achieve true equality. Either we respect everyone's right to be respected for what they want, or all we are is a race of hypocrites, and we will never come together, and we will never have true equality if that is the case.

There are other examples of what I am talking about, though. Take the videos online showing individual people getting beat up by groups of people. Now, I am not talking about videos of two people who both agree to fight each other, and then they film the fight to post on the internet. What I am talking about are videos of innocent people getting jumped and beaten up by someone, the videos where the victim obviously did not agree to get beaten up, but they do get beat up against their will while other people film the attack, as if this type of behavior is something to be proud of. Again, this is an example of something that is actively hurting people, because the people who want to make these videos are actively hurting people by finding someone to beat up, and then attacking them just so that they can film the attack. No one should have their wants and desires respected if what they want to do is to physically harm anyone, period. Having said that, please allow me to state something again, because while it applied earlier, it also applies to this topic as well.

Let me give you another prime example of people wanting to do something that actively hurts others, and they are becoming more and more prevalent in today's internet world. What I am talking about are people who make a sex tape of themselves having sex with their partner, and then they post it online once the relationship is over so that they can damage the reputation of the person who they broke up with.   As a matter of fact, there are now entire web sites devoted to people who want to post a video of their ex involved in a sex act with them.   Now I will be the first to admit that losing a love is one of the most painful things that we can go through.   We feel lost, and alone, and the pain is tremendous, and as wrong as it is, we want the person that we lost to feel the same pain that we are feeling.   Is it right, though?   How do we know that the person who we just broke up with is not feeling the same pain that we are feeling?

Here is the thing, though, and it has really helped me to keep my dignity and my sanity after a breakup.   It is also the main reason that I just mentioned making sex tapes in this chapter as well as earlier.   The one thing that I did not do was try to intentionally hurt my ex by actually doing something to cause them harm.   What do I mean when I say, *'causing them harm'*?   Actually doing something to take revenge on them that does cause them harm, and one of the worst things that I have seen concerning this is the publicizing of an intimate moment like a sex act for the world to see, because let's face facts, once something is posted on the internet, it is not only out there for the whole world to see at that time, but it is out there forever.

Which brings me to my main point.   Remember how we were talking about respecting everyone's right to feel the way that they want to feel, and having everyone's rights respected concerning what they want in order to achieve true equality, as long as they are not hurting anyone?   Well, the way that I see it is this.   No one should have their rights respected (as far as what they want) if what they want to do is post a video of a very private moment of intimacy that they shared with their ex-partner on the internet for the whole world to see in an attempt to hurt them by humiliating them or by ruining their reputation.   I feel so strongly about this that I actually think that there should be a law against it, and it should be a part of the Criminal Statutes, and I say that for this reason. I have actually seen just how bad this can cause harm to someone.

I knew a girl once. Just your normal, beautiful soul. Good student in the college that she was attending. Loved music. Loved reading. Was a good friend to those who were lucky enough to have her as a friend. She was an understanding and compassionate girl. She was the type of girl who was loyal to a fault. Loyal to her friends, and her boyfriend when she had one. She held religious beliefs and attended church on a regular basis. She was a good employee at the coffee shop where she worked, and the customers loved her. She was a great cook, and she was always open to learning everything that she could in order to better herself. Just your all-around great person, someone that I felt extremely privileged to have in my life as a friend. Then, one day, she found herself attracted to someone that everyone thought was the quintessential bad boy, the type of boy (again, not a man, like I said earlier in this book) who thought nothing of breaking every rule that he could, and she decided to start a relationship with him. We tried to tell her to be careful with him because of his reputation of hurting the women that he had been involved with, to include being violent with them and cheating on them, and because of his criminal record (and do not get me wrong, I do believe that people can change if they break a law, but this boy showed no signs of changing. He felt that the world should change, instead of him changing to better himself), but she would not listen. She felt that she could change him, and help him to be a better person, and she ignored all the warning signs that would tell most people that he was just a user, and that he was going to hurt her in the long run, as he had done to many other girls in his past.

As most abusive relationships go, she started to slowly

A Visit to the City in the Light

withdraw. From her friends, from her family, from everyone. She lost her job because she started not showing up for work, and because he would call her all the time while she was at work. He would even show up at her work, and he would have a problem with anyone who even looked at her in a way that he did not approve of. Her grades started slipping at school, and then she dropped out entirely. Then one day she showed up at one of our friend's house with a black eye. That was enough for me and my friends, and we wanted to go *'old school'* on his, well, *'behind'*, but she said no, that she was planning on ending the relationship, because at that point even she was done with him. So, we went over to where she was living with this boy, and we helped her get her stuff and move to a new apartment. We had even convinced her to return to college, and to find a new job, which we helped her get, because she really was a great person. We thought that what we had done to help her would be the end of it, but we were very wrong.

Apparently, he had talked her into making a sex tape, because as he put it, he wanted something to have on his phone to look at when they were apart. What he was actually doing with it was showing it to his friends while they were still together, bragging about how he *'owned her'*, and that she was just a *'ho'* that he was using for her money and a place to stay so that he would not have to work, and so that he could just stay home and play video games while she provided for him and gave him everything that he wanted. As such, the next thing we knew people started talking through the rumor mill concerning her being in a pornographic video. We eventually found it online, on a site that caters to people wanting to see videos of other people's exes in *'compromising positions'*. He even put a description on the video, talking about how she was just a *'sloppy ho'*, and that when he was done using her, he claimed that he *'kicked her to the curb'* because, as he put it, she was the worst sexual partner that he had ever had. He also went onto other social media sites saying all sorts of horrible things about her, in an attempt to ruin her in everyone's eyes.

We tried, as her friends, to have the video taken down, but as there are no laws against this type of thing at this point, and since, as we all know, once it is on the internet, it is there forever, we were unsuccessful, and what it did to her I will never forget. She withdrew from everything and everyone. She confided in me (and her other close friends) that she felt like everyone was looking at her when she would go out into public, and she stopped going anywhere. She even stopped going to church. She never returned to school, and she stopped working again. We tried to take care of her, and we even helped her make sure that her rent and bills were taken care of so that she would not have to worry about anything while she was getting over what had happened to her. At this point, though, she told us that she felt worthless and ashamed, even though we tried to tell her that he was the worthless one, and that she truly was a great person. Even though we did everything that we could to help her, she never recovered from what he did to her.

Then, one day, we went to her place to pick her up for a get together that we had talked her into going to, and that she had even helped plan.......but there was no answer at her door. When the police arrived, they found her in the bathtub where she had cut her wrists that morning before we got there. They found a note. It said, among other things, that she could not go on thinking that everyone thought that she was a bad person, and feeling like she was worthless (as he had claimed she was in the video), and that she could not live with the fact that, in her mind, everyone in the world had seen the video. Even today, when I think about her and what this boy did to her, it makes me both mad and sad. Now do you see just how much harm can come from making an *'innocent sex tape'*? Now do you see why I say that the people who want to share these videos without the consent of both parties should not have their wants and desires respected? I still miss her to this day; she really was an angel and a wonderful gift to the world.

Let me put it into perspective even more. Let's say that you are a woman (or even a man), and you catch someone creeping outside of your bedroom window watching you get undressed or having sex with someone. You would be upset, wouldn't you? Of course you would, because you did not give them permission to look at you while you are undressed or having sex, and your first thought would be to call the police and file a report and have the person who was doing it arrested and put in jail. Why should it be any different when talking about someone posting a sex tape of you on the internet without getting your permission to post it? You did not give you ex permission to post the sex tape online after the breakup (at least I've never heard of anyone giving their ex permission to post a sex tape of them online after a breakup, unless they are in the sex industry I suppose, but then maybe they would be ok with it because they might want the publicity, but just maybe, not definitely), and concerning most people that I have talked to about this, they never gave anyone permission to share it with the world while they were still in a relationship.

So why should anyone be able to share a sex tape of them and their ex on the internet after a breakup? In most instances, the main reason that I have heard of someone posting a sex tape online is to get revenge on their ex by ruining their reputation in an attempt to actually cause them harm, and to me, that's wrong, and it should not happen. As a matter of fact, I think that it should be included in a specific section of Tort Law as well, giving the person who did not give their ex-partner permission to post the sex tape online the ability to sue them in court for personal injury monetary damages, as well as them being able to press criminal charges as well. After all, we do have laws against *'Peeping Toms'* and people being perverts, don't we?

Now, again, concerning why I mentioned all of this in this chapter, I did it because this is another example of someone wanting to be able to do something that is actively hurting someone else. There arc women, right now, who are saying that they were sexually harassed because of something that someone said to them, whether it was on the job or in a social situation, and they say that it hurt them a lot, and I believe them when they say that it hurt them, because no one should ever be harassed sexually. At least to me, though, posting a sex tape online of someone (when they did not give their permission to have it posted online) is a lot worse than just saying something to someone. This is actually exposing someone to the entire world in the most intimate way without their permission. I look at it like this. This again, to me, is paramount to someone peeking at you when you are in, say, a changing room at a clothing store, or in a bathroom. You are naked, and you did not give anyone permission to look at you while you are naked, and it would upset you a lot if you found out about it, and you would want to call the police and have charges filed against the person who did it. So why should it be ok for someone to post a video on the internet of their ex involved in a sex act with them when their ex did not give them permission to do that?

True, they may have said that it was ok to take the video while they were in a relationship with someone, but does that mean that they wanted it to be shared with the whole world after a breakup, or even while they are still in a relationship with someone? I have heard many reasons that someone would agree to have their sex acts videotaped while they are in a relationship. Reasons like *"Well, I wanted to give my partner something to remember me by when we were apart."* or *"Well, I wanted to spice up our sex life."*,

263

but when they say that these are the reasons, they are not saying that *"Well, I wanted to give my ex something to embarrass me with after we broke up."* or *"Well, I want to give my partner, or my ex, something to try and ruin my reputation with by posting it on the internet for the whole world to see after we broke up."*, or anything else like that.

The bottom line is this. As long as anyone's wants and needs do not actually cause harm to happen to another person, or does not do something that would normally be considered illegal (again, you would want someone arrested for being a *'Peeping Tom'* for spying on you when you are in the bathroom or a changing room because it is a personal violation, then why aren't people being arrested for posting a sex tape online without both parties who are in the video agreeing to posting it), then everyone should have their wants and desires respected. As long as they are not like the child pornographer who wants to take videos of children being molested and then share them with his sick friends, or like the people who, along with their friends, want to attack someone just to film the attack to post on the internet, or the person who wants to post a video of a sex act on the internet just to humiliate and embarrass their ex in an attempt to ruin them and their reputation, or for any other reason that causes harm to come to another person, then they should have their wants and desires respected, just like we want to have our wants and desires respected.

Like I was talking about before, it is true, when we are talking about things like the statues that exist in the American South that represent a bad time in America's history, there are people whose feelings are going to be hurt when they see these things, because of what they represent, but ask yourself this. Do you want true equality? Do you want to have your feelings and wants respected? Then the only way that this can happen is if everyone's wants and desires are respected, again, as long as their wants and desires are not causing real harm to come to anyone. Otherwise, all we are is a bunch of hypocrites who will never get along, and at least to me, just a bunch of hypocrites who do not deserve to have our wants and desires respected, because we are not willing to do the same for others.

Now, I can hear people out there saying *'Well, does that mean that we should respect the wants and desires of the perverts out there who do not make child pornography, but just want to watch it?'*. In response to that, let me say that the way I look at it is like this. True, they may not be making or producing the videos of these things, but what they are doing is enabling the people who do produce these videos and images, and it is why the producers of these videos and pictures make them. This makes the *'consumers'* of these videos a definite part of the problem (at least in my mind), and they are just as guilty as the people who produce these videos and pictures, because they are the end consumers of these *'products'*. If it were not for them, the people who make these videos and pictures would not have anyone to make them for (except themselves, which is disturbing enough as it is). Therefore, in my mind, the people who want to watch these videos of children being molested are just as guilty as the people who make the videos and pictures of children being molested. Like I said, they are enabling the people who make these things, and as such, they should not have their wants and desires to watch these things respected either, because they are causing these horrible *'products'* to be produced, which causes real harm to happen to children.

Here is the thing. We need to accept the responsibility to make sure that those people who are causing harm to others (with their wants and needs) get shut down, because they are causing others to be harmed, which in this case are the children who are being molested.   Now, do we shut them down with violence?   No, because when we exhort to violence against others, then we are part of the problem (I mean, even though I will be the first to admit that I would love to kick the *'behinds'* of people who produce, distribute, and watch child pornography, I would rather have them put in prison, but not to be killed, like what happens to a lot of them when they are incarcerated.   I would much rather know that these perverts will have to live the rest of their lives in a small cage, just like the emotional cage that their victims will have to live in because of what happened to them).   I feel that the best way to shut them down is to be vigilant in exposing them for what they are doing so that they can be shut down legally.   This is why I say that the law needs to catch up with technology, so that good people stop having their reputations destroyed by others through the use of things like sex tapes.   Also, as far as where the law is concerned when talking about people like child pornographers, that is where we need to be vigilant in exposing these people where both the producers and consumers are concerned.   It should not matter who they are, if they are the producers and consumers of these *'products'*, then they should be exposed so that they can get shut down.

Now, while we are on this subject, let's talk about hate speech and videos that causes, or calls to cause, harm to others. Again, this is where the law needs to catch up with technology, because in my mind, real life bullying (which can be punished in the criminal statutes as *"Criminal Harassment"*, for one) is the same as *'Cyber Bullying'*, and yet, there are no criminal laws against bullying people online (none that I know of at least).   Why?   Now it is true, there are a lot of people who spew some very hateful things online against some very undeserving people but let me ask you a question.   How do those people who make these videos, and promote these attitudes, win?   More importantly, do these people (who promote hate speech) deserve to have their wants and desires respected?

You see, I respect the right of everyone to feel the way that they want to feel, as long as they don't call for violence to happen to anyone, and they don't cause actual harm to happen to anyone (like the child pornographers do), but to me, these people win the minute that they get the response that they are looking for from those who they are aiming their hate at. In my mind, the people who spew hate speech are doing it for one reason. They want the attention that their hate speech gives them, especially if they are spewing their hate speech on the internet. They want the *'Likes'* on the videos, they want the *'Shares'*, and *'Retweets'*, and everything else that their hate speech causes to happen, because when that happens, then they get the attention that they are seeking, and they win. Also, every time we respond by saying *"Wow, that hurt me a lot, and I am going to let everyone know just how bad it hurt me."*, the people who spew hate speech win as well, because in the end, that is exactly what they want to do. They want to hurt those who their hate speech is directed at, and they want those people to respond by saying that what they heard really did hurt their feelings, because that also gives them what they seek when they spew their hate speech.

Now, the way that I respond to these people is by not giving them the *'Likes'* and *'Shares'* and *'Retweets'* that they are looking for. What I do is think to myself *'Wow, what an ignorant attitude to have towards others. The people that they are directing their hate speech at want to be respected for who they are and the way that they have chosen to live their lives, and you don't want to give them the same respect that you want. You hate these people without even knowing them as individual people. I think that it is really sad that, in today's world, you hate people just because of who they are and the way that they choose to live their lives'*, and then I ignore them, because when I do something like that, it actually upsets **them**. They see that they are not getting the attention from me that they want, and that does not give them the response that they are looking for. Is it a perfect solution? No, but at least I know, in my heart, that my response does not let them win by giving them the response from me that they want, and it does not give them the attention that they are seeking. Now, that works concerning hate speech in general, because most of the time, hate speech does not call for actual violence against other people, but at what point does hate speech go too far?

Let's take a look at an example of what I am talking about. Let's say that someone posts a video of hatred against people who have an alternative lifestyle where their sex life is concerned, in other words, against the LGBTQ community. Let's go further to say that this hate speech is saying things like *'They will never go to heaven'* and *'God hates them'* and *'They are all perverts, full of evil and sin'*. Now, while this is definitely hurtful to those who are a part of the LGBTQ community and their supporters, does it accomplish anything other than that? When I hear things like this, I think to myself *'Well, first of all, it is not up to us who goes to heaven and who goes to hell, that is God's decision, and he alone will make that judgment when we all face him'*. Then, once again, I do not give them the attention that they are seeking, because when we do, the people who are saying these things win, because they get the attention and response that they are seeking.

You see, when the people who are the targets of hate speech (like the people who are a part of the LGBTQ community and their supporters) say that they are upset by what they are hearing, and that they want to go after those who say these things, the *'Cyber Bullies'* who are spewing this hate speech win, because that is the exact response that those who promote this type of hate speech are looking for. They want to see people get upset because they are looking for

268

a response that gives them the things that they want the most, which is the attention and the response that they are looking for, and they get that when people say publicly that they are hurt by what they are saying. That is why I refuse to give them the attention and/or response that they want, because while it does upset me to hear such blind hatred, I refuse to let them win (especially since I have many friends who are a part of the LGBTQ community. Now, am I saying that I belong to the LGBTQ community? No, I am not saying that. What I am saying is that I practice *"Acceptance"*, and that means that, while I am a heterosexual, I accepted the responsibility to get to know the friends that I have made in the LGBTQ community as individuals, and I judged them based on who they are as a person, instead of judging them on what they believe, and how they lead their lives. Remember the person "A" and person "B" theorem that I spoke of earlier? That is how I judge people, like the philosophy of *"Acceptance"* dictates).

Again though, how do we decide when hate speech goes too far? In my mind, it goes too far when it starts calling for violence against those who their hate speech is directed at, or it starts calling for physical action against those who their hate speech is directed at, or it calls for people to be actively and openly discriminated against in an attempt to take away their right to live their lives the way that they want to live them. Let me explain. Let's say that the people that I just mentioned (those who are spewing hate speech against those in the LGBTQ community) start saying things like *"We need to take these people and kidnap them, and then place them in psychiatric centers so that they can be 'cured' of the way that they lead their lives."*, or they say things like *"We need to rape these people so that they will become 'straight' again."*, or something equally as ignorant (and the reason that I use the word *'ignorant'* is because the people who say these things have no idea who the people are that they are saying these things about. They are not

269

allowing them the same respect to believe and live their lives that **they** want).   This is where hate speech goes too far, at least in my opinion, because now they are no longer expressing their beliefs, they are actively calling for people to cause harm to other people, and that is where they cross the line where hate speech is concerned, at least in my book.

   We need to accept the responsibility to discern when hate speech has gone too far, and to be vigilant where reporting it to the proper authorities is concerned.   There has to be warnings to people who are the targets of hate speech when it turns into threats of bodily harm, and if there aren't laws that address this type of hate speech and *'Cyber Bullying'*, then we need to accept the responsibility to create the proper Bills that will enact laws to make this type of hate speech illegal.   Now, I can just hear people out there saying things like *"Well, there goes the right to free speech."*, but **something** has to be done in order to make sure that hate speech that threatens violence is addressed, because these type of warning signs (speech that calls for violence against people) need to be addressed in order for us to be proactive in stopping hate speech that calls for violence before it turns into real violence (which, in some cases, it does, and good people end up getting hurt as a result).

   In too many instances violence, like mass shootings for example, start with warning signs that are usually posted on places like the internet.   Just look at the examples from our recent history. Usually (but not always) there are warning signs that herald that violence could be on the way.   Most of the time it is signs like manifestos being posted on the internet.   Manifestos that give clear warning signs that someone is close to the edge, and that there could be violence on the way at their hands.   There are usually other signs as well, and if we start caring about those around us, like the philosophy of *"Acceptance"* dictates that we do, then in a lot of cases we can see those signs if we look.   It absolutely breaks my heart every time I hear about a mass shooting, especially at a school.

This is why I can't say this enough.   We need to be diligent in watching for warning signs of hate speech that goes too far, and this is also why we need to really care about those around us.   If we care about our fellow brothers and sisters in our race, then we can recognize when someone may be having a problem (like when they start to say things that may herald violence).   This is especially true where school shootings are concerned.   In almost every situation that I have heard of people almost always said that they noticed something that did not seem right with the shooter before the shooting occurred.   I am not going to go any further into this here, other than to say that we have to really accept the responsibility to watch for warning signs, because if we do, then maybe we can prevent the next tragedy from happening altogether (at least I sincerely hope so).

To continue, though, these signs from regular people are bad enough, but when public figures start to call for violence, or even hint at the need for violence against someone, then it becomes even worse, because people, like politicians and celebrities, should know that there are people who will take what they say seriously because they look up to them.   These public figures should be smart enough to know that they should never call for violence against someone else, and they should not even hint at the need for violence against someone, because it could lead to trouble.

Take the 2016 American Presidential Election, for example. A lot of people did not like the outcome of the presidential race, especially politicians from the other side of the fence, but while they may not like what happened, the last thing that they should do (at least in my mind) is even hint at the need for violence against someone all because of the outcome. A politician even went as far as to say that the American President should be assassinated, and in my mind, that is just reckless and foolish, and here's why I say that.[12] Let's say that someone does take what this politician said to heart, because they are a fan of this politician and they did not like the outcome of the 2016 election, and let's say that they go out, buy a weapon, and actually shoot the American President (it almost happened at a rally that the American President was conducting just months before the 2016 American election, even before the other politician said that the American President should be assassinated. A British citizen tried to get a gun and was going to shoot him before police stopped him).[13]

It could very easily happen. There are people out there who feel that violence is the answer to everything that they do not like, which saddens me, but it is a fact of life in today's world. Then let's say, just for the sake of argument, that the American people get a new president in the next election that is from the opposite side of the fence. What would stop someone from the side of the fence that the assassinated President was on from saying to themselves *'Well, a politician called for our last President to be assassinated, and he was killed. So, maybe it is time for the 'score to be settled', and maybe the new President, who is on the other side of the fence, needs to be assassinated as well'*. I mean, it could happen.

My point is this. Where would the violence end? It could start out like that, and then it could escalate into not only politicians being killed, but also regular people being killed that are on the opposite sides of the fence. Then what? American's go from politicians being killed to regular people being killed to.......what, Civil War again? Also, before you think that things could not possibly get that bad, then just take a good look around the world. There are entire countries, right now, where their citizens are being

272

killed just because of the political parties that they belong to. Consider that before thinking that things could not get that bad in America. I have gone to, as well as studied, countries all over the world, and believe me when I say that there are countries where you can be jailed and executed just for criticizing the leaders of those countries. Believe me when I say it can get that bad. So, the real question becomes are we going to let it get that bad, no matter where it is happening, or are we going to stop all the violence by learning to get along by practicing *"Acceptance"*? Are we going to let things get completely out of hand, or are we going to finally accept the responsibility to learn how to put aside our differences so that we can come together for the peaceful evolution and advancement of our race?

I talked about this one topic (hate speech) for so long in this chapter because I want to really make everyone reading this book think about something, and that is this. Where do we draw the line where *'Equal = Equal'* and hate speech is concerned? I mean, we should all have the right to believe any way that we want to if we are ever going to have true equality, right? So, what do we do where hate speech is concerned? Do we allow it if it does not call for physical violence against anyone? Do we shut it down entirely, and take the chance of destroying the right to free speech? You know, this is why I wish that I had all the answers, but I don't. That is why I really hope that *"Acceptance"* takes hold and that everyone starts practicing it, because it will allow us to come together and solve issues just like this one.

To continue, though, I do not know how you feel, but here is what I think. See if you agree. I think that, unfortunately, it may be too late for our generation to stop hate speech entirely, but it is not too late for our future generations. That is why I talked about the importance of developing a good relationship with our children, because if we teach them how bad hate speech that calls for violence truly is, then there will be less people who do it when they are adults, and then they will teach their children, and so on, and so forth.   I know that it is not a perfect solution, and it is definitely not going to stop it now.   However, I feel that this step, along with the ones that I mentioned earlier, would be a good start, and we need to start somewhere.

Now, while we are talking about *'Equal = Equal'*, let's talk about something that I call *'Reverse Discrimination'*.   For a very long time (too long), people were discriminated against just because of things like the color of their skin, or their religious beliefs, or where they came from.   But does that mean that people who were discriminated against in the past should discriminate against others now, in sort of a retaliatory way?   Let me explain.   For many years it was commonplace for people with black skin color to be called many hurtful names and words (I will not mention them here, because I refuse to say them, but I am sure that you know which words I am talking about).   Now, it was finally determined that people would no longer use those words because of how hurtful and discriminatory they are.   So why is it ok for some people to use those words now, while it is not ok for others to say them?

If *'Equal'* is ever going to truly mean that things are going to be *'Equal'*, then either it should be ok for everyone to use these hateful words, or it should be ok for no one to use them.   An example of what I am talking about is what I heard and saw the other day.   A young black man was playing music loudly in public, and the lyrics were graphic.   As a matter of fact, every other word was one of the worst words that people have determined should never be said about black people.   So, why is this ok for him to do this (and for the musician to do it, for that matter) when, if a white man did it, he would be ostracized as a racist (personally, I do not think that anyone should say it, but that is just me).   That is why I say that this is a prime example of things not being equal, because if things were truly equal, then these types of things would not be happening.   We need to do what it takes to make things truly equal (as in, what is good for one should be good for the other, or what is not good for one should not be good for another) because anything less is not equal.   It is like this.......we either want true equality, or we do not want things to ever be equal, pure and simple.

Now, let's go one step further and talk some more about how things are further evolving into what I call *'Reverse Discrimination'*. For the longest time people have used the terms *'Black People'* and *'White People'* when describing people of those skin colors.   *'Black Man'* or *'White Man'*.   *'Black Woman'* or *'White Woman"*.   Then, one day, people started to say that *'Well, if you say 'black man' in a certain context, then you are using discriminatory language, and you must be a 'racist'.   If you say, "This black man is my friend." then it is ok, but if you say, "What's wrong with that black man?" or "Those black men are bad people." or "Where did this black man come from?", then it is wrong, because his skin color should have nothing to do with anything.'*.   So, as a result, white people started to be called bigots and racists when they used this type of language. So, please tell me, if things are ever going to be truly equal, then how is the following ok?

I saw a clip from a comedy television show one day (*'Sherman's Showcase', IFC, Season 1, Episode 7, entitled 'White Music'*) where the host (a black man) was saying things like *"Who is this white woman?"* in an episode where he was making fun of *'White People Music'*.   Now, if you are honest, then you are going to agree that, if a white man was the host of a comedy television show, and he was saying *"Who is this black woman?"*, and he was making fun of what he called *"Black People Music"*, then everyone would be saying *"Wow, that show is completely racist, and it should not be on the air!"*.   Now, if it would be considered bigoted and racist for a comedy show to make fun of black people and *'Black People Music'*, then how is it ok for a show to make fun of white people and *'White People Music'*, even if it is just a comedy?   Why is it ok for black people (who were discriminated against for so long, too long in my book) to reverse it now so that it is now ok for them to say things that would be considered bigoted and discriminatory if a white person said it?

My point is this.   Either we make things truly equal, or we just say that things will never be equal.   Personally, if it were me, I would have just said something like *"Who is this woman?"*, without bringing skin color into it at all.   At least that is me, because in my mind, there is no *'Black Man'* or *'White man'*, *'Black Woman'* or *'White Woman'*, *'Black Music'* and *'White Music'*, there is just *'a man'* and *'a woman'* and *'music'*.   In my mind, we are all brothers and sisters in our race, the human race.   If we cannot accept that simple fact, then we are doomed to never come together and achieve true equality, at least that is the way it seems to me.   How about you?

Now, speaking of another area where things not being equal is a problem, I would like to touch, just briefly, on another situation, and that's where celebrities, and their shows, are concerned.   Take this situation for example.   After the 2016 American Presidential election there were many people who were upset about the results, because they did not like the person who was elected president. One comedian, in particular, made a point of suggesting (in a *'joke'* post online, a *'joke'* in her mind, that is) that the new American President should not only be executed, but that he should actually be decapitated, and she did that by posting a picture of herself holding the decapitated head of the new president in her hand.[14]   How is this wrong and hurtful? Well, for one, why don't you ask the people who have lost loved ones to terrorist groups (because their loved ones were kidnapped and decapitated) if it is wrong for anyone to make *'fun'* of someone being decapitated, no matter what the reason is for the *'joke'*. There were even other comedians (as well as many in the public as well) who tried to defend her by saying that it is a comedian's job to push the limits of comedy.[15] Well, if that is the case, then why aren't all comedians (or celebrities for that matter) forgiven for making what they consider to be *'jokes'*, or saying truthfully what is on their mind, no matter how hurtful it is to some people? Take what happened to this next comedian, and her show, as an example of how things are not equal when they should be, especially if we ever want true equality.

This next comedian's show was attacked for an episode where the main character thinks that her neighbors are terrorists, all because they are of the Muslim faith.[16] She even goes as far as making fun of them, and where they are from, in the episode. Then, after this, this comedian made a *'joke'* (a horrible joke in my mind, but in her mind, a *'joke'* none the less) on *'Twitter'* about someone who was in the American Government, but in a former president's staff (she was an advisor for the former American President) by comparing her to an ape (which I found to be absolutely abhorrent).[17] However, because this comedian told a bad *'joke'* (again, a *'joke'*, at least in her mind) in a *'Tweet'* about someone (who was in a former President's staff), someone that she may not agree with politically, and because of the episode of her show that I just mentioned, her show was cancelled, and she was ostracized and admonished publicly for what happened. So, please tell me, if things are ever going to be truly equal, then how can one comedian be defended and forgiven by the public and her fellow comedians for suggesting that the murder and decapitation of anyone (especially when that person is the President of America) is a *'joke'*

A Visit to the City in the Light

when there are many people who actually like the present American President (and especially when the murder of anyone is anything but a *'joke'*, especially to those who have lost loved ones by them being decaptiated by terrorists), and yet, when another comedian makes a bad *'joke'* about someone on her comedy show (a *'joke'* about certain people's religious beliefs), and then follows it up with a *'joke'* (again, in her mind, a *'joke'*) about someone who worked for a former President, it causes her to be completely ostracized, and admonished by both the public and her fellow comedians for her *'joke'*?

Here is the way that I view it, see if you agree. First of all, **I don't care** about anyone's political views, and I am **not** here to preach mine. I practice *"Acceptance"*, which dictates that I accept everyone, no matter how they believe or feel (as long as their beliefs do not call for harm to happen to anyone, or whose beliefs actually cause harm to happen to anyone). I just feel that anyone who makes a joke that suggests that someone be murdered (especially by decapitation), **and** anyone who makes fun of someone just because of their religious beliefs, and who also makes a horrible joke about someone's looks (by comparing that person to an ape, for example), should all be treated equally, period. Either we allow all comedians to push the limits of comedy without ostracizing and publicly admonishing them, or we ostracize and admonish all of them for their horrendous *'jokes'*. Either we treat everyone equally, or we will never have true equality, pure and simple. Either we support everyone's right to Freedom of Speech, or we support no one's right to it. Either we accept each other, and we support everyone's right to believe the way that they want to believe, or all we are is a race of hypocrites who will never get anything meaningful done because we will never come together long enough to work together as a single race. Bottom line? Either we want true equality, or we do not. It is that simple. I know that I want true equality, the type of equality

278

that many great people have spoken about throughout our history. How about you?

Now, I would like to go back briefly to what I was talking about earlier concerning reverse discrimination, and the reason is that the instance I would like to mention here is what I consider to be the best prime example of this happening, and the best example of how it will keep us all apart until we stop it (and all forms of discrimination) once and for all. I learned of this incident just before I was ready to publish this book, however, I feel that this needed to be included, so I put it in at the last minute. As I was saying, not too long ago there was an incident that occurred at a college in America, and where it happened at the college was the thing that bothered me the most.

You see, at this college (like at many other colleges around America) they have a meeting place that is called the *'Multicultural Center'*, and by definition these places are there so that students can create a safe community where they can all (everyone, including people of all skin colors and cultures) go and be together so that they can deal with the issues that affect them, and so that they can learn about everyone's backgrounds and cultures in order to promote tolerance and togetherness. As a matter of fact, the college itself bills the space as a place to embrace and support the diversity of all the students at the college. Most importantly, like I said, is the fact that these places are meant for students of all cultures to go to, including students of all colors and nationalities, hence the name **Multicultural** Center. Anyway, at this one center there was a student, a young black woman, who stood up and announced to the entire center that there were just *'too many white people in here'*, and that *'this is a space for People of Color'* (and to be honest, I never really understood the moniker *'People of Color'* when describing a group of people, because white is a color, isn't it?).[18]

A Visit to the City in the Light

Now, again, these centers are meant to promote a coming together of all people, no matter what the color of their skin is, and yet, I even heard that there were students at that same college who, when she made this announcement, actually applauded her for what she said. Then there were the students at that same college who, when they were interviewed after the incident, told an interviewer such things as white people need to be aware that it is not a space for them, and that the woman who made the statement made a good point, and that white people need to be cognizant of the space that they are taking up, and that what she said was a very valid point because the university is full of history that's oppressing People of Color.

Now, if that is the case, and the students who said these things meant what they said, then how can they justify feeling the way that they feel (that oppressing people is wrong) when they are oppressing white people by believing that they do not belong there, especially when the place that they are saying should not include white people is called a Multicultural Center? I can guarantee you that, if it was a white person who stood up and made that statement (but did it by stating that there were *'too many black people'* in there) then there would have been outrage from everyone, especially from all the students at that college, and people would have condemned a white student for saying such an outrageous thing (like they should, because racism, discrimination, and bigotry has absolutely no place in our world).

Now, here is another thing about this incident that makes me really upset. Once upon a time, it was commonplace to segregate white and black people, especially in America. There were cafes, and schools, and other places where black people were told that they did not belong, and therefore, they were not allowed at these places. It was horrible, as it happened all because of the color of their skin.

A Journey There.......and Back Again with a Message of Hope

So, is this student (and the students who applauded her) saying that there should be a return to segregation? Is she saying that (even though some of the greatest people who ever lived fought against segregation, and won their struggle for the betterment of our race) we should now return to segregation, and separate our fellow human beings according to their skin color? I mean, she said that people who have a certain skin color should not be somewhere, didn't she?

In addition, there were students at that college who agreed with her when she made that statement. So how is that different from the segregation that once existed in our world? Like I said, there were many great people who fought hard against segregation (including, in my opinion, one of the greatest men who has ever lived, Dr. Martin Luther King Jr.), and they made many sacrifices in order to make segregation a thing of the past. So now are there really people who think that we need to return to segregation, essentially erasing the struggles that these great people went through in order to stop it once and for all? If that is the attitude of some people now, then it makes me sick, because the Equal Rights Movement was hard won, especially where segregation was concerned. This is why I stated earlier in this book that we should not erase the monuments that exist in places like in the Southern States of America, because the day that we forget our race's history **is** the day that we are doomed to repeat it.

Anyway, to conclude this chapter, please allow me to say this. If we are ever going to achieve true equality for everyone, then we need to make sure that things are truly equal. We need to stop profiling and discriminating against people all because of the color of their skin, or because of the way that they love, or because of what they believe, and the like. We need to stop profiling people in a discriminatory way by doing things like saying *'Hey, they are racists and bigots who believe in slavery, just look at what they call themselves.'* (remember the band that I talked about earlier in this book?). It is terrible that there were a bunch of horrible people in the past who thought that slavery was a good thing in a country like America, and so they tried to form their own country by taking over a part of America, and as a result, now there are many people who feel that the entire country is to blame for what they did. However, let us not forget the **thousands** of Americans who fought against them, and lost **their** lives, all because they thought that slavery was bad, and so they fought to end slavery in America forever. So, why is America not credited for their sacrifices when people say that the entire country of America is to blame for slavery? True, there are many things in America (and in other countries of the world for that matter) that are upsetting to look at because of the time period that they represent and what was happening then, but there are also good people who are not bigoted or racist in any way and that want to save those things and do things like display a flag from the past or save a statue that represents a certain time period. I mean, if we are ever going to have true equality, then aren't their feelings important too?

Let me sum it up like this. One of the greatest men who ever lived (at least in my opinion) spoke of equality, and he did it by delivering one of the greatest speeches that has ever been delivered. He was a man that I have always admired and looked up to, Dr. Martin Luther King Jr., and we sometimes forget his immortal words, but not me. I will never, ever forget them. In that speech he said the following things:

"I have a dream that one day this nation will rise up, live out the true meaning of it's creed: "We hold these truths to be self-evident, that all men are created equal." I have a dream that one day on the red hills of Georgia sons of former slaves and the sons of former slave-owners will be able to sit down together at the table of

A Journey There.......and Back Again with a Message of Hope

brotherhood."

"I have a dream that my four little children will one day live in a nation where they will not be judged by the color of their skin but by the content of their character."

King, Martin Luther. "I Have a Dream by Martin Luther King, Jr; August 28, 1963." *The Avalon Project*, Yale Law School, avalon.law.yale.edu/20th_century/mlk01.asp

He said many other things in this incredible speech, but to close, let me ask you a question. How will Dr. King's dream of equality ever come true if we refuse to make things equal by coming together and ensuring that things are truly equal? *'Equal'* **has** to mean *'Equal'*. Otherwise, things will never be equal, and Dr. King's dream of true equality may never come true. I, for one, sincerely hope that it does come true, and practicing the philosophy of *"Acceptance"* can make it happen if we all just give it a chance. I know that I will be doing my part to make his dream of equality a reality. How about you? You see, without true equality, and without making sure that equal truly does mean equal, then we will never be able to come together because we will be too busy trying to keep each other apart through our irrational hatred of each other. The philosophy of *"Acceptance"* is the way that we can bring our world together in true equality, which is why I am happy to practice it, and I will always teach it to anyone who is willing to listen, just as I was instructed to do when I went through the light.

Chapter Ten
Could You Accept Me?

Ok, while this chapter does not coincide with anything that happened to me when I went to the City in the Light, I think that it is important, because it will be kind of a test to see just how ready you are to practice *"Acceptance"*, and how much you would like to practice it as well.   I know, it is kind of unfair to spring this chapter on you, because it is like a pop quiz (and I hate pop quizzes) but here we go.

I have a question for you.   If you met me, and learned everything about me, then no matter who I am, or how I feel, could you give me enough respect (the same respect that you would want from me) to accept me in order to work with me to solve the problems of our world?   The ones that we need to solve in order to make our world operate better, and in order to advance our race into a better tomorrow?   Or would you hate me to the point where you could not work with me just because of who I am and how I believe?   In the spirit of *"Acceptance"*, if I was willing to give you the respect that you want (for the way that you want to believe and live your life), would you give me the same amount of respect in return (as long as I was not trying to cause anyone harm, or calling for harm to happen to anyone)?   Well, let's put it to the test.

Here is what I want to do.   I am going to describe to you who I am, and how I believe.......kind of.   Let me explain.   Some of what I am about to tell you about me is absolutely true, however, some of what I am about to tell you about me is not true at all.   The reason that I am going to do this is because I want you, with all sincerity, to ask yourself this question....... *"Could I accept this person into my life, and work with them to solve the problems that we all face, or could I not accept them because of how they believe and lead their life?"*. Would you be willing to set aside your feelings about the way that I live my life, and the way that I feel and love for that matter, in order to say *"Yes, I can, and will, accept you, and the life choices that you have made, and the way that you feel, worship, and believe, so that we can work together to try and solve all the problems of our race in order to help us evolve into a better future."*?

Let's start with something simple. Let's start with religion. Let's say that I believe the way that many religions around the world believe, the way that about 1.5 billion people on our planet believe. Let's say that I believe in reincarnation. I know that some may find this belief unbelievable, and some may say that anyone who believes in reincarnation is, well, crazy. But let's say that I believe, with all of my heart, that when we die, we go to a place that I call the City of Light where God waits for us because he rules the city and all of its inhabitants, and it is there that we will be judged for our actions while on this earth. As a matter of fact, let's take that one step further by saying I believe that, when we get there, if we have unfinished business that we were unable to complete while on this earth, then we can be given the opportunity to return to our planet so that we can finish our business. However, when we return, it will be in another body/life, and that the memories of what we did not get accomplished will be locked away in our subconscious when we return, waiting to be unlocked so that we can remember what we did not get accomplished in our previous life. Would you accept me for this belief, or would you think that I was out of my mind, and not want to work with me just because you would want to ridicule me for having this belief?

Let's go even one step further where reincarnation is concerned, and let's say that I believe that there is an incredibly good reason that we only use a small portion of our brain, and our brain power, and that reason is this.   It is because the rest of our brain is reserved, sort of *'taken up'*, by the memories of our past lives that are locked away in our subconscious.   Let's also say that I believe that we can tap into those areas of our brain if we discipline our minds, through trances, hypnosis, and meditation, to the point where we can recall those past life memories.   Would you call me crazy, or would you accept me and want to get to know me so that we could be friends and work together?

Let's examine the lives of famous geniuses like Albert Einstein, and people who (a lot of people say) could predict the future, like Edgar Cayce and Nostradamus.   Let's say I believe that, when they went into their trances in order to do the things that they did, they were actually tapping into the *'conduit'* that leads to the City of Light, and thereby, tapping into the vast knowledge that resides in the City of Light so that they could come up with their predictions and formulas.   Take Albert Einstein, for example. Let's say that I believe, when he was in his trances where he came up with his theories, like the Theory of Relativity, he was not actually conversing with aliens, like a lot of people claim, but that he was actually tapping, again, into the City of Light to come up with those theories.   Or maybe he was actually tapping into a past life when he came up with those theories.   Now, you might say, just **how** could it have been a past life memory when he came up with a future equation?   Well, let's say that I believe that he was tapping into a past life memory that occurred during a life of his that happened either when he was alive and we were visited by aliens in the past, or when he lived a past life that was not on this earth.

There are many who believe that we actually originated from a civilization that lived on Mars well before our human history started here on Earth.   So, let's say that, not only do I believe that to be true, but that I also believe that Einstein had disciplined his mind

287

A Visit to the City in the Light

to the point where he was actually tapping into the memories of a life that he actually lived back when we were still a civilization on Mars, and that his theories were those that he had learned while living that past life on Mars.   Could you accept me if I believed this, or again, would you call me crazy, and not want to even call me a friend of yours?   Would you want to have me in your life, or would you be embarrassed to be seen with me?

How about this.   Let's say that I believe, with all of my heart, that God not only exists, but that he, and our Lord and Savior Jesus Christ, were actually beings from another planet, sort of *'energy beings'* from the aforementioned City of Light, and that one day their race will return openly through what I call the *'conduit'* (which I believe to be something like a worm hole that allows us, and our souls, to travel through space back and forth to and from the City of Light).   Then let's say that I believe that, when they do return, they will let us know that they have returned so that they can see how we have developed as a race, to see if we are worthy to become a part of the universal family.   Would you want to work with me, and consider having me as your friend, or would you walk away from me thinking that I am just a nut case who is not to be taken seriously?   Would you consider that blasphemy just because of my religious beliefs where that is concerned, and would you hate me so much that you could never work with me?   There are those who believe that we are definitely not alone in the universe, and if that is the case, then why would they be considered sane while you would consider me to be a nut case for my beliefs?

Let's take that another step further and say that I believe that we already have been contacted by these *'energy beings'*, and it is them, and their race, that have been leaving signs like the crop circles that appear in fields in order to not only contact us, but to also, in some cases, warn us of other races of aliens and the harm that they could cause us.   Would you consider me crazy?   One example, I believe, was the infamous *'Alien Face with Message'* that was left in a field.   The message beside the face of the alien, which has been called a *'Grey'* by alien enthusiasts and scientists, was finally translated because it was written in binary code, and stated the following, *"Beware the bearers of false gifts and broken promises.   Much pain but still time.   Believe.   There is good out there.   We oppose deception.   Conduit closing.'.*   Now, it is believed that these crop circles are, in some cases, being made by what witnesses have called *'balls of light'* that seem to hover above the field, with the crop circles appearing almost instantaneously below them.   What if I told you that I believe, with all my heart, that these *'balls of light'* are what is making a lot of these crop circles.   That they are actually from the aforementioned alien *'energy'* race, and that some of these messages, in particular this one, was in reality a warning about the *'Greys'*.

Think about it.   When we want to warn a neighborhood, for example, about a sex offender (or another type of dangerous criminal) entering that area to live, or we want to warn a neighborhood about an escaped criminal that has been sighted in that area, what do we do?   We print up posters, with a picture of the criminal on the poster, along with a message warning us about the danger that has just entered our town or neighborhood, and then we distribute the posters to the area where the criminal is either presently living, or where the fugitive has been sighted.   We also do this on the internet, with web sites that list the names of sex offenders and the like.   If I told you that I believe that the *'Greys'* are an evil race of aliens, and that the *'energy beings'* are the good race that was trying to warn us about the *'Greys'* evil intentions towards us, would you still want to accept me into your life, and work with me to help advance our race?   Or would you just want to ridicule me, and discard me from your life as someone who you

289

A Visit to the City in the Light

would not want anything to do with, or ever take seriously for that matter?

Let's take that even one step further and say that I believe that the Gods of Olympus were also aliens from another world, and that they, too, could return to our world to try and rule us once again, because I believe that their powers were nothing more than advanced technology that they used to amaze our more primitive ancestors. Would you consider that a mad theory, or would you still be willing to accept me into your life as someone you could work with? Would you be willing to call me your friend? Or mad?

Ok, how about this. Let's say that I consider myself a *'rebel'*, someone who does not play *'by the rules'*, so to speak, and that, in order to display my rebellious nature, I have a confederate flag on the back of my vehicle. Would you still want to call me your friend, or would you just assume that I was a bigot and a racist and not want to have anything to do with me? Let's take that one step further and let's say that, along with that flag, I had other flags on the back of my vehicle, as a matter of fact, one flag for every flag that has ever represented America in the past, to include the *'Don't Tread on Me'* flag and others. Would **that** make a difference? Would you be able to call me your friend if I did that?

Ok, how about this. Let's say that, at one point in my life, I had been falsely accused of a very heinous crime, like rape, or maybe even child molestation. Let's go further to say that, while I did prove my innocence in court, my ex was living in my town, and she wanted to make me look bad. So, she told many people that I was a bad person, and that I had been found guilty of the crime that I had actually proven myself to be innocent of in court. However, according to her, I had gotten away with it because of a technicality.

A Journey There.......and Back Again with a Message of Hope

Would you shun me, and not trust me, or would you have the courage to seek the truth for yourself by actually looking at the court records, or by talking to me to get my side of the story, in order to see, for yourself, if I was innocent so that we could work together?

Ok, how about this. Let's say that, when people tell me that they were born in the wrong body, and that they should have been a girl when they were born a boy (or vice-versa), I believe them, and here is exactly why I believe them. Let's say that I believe that, when souls come down to Earth from the City of Light (that I mentioned earlier), they are either boy souls or girl souls. However, when they get ready to go into the body of an unborn baby, they find themselves without a body to go into, because the baby that they were supposed to go into was aborted or died from some other reason before the baby could be born. Then let's say that I believe that, because of this, the souls either go back to the City of Light, or because they want to live their life very badly, they actually go into the body of another baby, and that sometimes, the boy souls go into girl babies, and vice-versa, which is why some boys (or girls) say that they were born in the wrong body.

Let's take that one step further and say that I also believe that this is why some people are born with multiple personalities, because the baby that already had a soul in it was invaded by the soul of a boy or girl whose baby body (the one that they had been intended for) had either been aborted or died from some other reason, and therefore, they really do have multiple personalities because they have multiple souls in their body. Let's go even further by saying that this is why I believe that no baby should ever be aborted, because when a baby is aborted, then we are harming another baby by possibly having it born with multiple personalities, and/or because they are basically robbing the soul (that was intended for the deceased baby) of the life that they should have been able to

291

A Visit to the City in the Light

lead as a boy or girl had the baby not been aborted.   In other words, when a baby is aborted, it steals the life (that the soul should have been able to live) away from the soul that was intended for the baby. Would you consider me crazy or maybe a bad person for believing this, or would you still want to work with me, and accept me into your life?

How about this.   Let's say that I am really attracted to girls who are *'unique'* in the way that they look, as in, I like (**really** like) girls who dress like, well, naughty clowns.   Let's go further to say that, whenever I go to a circus, or I see a girl clown on television, it makes me very excited and nervous in a way that would be noticeable if seen in public, and while I do try to maintain my composure so that no one notices, I fail at times.   Would you be understanding, or would you call me a pervert, and not want to have anything to do with me?   Let's go further and say that I am also very attracted to girls who dress in a style that would be considered *'Goth'* or *'Emo'*, especially girls who wear things like black lipstick and have dyed hair, and that I am also very attracted to girls who dress in a way that would be considered *'Cosplay'* as well (especially girls who dress like, oh say, Elves or Pixies), and that I have the same response to them as I do to the girls who dress like clowns.   Would you call me a pervert, or would you accept me and try and be my friend?

Let's take that even one step further and say that I am also attracted to girl's legs, and in particular, their feet, and that, when I see a girl wearing something like sandals, or high heels, or just going barefoot for that matter, it really drives me crazy, and sure enough, there I go again.   Would you think that I was sick, or would you still want to work with me (and actually cover for me when that happens while we are in public) and accept me into your life?   Let's take this even one step further.   Let's say that I am also attracted to girls who are really feminine, and when I say, *'really feminine'*, I mean the ones who dress, talk, and act very *'girly'*. Girls who wear a lot of pink and white, and lace, and dresses, and ankle socks, and heavy makeup, and.......well, you get the idea. Let's also say that I just love it when they talk in a sort of petulant and pouty *'baby girl'* type of talk, and let's say that, if they talk with any type of accent as well, then.......yep, you guessed it, there I go again, even though I do everything that I can to make sure that I maintain my composure so that no one notices. Would this make you think that I have a problem because of these attractions? Or, since I do not cause harm to anyone when I responded in this way (because I do my best to maintain my composure), would you still want to call me your friend, and be willing to accept me and work with me in order to solve all the problems that we face as a race? In short, would you consider me a pervert, or could I be your friend?

Let's try one more thing. Let's say that I am the direct descendant of someone who owned slaves during the time period in the past when slavery was the order of the day in the American South. Let's go further to say that my ancestors were members of the KKK back then, and that they were responsible for killing many innocent black people. Let's go further to say that, even though I do not believe in slavery myself, and even though I have many black friends that I consider my brothers and sisters in our race, the human race, I still have family members today who are white supremacists and who are either in the KKK underground or are involved in the modern Neo-Nazi movement. Would you want to hate me, and consider me a bad person, or would you be willing to sit down with me *at the table of brotherhood*?

I could go on, but you get the idea. After reading all of this, ask yourself this. Is this someone that I could accept, and work with, in order to practice the philosophy of *"Acceptance"* and help

293

change our world, because while I have beliefs and likes that are, well, *'different'*, none of my beliefs and the way that I live my life cause, or calls to cause, harm to anyone?   Or would I be someone who you could never accept, or be a friend with and work with at all in order to solve all the problems that we face as a race?

Chapter Eleven
The Plan

"They got a good plan. Works every time." - My Dad, at the
football game.

My dad said this to me when I found myself at a football
game with him. He was always saying that, if you have a good
game plan, then you stand the best chance at winning, especially at
life. He would tell me to always think ahead when planning my
life. Live for today, but plan for tomorrow, because in order to
make sure that things go good for you, you need to think ahead.
Plan for your future. Think about where you want to be next year, a
decade from now, and when you retire. Plan out your goals, and
then when you have a good game plan, do everything in your power
to make it happen. I think that this is why I would like to talk about
the plan at this point (the philosophy of *"Acceptance"*), because if it
is true peace based on love that we want, then we need a good game
plan to make it happen, and I believe that *"Acceptance"* can make it
happen if we learn it and teach it, just like it was taught to us a long
time ago.

Ok, if you have made it this far through this book, then
maybe there is hope for all of my brothers and sisters of the human
race, because if you have made it this far, then it shows that you are
truly open to the philosophy of *"Acceptance"*. Open enough to, at
least, consider the philosophy and consider putting it into practice in
your lives. In addition, if you, as the reader of this book, are open
to this philosophy, and putting it into practice, then maybe others
will as well, and as such, it will be the first step of a much longer
journey for all of us. I hope so, because it has made my life, and
my world, an absolutely wonderful place to live in, and I hope that,
if you do decide to put *"Acceptance"* into practice, it will do the

same for you. I also hope that, eventually, everyone will not only consider putting the philosophy of *"Acceptance"* into practice in their lives, but that it truly does become a universal practice. I honestly believe that once everyone does, then we will **finally** come together as one race, and it will put us on the path towards the evolution of our race into the future. Like I have said many times, I genuinely believe that we are at a crossroads in our evolution, and that we can either advance into a brighter tomorrow, or we can perish into history, eventually destroyed by our own hands through war and hatred. Now, like I said earlier in this book, if you see a plan that works and that can help us all, does it really matter where it came from? Whether it came from me, or whether it is backed up by another source, maybe one that you do not even believe in? If you really do mean that it does not matter where the plan of *"Acceptance"* came from, that you are willing to listen and put this philosophy into action, then please, finish reading this book all the way until the end with an open mind, and an open heart.

Before I tell you about where the plan and philosophy of *"Acceptance"* was spoken of in the past, I wanted to share something with you. You see, I did not share the end of the story that I told you at the beginning of this book. You remember, the story of the student/teacher at the school who taught the students how to learn through cooperation and caring? Well, I want to share the rest of that story with you now, because while I was given the plan when I had my *'Near Death Experience'*, and while I was told to spread this message to the world at that time, it is also similar to a message that was taught to our world a long time ago by an incredibly special student/teacher from our past. I wish that I could say that the story has a happy ending, but life sometimes does not have a happy ending. I will say this. Because of whom he was, and what he taught, his legacy has a happy ending, even if his ending was not.

296

A Journey There.......and Back Again with a Message of Hope

To continue the story though, it goes like this.   When the students saw the difference that the student/teacher had made in their lives, they realized that he truly had a wonderful plan. Realizing this, they all decided to try and find the student who was actually the teacher, because he had taught them how to come together, and work together, for the betterment of all mankind.   So, they went back to the school to try and find out where he went to after school so that they could all say *'thank you'* for teaching them how to come together through the lessons that he had taught them.......and it was then that they found out the news.

You see, there was another clique that was at that school, only this group was operating in a different way than the other cliques.   You see, this group made money at the school, but not by working.   They made their money by doing things like selling test answers, and other devices to help students cheat.   They made a lot of money from other students, and that gave them true power and influence.   They were the real ones in charge at that school, and they made sure that everyone knew that, and if anyone had a problem with that, then this group would expose them as cheaters, and they would destroy them in the eyes of everyone, and they would be ruined.   They wielded their power from a central fraternity, and everyone knew them, and what they could do.   Then, one day, the fraternity realized that students were starting to come to them less, and they started losing money.   So, they decided to find out who was responsible for instigating this *'rebellion'* against them.

It was then that they learned of the student/teacher who was showing the other students a new way to learn, the one that was causing the fraternity to not only lose money, but to also lose the power and influence that they had.   They knew that if this kept up, then they could end up losing everything, including the fraternity, and so they decided to do something about it.   They decided to end

297

what he was doing, but they knew that they had to be careful, because he had made some very close friends, about 12 in all. They would spend all of their time with him, helping other students learn the studying method that he was teaching, and thereby, helping all the students to come together in peace and harmony. They loved him due to his teachings, and they would spend all of their time with him. As a result, the fraternity decided that they needed to be careful about what they were planning to do to him.

So, one night, when he and his friends were just leaving the library, the fraternity approached them *'en masse'*, and seeing the throng, his friends ran for cover, but he was captured, and brought by force to the fraternity. Then, because they even had dirt on the faculty, they told the faculty to kick him out of school. Because he was already so well-known though, the faculty told the fraternity that they had to deal with it, because they could not cause any harm to someone that was seen to be an innocent. So, to make a long story short, he ended up being taken out to a field and beaten mercilessly, and then the members of the fraternity just left him there to die. He was found the next day by his friends, and his own mother, and they brought his body home to be buried. His friends were upset about what had happened, and so they decided to go to other schools, and spread the teachings that he had taught them in order to help other students, and people in general, around the world to come together in peace and love. They made many enemies, because every school had their own bullies who made money off the students, but his friends did not care. All they cared about was spreading the word on how to learn through cooperation, peace, and caring. In the end, it helped a lot of people, and it actually changed the world by bringing people together through peace and love and cooperation.

Does the story that I just told you about the student/teacher

A Journey There.......and Back Again with a Message of Hope

sound familiar to you? It should. It is, in all actuality, a loosely
based (very loosely) version of another tale, placed in modern times
and in a modern setting, of what happened to the student/teacher that
originally gave us a plan to come together in peace and love and
cooperation. The special student/teacher whose story has been
shared throughout millennia, and now, I would like to share with
you how his teachings actually back up the philosophy of
"Acceptance" that I was given to spread to the world, and how it
can truly save our world, if we all just give it a chance.

Now, I know that the philosophy of *"Acceptance"* might
seem like a new idea. Something that has not yet been
disseminated worldwide. Also, it may seem like *"Acceptance"* is
something that will never work. However, not only can it work, but
the message has been around for a very long time, and it was first
disseminated by, in my opinion, the greatest man who has ever
lived.......my Lord and Savior Jesus Christ. Now, I will say this one
true thing about myself, and that is the fact that I am a believer in
God as the one true and only God, and I am also a believer in our
Lord and Savior Jesus Christ, and the reason that I am a believer is
because I have studied the word of God and our Lord and Savior
Jesus Christ my entire life. In addition, I am also convinced that
when I had my *'Near Death Experience'* it was actually Heaven, or
as I call it, the *'City of Light'* (based on how it looked to me when I
was there) that I visited. I have studied the plan that was laid out by
God, and taught to many by Jesus, and I have come to the
conclusion that the plan that was laid out truly is a plan that can save
not only our race, but also our world, by bringing us all together
using love and compassion, whether you are a believer or not. I say
that because I have seen it work in many places around the globe.

There are places in our world where the people who live
there do not have a lot of worldly goods. They do not have a lot of

money and they do not have the electronic toys that most of us take for granted. As a matter of fact, they do not have much of anything at all. What they do have, though, is a deep love for each other, and they utilize that love to build a bond of cooperation that keeps them together in peace. They work together, they accept each other, and they watch out for each other. Everything that they do is concentrated on making sure that they not only survive, but also thrive as a group. They do not look for fame or possessions. Instead, they come together as a group, and they accept each other. Why can't we do that?

Now, before you just stop reading, or throw this book away and say, *'Oh boy, here we go, all this has been is just an attempt to convert me to Christianity'*, please hear me out, and then make your own decision, because that has not been my intention. My intention was to spread the message that was given to me when I had my *'Near Death Experience'*. My intent was never to convert anyone to Christianity, or to have anyone change from their own beliefs at all (now, if it does happen, and this book does cause someone to convert to Christianity, then it will make me happy, but that was never my goal. What my goal has been is to try and bring us all together through utilizing the philosophy of *"Acceptance"* in the hopes of bringing us all together in peace and love). However, if you see or hear something that can work, like a plan or a way of doing something that you would like to accomplish, then you will want to put it into practice, even if it is a plan that was originally given to us by someone else. Someone that you may not like or even believe in for that matter. The reason that I am saying this is because it will take all of us practicing *"Acceptance"* in order to bring us together, and when I say, *'all of us'*, I mean all of us, believers and non-believers alike.

Take this as an example. Let's say that you are a musician.

A Journey There.......and Back Again with a Message of Hope

Let's go further and say that you really want to be a great musician, and you also want to be a great song writer and soloist. Good enough to have the world take notice of your music. However, let's say that you are having trouble being able to play certain music, because whenever you try, you just cannot seem to pull it off. Then, one day, you see another musician that can pull it off, and they are really great at playing music and soloing. So, you go to this person, and you ask them how they are able to play the music that you are having trouble with, even though they are your competition in the music world and you really don't like them. Then, much to your surprise, they see your dilemma, and they decide to show you a way of practicing and playing your instrument that you never thought of trying before. So, you try it.......and it works! You are suddenly able to play like you have never been able to play before, all because of the method that the other musician showed you.

Or say that you are a baker, and you always seem to have trouble making your wedding cakes look exactly right because of the problems you are having with the icing. Then, one day you decide to talk to another baker who is not having the same problem that you are having, even though they are your competition. However, to your surprise, they decide to help you, and they show you a method of making your icing so that it works really well when you are making wedding cakes. So, you try it, and suddenly you are able to make your wedding cakes in any style that you want, all because of the method that the other baker showed you.

That is what my goal has been by writing this book. To spread the message that was given to me in order to help our race by bringing us together in peace and love and cooperation, no matter how we believe and live our lives. You see, I believe that the plan can work by uniting us in a way that has never happened before. In

A Visit to the City in the Light

short, my intent has been to show that *"Acceptance"* can not only work to bring us all together, but that the message has been around for a very long time.

You see, we will all need to come together if this plan is to work. It will require non-believers to try a plan that was originally disseminated to our world by our Lord and Savior Jesus Christ, and it will also require Christians to do this as well, which may be a challenge, whether we want to admit it or not. Please let me explain. You see, many people today say that they are a believer in God, and in our Lord and Savior Jesus Christ, but then, a lot of times, their actions speak otherwise, at least to me. It has been said that one of the hardest things to do in this life is to be a believer, to be a Christian, because it requires people to actually do more than just attend church or carry a bible. It requires people to follow the word of God and our Lord and Savior Jesus Christ with a heart that operates on pure faith alone. Faith in God, faith in Jesus, faith in their fellow humans, and most importantly, faith in themselves to do the right thing. It can be hard, especially when there is so much hatred in the world, and so much hatred harboring in the hearts of our fellow human beings. People do something that upsets us, whether it is doing something like trying to hurt us or take advantage of us, and all we want to do is hurt them in return, to make them feel as much pain as we are feeling. To show them that we are not weak, that we are strong enough to take them on, no matter what, and no matter what we have been told is 'doing the right thing'.

Let me explain what I mean while showing you how the philosophy of *"Acceptance"* parallels what was taught to us in the Bible. Take what I said in many sections of this book when I said that we should respect each other, including our wants and our desires, as long as we do not advocate violence against anyone, and as long as what we want does not cause harm to another person. In the bible, in **Matthew 7:12**, it states that Jesus said, when he gave his Sermon on the Mount, that:

Matthew 7:12 - *"So in everything, do to others what you would have them do to you, for this sums up the Law and the Prophets"*. New International Version (NIV)

This is better known as **The Golden Rule** to most people, and it's message can be found in many parts of the Bible. In addition, in **Ephesians 4:31-32**, the Apostle Paul, during his ministries to the world of the word of Jesus, said that we should:

Ephesians 4:31-32 - *(31) "Get rid of all bitterness, rage and anger, brawling and slander, along with every form of malice. (32) Be kind and compassionate to one another, forgiving each other, just as in Christ God forgave you"*. New International Version (NIV)

Another excellent passage from the bible where it mentions that being violent towards others should never happen can be found in **Hebrews 12:14**. Hebrews was written (according to most scholars) during a time when, if you followed Jesus' plan and you were a Christian, it meant that you might have to suffer everything from beatings to being executed, and while in most nations today this is not the case, unfortunately, it is still the case in a few modern countries. I know of some countries where you can still be jailed just for carrying a Bible, let alone being a Christian, and yet, this passage speaks to everyone in our world, whether you live in countries where it is acceptable or unacceptable to be a follower of Jesus and his word and plan. In this passage, it says to:

Hebrews 12:14 - *"Make every effort to live in peace with everyone and to be holy; without holiness no one will see the Lord."* New

303

A Visit to the City in the Light

International Version (NIV)

This is passage states what I was trying to relay when I spoke about not being violent towards anyone who might feel differently than you do, or who holds different beliefs than you do, or who live their lives differently than you do. Everyone has the right to live their lives in the way that they want to. So why call for violence against another person just because they do not believe, or live their lives, like you do?

Here is what I would like to do. I want to try and break each chapter down by showing which scriptures apply to what I said in each chapter so that you can see how the philosophy of *"Acceptance"*, in a lot of ways, parallels what the Bible teaches us. Again, I call our Lord and Savior Jesus Christ our *'student/teacher'* because I believe that everything he taught to us came from God, and then Jesus taught it to us. So, if you have made it this far through this book, and you like the idea of *"Acceptance"*, then no matter how you believe religiously, then please keep an open mind and open heart and allow me to explain how the plan of *"Acceptance"* parallels what the Bible teaches us by citing scripture. Then, if you do decide to put the philosophy of *"Acceptance"* into practice in your life, and someone questions you about it and where you learned it from, you can even tell them that you learned it from the Bible (even if you are a non-believer), and that it was the message that was given to us by God and taught to us by our Lord and Savior Jesus Christ.

One last thing. People may question why I decided to quote scripture from the New International Version of the Bible, and not from other versions like the King James Version. Well, I decided to use this version of the Bible because I have had many people tell me that other versions are sometimes confusing as far as what each piece of scripture truly means, and in other instances they told me that they became frustrated with trying to interpret just what each piece of scripture means, and as such, they eventually just put the Bible down and stopped reading.

I did not want to take any chance of that happening, because this message is just too important, and so that is why I decided to use the New International Version, because it puts scripture in the most easily to understand language possible. That is not to say that I think that people are not intelligent, because I know for a fact that people are intelligent, but again, I am basing my decision on what people told me in my travels around the world. So, I wanted to make sure that I used a version of the Bible that everyone told me was the most understandable and easiest to read.

Chapter One

Remember when I talked about being a good person, as well as helping each other when we can? Well, in **Galatians 6:2**, it says that:

Galatians 6:2 - *"Carry each other's burdens, and in this way you will fulfill the law of Christ"*. New International Version (NIV)

This tells me that we should not only be a good person, but good to each other as well. That is what the philosophy of *"Acceptance"* is all about. Being good to each other so that we can all get along. Otherwise, we will not get anything done because of all the fighting, and it could cause us to continue with all the hate forever. I think that this next piece of scripture talks about that the best, because if we do not start being good to each other, then only bad will happen to us, and we will only have ourselves to blame when bad things happen do happen due to bad things that we do in life, just like this says:

Galatians 6:7-10 - *(7) "Do not be deceived: God cannot be mocked.* ***A man reaps what he sows.*** *(8) Whoever sows to please their flesh, from the flesh will reap destruction; whoever sows to please the Spirit, from the Spirit will reap eternal life.* ***(9) Let us not become weary in doing good, for at the proper time we will reap a harvest if we do not give up.*** *(10)* ***Therefore****, as we have opportunity,* ***let us do good to all people****, especially to those who belong to the family of believers."* New International Version (NIV)

This is what I was talking about when I said that we should take responsibility to be a good person. Accepting the responsibility to be good is a part of God's plan for us, because he genuinely wants us to be good people, and good to others also. He wants us to succeed as a race. He wants us to do it so that we can all get along and work together, so that we can succeed. As I said, it starts with all of us taking responsibility to be good to each other by being a good person, the type of person that everyone wants in their life.

Now, where I mentioned taking responsibility for our actions, especially when talking about how we treat other people in our lives no matter how they treat us (instead of just trying to retaliate against other people when they treat us bad), I think that this piece of scripture pretty much says it all, even when others are bad to us and we feel the need to judge them or retaliate against them:

Galatians 6:4-5 - *(4) "Each one should test their* ***own*** *actions.* ***Then they can take pride in themselves alone, without comparing themselves to someone else, (5) for each one should carry their***

own load." New International Version (NIV)

You see, only we can, and should, be held responsible for our actions. No one can be held responsible for what we decide to do. We have to be held responsible. That is what is meant by saying that we should test our *"own actions"*. In that way, we can take pride in the fact that we are good people, and we do not have to compare ourselves to others when making that determination. This is especially true when it comes to carrying our *"own load"*, or to put it bluntly, when we are responsible for being good people during our lifetime.

Now, remember when I talked about young people who are in love and in a relationship? When I mentioned that they should really take their time before doing things like having a child in order to make sure that they can love each other in a way that shows that they both truly do care about each other completely? Well, there are many pieces of scripture that talk about young love and treating each other in a way that proves that we do love each other completely, and how to have that level of love for your partner. However, I think that these pieces of scripture say it best:

Ephesians 5:22 - *"Wives, submit yourselves to your own husbands as you do to the Lord."* New International Version (NIV)

Ephesians 5:28 - *"In this same way, husbands ought to love their wives as their own bodies. He who loves his wife loves himself."* New International Version (NIV)

Ephesians 5:33 - *"However, each one of you also must love his wife as he loves himself, and the wife must respect her husband."* New International Version (NIV)

A Visit to the City in the Light

Now, I know that these talk about young couples who are already married, but I believe that it also applies to both partners in a relationship who are not married in today's world as well. Let me explain. Before anyone makes a serious commitment to their partner, and before both of them think about having a child, they really should ask themselves these questions. *'Do I love this person enough to stay with them forever, or do I need more time before making such a commitment? Also, does my partner love, respect, and care for me as much as they love, respect, and care about themselves? Does my partner love me completely, and do I love my partner completely? Enough for us to be together for the long haul?'*. I say that for a couple of reasons.

The first is because we all want to have our partner love and care for us completely, and that means that we need to love our partner for more reasons than just wanting to have sex with them. It means that we love each other because we completely care about each other, more than we care about anyone else on Earth, including ourselves. It also means that we respect each other completely. If you look at yourself in the mirror, and you think that there is any chance that you cannot respect and care for your partner to the point where if your partner is hurting (or needs you in any way, especially emotionally) you cannot be there for them completely, then maybe you don't love and care for your partner, and if that is the case, then one of two things need to happen, especially if you want a love that lasts forever. The first would be to figure out what needs to happen (as in, what personal changes do you need to make to yourself so that you can love and care for your partner completely) in order to make the love that you have for your partner grow to the point where you can love and care for them completely, like they deserve to be loved. However, if you cannot do that, and there is no way that you can love and care about your partner completely, then the second thing would be to accept the responsibility to admit to yourself that you do not love your partner completely, and that it would be better for the both of you to make a clean break so that you can find a new partner that you can love and care about completely, like they, and you, deserve to be loved, and this goes for both partners in a relationship.

Now, there are a few reasons that this is so important. The first is because you (and your partner) deserve to be loved completely, because love is so important to us as a race. It motivates us to be better than we thought that we could ever be. It energizes us so that we can do more than we ever thought we could be capable of doing. Most importantly, though, is the fact that love is one of the most basic of our needs as a human being. Nothing feels better than knowing that our partner truly does love us, and that they accept us and do care about us completely.

Another reason is this. The love that we have for each other affects so many people around us, especially our children. If there is any chance that our love will produce a child, then we need to make sure that our love is real and can last a lifetime. If we think that there is any chance that our love will not last, then we need to take whatever precautions are necessary in order to make sure that we do not have a child until we are absolutely sure that our love will last. They deserve to grow up in a home with parents who are with them during their entire childhood, and who can teach them, through example, what a real love looks like. There are many other reasons that we, as a couple, need to make sure that our love can last, but this reason is one of the most important because it will it affect our children for their entire lifetime.

Your see, I have always believed that one of the most difficult things that anyone can do is raising a child as a single parent, and if the love that we have for our partner is not strong enough to last a lifetime, then that is exactly where we will find ourselves. Being a single parent trying to raise a child. It is hard, even with things like child support. So, before any man makes the decision to have unprotected sex, or before any woman makes the decision to allow her partner to have unprotected sex with her, they should ask themselves these questions. *"Could I raise a child on my own?"* and *"Do I have what it takes to be a single parent?"*. If any man thinks that he could not do it because of what he would miss out on, and if any woman thinks that she would not be able to do it without missing out on a lot of her life as well, then they should accept the responsibility to not have a child until they are ready to make a lifetime commitment. Also, both partners should give each other the time to prove that they truly do love each other completely before they have a child. People can only put on a fake face for so long. So, make sure that what you are being told by your partner is not just *'flowery words'*. That when your partner tells you that they love you completely, like you deserve, then they prove it to you through their actions, even after the initial *'wow'* time period ends.

Now, remember when I was talking about making excuses for the bad things that we do, and how excuses could cause us problems? Well, I have a parable to share with you concerning making excuses that could cause us to experience bad results in our lives, one that was shared by our Lord and Savior Jesus Christ:

Luke 14:12-24 - *(12) "Then Jesus said to his host, "When you give a luncheon or dinner, do not invite your friends, you brothers or sisters, your relatives, or your rich neighbors; if you do, they may invite you back and so you will be repaid. (13) But when you give a banquet, invite the poor, the crippled, the lame, the blind, (14) and you will be blessed. Although they cannot repay you, you will be repaid at the resurrection of the righteous. (15) When one of* *those at the table with him heard this, he said to Jesus, "Blessed is the one who will eat at the feast in the kingdom of God." (16) Jesus replied: "A certain man was preparing a great banquet and invited many guests. (17) At the time of the banquet he sent his servant to tell those who had been invited, 'Come, for everything is now ready.' (18) But they all alike began to make excuses. The first said, 'I have just bought a field, and I must go and see it. Please excuse me.' (19) Another said, 'I have just bought five yoke of oxen, and I'm on my way to try them out. Please excuse me.' (20) Still another said, 'I just got married, so I can't come.' (21) The servant came back and reported this to his master. Then the owner of the house became angry and ordered his servant, 'Go out quickly into the streets and alleys of the town and bring in the poor, the crippled, the blind and the lame.' (22) 'Sir', the servant said, 'what you ordered has been done, but there is still room.' (23) Then the master told his servant, 'Go out to the roads and country lanes and compel them to come in, so that my house will be full. (24) I tell you, not one of those who were invited will get a taste of my banquet.'"* New International Version (NIV)

Now, I know that was a long parable, but what does it tell you about making excuses instead of doing what is right? I will tell you what it tells me. It tells me that no good, and no reward, will ever come for making excuses. We need to keep our word, and be good people who never make excuses, especially if we want everyone to trust us enough to come together and work with us so that we can implement the philosophy of *"Acceptance"*. How can we expect others to trust us if all we do is make excuses?

Ok, remember when I talked about helping others? Well, here are some scriptures that talk about that as well:

Hebrews 13:16 - *"And do not forget to do good and to share with* *others, for with such sacrifices God is pleased."* New International Version (NIV)

Doing good for each other is more than just a hug or a kind word. It is really doing things like sharing what we have with others who may not have that much.

Philippians 2:3-4 - *(2) "Do **nothing** out of **selfish ambition** or **vain conceit. Rather, in humility value others above yourselves, (4) not looking to your own interests but each of you to the interests of the others**".* New International Version (NIV)

In order to fully put *"Acceptance"* into practice, we are going to need to look to the needs of others rather than only looking just to our own needs, and we do that by valuing others more than we value ourselves.

Galatians 6:2 - *"**Carry each other's burdens**, and in this way you will fulfill the law of Christ".* New International Version (NIV)

Again, if you see someone who is burdened with difficulties, like trying to survive on a little money or just to get something done, then by helping each other during these times we can bring everyone together, like *"Acceptance"* dictates that we do.

John 15:12 - *"My command is this: **Love each other as I have loved you**".* New International Version (NIV)

Having love for our fellow human beings is going to be important in trying to bring us all together. This does not mean that we need to actually be in a romantic relationship with others but love for our fellow human beings means that we care about each other to the point where we want to help each other, and be there for each other, and care about each other, like *"Acceptance"* dictates that we do.

But my favorite piece of scripture concerning helping each other is this:

Acts 20:35 - *"In everything I did, I showed you that by this kind of hard work* ***we must help the weak****, remembering the words the Lord Jesus himself said: '****It is more blessed to give than to receive****'"*. New International Version (NIV)

Like I said, if we really want to place *"Acceptance"* into practice in order to bring our race together using peace, caring, and love, then our reward, by ***"giving"*** versus ***"receiving"***, will be the fact that we will finally be brought together as one race in the bonds of love and peace forever.

Chapter Two

Again, when talking about cultivating good relationships with our loved ones, the piece of scripture that I mentioned earlier, **Ephesians 5:28**, pretty much applies here as well, and it also applies to both partners. We should always want to love our partner just as much as we love ourselves, because if both partners live their lives with this type of love in their hearts for each other, then they have the makings of a wonderful love story, one that can last a lifetime. Think of it like this. If you do something that would cause your partner pain in any way, including emotionally, then it should cause you pain just to see them in pain. Conversely, if you do something to make them happy, then do it because you truly do care about them as much as you care about your own happiness. If you do this, then it should give you happiness. Treat them like you would treat yourself, with love, care, and compassion.

A Visit to the City in the Light

Now, I realize that there are prevailing attitudes in today's world that say that sex is necessary in order to have a relationship with someone you are not married to, but there is some wisdom in waiting so that you can truly get to know the person that you are dating. Do not ever let anyone tell you that, if you love them, then you will have sex with them when you are just starting your relationship, or even after you have been together with them for a while. If that's your love interest's attitude (that sex is the most important thing to them in your relationship with them), then they do not care about you and your feelings, they just care about their own wants and needs. Also, just to be clear, I think that there is a real difference between sex and intimacy. You can be intimate with your partner without sex being involved. Things like kissing, and cuddling, and holding hands, are different than actual sex, at least to me (again, though, just to be clear here, I am talking about activities with your partner, and not with someone that you are not in a relationship with. You should never have any intimacy with someone who is not your partner. Look at it like this. You would be extremely hurt if your partner had intimate contact of any kind with someone other than you, so why would you do it to them? At least that is the way that it seems to me, because I want my partner to know that I do have a strong character, and that my word truly does mean something when I give it to them). There should be intimacy in any love relationship because it helps show our partner that we really do love them, and that we want our love to grow bigger and to be strong. Wanting intimacy from our partner is different than telling them that we need to have sex, and that sex is the most important thing to us, at least to me. Again, if your partner does care about you, then they will want to do things, like being intimate with you, to make your love grow. However, when your partner tells you that sex is more important than intimacy to them, and especially if your partner only spends time with you if they want sex with you, then that is when you should ask yourself if your partner really loves you completely, at least in my opinion. How do you feel about this?

To continue, courting is a dying art with a lot of young people. There is something to be said for getting to know a person before you jump into bed with them. Also, like I said, if they truly care about you, and they genuinely care about getting to know you completely in order to know what makes you happy, then they will want to wait as well in order to truly learn all about you, including what makes you happy. Now, I know that being chaste in today's world is not a popular attitude, but like I said, waiting until you truly get to know someone before you have sex with them will pay off in the long run, because you will know if the person that is interested in you is genuinely interested in you, and not just using you for their own selfish needs. Here is some scripture that I have found that speaks to taking your time before having sex with someone, and not being fearful of them leaving you if you do not have sex with them right away:

Matthew 5:28 - *"But I tell you that **anyone** who looks at a woman lustfully has **already committed adultery with her in his heart**."* New International Version (NIV)

If your partner only looks at you with lust, then they do not have your best interests in mind, only their interests and their lust. Also, there is this:

2 Timothy 1:7 - *"For the **Spirit** God gave us **does not make us timid**, but **gives us power, love and self-discipline**".* New International Version (NIV)

God gave our Spirit the *"power"* to wait to have sex until we develop our love for each other, and he also gave us the *"self-*

315

discipline" to wait as well. If we truly do care about our partner, then we will be more interested in making our love grow with them, instead of only being worried about having sex with them. We do that by being interested in learning about our partner, and what makes them happy, and if our only desire is to have sex with our partner, then it is a clear sign that our partner (who is pressuring us to have sex with them) may not care that much about us at all.

Remember when I talked about setting a good example for our children? Well, here is a piece of scripture that pretty much states that, if we teach our children through example, and show them how they should be in order to be a good person, then they will know how to conduct themselves when they are running our world one day. In addition, when they pass their knowledge on to their children, they their children will know how to be good people as well:

Proverbs 22:6 - *"Start children off on the way they should go, and even when they are old they will not turn from it"*. New International Version (NIV)

Ergo, if we want our children to have good lives, and good relationships, then we should teach them how to have those things by setting a good example for them to see and learn from. So that they will learn how they happen. Then, when they are older, they will be able to teach these things to their children, because they will still be setting the example that we taught them when they were children. This is especially true if we want *"Acceptance"* to be a universal practice because they will see the importance of accepting each other in order to help our race advance and evolve into the future by working with each other.

Remember when I was talking about not doing things to hurt

our partners, or ex-partners?   Hurting them is not something that someone (who truly has, or had, love in their heart for them) would ever do, because it is not doing anything good for them, it is only doing something good, or self-seeking, for the person who is hurting them, like it says here:

James 3:16 - *"For where you have **envy** and **selfish ambition**, there you find **disorder** and **every evil practice**"*. New International Version (NIV)

We should never have *"envy"* or *"selfish ambition"* in our heart towards the person that we say we love, or that we say we loved in the past.   If we do, and we do something to hurt them, then it can cause *"disorder"* and *"every evil practice"* to happen to them, and it can really hurt them in unbelievably bad ways (remember my friend that I told you about, who was so affected by her ex posting the sex tape of her that she committed suicide?).   Again, we should treat everyone the same way that we want them to treat us.

Where keeping our word is concerned, think about this:

Deuteronomy 23:23 - *"**Whatever your lips utter you must be sure to do**, because **you made your vow freely** to the LORD your God **with your own mouth**."* New International Version (NIV)

Look at it this way.   If we are ever going to come together through utilizing *"Acceptance"* in order to help our race evolve into the future, then we are going to need to be able to trust each other, and how can we trust each other if we can't even keep our word to each other?   If we make a promise to someone, or we give our word to someone, then we should make sure that we keep our word to that person.   Like this says, we made the promise, or we gave our word, ourselves with our *"own mouth"*.   We did so *"freely"*, without being pressured to do it, so we should keep the word or promise that we gave to anyone that we give it to. It is one of the biggest ways that we will prove to others that we can be trusted.

In addition, where earning trust is concerned, I think that this is a great piece of scripture that states one of the things we should look for when having someone earn our trust:

Proverbs 11:13 - *"A gossip betrays a confidence, but **a trustworthy person keeps a secret**."* New International Version (NIV)

Therefore, we should not only strive to be a trustworthy person, and never betray others, but we should **also** look for these qualities in anyone who is earning our trust so that we know that they are a *"trustworthy"* person, and that they are not going to betray us. Again, we are going to need to be able to trust each other if universal *"Acceptance"* is going to have any chance to succeed.

Chapter Three

Remember when I spoke about being happy with our job, no matter what it is. Here is some food for thought concerning being happy with our job, and doing it to the best of our ability:

Colossians 3:23-24 - *(23)* ***"Whatever you do, work at it with all your heart, as working for the Lord, not for human masters**, (24)* *since you know that you will receive an inheritance from the Lord as a reward. **It is the Lord Christ you are serving**."* New International Version (NIV)

Like this says, we should work our job with all our heart, as if we are doing it not for our *"human masters"*, but as if we are doing it for *"the Lord"*. If we approach our jobs like this, then we will do a great job, and doing a great job will not only make us a success, but it will also make us great at doing our part to make sure that our race operates at maximum efficiency. This is especially important in order for our race to evolve, which is what *"Acceptance"* is all about.

Also, as I mentioned, one of the worst things that anyone can do to another person at their work is to harass them or try to take advantage of them in any way. For that, just remember **The Golden Rule**, as it is stated in multiple passages, including this one:

Luke 6:31 - *"Do to others as you would have them do to you."* New International Version (NIV)

If you do not want to be harassed at work, and you do not want to have anyone that you care about harassed, then this piece of scripture says it all. Again, how can we all work together through practicing *"Acceptance"* if we cannot even trust each other enough to work together?

Chapter Four

Now, there are even Bible passages that talk about the importance of having fun. Here is a good piece of scripture that talks about that:

Ecclesiastes 8:15 - *"So I commend the enjoyment of life, because there is nothing better for a person under the sun than to eat and drink and be glad. Then joy will accompany them in their toil all the days of the life God has given them under the sun"*. New International Version (NIV)

Enough said concerning how the Bible feels about the

importance of having fun in our lives, wouldn't you agree? I mean, we need to make sure that we have fun for our own emotional needs, and it can be a powerful tool for us to use when we are trying to help others, and when we are trying to foster good in all of our relationships.

When talking about doing something to care about elderly people, or doing something nice for them, this is a good passage to consider:

1 Timothy 5:1-2 - *(1) "Do not rebuke an older man harshly, but exhort him as if he were your father. Treat younger men as brothers, (2) older women as mothers, and younger women as sisters, with absolute purity."* New International Version (NIV)

In other words, it should not matter if the elderly person that you are considering doing something nice for is your relative or not, we should do it in order to make sure that we are good to everyone. Even if it is just to visit them to give them some company at someplace like a nursing home, or just watching a movie with them, or even helping them when they are at the grocery store. Be kind, be compassionate, be caring, and above all else, accept the responsibility to be a good person to them. It can make a difference, not only in their lives, but in yours as well. As a matter of fact, this also applies to being good to all men and women, young and old alike. Treat them as you would want others to treat your own father, mother, sister, brother, son, or daughter. It will really help us all come together when we start practicing *"Acceptance"*, because being good to each other will help us all come together in peace and love so that we can work together for the benefit of our race, and isn't that what we all want? Universal *"Acceptance"* in order to bring us all together?

Chapter Five

Now, I already gave some great scripture about teaching our children, so I will not repeat it here, but what about education, and the value of it in general? Well, here is some scripture that I would like to share with you concerning that:

Proverbs 18:15 - *"The heart of the discerning acquires knowledge, for the ears of the wise seek it out"*. New International Version (NIV)

Proverbs 4:13 - *"Hold on to instruction, do not let it go; guard it well, for it is your life"*. New International Version (NIV)

Proverbs 9:9 - *"Instruct the wise and they will be wiser still; teach the righteous and they will add to their learning"*. New International Version (NIV)

The Bible is replete with examples of the importance of education, which is why I truly hope and pray for the day that it is available to all who seek it. We can figure out a way to do this if we all work together to figure out a way to make education as affordable as possible for everyone. Everyone will need to be able to access learning and higher education if we are ever going to truly take advantage of the opportunity that *"Acceptance"* will afford us. After all, if we are all going to work together in order to solve our race's problems, then don't we need to identify everyone who has the high intelligence levels in our race so that we can ensure that they have access to the education that they will need to help us solve all of our world's most pressing problems, no matter whether they come from upper class, middle class, or poor neighborhoods?

Chapter Six

A Visit to the City in the Light

Ok, this was about the longest chapter in this book, with good reason. Following the law is too important because of how much it can affect our lives. However, this chapter can be summed up with just a few pieces of scripture:

Romans 13:1-5 - *(1) "Let everyone be subject to the governing* **authorities**, *for there is no authority except that which God has established. The authorities that exist have been established by God. (2) Consequently, whoever rebels against the authority is rebelling against what God has instituted, and* **those who do so will bring judgment on themselves. (3) For rulers hold no terror for those who do right, but for those who do wrong. Do you want to be free from fear of the one in authority? Then do what is right and you will be commended.** *(4) For the one in authority is God's servant for your good. But* **if you do wrong, be afraid**, *for rulers do not bear the sword for no reason. They are God's servants,* **agents of wrath to bring punishment on the wrongdoer. (5)** *Therefore,* **it is necessary to submit to the authorities, not only because of possible punishment** *but also* **as a matter of conscience**." New International Version (NIV)

Titus 3:1 - *"Remind the people to* **be subject to rulers and authorities, to be obedient, to be ready to do whatever is good**." New International Version (NIV)

Romans 3:31 - *"Do we, then, nullify the law by this faith? Not at all! Rather,* **we uphold the law**." New International Version (NIV)

We should all follow the law, as long as it is an active law on the books. Should it be voted out, replaced, or even modified, then we should follow the new law as diligently as we did the previous law, because they are there to protect us and our loved ones. Chaos will never bring us together, because with total chaos and lawlessness we will never have the chance to come together peacefully in order to solve the problems that we face as a race by utilizing *"Acceptance"*.

Now, remember when I spoke about how everyone should be treated equally, especially when talking about the law and making sure that everyone is punished the same? If we are ever going to have a justice system that we can trust, then everyone should be treated equally under the law. It should not matter if you are a man or a woman, it should not matter what the color of your skin is, it should not matter what language you speak. Until we have a justice system where everyone is treated equally under the law, then we have a major problem, because it should not matter who we are.

What should matter is if what we have done is a crime, like making false allegations and filing false reports against others, or like committing a sex crime, especially against a child, and then (if we are found guilty of committing that crime) making sure that everyone is treated equally by facing the same judgment that anyone else would face for committing that crime. Therefore, here are some passages that talk about the importance of everyone being treated equally:

Acts 10:34 - *"Then Peter began to speak: 'I now realize how true it is that **God does not show favoritism**'"*. New International Version (NIV)

And neither should we, especially where the law is concerned. Everyone who breaks any crime that is on the books should face the same punishment. Another one is this:

Romans 2:11-12 - *(11) "For **God does not show favoritism**. (12)*

A Visit to the City in the Light

*All who sin apart from the law will also perish apart from the law, and **all who sin under the law will be judged by the law**.".* New International Version (NIV)

Therefore, to repeat, we should not show favoritism, especially where the law is concerned. In addition, we should judge all law breakers equally instead of punishing some with prison time and then letting others just get something like probation for committing the same type of crime. It should not matter what sex we are, or what color our skin is, or any other reason that we consider ourselves different than others. If we commit a crime, and it has been proven that we committed the crime, then we should all face the same punishments (as in, prison time for everyone who is guilty, instead of only for some). Now, I know that the prevailing attitude amongst the police is that, if a woman were to be punished for filing a false criminal allegation against a man, then it might discourage the next woman from reporting a crime for fear that she will not be believed.

Here is the way I look at it, see if you agree. If a woman is telling the truth, and she really did have a crime committed against her, then she has nothing to fear, because she is telling the truth. However, if she is lying, and it is proven that she is lying, then she should have everything to fear. In other words, as far as I can see, the only women that it should stop from reporting a crime are the ones who know that they are lying about the accusations. Refer this thought back to what **Romans 13:1-5** states above, where it says, in part, that *".......if you do wrong, be afraid......."*, because everyone who lies to the authorities by making a false police report should be punished equally, just the same as everyone who commits a crime should be punished equally. If a woman (or a man for that matter) lies to the authorities, and it is proven that she lied when filing charges against someone, then she should face the same punishment that a man faces for making a false criminal accusation against someone.

This is not limited to just those who file false charges though, because there are many more instances where justice needs to be equal, and presently it is not. Let's think about all the minorities who are in jail right now, with a lot of them now being proven to be innocent. Should a man or woman be treated differently just because of the color of their skin? Like I stated in an earlier chapter, the last time I checked, people of every skin color are committing crimes. So, we need to ask ourselves, why is it that there are so many minorities in jail, especially when a lot of them are now being proven to be innocent? Is it because minorities are committing the majority of the crimes, or is it for another reason? We need to know the answer for sure by examining the facts, so that there is no more guessing by anyone as to why this is happening.

Or let's consider the people who have sex with underage students, and it turns out that a lot of them did it because they were the student's teachers, or they were someone who had another type of position of authority over the students that they had sex with. There are many instances where some of these teachers get way less time in jail (if they get any jail time at all) than other teachers who have sexual contact with underage students. Why is that? If a person is a pedophile, then they are a pedophile, and they should all face the same punishments no matter what the circumstances were. Now, I am not trying to be an advocate for criminals here. What I am trying to do is show that, until we all come together to answer these questions in order to obtain equal justice for all, then we will never come together as a race, because like I said, nothing can affect a person's life more than the law. That is why I pray that we all do come together in order to answer these questions and then solve these problems, and the best way to do that is if we stop the fighting amongst ourselves in order to work with each other, and we can do that by practicing *"Acceptance"*. It will bring us all together, and it will give us the best chance of solving these problems once and for all.

Here is another piece of scripture that talks about how everyone should be treated equally:

James 2:1-4 - *(1)* *"My brothers and sisters, **believers in our glorious Lord Jesus Christ must not show favoritism**. (2) Suppose a man comes into your meeting wearing a gold ring and fine clothes, and a poor man in filthy old clothes also comes in. (3) **If you show special attention to the man wearing fine clothes and say, 'Here's a good seat for you', but say to the poor man, 'You stand there' or 'Sit on the floor by my feet', (4) have you not discriminated among yourselves and become judges with evil thoughts?** "*. New International Version (NIV)

To me, this is self-explanatory. Like the other pieces of scripture above state, God does not show favoritism, and neither should we, for when we do, have we not discriminated amongst ourselves and ***"become judges with evil thoughts"***? If we become judges with evil thoughts, and we discriminate amongst ourselves, especially in places like where sentencing everyone equally is concerned (especially where it concerns things like punishing all pedophiles equally) then how are we ever going to come together and get anything done? We need to have a justice system that we can trust, for without that, how can we ever trust each other enough to come together and solve all of the problems that we face? If we cannot trust our justice system, then we are facing chaos, and we will never come together if our world is being controlled by chaos and distrust instead of being adjudicated by equal justice for all, like our world should be. Again, though, that is why we need to come together as one race, and again, I feel that the best way for us to do this is to adopt the philosophy of *"Acceptance"* so that we can come together to solve these, and all the other, problems that our race faces today.

Now, again, remember when I spoke about people falsely accusing other people of crimes that they did not commit, and the fact that this needs to stop because there are already too many innocent people in prison? This is a problem that needs to stop, especially if we are ever going to trust each other enough to come together to solve our race's problems, especially this one. Well, here is a piece of Bible scripture that talks about that as well:

Proverbs 25:18 - *"Like a club or a sword or a sharp arrow is one who gives false testimony against a neighbor.".* New International Version (NIV)

The people who make false criminal allegations against an innocent person are like weapons that are being wielded against that person, because they can harm the person that they are making their false charges against just as surely, and in some instances as mortally, as any weapon can. Here is another piece of scripture that talks about making false allegations against an innocent person, one that gives us something additional to think about when this happens:

Exodus 23:1 - *"Do not spread false reports. Do not help a guilty person by being a malicious witness."* New International Version (NIV)

Always remember, when you make false criminal allegations against a person, not only are you harming the innocent person who you are making your false allegations against, but you could also be helping the person who was really guilty of committing the crime by helping them to remain free in order to continue to commit that, and other, crimes without being stopped and held responsible. Now, if making false accusations does not mean that much to you, then consider this. Heaven forbid that this would ever happen to you, but let us say, just as an example, you are raped one day. Then, for whatever reason (let us say, for the sake of argument, that you do not like your ex-partner), you decide to tell the police that it was your ex-partner who committed the rape against you (this does happen, especially if the breakup was particularly contentious). Then, because you falsely accused your ex of committing the rape, the real rapist remains free so that they can continue to commit even more rapes against other innocent people, people who would not have been raped if you had not falsely accused your ex-partner. Would it make a difference to you then?

Making a false criminal accusation is like throwing a rock into a pond. The ripples will spread affecting more and more people in a bad way. An example of that would be the one that I mentioned earlier in the Law chapter. Let us say that you find yourself falsely accused of sexual assault. Let us go further to say that, because you were falsely accused, you find yourself losing everything that you had worked your whole life for, especially your reputation, all because of having to defend yourself against these false accusations. You see, something like this does not just affect you if you are falsely accused of a crime like this (or any other crime for that matter). You could also lose (among other things) your family, your children (to social services, for example), your job, and maybe even your freedom while the charges are being adjudicated. This could happen all because someone decided that they wanted to make a false charge against you in order to get the things that they want (like the people who have filed false criminal sexual allegations just so that they can get things like money from victim's relief funds. Then, even if you do prove yourself to be innocent in a court of law, you will still face the stigma of being accused in the first place.

People will look at you like they are wary of you, like you are someone who cannot be trusted, and you may never have things fully return to normal for you.   All because someone falsely accused you of a sexual (or any other type, for that matter) crime for their own selfish reasons, with no regard of how much it affects you and those around you.   Now, in this instance, who is the *"guilty person"* that is being helped by someone spreading the *"false reports"*?   In this instance, it is the person who made the false accusation, because they made the false accusation knowing that you did not commit the crime in order to get what they wanted. This is why I say that anyone who knowingly makes a false accusation against someone (no matter who they are or what they are falsely accusing someone of doing) should be punished for filing false charges, like the law states that they should.

The bottom line is this.   False criminal allegations against innocent people needs to stop, because there are good people, everyday, who are having their lives absolutely destroyed by false allegations.   We need to do something to make it stop happening, even if that means that we need to make some hard decisions in order to stop them once and for all.   Hard decisions like having anyone, male or female, suffer punishment for making false criminal allegations, like the law says they are supposed to be punished.

Here is another piece of scripture to consider when talking about filing false charges against someone:

Exodus 23:7 - *"Have nothing to do with a false charge and do not put an innocent or honest person to death, for I will not acquit the guilty."*   New International Version (NIV)

329

A Visit to the City in the Light

Think about this for a moment, because we are not just talking about having an innocent person placed on death row because of false charges (which has happened too often). We are also talking about the way that a person's entire life can be destroyed by false accusations. Like I mentioned earlier, one of the biggest areas where this can destroy a person's life is if false sexual abuse charges are levied against someone. It can take a normal person who leads a normal life (who works a normal job, who has a normal family, who has a regular circle of friends, etc.) and it can literally destroy their entire world, and if that is not like putting an innocent person *"to death"*, then I do not know what is. They will never be the same again, and the entire world will never treat them the same way again either. It is literally like putting *"an innocent or honest person to death"*, all because the accuser who made the false allegation might have a hidden agenda which is causing them to make the false allegations against an *"innocent or honest person"* who did nothing wrong. It needs to stop if we are ever going to all come together through *"Acceptance"*, because again, how will we ever work together to solve our race's problems if we cannot even trust each other?

To continue, though, my favorite piece of scripture concerning not making false accusations or charges against an innocent person is this commandment found in The Ten Commandments that were given to Moses on Mount Sinai to deliver to the Israelites:

Exodus 20:16 - *"You shall not give false testimony against your neighbor."* New International Version (NIV)

How can it be any plainer that this? It is my firm belief that God does not make mistakes, that he is infallible in everything that he does (and before anyone says it, I do not believe that the platypus was a mistake.   More of an experiment than anything).   He knows that we are the ones who make mistakes, and as such, he gave us commandments to follow so that we could have the best chance to succeed as a race.   He loves us, and he wants us to succeed, and as such, he recognized just how much harm making false allegations against each other can cause to happen to our race.   Again, how can we trust each other enough to work together as a race in order to succeed if we are destroying each other by making false allegations against each other?   He wants us to be able to look at each other and say *'Yes, you are my brother/sister in the human race, and therefore, I will not try to harm you.   On the contrary, I will do everything in my power to show you that you can trust me to not cause you harm.   Therefore, I will not **"give false testimony"** against you in an attempt to destroy you and your life because we need to be able to work together in order to help our race succeed, and we can't trust each other enough to come together if we are trying to harm each other through false allegations'.*

Now, again, why did I just concentrate on allegations concerning sexual abuse where these scriptures are concerned?   I did this for two reasons.   The first is the fact that this seems to be a huge issue in today's world.   There are more and more people who are being accused of sex crimes currently, and while I would like to believe all women when they say this, I am also fully aware of the fact that there are women who are lying about these allegations as well.   We cannot believe all people when they make a criminal allegation, men and women alike.   That is why we have a justice system, and that is why the standard in a criminal court is supposed to be *'innocent until proven guilty'*, because having that standard is the way that we find out who is telling the truth when they make a criminal allegation, and more importantly, who is lying.   Therefore, as recent events have shown, we cannot believe all women who make these allegations.   Just because it is a woman who is making these types of allegations does not mean that they are being truthful. If we keep saying *'Because it is a woman who is making these types of allegations then it must be the truth.'*, then we are in big trouble. The sex of a person should not be the determining factor when deciding whether or not an accuser is telling the truth about a criminal allegation, rather, the facts of the case should be the determining factor. This is why we have a criminal justice system, and this is also why, again, the standard in any criminal court is supposed to be *'innocent until proven guilty'* and *'proven to be guilty beyond a reasonable doubt'* because people do lie about allegations.

The second reason is the fact that this is the one type of criminal allegation that can, and does, change and destroy the life of the person who the allegation is made against, and that is because of the social stigma that comes along with being accused of this type of crime. Again, it does not matter if you have had your day in court, it does not matter if you are found innocent, it does not matter if the court dismisses the charges with prejudice. If you are accused of a sex crime, then people will never treat you the same way again. They will never trust you again, they will treat you like you are a bad person, and like I said earlier, you will lose a lot, even if you are innocent. All because of the nature of this type of accusation.

This is why I honestly believe, with all my heart, that all people who are proven to have lied about this type of allegation should face criminal prosecution. If we do not, then we are basically telling the people who are making false criminal accusations that it is ok for people to lie about criminal allegations because nothing will happen to them if they do lie. If it is proven that someone made a false criminal allegation against someone, then they should be punished, otherwise more and more innocent people will have their lives ruined by false criminal allegations, and we will never see the end of it.

Tough choices are going to have to be made if we are ever going to stop false criminal allegations from happening, and I believe that this is one of them.   After all, there are laws that state that it is illegal to file false charges.   So why aren't we enforcing them where everyone is concerned?   Like I said in an earlier chapter, the day that we forget our history is the day that we are doomed to repeat it.   So why is it that we seem to have forgotten what happened during the *'Salem Witch Trials'* in America, and during the *'Spanish Inquisition'* for that matter?

True, people are not being hanged and burned at the stake if they have a false criminal allegation made against them today, like they were during the *'Salem Witch Trials'*, and they are not being tortured to death like they were during the *'Spanish Inquisition'*. However, if having your entire world ruined because of a false criminal allegation of a sexual nature is not a type of death, then I do not know what is, because once an allegation of this type is made against you, your chance at having a normal life will virtually be gone, and nothing will ever be the same way for you again. People will never trust you again, and you will be treated like a bad person for the rest of your life.

Look, it is really simple.   Do not lie about people where crimes are concerned, and if you do, then you deserve to be punished, just like the person who you falsely accused of a crime would have been punished if they had actually committed the crime you falsely accused them of.

Chapter Seven

Remember when I talked about being faithful to our beliefs,

no matter what they are?   I believe that we should do so with
something like this in mind:

Revelation 2:10 - *"Do not be afraid of what you are about to suffer.
I tell you, **the devil will put some of you in prison to test you**, and
you will suffer persecution for ten days.   **Be faithful, even to the
point of death**, and I will give you life as your victor's crown."*
New International Version (NIV)

You see, this passage talks about how Jesus had predicted
further suffering for the church at Smyrna, and how he had predicted
that believers would encounter many sufferings, like imprisonment
and even death.   Therefore, we should hold our own personal
beliefs faithfully, and I believe that this should apply to whatever
our beliefs are, because there are those who will test you, and hate
you for your beliefs.   However, if we are faithful to our beliefs
(even if they are different than what my belief is) then you will be
ok.   It is not our place to judge each other for our beliefs.   It should
be our place to live our lives the way that we want to (as long as our
beliefs do not cause, or calls to cause, harm to others) instead of the
way that others want us to.   Then, after that, it is my firm belief that
God will judge all of us at the end of our time here on Earth.   How
do you believe?   I can say this.   Whatever you believe, I will
accept you.   Will you accept me?

Now, where sharing our beliefs with someone else is
concerned, even with someone who does not believe in God and our
Lord and Savior Jesus Christ, this is a good passage to keep in mind
while doing it:

1 Peter 3:15 - *"But in your hearts revere Christ as Lord.   **Always
be prepared to give an answer to everyone who asks you to give a
reason for the hope that you have.   But do this with gentleness**"*

and respect". New International Version (NIV)

Therefore, when talking to others about your beliefs and their beliefs, always remember to do it with *"gentleness and respect"*, with love and compassion by utilizing the philosophy of *"Acceptance"*, because everyone should be respected for their beliefs, again, as long as their beliefs do not cause, or calls to cause, physical harm to anyone else. Nothing but hate will come from us fighting over our beliefs, and that is why, if we really want to all come together in peace so that we can work together to advance our race into tomorrow by utilizing *"Acceptance"*, then we need to be able to come together by stopping all the fighting over our beliefs.

Now, where the freedom for us to live our lives the way that we want to, and more specifically, where religious freedom is concerned, especially concerning the fact that we should be supportive of one another's right to live our lives the way that we want to, keep these passages in mind:

Galatians 5:13 - *"You, my brothers and sisters, **were called to be free**. But **do not use your freedom to indulge the flesh;** rather, **serve one another humbly in love"**.* New International Version (NIV)

Like this says, we should have the freedom to live our lives the way that we want to, as long as we do so *"humbly in love"*. However, if we want to live our lives in a way that causes, or calls to cause, harm to others, then we should not be allowed to have the freedom to do that. How can we *"serve one another humbly in love"* if we are trying to cause harm to others? For that matter, how can we come together in *"Acceptance"* if we are trying to use our freedom to cause harm to others?

Galatians 5:1 - *"It is for freedom that Christ has set us free. Stand firm, then, and do not let yourselves be burdened again by a yoke of slavery."* New International Version (NIV)

　　We should strive to ensure that everyone has the freedom to live their lives the way that they want to without being burdened by *"a yoke"* that keeps us from being free to live our lives, and that is especially true where religious freedom is concerned, again, as long as that means that we are not trying to use our freedom to cause harm to others.

2 Corinthians 3:17 - *"Now the Lord is the Spirit, and where the Spirit of the Lord is, there is liberty."*. New International Version (NIV)

John 8:36 - *"So if the Son sets you free, you will be free indeed."*. New International Version (NIV)

Psalms 119:45 - *"I will walk about in freedom, for I have sought out your precepts"*. New International Version (NIV)

　　What these passages say to me is that we should all be free to seek the freedom, and the religious freedom, that we want, and to be able to do so with *"liberty"*, no matter where we live, because that is the freedom that the Bible says that we should all have. In addition, that freedom should be protected by *"the Spirit of the Lord"*, as in, protected with the love and peace of the Lord for all of us. What better way to do that, and ensure that, than by practicing *"Acceptance"*.

Chapter Eight

　　Remember when I talked about people not being better than

other people just because of the job that they do and the like? Well, here are some passages that talk about humility when we think that we are a better person just because of what we do for a living, etc., instead of being based on our actions proving that we are a good person. You see, we prove that we are a good person through our actions, especially our actions towards others, like these passages state:

Proverbs 22:4 - *"Humility is the fear of the Lord; **its wages are riches and honor and life**".* New International Version (NIV)

Romans 12:3 - *"For by the grace given me I say to every one of you: **Do not think of yourself more highly than you ought**, but rather **think of yourself with sober judgment**, in accordance with the faith God has distributed to each of you".* New International Version (NIV)

Proverbs 16:18 - *"**Pride goes before destruction, a haughty spirit before a fall.**".* New International Version (NIV)

Therefore, we should not think that we are better than anyone else because of what we do for a living and the like. We should think of ourselves with *"humility"*, because it is our actions that make us a good person, not our *"pride"* in what we do for a living, or anything else that is superficial.

Now, when I mentioned how we should not be glorifying war, because of the horrors that come with war, here is something to consider:

Hosea 4:2 - *"There is only cursing, lying and murder, stealing and adultery; they break all bounds, and **bloodshed follows bloodshed**".* New International Version (NIV)

A Visit to the City in the Light

So, what is more important, glorifying war, or loving peace? You see, when we glorify war, then it truly becomes a situation where *"bloodshed follows bloodshed"* when it actually happens, and if it does happen, it could continue until we are all destroyed, especially in today's world where many countries have weapons like nuclear warheads (and if you think that this thought is extreme, then consider the fact that all it will take is one country using one nuclear weapon for it to start, and with some countries continually fighting others, especially for religious reasons, someone could make the decision to go for the *'win'* by firing one device, especially if they think that they are going to lose their war).   How are we ever going to come together in peace and love through *"Acceptance"* if what we do is glorify something as hateful and destructive as war?

Now, when I was talking about helping others, especially to make a living by doing things like giving them tips, consider this:

Romans 12:6-8 - *(6) "We have different gifts, according to the grace given to each of us. If your gift is prophesying, then prophesy in accordance with your faith; (7) if it is serving, then serve; if it is teaching, then teach; (8) if it is to encourage, then give encouragement; **if it is giving, then give generously;** if it is to lead, do it diligently; **if it is to show mercy, do it cheerfully**."*. New International Version (NIV)

So, remember, if you have the opportunity to share something like money with someone who is working a lower paying job by giving them something like a tip, then do so *"generously"*, and show your *"mercy"* to them *"cheerfully"*.   Everyone deserves to be able to survive, and thrive, no matter what job they are doing for a living.

A Journey There.......and Back Again with a Message of Hope

Chapter Nine

Where treating others equally is concerned, especially when talking about respecting each other for the way that we want to live our lives (as long as the way that we want to live our lives does not include harming others), this piece of scripture, and the others that are like it, is pretty self-explanatory:

Luke 6:31 - *"Do to others as you would have them do to you"*. New International Version (NIV)

If you want to be treated equally and respected without being discriminated against or harmed in any way, then treat others the same way.   It is only fair, and it will be the only way that things will ever truly be equal.

Now, if someone says *"Well, we were discriminated against for a long time, so we should be able to now discriminate against those who discriminated against us (as in, taking vengeance against them)."*, consider this:

Romans 12:19 - *"**Do not take revenge**, my dear friends, but leave room for God's wrath, for it is written: **"it is mine to avenge; I will repay"**, says the Lord"*. New International Version (NIV)

Leviticus 19:18 - *"**Do not seek revenge or bear a grudge against anyone** among your people, but **love your neighbor as yourself**. I am the Lord"*. New International Version (NIV)

So, if you truly do want a world without discrimination, and a world where we have true equality, then hold these scriptures near to your heart.   Always remember, if we seek retribution by means of discriminating against those who have discriminated against us in the past, then we are no better than the people who discriminated against us. We should strive to set the example by being the example, not the problem. We should strive to prove that we are better than those who used discrimination in the past, and we can do that by utilizing forgiveness.

Chapter Ten

Ok, now I know that while this chapter was basically a chance to see if you could accept me no matter how I believed, and while I did say that some of what I wrote in this chapter was true, while other things were, well, *'fantasized'*, let me give you this food for thought the next time you are trying to decide if you can accept someone:

Matthew 7:2 - *"For **in the same way you judge others, you will be judged**, and with the measure you use, it will be measured to you."* New International Version (NIV)

So please, before you judge others, and in doing so, possibly make the decision that you cannot accept them, even though their beliefs do not cause harm to anyone, think of this passage. It is based on bringing us all together in peace and love instead of having us judge each other wrongly just because we do not agree with others and the way that they believe and want to live their lives.

Chapter Eleven

Remember when I said that my Lord and Savior Jesus Christ was our *'student/teacher'*, well, this piece of scripture pretty much says it all:

John 8:28-29 - *"So Jesus said, 'When you have lifted up the Son of*

A Journey There.......and Back Again with a Message of Hope

*Man, then you will know that I am he and that **I do nothing on my own but speak just what the Father has taught me.** The one who sent me is with me; he has not left me alone, for **I always do what pleases him'**".* New International Version (NIV)

Like this says, Jesus did not speak or teach on his own. Every single thing that he taught to us came from *"what the Father"* taught him. It came from God, and Jesus taught what God told him to teach to the world in the hopes of saving us all.

So, there it is. The philosophy of *"Acceptance"* backed up by Bible scripture. Now, having shared these wonderful scriptures with you, my brothers and sisters in our race, I now have a challenge for you. Call it a *'mission'*, or a *'task'*, or whatever, just as long as you are willing to try it. Here it is. I want you to think about other areas in your own personal life that you may have questions about, areas that you want to check to see if they are mentioned in God's plan for all of us in the Bible. In order to be able to apply them to your own life and the plan of *"Acceptance"*, and to bringing us all together with peace and love. Then, I want you to go out and get a Bible (you can find them for free everywhere, at churches, online, etc.), and I want you to see if you can find more scriptures like the ones that I shared in this chapter that either support you and how you live your life and how you believe, or that support the philosophy of *"Acceptance"*. Then, I want you to go through your copy of the Bible and mark the pages (that the passages you found are on) with *'sticky notes'*. The passages that apply to you and your life the most. Then I want you to keep that copy of your Bible where you can access it when you need it the most (like next to your bedside, or maybe in a desk, or somewhere else where you can access it quickly and when you truly need it the most). Times like when you have had a bad day, and you need some inspiration, or maybe even just some reassurance that the Bible talks about things

A Visit to the City in the Light

in your own personal life.   Things that support you and being
accepted for the way that you have chosen to live your life.   You
would be amazed at just how many things you can learn about
bringing our world together in peace and love in the Bible.

Now, again, I am not trying to convert anyone to
Christianity, although it would be nice to know that I had a hand in
bringing someone closer to God, closer to my Lord and Savior Jesus
Christ, and closer to God's plan for all of us.   If all I do, though, by
sharing the philosophy of *"Acceptance"* with everyone is spread the
word that I was given to my brothers and sisters in our race in order
to try and bring us all together in peace, then I will be happy.   In
addition, if I am able to convince all of you, my brothers and sisters,
to come together with love, and peace, and cooperation through
"Acceptance", then I will be happy with that as well, because I truly
do want our race to stop all the fighting, war, and hate, so that we
can evolve and advance into a better tomorrow.   I truly do believe
that we should all be able to live our lives the way that we want to,
and most importantly, that we should all be able to believe any way
that we choose to, as long as we never cause harm to anyone.
Therefore, if you agree with the philosophy of *"Acceptance"*, and
you like the way it shows how we can all come together in peace
and love, then again, let me ask you a question.   Does it really
matter where the plan came from, even if you believe differently
than I do concerning religion?   Isn't bringing our race together in
peace and love the ultimate goal for all of us?

Now, why am I advising everyone to get a physical copy of
the Bible, and not just look scripture up on the internet?   Well, true,
you could look Bible passages up online, but I have always found
that, if I have an actual copy of the Bible with me where I can access
it quickly when I need it, then it means more to me to actually have
'sticky notes' on the pages marking the passages that apply to me

342

and my life, because on those sticky notes I can write personalized notes that help me to understand just how those Bible passages apply to me and my personal life (by putting it in my own words on those notes). It makes the passages more personal to me. If I tried to do that with, say, a tablet, or a computer, or a smart phone, then I would have a pile of sticky notes with an electronic device somewhere underneath, and instead of being able to read the passages with the personalized notes attached, I would never remember just what passages applied to the individual sticky notes, and on what pages those passages were on. In addition, it is just easier to turn to the page with the passage that the sticky note is on (and read it along with the note) than it is to try and find a passage online and then match it up with the note that applies to it because, again, there would be a pile of them to go through, and that would just lead to frustration instead of personal revelation.

Now, if you don't want to pick up a free Bible and keep it with you where you live because you may be afraid that those around you, like your partner, or friends, or family members, would ridicule you because you have an actual copy of the Bible with you, then I suppose that another way to do it would be to keep a diary, and then look passages up online to go with the entries in your diary. Let me ask you a question, though. If you are afraid that people would ridicule you, then consider this. Do those people really love you, or even care about you for that matter? Do they genuinely care about bringing our race together through love, cooperation, and caring, especially if they are just interested in ridiculing you for wanting to learn about a plan that would bring us all together? If they really do love you, and they really do care about you and your wants and needs, then they will care enough about you to respect you for wanting to learn for yourself how God's plan can bring us together, and they will care about your happiness in wanting to learn a way to bring us all together. Again, to repeat, these scriptures say

A Visit to the City in the Light

it all, starting with this one:

Luke 6:31 - *"Do to others as you would have them do to you"*.
New International Version (NIV)

     If your friends, partner, or family ridicule you, then they do not care about you or respect you, and they do not care about making you happy.   I mean, how can they if they do not care about what you want, and what is making you happy?

1 Peter 3:15 - *"But in your hearts revere Christ as Lord. **Always be prepared to give an answer to everyone who asks you to give a reason for the hope that you have. But do this with gentleness and respect"***. New International Version (NIV)

     Be a good person if people ridicule you for wanting to learn about a plan to bring us all together by having a Bible with you. Also, defend your reasons for wanting to bring us all together with love and peace, but be sure to set the example as defined by the philosophy of *"Acceptance"* by defending your reasons with ***"gentleness and respect"***.

Proverbs 18:15 - *"**The heart of the discerning acquires knowledge**, for **the ears of the wise seek it out"***. New International Version (NIV)

     Again, learning is not just limited to learning things like an occupation.   All learning is good and learning how to bring our race together with peace and love is too important to ignore, even if others want to ridicule you for wanting to learn it from the Bible.

Ephesians 5:28 - *"In the same way, **husbands ought to love their wives as their own bodies**.   He who loves his wife loves himself."*.

A Journey There.......and Back Again with a Message of Hope

New International Version (NIV)

Ephesians 5:22 - *"Wives, submit yourselves to your own husbands as you do to the Lord."*. New International Version (NIV)

Ephesians 5:33 - *"However, each one of you also **must love his wife as he loves himself**, and **the wife must respect her husband**."*. New International Version (NIV)

While these passages refer more directly to our relationship with a romantic partner, they also apply to all relationships in the fact that, if we love those around us, to include our brothers and sisters in our race and our family members, then we should love them the way that we love ourselves. Now, just as importantly, if they really do love us, then they should love us in the same way as well by not ridiculing us for doing something that makes us happy, like learning how to bring us all together with peace and love from the Bible.

So again, my brothers and sisters, my challenge to you is to go out, find a Bible, and learn how the passages in it apply to you personally, and just as importantly, applies to bringing us all together in order to stop all the hate through love, caring, respect, and of course, *"Acceptance"*.

Chapter Twelve
Time to Get to Work

"You got a lot of work to do kid, and we've got to go." - My Dad, in front of the City.

This was one of the last things that my dad said to me just before he went back into the city. I believe that he said this to me because he knew what the man standing in front of the city was going to tell me to do. He knew that, for our race to advance into the future peacefully, we would need to get to work now to make it happen. So, at this point I would like to talk about putting the plan of *"Acceptance"* into action. It will not be easy, and it will not happen overnight. However, if we start now by accepting it and practicing it, eventually it will happen for all of us.

So, now that we have talked about putting *"Acceptance"* into practice in our own lives and relationships, let us talk about how we can all get together to put it to work. I want to separate this chapter into sections, because I want to give some of my suggestions showing how we can use *"Acceptance"* to make our world a better place, and to fix some of the problems that we face daily. Now, I know that there may be more areas than the ones that I am about to mention, and I am sure that you will think up some of those yourself. That is what I am hoping that you will do, because when we all start working together to come up with new ideas to solve our world's problems, then we are all accepting the responsibility to make our world a better place, and that is one of the main ideas behind *"Acceptance"*. Having all of us accept the responsibility to come together in order to come up with ideas to solve our problems, because if we do not accept that responsibility, then who will?

So here are some of my ideas on how we can use

A Visit to the City in the Light

"Acceptance" to fix some of our world's most pressing problems. I know that there may be ideas here that you love, and there may be other ideas that you feel could be better, and there may be some that you do not agree with at all. However, again, that is the whole idea behind *"Acceptance"*. Getting all of us talking about how we can put a game plan together to solve our problems, and then actually coming together without fighting so that we can solve them. So that we can finally come together in peace in order to advance us into a better tomorrow.

<u>Stopping Hatred</u>

Ok, there are a lot of things that I want to cover in this one section, and I will try and tackle all the ones that I can think of. Let us start with *"Racism"* and *"Bigotry"*, since this is a bigger problem than a lot of people want to admit. I never really understood how anyone who calls themselves a good person can say that they hate people of their own race (The Human Race) just for being alive, and for trying to live their lives the way that they want to. However, there it is, people do, and it has caused unspeakable violence in our history. There are a lot of people who hate each other under the guise of *'They are different than me, they look and talk differently than I do, and therefore, they are inferior to me, and I hate them'*. We truly need to stop thinking about ourselves as being different races, because we are all the same race, and once we accept this, and I mean truly accept this in our hearts, then we will realize that *"Racism"* and *"Bigotry"* cannot exist. I mean, how can we say that we hate other people of a different race if we are all the same race (now, I do understand that there are going to be scientists out there who will be crying in their pillows while saying that *'We are all the same species, not the same race!'*. However, that is a big part of the problem, because we keep thinking that we are different, instead of changing the way that we think so that we start thinking that we

348

are all the same.   That is what *"Acceptance"* is all about, though. Changing the way that we think about each other so that we stop thinking that we are different and start thinking that we are all the same race so that we can finally accept each other).

Now, I understand that this leads to people saying things like *'Well then, I hate them because they are a different nationality than me, and/or they look differently than me, and/or they talk differently than me, and that makes them inferior to me.'*, but this is the same as I said before.   We are all the same race, so how can people hate others because they are different than us?   True, they may look differently, and they may talk differently, but they are not different where race is concerned, at least in my opinion.   Therefore, rather than saying *'They are different than me, and therefore I hate them.'*, what we should be saying is *'They are different than me, but because we are members of The Human Race, I want to learn about them, and how they live their lives.'*.   I mean, isn't that what love for our race is all about?   Not only that but think about how much we can learn about our race and how people from different areas live their lives by just accepting them.   I mean, we all say that we want to learn and be educated about our world, right?   What better way to do it than by accepting them and truly talking to people from other parts of our world?

In my travels, for example, I wanted to learn about how other people cook their meals, and what they eat in general.   The things that I learned were astonishing, and I picked up some great recipes along the way.   Another thing that I wanted to learn about was history.   After all, there are some incredibly great historic places around the globe that are still standing today.   My favorites are the many ancient castles that are still standing in parts of our world.   I mean, it is one thing to read about these castles, but to really see them in person is a very inspiring experience indeed.

349

A Visit to the City in the Light

Now, I understand that not everyone can afford to travel, because it is expensive, but there are other ways to do this that are a lot less expensive, we just need to use our imaginations in order find them. Joining the military is one way. Even though there are some people would not consider joining the military, it is a great way to see many areas of the world. Another way is to make a friend in another country, and then find inexpensive ways to travel to where they live. There are ways to do this. One used to be to travel on *'standby'*. In other words, you basically lived in an airport until someone canceled their reservation, and then you got their seat. It cost a lot less because the airlines said to themselves *"Some money for the seat is better than no money."*, and a lot of times you could get those seats for a big discount. Once there, you could stay with the friends that you made online, and what better way to learn about history than to not only be in a country where history comes alive, but to also be able to talk to the people who live there, because they will know these places better than anyone else. In addition, I have learned that people who live in other countries that you want to travel to know of *'hidden secrets'*, like places that are not advertised to the normal traveler, and seeing those places are worth whatever you have to go through to see them.

Another way to travel is to do volunteer work, maybe through a church or another organization. There are churches who send their members to other countries to perform *'missions'* in order to spread the word of God and our Lord and Savior Jesus Christ, and while their members are doing that, they get a great opportunity to experience other countries and other cultures for themselves while also making friendships that can last a lifetime. There are other NGOs (Non-Governmental Organizations) that send people to other countries as well in order to help the people who live there by doing everything from building schools to hospitals. Just do a search online. I am sure that you can find an organization that could use your help, and it will give you an opportunity to travel to other countries where you can help your brothers and sisters in our race in many ways.

There are other ways to make friends from other countries as well. We live in a wonderful age, because for the first time in human history we can make unlimited friends in other countries, and learn all about how they live their lives, and it is thanks to the internet. Now we can sit in the comfort of our homes and really talk to people halfway around the world. We can learn about how they live their lives, what they eat, what they do at their jobs, what they do for fun, and we can do this while really seeing them thanks to video chat services. Therefore, instead of just saying *'I wish that I could go there and see how other people live.'*, now we can say *'I think that I will make a friend in (insert country name here) and learn how they live their lives directly from them.'*. Look, in order to make *"Acceptance"* work, and bring our race together using unity based on peace and love, we need to be able to contact other people around the world and really get to know them. We need to let them know that we want to have them in our lives, and what better way to do that than to make as many friends as possible all around the world utilizing the internet? Now, you will want to check with the legal side of this (again, anytime there is a legal question, talk to an attorney), because there are some countries that our individual governments do not want us to contact due to political restraints, but again, the end result (making friends from around the world in order to practice *"Acceptance"*) is worth whatever trouble you have to go through (like getting permission from the Consulates or State Departments, for example) in order to make *"Acceptance"* a world-wide reality for everyone in our race.

Now, if you do make friends in other countries via the internet, then unfortunately, I need to give you a warning as well.

351

A Visit to the City in the Light

You see, there are those who will try and befriend you just so that they can do things like steal your personal information, or just so they can try and take advantage of you by doing things like scamming you out of money, or if you are a minor, they may try to talk you into doing something like running away from home in order to be with them.   There are even those who will try and tell you that they want you to come and visit them without anyone coming with you, and then if you do go alone, they might try and do something horrible like sell you into sex slavery.   It is just a tragic fact in today's world, and it can really cause you harm.   However, if you do things carefully, like going with a group of friends that can protect you (because, after all, there really is safety in numbers), and by carefully checking out the people who want you to come to visit them, then you should be ok.   Also, be sure to keep in contact with your family back home.   The bottom line here is this.   Be careful by being safe.   If you do these things (and take every additional precaution available to you, like going with an official organization or church) to safeguard yourself, then it could be a life changing experience, one that you will remember and cherish always.   So, again, if you do make a friend in another country via the internet, then be careful by taking precautions.   Do not give them your personal information and be wary if they suddenly start asking you for things like money, or if they ask you to come alone for any reason (and be sure that you check to make sure that you are not going to a country where rampant violence is taking place.   Again, be careful by being safe).

Now, as I said earlier, another area of hate that we need to deal with is bullying.   Again, though, if we would all take the time to just be a hero, instead of only idolizing them, then we could really make a difference where this is concerned.   Believe me, it can, and does, make a difference, especially in the life of the person who is being bullied.   What can we do about the law catching up with cyber-bullying though? It is a real problem, especially in today's world. In the past, people could not bully other people unless they were there in person. Now it is so easy for bullies to pick on other people from the comfort of their own home thanks to the internet (does the term *'internet troll'* ring any bells?). My question is this, though. When is the law going to catch up with internet crimes? I say that because I feel strongly that all bullying should be a crime, including internet (or cyber) bullying, because it can destroy a person's life, and it should never happen to anyone.

Why is it that a lot of people in today's world feel the need to say horrible things about other people on the internet? True, when politicians and celebrities become famous, they are basically opening themselves up for others to comment on them, but where do we draw the line? Here is an example of where I think that the line should be drawn, see if you agree. Let's say that a politician does something that people do not agree with. Now, I understand that people want to let their feelings known about what they did not like concerning what a politician did politically, but we should never make comments that could be construed as a call for violence against the politician. Like I mentioned earlier in this book, saying that you do not agree with what Politician "A" did or said is one thing, however, when Politician "B" suggests that Politician "A" should be assassinated (or if anyone says it, for that matter), that is crossing the line. We should never allow anyone to suggest that someone else should be caused harm, ever.

Like I mentioned earlier in this book, expressing our opinion is one thing, but suggesting that someone be harmed or attacked is an entirely different situation, and it should never be allowed or tolerated. This is another area where I think that the law needs to be updated. Hate speech (or speech in general) alone is not violence. Hate speech (or any speech) that truly calls for violence

353

to be committed against someone (or causes harm to happen to anyone) is unacceptable, because it can cause someone to be hurt, or even killed. It is not just politicians threatening other politicians with physical violence, though, it is also normal people threatening other normal people as well, especially where young people are concerned. It is just too easy for bullies to threaten other people on the internet in today's world, and it can have tragic results.

That is why I feel that there needs to be new laws concerning cyber-bullying, and I think that these laws really need to be stricter than any law concerning face to face bullying, because of how easy it is for cyber-bullying to exist in today's technological world. The bottom line is this. In order to make bullies think twice about being bullies, the law needs to take action in order to stop bullying in its entirety. Now, I can just hear people out there saying things like *'Well, there goes the right to free speech.'*, but let me ask you this. If it were someone that you cared about (like your mother, sister, daughter, or anyone else that you love) who was being bullied, you would want to take action, right? You would want something done about it, right? There are laws on the books currently that say that it is a crime to threaten someone with bodily harm, or to stalk someone, or to harass someone. So why is it ok to do these same things to someone on the internet? Why would anyone even suggest that cyber-bullying should ever be ok, or protected by Freedom of Speech? Harassment is harassment, threats are threats, and bullying is bullying. It should all be stopped if we are ever going to end bullying once and for all. Thanks to the internet, it has become too easy for bullies to get away with harassing people. We need to put a stop to it once and for all, and that means tougher laws that address all forms of bullying.

So, how do we do it? Well, I have a suggestion. You may not agree with it, but at least it is a suggestion. If you can come up with a better one, then please do, because that is what *"Acceptance"* is all about. Keeping that in mind, see if you agree with my suggestion. Question - how do we catch these cyber bullies? Well, you know what they say, once it is on the internet, then it is there forever. Therefore, if it takes watchdog groups, then so be it. Now, what do we do about protecting everyone's right to privacy where this is concerned (because we do not want to have our governments reviewing all of our posts. We should all have some privacy)? Well, how about this. How about we all accept the responsibility to stop this type of bullying by reporting it when it happens? It would be easy because, if someone is being bullied, then they (or others) should be the ones who report it. Then, instead of having watchdog groups reviewing all of our posts, they can just review the ones that have been reported as bullying. Now, just like the laws concerning false allegations, if people try to take advantage of the new laws by saying that someone is bullying them when they are not, then the people who made the false report should be held accountable for their actions as well. Also, to repeat, I am not talking about posts where people express their disapproval for someone's actions. What I am talking about are the posts where there are actual threats of physical harm, or the ones that call for people to commit acts of violence against other people, or even to themselves (by telling them things like they should commit suicide, for example, because it can send someone over the edge).[19]

Is it a perfect solution? Probably not. Here is the thing, though. We need to accept the responsibility to put an end to all types of bullying once and for all, because it can destroy a person's life (remember the girl that I spoke about? If ruining a person by posting a sex tape of them on the internet, without their permission, is not a type of bullying, then I do not know what is). Well, that is my suggestion. I know that it is not perfect, but at least it is a start, and I know that there are a lot of very smart people out there who

355

could come up with better solutions.   So please, come up with your own suggestions and write them down.   The bottom line is this. We need to put an end to bullying before any other good people are harmed by a bully.

Now, back to the example that I was using before (concerning posts on the internet about celebrities and politicians), and where comments cross the line in my opinion.   Making comments about something that a politician (or celebrity) did or said is one thing, and suggesting that violence happen to that person truly crosses the line in my book, but another area that crosses the line is when people start making bad personal comments about them as a person, or as some people are calling it, *'publicly shaming'* them in a way that has nothing to do with something that they said or did and is meant to just attack them personally.   To me, this is the same as being a bully to them.   Disagreeing with what they said or did is one thing, and we should have the right to express our opinion about those things.   Attacking them personally, however, takes it from being critical of what they said or did and turns it into a situation that becomes bullying, and it can cause harm to come to someone who is their target.   Where it becomes a much worse problem is where the bullies not only attack the person that they are making the comment about, but when they also attack their family members as well, like their partner, or maybe their children.   Did **they** do something to earn a personal attack?   If the only thing that they did is the fact that they are married to a politician (or another public figure) that did or said something that you did not agree with, then why should they be attacked?   In a lot of cases, these attacks are very personal, and include things like *'That person is ugly'* or *'That person is fat'* or whatever else the bully can come up with in order to just attack a person for no reason.   It is wrong, it should not happen, and it should not be tolerated because it is bullying, pure and simple.

356

A Journey There.......and Back Again with a Message of Hope

Look, the bottom line is this. We need to put a stop to bullying in all forms, and that is why I feel strongly that the law needs to step in and get up to date where the internet is concerned. Until it does, then bullying will never stop, and if we are ever going to start caring about each other and finally come together as a race, then we need to put a stop to bullying once and for all. We are the ones who can do it, as long as we are truly ready to do whatever it takes to end bullying forever.

Now, while we are talking about stopping hate in all forms, let me go even further on the topic I was talking about, where hate speech, especially on the internet, is concerned. Now, I do realize that not all hate speech causes violence, some of it is just ugly and sickening. However, there is hate speech that does cross the line, like I said previously, because it calls for violence to be committed against people. In addition, hate speech does not just involve ugly words, some of it suggests that it is ok to for people to do some ugly things to other people, mainly because of what it encourages to happen to people, especially to women. What do we do about this? Well, this is another area where I truly feel that the law needs to catch up with technology, because this type of hate is really becoming a problem as well. Want a prime example? Well, how about this.

Question - what is one of the biggest problems that we, as a race, face today? Well, one of the biggest problems that I see in today's world is the problem of women being taken advantage of sexually. This happens for a lot of reasons, but in my mind, one of the biggest reasons that it is happening is because of a lot of boy's attitudes towards women (and again, I do not think of males who take advantage of women sexually as men because a real man values the people around him, especially women, and that is why any man who would take advantage of a woman sexually is a boy in my

357

A Visit to the City in the Light

book).   They do not look at women as people who are intelligent individuals and worthy of the same respect that they want.   On the contrary, they look at women like they are someone that they can use to satisfy their needs, in this case, their sexual needs and their need to dominate someone.   Now, where do these boys get these attitudes?   Well, one of the places that I see promoting these hateful attitudes towards women is on the internet, and more specifically, on pornography sites.   Hear me out on this, because I really feel that there are some truly scary videos out there that promote hate and violence towards women, and some of the worst that I have found are located on pornography sites.   Also, I am not talking about pornography sites in general, what I am talking about are the ones that I am about to mention here because they, and the attitudes that they promote, are absolutely horrifying in my opinion.

Anyway, let me give you a few examples of why I feel that some of the worst hate speech videos (in particular videos that promote hateful attitudes against women) are found on pornography sites (and just to be clear, like I said earlier, I am most attracted to a women who exhibits what I call *'confident feminine intelligence'*, as in, a woman who is proud of her femininity while displaying her intelligence by confidently talking to me about her plans to achieve her goals and dreams and, more importantly, the world around us, while also educating me on things that I might not know about.   I say that because, even though there are some people who like to think that they know everything, no one knows everything, and it is exciting to me when anyone teaches me about something that I do not know about.   Like I said, if a woman can stand beside me and defend me when I am right or stand toe to toe to me while explaining to me why I am wrong without fighting or name calling or starts a conversation with me by saying something like *"Did you know......."* or *"Guess what I learned today?"*, then she has my complete undivided attention, so pornography sites hold little interest to me). Now, again, I am not saying that all pornography videos promote hate towards women, because a lot of these videos are made voluntarily by the women who star in them, and they do not depict or promote violence against women. However, let me give you a few of examples of when I think that these videos do promote hate and violence against women, and thereby, go too far. Let us take a look at what I am talking about through these following examples.

Let us say that we have a boy who we will call **"Boy A"** and let us say that he spends most of his evenings at home because he is never successful at attracting, or having a relationship with, a woman. Therefore, he has a low opinion of women, because he feels that they are the ones who are responsible for the lack of intimacy in his social life (these boys do exist in today's world. They consider themselves *'involuntarily celibate'* because they have a hard time getting relationships with women). So, instead of assessing himself to see how he can become more attractive to women, he becomes bitter and angry towards all women in general. Then, one day, he looks at a pornography site, and instead of seeing people just engaged in sex, he sees videos that depict violence against women, or that promote the idea that women are nothing more than just property to be taken advantage of sexually (now, I do understand that there are people who are attracted to the idea of Bondage in sex, but I am not talking about that, as I will illustrate). Then, because of his rising hatred towards women, he starts to think to himself *'Gee, I wonder how I can take advantage of women for my sexual needs?'*.

So, then boy "A", who let's say is the manager at the company he works for, decides that he is going to try and take advantage of one of his co-workers by letting her know that, if she wants to keep her job, then she needs to go out with him and have a sexual relationship with him. Or worse yet, let us say that he decides that he is just going to attack a woman and rape her in order to get what he wants, and then he makes the horrific decision that, if he has to kill her afterwards so that she won't tell anyone about what he did to her, then so be it, because all women are responsible for his lack of a sexual relationship, and they *'have it coming'* to him. In his mind, it is just like the videos that he saw on the pornography sites that he was looking at, and so he thinks that it is ok, because women are the cause of his problems, and they *'deserve to be punished'* for not wanting to have anything to do with him. Think that this is an extreme example, and that pornography videos of this type do not exist? Well, consider this.

Right now, on pornography web sites, there are videos that depict women being tortured, and beaten, and strangled, and shot, and stabbed, and hung, and killed in many other ways, after the killer has raped her of course (and in some of these videos, the killer rapes his victim while he is killing her).[20] Even worse, in some of these videos, the woman who is the victim is raped after she is killed (now, I do realize that these videos proclaim themselves to be fake, but still, at what point did we decide, as a race, that raping and then killing a woman is a turn on?). How is this a turn on, especially when, in a lot of these videos, the woman who is being raped and killed is being portrayed as the killer's daughter, or as a babysitter, or as some other type of young woman? In the videos that I saw portraying this, the killers are all men, and they are the ones who are making these videos. However, let me tell you about another example of videos that promote hate against women, only this time made by both women and men.

Again, what is another reason that boys are attacking women and taking advantage of them? In my mind, they are doing it because they feel that women belong to them, and therefore women, in their minds, are nothing more than just property to be controlled and used sexually. Here is an example. Right now, again on pornography sites, there are videos, made by men and women, that state that women belong to men (and I am not talking about BDSM or "Submissive" videos. I am talking about videos that just say that women belong to men with no BDSM involved. Also, these videos say that only women of a certain skin color belong to men, but since I practice *"Acceptance"*, I refuse to say what skin color, or what skin color the men are who are saying this). Now, let me tell you all the reasons that these videos bothered me, and then let me tell you my idea for stopping things like this.

First, the last time I checked, no one belongs to anyone because slavery was abolished a long time ago. Second, this is another type of speech that we need to put an end to if we are ever going to advance as a race, because like I said before, it should never be white men, and white women, and black men, and black women, or any other skin color for that matter (like these videos state when they say that only women of a certain skin color belong to these men). It should just be men and women, period. In addition, it is this type of attitude that promotes the idea that women should be assaulted. Think about it. There are many boys (as I said earlier in this book, I don't consider the males who have this attitude men at all, because a man, in my book, never, ever, contemplates treating women like they are property) who have the attitude of *'She is my property, so therefore I can do what I want to her'*, and it causes these boys to treat women like they have no value, and like they can do whatever they want to them. Also, it does not just have to be women in pornography. If you think about it, if the boy is a woman's supervisor at her job and he feels like this, then, in his mind, he owns her, just like the boys who made the video that I just mentioned feel. Therefore, he feels like he can do whatever he wants to do to her, including harassing her, or even

361

A Visit to the City in the Light

forcing her to have sex with him, after all, women *'belong to him'*.

The bottom line is this.   The only person who should own a woman is herself.   As a matter of fact, everyone should be able to say that *'The only person who decides who I have sex with is **me.***'*, because no one should ever be forced to have sex with anyone else unless they want to.   It all comes down to respecting each other by treating others the way that we want to be treated.   But until the attitudes of *'I own her'* or *'Women belong to us'* ends, then women will continue to be taken advantage of sexually, because it is that attitude that promotes the idea of women being assaulted.   These boys feel that women belong to them, and that they can do whatever they want to them, including owning them, raping them, and even killing them, and therefore, they will do whatever they want to them to get what they want, which in this case is sex.

Look, if we are ever going to come together in order to advance our race into a better tomorrow, then we are going to need to accept the fact that women (and men) deserve to be respected, not owned, or used, or abused.   As far as I am concerned, women are beautiful to me (and not just because of looks, at least in my book), and they are worthy of our respect, just like good men are.   They are intelligent, wonderful members of our race.   They are the mothers, the sisters, and the daughters of our race.   Without them, and men for that matter, we would not even exist as a race.   They are incredibly valuable members of our race (just as valuable as men), and to have a group of boys say that they belong to them is just ugly, just as ugly as videos that suggest that it is a turn on to watch a woman being raped and killed.   In addition, it is the attitude of *'women belong to us'* that sex slavers have as well, and we all know how bad sex slavery is.

Speaking of which, why is it that they said that only women

of a certain skin color belonged to them? Aren't all women equally beautiful to them? Or are these boys so prejudiced and biased that they only want women of a certain skin color to belong to them? Like I said, ugly, pure and simple, and it is this type of speech that we need to get rid of if we are ever going to come together with love, compassion and cooperation. Like I said, all hate speech that even suggests that violence should happen to anyone needs to be stopped (and even suggesting that women belong to anyone suggests that women are nothing more than property, which makes what they said just as ugly as sex slavery is in my book). I especially wanted to mention this here because, in my opinion, these videos are so disrespectful to all women, and such a dangerous attitude to have that I felt that these are prime examples of the type of hate speech that is only meant to keep us apart, and the type of hate speech that we need to put an end to, because it can lead to violence against women, and no woman should ever have violence committed against her.

So, what do we do about this in order to stop it? Well, again, what I did was I ignored their posts, and I did not give them the *'Likes'* and *'Shares'* that they wanted. In addition, I did not tell them how bad it upset me (to have anyone even suggest that a woman belongs to anyone, or that women should be raped and murdered), because if I did those things, then they would have won, because those are the responses that they are looking for. How can we stop this type, and all types, of hate speech that can cause harm to anyone though? Well, here is my suggestion, and it goes back to what I said earlier.

First, where all types of hate speech (that even suggest that violence of any type should happen to anyone) is concerned, we need to have the law catch up with the internet. We need to draft Bills so that the purveyors of hate speech (that suggests that violence

363

happens to anyone) are held accountable for their actions. In addition, we need to include specific language in these new laws that not only shut down the hate speech videos, but also call for specific punishments for any type of hate speech that calls to cause, or causes, harm to happen to anyone. That also means that we need to report hate speech that crosses the line so that the people who make these videos can be stopped (and again, if you think that videos suggesting that women are nothing more than property to be used sexually by boys, or depicting the abuse, torture, rape, and murder of women just to satisfy boy's sexual needs, should be covered by Freedom of Speech, then maybe you need to really think about reassessing what your idea of a turn on is. Anyone who thinks that women should be treated as property, or that young women should be raped and murdered, even by their own fathers, in order to satisfy their sexual needs, has a problem, at least in my book). Is it a perfect solution? Maybe not, but at least it is a start, and we do need to do something that halts hate speech that crosses the line. Again, though, this is what *"Acceptance"* is all about. Having all of us come together so that we can come up with solutions to solve the problems that we face today.......and believe me when I say that we truly do need to solve the problem of women being abused, raped, and murdered just to satisfy a boy's sexual needs.

Now, I am sure that you can come up with many more examples of the types of hate that we, as a race, need to put an end to when we finally do come together, but let me close this section by saying this. Until we do come together to come up with ways to stop hate in all of its forms, we will just continue to fight until we destroy ourselves. No civilization that has rampant hate as a part of its history can ever survive, because all hate does is cause people to tear themselves apart. It is destructive, and it will keep us from coming together forever.

A Journey There.......and Back Again with a Message of Hope

<u>**Protecting Our Home**</u>

Ok, what do I mean by this? Well, it is the fact that we have only one home, our planet, and if it goes, we all go as well. Let me explain, because I do not want anyone to think that I am just talking about ecological issues here. I am also talking about things like protecting the other species that live here with us, and even preventing war. Also, before anyone thinks that I am just a *'tree hugger'* because I am talking about saving our home world, let me just state, for the record, that I consider myself a *'Defender of The Human Race'*. What that means is that I am a defender of everyone and everything that helps our race to keep operating and thrive, and that includes defending our home world.

Let me explain. The most obvious topic that needs to be dealt with when talking about protecting our planet is our natural resources. Now, let's think about this for a moment, because I am not suggesting that we immediately stop using our natural resources, because due to present technology, we need to use the resources that we are using, at least until we come up with alternatives that would allow us to do things like stop using wood for homes and heat, stop using oil for things like powering our vehicles, and other things that we are presently using them for. That is also why I refuse to condemn the people who run the factories that manufacture things using these natural resources, because if it were not for them and what they do, then we would not be able to get much done presently. However, if we deplete our natural resources, then our planet will die. Our planet is a living thing, and like anything that is living, if we kill almost everything on it, then our planet will react. Let us take the plants, for example. Our lives depend on the oxygen levels that make up our atmosphere. Those oxygen levels, and maintaining them, are dependent on plant life, and if we destroy those plants (or the majority of them), then it will have catastrophic

365

effects on the oxygen that make up our atmosphere. Again, if it goes, then we go, because we need oxygen in order to survive (as do the other species that live on our planet).

Now I know that, considering our present situation, this might seem like an extreme attitude to have, but consider this. As a race, we are continuing to grow. Recent data states that there were approximately 7.7 billion people on our planet in 2019. However, think about this. How many more people will be living on our planet in, say, 50 years? 100 years? 500 years? Our population will continue to grow, and while there are many people dying each day as well, it is still a fact that there are more people being born than there are dying each day.[21] Now, those numbers will only increase as we solve other problems that afflict our race, like finding cures for diseases. So, the oxygen levels in our atmosphere, and having them depleted by the death of plant life, may not matter presently, but how will it affect our future generations? You see, the more of us that there are, the more space that we will take up, and as a result, the more natural resources we will use, which will cause more plants to die as a result, and as a result there will be less oxygen released into our atmosphere, and.......well, you get the idea.

If we are going to deal with this, then we need to keep trying to come up with things like alternative fuel sources to make sure that we do not use up our planet until it dies. Again, though, I refuse to blame anyone who uses our planet's natural resources to manufacture things that we presently need, like gas for our vehicles and the like, because they are the ones who are keeping us going for now. We do need to start to deal with this, though, so that we can ensure that our future generations will be able to keep going as well. That is just one of the reasons that I say that we need to come together now and learn to get along so that we can solve these problems. I am encouraged each day, though, when I hear about things like electric cars and alternative heating sources, because it shows that I am not alone when I say that we need to do these things in order to save our planet. In addition, I am encouraged when I hear about the fact that we are starting to work on going back to the moon, you know, eventually more space for more people. Again, though, I feel that we truly need to stop all the fighting so that we can all put our heads together to solve these issues, and the best way that I think we can do that is by adopting the philosophy of *"Acceptance"*. It will allow us to come together and start working on problems like these now, before it becomes too late to do anything about them.

Another thing that we need to come up with a solution for is all the fighting that we do amongst each other, and that includes all the war that ravages our world. Let me explain exactly what that has to do with protecting our planet. As we all know, war ravages our world, and any country that is the site of a war as well. From the beginning, every war that has happened has gotten worse and worse concerning how we fight each one. Weapons have been getting more devastating, and the worst of it, at least in my opinion, is when we first developed, and used, nuclear weapons. To put it poetically, I truly feel that when we first split the atom, the Earth cried, because she knew what was coming. With each nuclear weapon that has been unleashed, it has caused our world to become poisoned with things like fallout. Ever since we first utilized nuclear energy there have been accidents that have poisoned areas of our world to the point where they have become uninhabitable due to what they left behind. Then there are such things as nuclear waste to consider. A lot of these piles have half-lives that run from 30 years (for Strontium-90 and cesium-137) to 24,000 years (for Plutonium-239) before they are declared to be safe again, making the waste sites dangerous places to be.[22]

A Visit to the City in the Light

Now, again, my attitude may seem a little extreme, but consider this. Let's say that a nuclear war erupts in the future, and everyone starts punching buttons like they are playing pianos. It is not that farfetched. There are many countries that have nuclear weapons in today's world. What if it happened? We could destroy our world and make the majority of it uninhabitable in just one day. That is why I say that our world leaders truly need to become *'World Leaders'* by coming together and making sure that we do everything in our power to stop major wars before they start, which would be an easy thing to do if we all came together through the philosophy of *"Acceptance"* and actually started caring about each other, instead of only caring about our individual countries.

Now, the United Nations was a good start, and Nuclear Arms Deals have also helped, but I still think that we can do better. How? Well, again, I wish that I had all the answers, because the last thing that I am suggesting is that our world leaders become all powerful tyrants who utilize dictatorships to control everything, because it is my opinion that our leaders should be representing us, not ruling us. Now, as I said, Nuclear Arms Deals were a good start, but are they enough, especially when there are countries who do not honor the deals that they make? I truly wish that I had all the answers, but I do not. We need to do something though to, at least, start addressing this situation on a world-wide scale even more than we are now, because nothing will ever get done if we do not start coming together to solve these problems.

Another area that we will need to address when we all come together is protecting the other species who live on our planet. That includes the ones that live in our oceans, because they are in just as much danger as those who live on land. As everyone knows, pollution in our oceans is increasing every day. Here is the thing. We need water to survive as well as oxygen, and if we poison our oceans, then eventually it will affect us. Maybe not in our lifetime, or in the next few generation's lifetimes for that matter, but eventually it will affect us in bad ways. That is why I say that we should not ignore it just because it is not greatly affecting us now. We should be the generation that starts to address it and comes up with solutions to solve these problems, because we cannot continue to pollute our oceans. Now, I have seen many promising signs that some of us are starting to address this, and who are doing something about this, but again, what about the rest of us? Why aren't the rest of us pitching in as well, even if that is just by picking up our trash when we go to the beach?

Just as importantly, though, is the fact that we cannot keep watching our animal friends succumb to extinction when we can work together now to come up with solutions in order to keep their species alive. Again, this may seem like an extreme attitude to have presently, but I still feel strongly that we should be the generation that at least starts to come up with solutions instead of just giving more excuses as to why we are not all working together to address and solve these issues now. Now, I am not saying that we should do things like discontinue all hunting, because there are animals that some people hunt in order to feed their families (yes, this is still true, as there are families who live in rural areas that depend on activities like deer hunting to feed their families), but that does not mean that we should allow things like *'trophy hunting'* for animals that are in limited numbers or allow animals to be hunted for things like their ivory and fur, for example.[23] That type of hunting should be stopped permanently, at least in my opinion. So, what do we do in order to protect the other species? Tougher world-wide laws maybe? Well, again, I wish that I had all the answers, but I do not. However, I truly feel that this is another area that should be addressed when we all come together.

A Visit to the City in the Light

Like I said, I wish that I had all the answers, or at least a *'magic wand'* that I could use to come up with solutions to these, and all the other problems that we face concerning protecting our home world, but I do not. I am sure, though, that you can come up with other problems that we will need to address, and solutions as well, and that is why I pray that we all adopt the philosophy of *"Acceptance"* so that we can all work together, utilizing mutual respect, to solve them.

Helping All of Our Brothers and Sisters

There are so many ways that we need to help our brothers and sisters in our race, and to be honest, I do not know where to begin when talking about this. There are many problems, like homelessness. No one should ever have to face a single night living on the streets without a home, especially if that homeless person is a child. It should be a basic right that everyone should have a place that they can call home, especially a child. It absolutely breaks my heart to think of any child having to live on the streets. It is scary enough to be an adult without a home, but when you are a child and you are still learning how the world should be, it must be terrifying. No child should ever have to live in fear. This is one of the problems that I truly feel that we, as adults, should solve first when addressing the problems that we face.

Now, having said that, here is my suggestion for one possible solution to the problem of homelessness. If you can think of a better one, then write it down and share it, because again, that is what *"Acceptance"* is all about, having us all come up with ideas to solve our race's problems, and then working together to solve them. Here goes. You see, I have always lived my life by the philosophy of not giving someone a handout, but instead, giving them a hand up. What that means is that, if we help someone by giving them a handout (say, with a few dollars), then we are not solving their problem, because all we are doing is helping them temporarily instead of helping them permanently. There are many reasons that people find themselves homeless, and what we really should be doing is helping them permanently by helping them solve the reason that made them homeless in the first place. So that they can stand on their own two feet again. When we do that, we are helping them by making sure that the original problem that caused them to be homeless in the first place is now solved and no longer a problem.

You see, one of the things that I have always believed in is an old saying that goes *"If you give a man a fish, he will eat one meal. If you give a man a fishing pole and teach him how to fish, then he will not go hungry again."* (variation - origin from assorted sources), and there is a lot of truth in that statement. If we want to solve the problem of homelessness, then we need to help the people who find themselves homeless by helping them get back on their feet, and we do that by solving the original problem that made them homeless. Consider this. Every day I see buildings that are vacant, and if we could just remodel them so that they could be used to give homeless families a home, even if it is with just a basic apartment, then what a blessing it would be to everyone. Here is what I mean. We could renovate these buildings, and then offer an apartment to people who are homeless, if they are willing to earn it (do not give anyone a hand out, give them a hand up if you want to help them). Let me explain.

Let us say that we take one of these buildings and renovate it so that it now has basic, but livable, units in it. Then we could offer these units to families who are homeless. Now, what about single people, men and women? Well, we could renovate some of these buildings to be like the open bay barracks (some for men, others for women), so that they could have a place to live while they are

371

getting back on their feet. Now, we would have to make sure that the people moving in understand that, if they have any problems like drug addiction, then they would have to undergo treatment in order to beat their addictions so that then they could obtain employment with our help. In that way they would have the opportunity to become independent and then move to a better place, because they would be basic living quarters, made specifically to give these people a place to live while they get back on their feet.

Now, when I say if they are willing to *'earn it'*, here is what I mean. First, like I said, they would have to beat their addictions if they have any (with our help), and they might even have to live in recovery centers if they have severe mental problems in order to get them the help that they may need. Second, they could use the time they spend living in these quarters to also get over another type of problem that all homeless people face, and that is what I call the problem of being in *'Survival Mode'*. One thing that I have learned about being human is this. When we are faced with an extreme situation like being homeless, and it backs us up into a *'corner'*, then we stop caring about anyone else, and the only thing on our mind is wondering how we are going to eat that day, and where we will sleep that night, and we find ourselves doing whatever it takes to make sure that we accomplish those goals. Even if that means that we need to lie, cheat, and steal to make it happen.

We do things like we stop trusting anyone, and we find ourselves looking at other people like they are either our enemy, or like they are someone we can take advantage of, all because basic survival is our only goal. It is natural to feel this way, it is human to feel this way when we are homeless, and I ought to know, because at one point in my life I was homeless. However, the way that I solved my problem was to learn how to trust people again. I realized that they were not the reason that I was homeless, it was what had happened to me in my life (in my case, I became homeless because I lost a job, and I could not pay my rent).   After I realized that, I started to look for ways to pull myself out of homelessness by doing whatever it took to find a job so that I could stand on my own two feet again.   Now, there are many ways to do this, but the way that I did it was to walk into a construction company one day, and I went up to the foreman and told him that I needed to work so that I could get myself back on my feet again.   I also told him that I was willing to do whatever he wanted me to do (within the law, of course) in order to be able to earn a paycheck once again, and that he would not regret giving me a chance because I would work hard for him.

I told him if he wanted me to pick up garbage from construction sites, then I would do it.   If he wanted me to wash construction equipment, then I would do it.   I told him that I would do anything for a paycheck (again, within the law of course), and that I would work hard to earn that paycheck.   He took pity on me, and so he gave me a hand up by starting me out at minimum wage, doing things like picking up the garbage at construction sites, and washing vehicles, and anything else that none of the other contractors wanted to do.   It was hard work, and it did not pay much, however, what it did do was help me to start earning money again so that I could get back on my feet.   It started to pay off after then because the contractors started seeing what I was doing, and they took pity on me (again, sometimes we need to let go of our egos in order to be successful, and we should not look at people taking pity on us as something bad but as an opportunity), and as such, they started teaching me how to do things.

Things like how to hang drywall, and run electrical wiring, and pouring concrete, and everything else that it takes to build something.   After a while, the foreman started using me to do those things by working with the contractors as an apprentice, and eventually I was a success again, because while it did not make me rich, what it did do was allow me to solve the reason why I had become homeless, and I have never been homeless since then. This is what I mean when I say that we should be giving homeless people a hand up, and not a handout, because if we really want to solve the homeless problem once and for all, then again, we need to do things that not only pull people out of homelessness, but also allow them to stand on their own two feet so that they are never homeless again.

Now, as I was saying, once we have homeless people move into these basic domiciles, and we get them the help that they need in order to help them beat any addictions that they may have (and that includes helping them to pull themselves out of *'Survival Mode'*), then we need to help them get jobs so that they realize that they can make it on their own again. If you think that this will not work, then consider this. Back in America's history, between the years 1933 to 1942 (during the Great Depression), there were many young men who found themselves unemployed, and as such, they and their families were facing homelessness on a massive scale. The American President at the time, Franklin D. Roosevelt, decided that something needed to be done about this, and so, on April 5th, 1933, he signed a piece of legislation that started what was called the Civilian Conservation Corps (better known as the CCC) as a part of his *"New Deal"* legislation.[24] The way it worked was like this. Young men between the ages of 18 and 25 were given the opportunity, thanks to this piece of legislation, to work on environmental projects for the government by doing everything from planting trees to building campgrounds and everything in-between. The young men included Army veterans, skilled and unskilled foresters and craftsmen, and all other young men who were facing homelessness and hard times during the Great Depression. These men were given basic places to live, and they were given the opportunity to volunteer for a period of six months (and I do mean volunteer, because none of them were forced to do this), and part of the requirement was for them to send most of their pay back home to their families so that their families could survive without becoming homeless. In addition, while they were there, they also learned trades that allowed them to succeed once they left the CCC, so that they could continue working their trades in the private sector.

They were given a hand up, instead of a handout, and not only did it help them and their families by making sure that they could survive instead of being homeless, but it gave them the tools to succeed once they left the CCC. It helped the American Government by helping to get things done (like developing more than 800 parks in the American National Park System), and it helped these young men learn trades as well in order to provide for themselves and their families. It was a win/win situation for everyone. So, if we really want to help homeless people pull themselves out of homelessness, then why can't we do something like that now? Why can't we come up with a plan that helps people to survive and succeed like the CCC Camps did back then? Look, if we are serious about solving the homeless problem once and for all, then we need to do more than just give someone a handout. We need to give them a hand up, and this sounds like a good idea to me, especially when a similar program has already proven in the past that it can work. Is it a perfect solution? Maybe, maybe not, but at least it is an idea, and if we are ever going to solve the homeless problem, then we need to do more than just *give a man a fish*. We need to give him a fishing pole and then teach him how to fish so that he can succeed.

Now, these ideas are good as far as helping homeless adults, but what about helping children who are homeless? What can we do when it is a child who is homeless? Again, I truly wish that I had all the answers, but I do not. What I do know, with all certainty, is that we cannot just stand by anymore when we know that there are children on the streets, every single night, who are hungry and scared. Again, though, that is why I truly do hope that the plan of *"Acceptance"* takes effect, and that everyone practices it, because I know that there are very smart people out there who can come up with the answers. Coming together with love and compassion will help us solve this problem and solving the problem of homeless children needs to be a top priority when we do come together as one.

Homelessness is not the only thing that we need to solve, though. Another thing that makes me sad is when I see or hear about people going hungry, especially children. Everyone should have three meals a day, especially children. How can we say that we care about all of our brothers and sisters in our race when, every day, there are children who wonder when they will eat again or what they will have to eat? I am blessed enough to have a home, and to be able to eat every day, and it really makes me feel guilty about that fact. If I knew that, by cutting myself back in food to one meal a day in order to ensure that no child ever goes hungry, then I would be happy eating only one meal, because no child should ever have to worry about things like if they are going to eat today.

Now I know that there are things like food warehouses that families can go to in order to get food, but why is it so hard for some people to get that food? There was a time in my life when I had to go to one of these places in order to get some food, and I noticed that it was hard to get that food. One of the biggest stumbling blocks was that you needed to have an address in order to get the food. So, what do you do if you are homeless? I mean, some families are absolutely terrified to go to these places because they know that, if they do, then they could have their children taken away from them all because they are down on their luck and they are homeless. We truly need to stop punishing people for being homeless or poor. People can lose their place to live for many reasons, including losing their jobs due to cutbacks (like what happened to me), and when that happens, they find themselves worried that they will be punished by having their children taken away from them if they do seek help. We need to start caring for everyone, including those who find themselves homeless. We need to stop making poverty a crime and start caring for people who find themselves in a bad situation. We can do that if we all come together in *"Acceptance"*.

Another area that we need to come up with solutions for is where disease is concerned, especially when children are afflicted. I know that I keep mentioning children in this part, but they are our future. They have not even had the chance to do the things that we have gotten to do as adults, like going to High School, or College, or falling in love, or anything else that we, as adults, take for granted. Then, to make matters worse, one day someone tells them that they have a terrible disease, like cancer. I remember how I felt when I was told that my dad had cancer. I remember what he went through during his battle, and how he died from the disease. It absolutely breaks my heart whenever I think of a child going through what he went through. We need to come up with cures for this, and many other, diseases that afflict us all, because no one (especially a child) should ever be told that they may not have a next birthday.

Like I said though, there are other diseases that we need to come up with cures for as well. Another one that comes to mind is Alzheimer's Disease. Now, this is one that does not affect children directly, but it is still devastating to a family, and the children in the family. How do you explain to a family member, especially a child, that Grandpa or Grandma, for example, does not know who they are anymore? Look, we need to come up with cures for these, and other, diseases. If we really care about our brothers and sisters in our race then we need to do this, and I believe that we can do it. Unfortunately, this is going to take a lot of money. Please, hear me out. Everyday there are people being told that there is a chance that they, or their loved ones, could be cured of a disease, but only if they have the money, or the insurance, to pay for the cure. How do you tell anyone that, especially if you advertise your medical services by saying that you *'care'*?

Now, I am not saying that we should all receive free medical care, because just like I said about colleges in an earlier chapter, it takes a lot of money to provide medical care. The doctors, and others, need to be paid. However, there has to be a way to make sure that they get paid while the people who need the medical care (especially children) are able to get the care that they need. Do I have a suggestion on how we can do this? Well, something I do is donate to children's hospitals so that they can provide care to sick children. Another thing that we could do is for all of us to donate to medical centers so that they could have a surplus to draw off of (like a *'slush fund'*) in order to use that money to provide medical care to people who cannot afford it (I mean, in America, there were, as of 2019, approximately 328.2 million people according to the Census Bureau.[25] Even if only half of those people donated $1.00 a month to these medical *'slush funds'*, then that would give the hospitals $164.1 million dollars extra a month to help people get medical care. It would allow, at least, the children to have a chance to get medical care. Is $1.00 a month too much to ask for in order to ensure that, at a minimum, all children receive medical care? If no one else will take care of us, isn't it time that we did?) Do I have any other suggestions? I wish that I did, because illnesses can be devastating, especially to families, and not being able to get medical care is wrong.   Again, though, these are all problems that I know we can come up with solutions for if we would come together through *"Acceptance"*.

There are so many more problems that need to be dealt with in order to help our brothers and sisters in our race.   Stopping hatred, taking care of our home world, and helping our brothers and sisters are just the tips of the iceberg.   We can solve all of these, and many more, problems that our race faces every day, but we will never solve anything until we are willing to put aside our differences and finally come together to solve them, and I truly feel that *"Acceptance"* can make this happen, if we are all just willing to give it a chance.   I know that I am doing it.   How about you?   Will you be willing to do it as well so that we can all finally come together in peace to solve all the problems that we face?

Chapter Thirteen
One More Word of Hope

Now it is up to all of us. I really believe that, if we are to survive as a race, then we need to roll up our sleeves and get to work. Do I have all the answers? No, not at all. I do believe that *"Acceptance"* is a good starting point, though, if we are all going to come together, and that is exactly what we need to do in my opinion. This is why I feel that I was given the plan of *"Acceptance"* to spread to the world. God loves all of us, whether we believe in him or not, and he truly does want us to succeed. He wants us to have a plan to make that happen. That is why I believe that I was given this message when I went to what I believe was Heaven, and why I believe that it was an Angel who implanted this message in my head, so that we can utilize this plan to come together in order to make it a better tomorrow for all of us.

Like I said, everyone keeps saying *'we need to put a stop to'* everything from bullying to war. People keep saying that we need to *'branch out to the stars'* in order to advance our race into the future. People keep saying that we need to *'put a stop to hate'* in all forms, to *'put a stop to sexual harassment'*, to *'put a stop to violence and bullying'*, to *'find a cure'* for diseases like cancer, but no one says exactly how we are supposed to do it. Most of the time this happens because we hear these messages, and while we do agree with them, the majority of us just hear them, and then we go back to our own lives and figure that we don't have the time deal with it, or that there is nothing that we can do because we aren't in a position (like having a specialized job) to do anything about these problems. Or even worse, we just figure that someone else will solve these problems without our help.

I really believe that this attitude is a big part of the problem,

A Visit to the City in the Light

though, because it falls into the old *'out of sight, out of mind'*, or *'it's someone else's problem to figure out'* attitude, and it is that attitude that is a major part of our problems never being solved. True, we may not have the type of job that would allow us to do things like cure certain diseases, but there are things that we can do. Things like donating money to help the scientists who are trying to find the cure for certain diseases and donating to children's hospitals. We can even do something small like visiting a local children's hospital to give sick children something to make their day a little happier, like playing a game with them, or even just letting them know that we do care (again though, make sure that you get permission to visit the sick children from the hospital and the parents, and that you cooperate with them if they want to check you out). One thing that I have learned is that a positive mental attitude can really help someone who is sick, and letting a child know that they are not alone, and that we care, can really help them in their fight against disease. Another thing that we could do is identify all the people in our race who have high intelligence levels so that they can work on solving the problems, and we can do that by making sure that education is something that everyone can afford.

If we are ever going to solve the problems that we face currently then we need to accept the fact that it is our responsibility to do it. No one is going to do it for us. There is no *'magic wand'* that we will be able to pull out to make these problems go away. We need to solve them by accepting each other in order to get along through the utilization of mutual respect for everyone.

We have an opportunity here to change our future for the better on a massive scale. But it will take a lot of work. We will need to change our way of thinking. *'Looking out for number one'* will no longer be an option if we want to change the course of our history. It will take time. We need to not only change the way that we think, but we will also need to educate our children to think differently, so that they will *'pick up the ball and run with it'* when they run our world.   So that they can make the right decisions to lead us into tomorrow by using global cooperation and unity based on love, compassion, and understanding.

Now let me be clear.   When I say that we all need to change the way that we think, I am not talking about changing the way that individual people think by changing the beliefs that they hold, or the way that they live their lives, or anything else that would change them as an individual.   What I am saying is that we need to stop fighting each other, and we do that by changing our confrontational attitudes towards each other, which happens because of our differences.   We need to start accepting each other by accepting the differences that make us unique as individuals, so instead of saying things like *'They believe differently than me, so that makes them my enemy'* or *'They look different than me, so they are my enemy'*, we start saying things like *'I will work with them, and accept them as they are, in order to bring our race together in peace, love, and compassion.   I will accept them so that we can get the things accomplished that we, as a race, need to get accomplished, as long as they never want to cause harm to anyone'.*

Love, compassion, mutual respect, and understanding are more powerful tools than most people can possibly imagine.   They can end people's hate towards each other.   They can help us heal our emotional wounds so that we stop hating everyone who is not exactly like us.   Now, I am not just talking about hate because of physical violence that has occurred towards each other in the past, I am also talking about the hate generated by the words that people say towards others.   Let me explain.   As I said, I am a fan of *'Science Fiction'*, and in many of those stories, many of the characters say one common thing, and that is the fact that they had

383

stopped becoming upset about hurtful words. They realized that words alone do not hurt us if we do not allow them to (and again, I am not talking about hate speech that calls for violence or causes people to get hurt physically. I am talking about words in general, especially distasteful words).

Think about that. I touched on this earlier when I was talking about hate speech, and not giving the people who are responsible for hate speech, or hurtful words in general, the response that they are looking for. However, I also mentioned that, where hate speech crosses the line in my book is when the words start calling for violence against anyone, because when they do, then they go beyond being just words, or hate speech in general.

Words alone, though, should be taken for exactly what they are. Words, and words alone cannot hurt us if they do not call for violence in any form, and they cannot hurt us if we do not allow them to. True, they may hurt our feelings, and make us upset, but the words alone cannot hurt us physically. All they do, especially in instances like generalized hate speech, is prove the ignorance of some people who are spewing their hateful words towards others that they do not even know as individual people.

Now, this may seem like a contradiction to something that I mentioned earlier when I was talking about the hate speech videos where the people making them said that women belong to them now, but hear me out on this, because I truly feel that the people making those videos were calling for violence against women. Just like the violence that has been occurring to many women by boys of all skin colors (again, not men in my book, because true men never physically hurt women. Real men respect and value women). The same boys who have harassed and raped women because these boys feel that women *'belong'* to them, which is just like the attitude that the people have who traffic sex slaves.   You see, as I mentioned earlier, no woman belongs to anyone, they only belong to themselves, and when people start thinking and saying that women belong to someone, then it makes some boys say to themselves *'Well, if that's true, then this woman belongs to me'* or *'That woman belongs to me'*, and then they start thinking that they can do whatever they want to do to all women, including acts of violence.

You see, it is then that the boys watching these videos become capable of doing all sorts of horrible things to women, because they start thinking that all women are now their *'property'*, and that they can do whatever they want to do to them.   That is an extremely dangerous attitude to have towards women, because the boys who have this attitude can start acting on the theory that women belong to them by doing things like abusing, kidnapping (including for the sex slavery trade), raping, and even murdering them.

So, you see, those hate videos that say that women belong to anyone (and again, I am not talking about BDSM videos) are quite different than just hate speech that does not call for violence, or hurtful words that some ignorant people spew against people that they don't even know.   What proves my point is all of the harassment, rapes, kidnappings (especially for the sex slave trade), and murders that have happened to women, perpetrated by boys who have this dangerous attitude against women, and have had this dangerous attitude towards women for quite some time now.   Like I said, words alone do not hurt, but when those words call for violence in any form against someone else, or they cause violence to happen to anyone, then that is when their hate speech has crossed the line, at least in my opinion.

To continue my earlier thought though, love, compassion,

385

caring, and everything else that *"Acceptance"* is based on can bring us all together in ways that are the answers to all of our dreams. They can stop hate, violence, and all of the conflicts that plague our race. They can bring us together and unite us in ways that we cannot possibly imagine. But it will never happen until we make the conscious decision to start now to bring us all together so that we can be the generation that starts to lead our race into the future. Like I said before, it will take time, it will not take effect overnight, but as long as we are willing to take those first steps then we can lead our world into a wonderful future for all of us. To make our world a wonderful place to live in for everyone. I truly feel that this is why I was given this message to spread to the world, because God loves all of us (believers and non-believers alike), which is why I am convinced that it was an Angel who touched my head when I had my *'Near Death Experience'* in order to give me the message, so that I could share it with the world in order to help our race come together in peace, love, and caring for all time.

Think about this. Imagine being able to visit lands where, up to now, we have not been able to visit because of irrational hatred directed towards others. Imagine people being able to live where they want to live, instead of having to be refugees and leave their homes (due to not being accepted for the way that they hold their religious beliefs for example), all because their leaders have become true *'World Leaders'* who work within the boundaries of their own countries to take care of their citizens better than they have ever been taken care of before. Because they allow their citizens the freedom to live their lives the way that they want to live them without fear of persecution in any way. Imagine being able to walk the streets at night, without having to fear for your own safety, because the problem with criminal activities in those areas has been eradicated. One place that comes to mind is Germany when talking about combating criminal activity.

A Journey There.......and Back Again with a Message of Hope

I remember the last time that I was there many years ago. I could walk down any street, day or night, and not have to worry about being robbed or attacked, all because of the ways that the laws are written, and more importantly, enforced there. You see, one thing that I noticed was that criminals knew better than to commit crimes in the cities that I visited in Germany, because they knew that the police force there would not tolerate people committing crimes, and when they would catch a person committing a crime, they made sure that the criminal was dealt with accordingly (I'm not saying that there was absolutely no criminal activity there, because there are criminals in every country in our world, but I was absolutely amazed at just how little violent criminal activity there was in the places that I visited [26]). Now, I know that this may cause concern to people, because they do not want to live in anything that even remotely resembles a police state, but that is not the case. The police (or Bundespolizei) in Germany are some of the nicest people that you could ever want to meet (at least in the areas where I visited) unless they catch someone committing a crime, because they do not tolerate anyone committing crimes at all, and if they catch a criminal, then rest assured, they will deal with them so that they, and the general public, are assured that they will not be on the streets to commit any more crimes, mainly because the criminals are dealt with to the full extent of the law. My question is this. What are we willing to do in order to end crime? We have to do something. So, what will that be? Again, I wish that I had all the answers, especially where stopping crime is concerned, but I don't. However, this is a problem that we need to come together and solve.

Speaking of crimes, what do we do about the illegal drug problem? Well, how about this scenario. Imagine, just for a moment, how much better the world would be if those people who make the illegal drugs that destroy our race would instead use that knowledge to try and come up with legitimate uses for those drugs, like medicines that could help the sick, or even help our animal friends. Can you just imagine how much legitimate money that they could make if they did that, instead of just using their knowledge to hurt our race through addiction? On that subject, imagine the other uses that they could come up with for those drugs, and the plants that grow them. Uses that could change the way that we live and change our world for the better. Maybe there are uses that could even help with clothing people, or help with building homes and furniture, all of which come from those same drugs and the plants that grow them. For example, hemp can be used to do all sort of things, like make clothing, and items like rope, and best of all, it can be regenerated rapidly, much more rapidly than trees.

I think that, again, if I had a *'magic wand'* and I could change things so that they happened the way that I wanted them to happen, then the first thing that I would do is figure out a way to convince the people who make illegal drugs to stop making them, and then to have them start using their genius to come up with uses for those drugs that would benefit all of our race. Please, hear me out on this. We have many problems where diseases and the manufacture of pharmaceuticals are concerned, one of the biggest being the cost of medicines that are presently on the market. Can you imagine just how much it could benefit our race if the people who manufacture illegal drugs started coming up with ways to make legal pharmaceuticals, especially if they could make those legal medicines more affordable than the medicines that are presently on the market?

Unfortunately, I don't have a magic wand, and I don't have the power to change things. However, I do believe that, if the people who manufacture those illegal drugs would just start coming up with ways for their drugs to benefit us, then we might just come up with ways help many patients. If that happened, if they stopped producing illegal drugs and they put all of their efforts into producing legal pharmaceuticals that are more affordable than what is on the market now, then I am convinced that they could really help our race advance into a more compassionate tomorrow for all of us. How about you? What would you be willing to do, and what ideas could you come up with, to help our race medically and medicinally, especially if it were your child that was sick?

To continue, though, speaking of natural building materials that can re-grow much faster than trees, how about bamboo? It grows much faster than trees, and it is much stronger than a lot of trees that we now use to build with (actually stronger than steel in tensile strength [27]). In addition, if we started utilizing bamboo more, it would help to keep us from destroying our forests, or even just cutting down too many trees, as they are particularly important to all of us where making sure that our planet has a constant supply of oxygen, especially when talking about future generations and how many more people will be on our planet at that time. Now, I do realize that having enough oxygen for all of us is not a problem presently, but again, how about for our future generations? We are only getting larger where our world population is concerned. Will future generations look back at our generation and say, *'I wish that they had started to do something back then.'*, or will they say *'Wow, even though they did not have that concern in the past, that generation still took action to make sure that our forests were not threatened so that we would still have a livable planet now.'*.

Now, I am not saying that we should just stop using trees entirely, or we should shut down the people who manufacture trees for the things that we need to use, because there are things that we need presently that are made of wood, and we need those people who manufacture the things that we need to keep doing it, because it does benefit all of us presently. What do we do, though? Do we

stick our heads in the sand and ignore it, or do we all come together and come up with solutions for this and all the other problems that our planet faces?   After all, right now, this is our only home.   So, what do we do?   These are just some examples of how we can make things better for all of us by coming together utilizing *"Acceptance"* in order to come up with solutions that will benefit us all.
However, none of it will ever happen until we all accept the fact that it is our responsibility to make these changes happen for the betterment of our race by coming together now, and again, and we can do that by practicing *"Acceptance"*.

Now, I know that I keep mentioning things like *'If I had a magic wand, then I would probably do this'*, and some may be wondering who I am as a result, but as I said previously, I feel that it is important that this book not be about me, or any one person for that matter, because it is easy to see a person responsible for a message, and then lose sight of the message, no matter how important the message is, because the focus shifts from the message to the person who is delivering it, and no matter how important the message is, it can get lost.   Like I said earlier, I was entrusted to spread this message to the world while ensuring that I wrote this book humbly, and I believe that I know the reason for that.   You see, someone may have something incredibly important to say, something that really matters and is a great message to deliver to the world, bettering ourselves if we place it into practice, but then the message gets lost just because we have an opinion about the person delivering the message.

Let's say, for example, that someone comes up with a plan to stop world hunger.   It may be a great message and plan, but then we learn that the person delivering the message is the CEO of a food processing plant, and because of that, people might stop listening to the message and focus on the person delivering it because they feel that the person is just trying to make money for his food company and himself. Or let's say that a person comes up with a plan to stop sexual assault of all kinds, but then it is discovered that the person delivering the message and the plan is actually a convicted rapist. We would stop listening to the plan, and instead, focus on the man delivering the message because of his criminal past, and because of that, we might not want to listen to him, even though his plan might be an incredible plan to stop sexual assault. We would be so focused on the fact that he is the type of person that people hate that the message could get lost.

Now, I am not saying that I am a bad person. As a matter of fact, I have never committed a crime in my entire life. However, I really feel, in my heart, that this message is too important to be about any one person, especially if we are to evolve into the incredible race that we could be. I believe that this is the reason that I was instructed to write this book humbly, because this message is way too important to be distracted by anything or anyone. I do not want to take even the slightest chance that this message gets lost due to the focus of the message shifting from *"Acceptance"* to me. I have seen the philosophy of *"Acceptance"* work in many areas of our world, and I do not want to do anything that might derail the message. That is why I decided to write this book anonymously, because I do not want this message to be lost because people may want to focus on me. That is also why I have tried to not give my opinion on too many issues that I have raised in this book. I tried to offer my suggestions in certain areas, and I included some personal experiences as well, but again, I did not do it to try and shift the focus to me. I did it because that is what *"Acceptance"* is all about. All of us working together to come up with ideas to solve all our race's problems.

Having said that, please allow me to say that I truly feel that

A Visit to the City in the Light

the philosophy of *"Acceptance"* can really help to change our world for the better, because it is not about what I think should be done as an individual, even though I have offered suggestions in this book. It is about all of us accepting each other as individuals so that we can come together to solve all our problems without fighting amongst ourselves. You see, one of the things that I have noticed is how easy it is for us to hate other people all because we have problems in our lives that have caused our hearts to harden towards other people, and as a result, we shut people out of our lives, or worse yet, we go out of our way to hate other people, and to try to cause them harm. This could be for a number of reasons, but all I know is that, when we allow our hearts to be hardened against other people for whatever reason (like maybe they remind us of someone who caused us hurt in our lives, or they remind us of someone who believed the way that the person who hurt us in our past believed, and then we hate them irrationally instead of getting to know them as individuals), it can not only cause us harm, but it can have harmful effects on others around us, effects that can harm them in very painful ways.

I believe that what I am about to tell you is a prime example of what I am talking about. You see, one of my favorite movies of all time is a movie from 1921 called *"The Phantom Carriage"* (Directed by Victor Sjorstrom. Performances by Victor Sjorstrom, Astrid Holm, and Hilda Borgstrom. Produced by Charles Magnusson, 1921). It is a silent film, but one that I would recommend everyone watch because of the powerful message that it conveys. Now, I do not want to spoil it by telling everything about it, but it is a prime example of what can happen to us, and to those around us, when we make the conscious decision to let our hearts become cold towards the world, all because of something that happens to us, as in, when we go through a very trying time caused by our actions, even though we have decided to change our ways and try to be a better person.   Again, I do not want to spoil the movie, but I will say this.   Letting our hearts become cold towards everyone, even against those who do care about us and are trying to save us, can destroy everyone and everything that we touch, and this movie illustrates that in a way that will change your way of thinking once you watch this hidden treasure.   This is what *"Acceptance"* is all about.   Opening our hearts to all our brothers and sisters in our race instead of letting our hearts become cold towards others.   It is when we start caring about others, even those that we do not know, that love can make a difference, and when it can change our lives for the better, and forever.

Like I said many times in this book, I know how bad it hurts to lose someone that we love.   I have lost love many times, and each time it has caused me to think that I no longer wanted to care about others, because I felt that no one cared about me, and I felt that, every time I cared about someone, anyone, then they would betray me as well.   So why should I care about anyone else.   Then, however, after giving myself time to heal I would realize, each time, that I am a good person, someone who is worthy of love, and that I just needed to find that one special person who would love me as much as I love them.   As a result, I would allow my heart to warm back up to caring and love.   In the end, I found that I was a much stronger person because I had lost the person that I loved, and it was because I made the conscious decision to allow myself, and my heart, the time to heal completely instead of just going back out there immediately and trying to find a replacement for the love that I just lost because I felt that I could not be alone.   It is easy to do. We lament our lost love, and we feel that, if we do not go out immediately and find someone to replace the love that we lost, then we cannot even function as a person, when in reality, being alone for a while and allowing our heart to heal is exactly *'what the doctor ordered'* for our broken heart.   We cannot love someone new if we are not happy with ourselves and we do not love ourselves, because our new love will be based on a lie, at least in my opinion.

I know that I spoke about this before, but please allow me to say this again, because I think that this also applies to helping us all come together through *"Acceptance"*, because we truly need to forgive each other for whatever we may feel that the world has done to us. So that we can be open to loving each other again in order to bring us all together. You see, losing a love is a truly dangerous time in our lives, because we can make bad decisions based on our need to feel wanted and valued, and we can decide that, if we don't find a new love immediately to replace the one that we lost, then it is because of something that we did, or something that the world did to us, and that is when we can make the decision to get revenge on the world by hating everyone. That is when things can get bad for us, and for everyone who do care about us. I see it every day. People lose love, and so they decide to hate everyone, or worse yet, they decide to hate those who are potential partners for them, when in reality, it is not their fault.

As a result of this decision, we can decide to spread hate everywhere we go. Or worse yet, we might decide to be a bad person to a new partner by doing things like trying to control them, or even trying to hurt them through physical or emotional abuse in order to make sure that they do not hurt us like our last partner did, and like ripples in a pond, this can cause our new partner to hate everyone, which affects those around them, and so on, and so forth. In the end, we could end up spreading so much hate that it could stop anything good from ever happening in our lives, and worst of all, it could cause our children to grow up thinking that they should hate everyone around them, and treat everyone around them bad as well, and.......well, you see how just one drop of hate can spread until it is an ocean of sadness. We can change that, though, if we just accept the responsibility to love instead of hate, to care instead of hurt, and most importantly, to care about others as much as we care about ourselves. If we accept the responsibility to do that, then our world will change for the better, and we will be remembered as the generation that was responsible for bringing our world together through *"Acceptance"*, which brings with it peace, caring, mutual respect, and of course, love.

If I have any last message before I go, I believe that it is this. We can make our world a better place. We can stop hatred, in all its forms. We can make everything from war, hunger, sickness, bigotry, bullying, discrimination, and all the other problems that we face as a race disappear forever. We can do it by adopting a simple philosophy. One that will finally bring us all together and allow us to progress, and evolve, into a better and brighter tomorrow for all of us. I firmly believe that we can achieve this better future for our race, and we can do it by adopting one simple set of beliefs, one simple philosophy. The philosophy of *"Acceptance"*.

We can accept others for who they are, and how they want to live their lives, by simply accepting who they are, instead of trying to change them to whom we want them to be. We can accept the fact that, while people may look different than us, they are just like us, because we are all truly one race, and by doing so, we can make racism a thing of the past. After all, it is hard to be a racist when we accept the fact that we are all one race. We can make bullying a thing of the past when we accept the fact that we would rather be a hero than a bystander. We can solve many of the world's most difficult problems when we accept things like the fact that education should be made available to all by making it as cheap as possible (while ensuring that the people who rely on the jobs that keep a school operating get paid), and especially made available to everyone who has the high intelligence levels. There could be

395

someone out there, right now, who may hold the key to eradicating some of the world's most horrible diseases because they have such a high intelligence level, but because they cannot afford to go to college, they may never be allowed to get the education that they need.

We can do this, and a lot more, if we are brave enough to take that first step towards a better tomorrow for all of us. That first step into the paradise that our world could be, and that our race could enjoy together. It will not be easy, nothing good ever is, and it will not happen overnight. It will take a lot of work. We can do it, though, if we all just come together finally with faith in our fellow humans, mutual respect, love, and understanding. We can do it if we just take that first step, the step called *"Acceptance"*. Love is the key, the future is the door. All we need to do is cross that threshold and accept the fact that it truly is our responsibility to change our world by accepting all our brothers and sisters in our race.

Let me leave you with this. I call these the ***"Core Values of Acceptance"***. I read these core values every day before I go out into the world, and they help me to remember the best way that I can practice *"Acceptance"*. They are as follows:

Core Value #1: **Mutual Respect**. I will respect everyone that I meet, as long as they don't want to cause me, or anyone else, harm in any way. If they want to express a different opinion than me, then I will listen to what they have to say, without trying to stifle them in order to keep them from expressing their views, because I would rather have a mutually respectful exchange of ideas when talking to others. I will not argue with them, however, after they express their opinion, I will talk to them about how I feel, and then we can debate our differences in a polite, and mutually respectful, manner.   I will not try to stifle them by yelling at them, or by trying to keep them silent through violence or disrespectful actions, because I want them to respect me for my opinion, and if I want them to respect me, then I will respect them.   I will treat others the same way that I want to be treated in all things.

Core Value #2:   Love not Hate.   I will treat everyone like they are worthy of love, because when we have some level of love for each other, then we genuinely care about each other, even if we are not in a romantic relationship.   All hate does is cause us to fight each other and fighting amongst ourselves will never allow us to come together in peace.   Therefore, I will treat everyone with some level of love, as long as they do not want to cause any harm to anyone, because when I do have some level of love for someone, then I truly do care about them.   Caring about everyone in our race will be necessary if we are ever going to come together as one to solve all our problems.

Core Value #3:   Caring by Sharing.   I will show others that I do care about them, even if I am not in a romantic relationship with them.   I will do this by sharing what I have with them when I am able to.   If I see someone who is trying to make it on a small salary, then I will help them if I can, even if that is just by giving them something small like a tip.   I will donate to charities that help those in need, especially when they help sick children, because children deserve to have the chance at a long life.   I will help people who have fallen on hard times and are homeless by trying to give them a hand up instead of a handout, even if that means that I volunteer my time to help them get the help that they need to beat addictions, and even help them look for work if they need a job.   If I genuinely care about them, then I want to help them by helping them to solve the situation that made them homeless in the first place so that they are not homeless anymore.   By caring for those in need, it will help all

397

of us come together by helping us make it in this life.   If I ever expect anyone to help me should I need it, then I will help those who may need it.   If I want people to care about me, then I need to care about them.

Core Value #4:   Be a Hero.   If someone needs me, then I will be there for them if I can, as long as it does not put me into physical danger of being injured.   These include things like if I see a robbery, then I will be the hero who calls the police immediately without putting myself into danger of being physically harmed.   If I see someone being assaulted, or I think that they are being assaulted because I hear it, then I will call the police so that they can get the help they need, instead of just ignoring the screams.   If I see or hear of any crime being committed, then I will call the police.   If I want someone to care enough about me to get me help if I am in danger, then I need to care about them enough to get them the help that they need.   If I see someone being bullied, I will do what I can to stop it. If I see someone having trouble with something, even something small like getting something off a shelf at a store, then I will help if I can.   If I want others to help me when I need it, then I will help them if I can, because caring about each other will help to bring us all together in peace and love.

Core Value #5:   Learn and Share Knowledge.   I will try to learn something new every day, and then I will share that knowledge when I can, without sounding arrogant about what I know.   If I see someone having a problem doing something, and I can help them by showing them a better way to do it, then I will share my knowledge, but I will do so in a friendly manner.   I will not use my knowledge or wisdom to try and show someone up, or to try and make them feel like I think that they are inferior to me.   I will listen to people when they share their knowledge with me, and I will not let my ego get in the way.   It is through the sharing of knowledge that we advance as an individual, and as a race.

Core Value #6:   **Be a Friend**. I will try to be friendly with everyone that I meet, as long as they are not trying to cause harm to me or anyone else.   I will accept the fact that, even though I am trying to be a friend to someone, I do not have to have a romantic relationship with them, and I will not try and force anyone to have a romantic relationship with me.   I understand that people may not want to have a romantic relationship with me, and I will respect their right to choose who they want to have a relationship with, just as I want others to respect my right to choose who I want to have a relationship with.   If I want to have people understand the fact that I want to take my time getting to know them before I can trust them, then I will allow others to take their time getting to know me before they decide to trust me.   If we are all friends who can trust each other, then we can accomplish many things that will benefit us all.

Core Value #7:   **Never Take Advantage of Anyone**. I will not try and take advantage of anyone for my own selfish needs.   I will treat everyone with respect, especially my co-workers, and I will not try and take advantage of them by forcing them to do things that I would not want anyone to force me, or someone that I care about, to do.   Things like trying to force them to have a romantic relationship with me.   I will not try and force someone to love me, because control is not love, it is hate.   I will not try and use things (like sex tapes) to force someone to do anything, like stay in a relationship with me, and I will not use those same things in order to cause anyone, like my ex-partner, harm.   I will not steal, or commit any crime against anyone, because if I do not want anyone to commit a crime against me, then I will not commit a crime against anyone else.   In this way I will prove that I am a good person, and if we are all good people who treat others the way that we want to be treated, then it will help us all come together in peace.

A Visit to the City in the Light

Core Value #8:   **Set the Example**.   I will try and set the example in everything that I do and say.   I will show people how to be a good person by living the life of a good person, without acting arrogantly in my actions or acting like I am better than anyone else. I will treat others the way that I want to be treated.   I will teach children by instructing them, and more importantly, showing them how to be a good person, and how to have good relationships in their lives.   How to be responsible for their actions, as well as the value of hard work and a good education.   I will be a good person to my partner at all times, and I will never treat them badly.   This includes never betraying them by going to another person for intimacy while we are in a relationship, because I do not want my partner to betray me in this manner.   This also includes never saying hurtful things to them or being violent to them by physically harming them.   I will communicate with my partner and show them, through my actions, that I really do care about them at all times, because I want my partner to treat me the same way.   I will respect other people, even if the way that they believe and live their lives is completely different from the way I believe and live my life, because I want other people to respect me for the way that I believe and live my life.   I will not discriminate against others, especially where religion is concerned, because I do not want anyone to discriminate against me.   I will always be there for others in order to help them when and where they need it (if it does not involve helping them to commit a crime, or helping them to cause harm to anyone), especially if I want others to be there for me if I may need it.   I will do these things because if we are all good to each other in this way, then we will be able to come together as one race in order to work together to solve all our race's problems.

Core Value #9:   **Spread the Word**.   I will talk to people about the philosophy of *"Acceptance"* every chance that I get.   I will do this to try and bring us all together in peace, mutual respect, love, and cooperation. I will try to show people that, by all of us coming together, like the philosophy of *"Acceptance"* dictates, then we can join together to solve all of our race's problems. In order for *"Acceptance"* to become a universal practice to benefit us, then it needs to be disseminated, and I will do my part by talking to others about it every chance I get.

We can do it. We can bring our world together in peace and love. I believe, with all my heart, that all we have to do is one simple thing, and that thing is to come together through *"Acceptance"* and genuinely love and care about each other. As I said earlier, I know that this message was given to me to spread to our race for a reason, and I believe that the reason was that God saw how we are tearing each other apart. God wants us to succeed and become the fantastic race that we could be, whether we believe in him or not. God wants us to evolve and advance into a better tomorrow, one that will see us do the many incredible things that we are capable of doing. That is why I am convinced that God had, who I believe was an Angel, place the plan into my head when I went to the *'City of Light'*. We cannot do anything, though, until we all make the decision to finally stop hating each other and start working together. I believe that is why this message is so important, because it is the key to bringing us together. I am not completely sure just why I was chosen to spread this message. After all, am I anyone important? No, I am just a normal, average human. I do have a theory, though. I think that I was chosen because I am just a normal, average human.

I mean, if I were a religious leader, then maybe people would see that, and then they might say that all I am trying to do is spread propaganda for my individual church. Or if I was a famous person that a lot of people know and listen to, then a lot of people might say that all I am doing is trying to gain more popularity for myself. No,

A Visit to the City in the Light

I think that the reason was because I am just a normal average human being, and that is important, because this message is way too important to have it distracted by who I am.

At any rate, that is it. I do only have one last question to ask, though. I am doing everything that I can to spread this message. My question is this. Will you help me spread this message? I do know this. It is the fact that I truly do care about you all, because you are my brothers and sisters in our race, and I will accept you into my life. Will you accept me, and help me now that our race needs us the most? I sincerely hope so, because I truly cannot wait to see all the incredible things that will happen for our race once we all come together in peace and love in order to advance our race into a better tomorrow. Take care, and may you all be accepted, cared about, and loved.

Chapter Fourteen
Final Thoughts for Accepting Souls

I just wanted to add something here, in case you need some inspiration to help you on your way to spreading love, caring, and compassion to our brothers and sisters in our race. This time, though, I wanted to share some scripture with you that deals with the core values of *"Acceptance"* directly. Just in case you need something to share with other people. So, they can see that *"Acceptance"* truly is a plan that has been around for a very long time. A plan that can work if we all just give it a chance. Now again, it has never been my intention to change the way that you believe religiously by showing you how *"Acceptance"* came from the Bible and the teachings of God and our Lord and Savior Jesus Christ, but if anything that I have said in this book does make you want to become a Christian, then it would make me happy to know that I have done something to bring someone closer to God.

Anyway, I truly wish that all of you have a wonderful and blessed life, and that maybe I have touched you in some way with the message that I was told to spread to our race, because I really do feel that *"Acceptance"* can change our world for the better. I know that it has changed my life, as well as the lives of those who I have taught it to, and I am sure that it can change your life, and the lives of those who are close to you, through its message of love and hope for all of us. Thank you for being my brothers and sisters, and I truly do love you all. May you all have a blessed life, full of love, and caring, and of course, *"Acceptance"*.

Accepting Others

A Visit to the City in the Light

I wanted to share these for the times in this book where I mentioned that we should be more accepting of each other, even though other people may hold beliefs, and live their lives, in ways that are much different than us.

1 Peter 3:8 - *"Finally, all of you, be like-minded, **be sympathetic, love one another, be compassionate and humble**"* New International Version (NIV)

We should be compassionate towards all our brothers and sisters in our race and love one another (as long as they are not trying to harm others), and we can do that by accepting each other.

1 Peter 3:9 - *"**Do not repay evil with evil or insult with insult**. On the contrary, **repay evil with blessing**, because to this you were called so that you may inherit a blessing"* New International Version (NIV)

If we treat others in our race with scorn (*"evil"*) or in another bad way that would keep us apart, then we will never achieve the peace and love that we all want in order to bring our race together. Conversely, if we repay *"evil with blessing"*, or in other words, when someone does something bad to us then we do not retaliate against them, then not only will it end the cycle of revenge, but it will also set a good example for our children to follow.

Romans 2:11 - *"For God **does not show favoritism**"*. New International Version (NIV)

Neither should we when dealing with those who believe differently than we do and live their lives differently than us. We should love all our brothers and sisters in our race equally, without showing favoritism to those who believe exactly the way that we do.

A Journey There.......and Back Again with a Message of Hope

If we are ever going to come together in peace and love by accepting each other, then we need to treat everyone equally.

Romans 14:1 - *"Accept the one whose faith is weak, without quarreling over disputable matters"*. New International Version (NIV)

If we want others to accept us and the way that we believe, then we should accept them no matter how they believe *"without quarreling"* with them. In doing so, we will be able to finally stop all the fighting amongst ourselves, and we will be able to bring us all together. After all, that is what *"Acceptance"* is all about. Bringing us all together, even if we believe differently than others, or in other words, when their *"faith is weak"* in what we believe as individuals.

Colossians 3:12-14 - *(12) "Therefore, as God's chosen people, holy and dearly loved, clothe yourselves with compassion, kindness, humility, gentleness and patience. (13) Bear with each other and forgive one another if any of you has a grievance against someone. Forgive as the Lord forgave you. (14) And over all these virtues put on love, which binds them all together in perfect unity"*. New International Version (NIV)

We should treat others the way that we want everyone to treat us, with *"compassion, kindness, humility, gentleness and patience"*. We should forgive others if we seek it from anyone, and we should wrap all these traits up with *"love"*, for love can bring us all together, and it really *"binds"* us all in peace and love forever. This is what *"Acceptance"* is all about.

Spreading Love to All of Our Brothers and Sisters

A Visit to the City in the Light

1 Corinthians 13:4-7 - *(4) "Love is patient, love is kind. It does not envy, it does not boast, it is not proud. (5) It does not dishonor others, it is not self-seeking, it is not easily angered, it keeps no record of wrongs. (6) Love does not delight in evil but rejoices with the truth. (7) It always protects, always trusts, always hopes, always perseveres"*. New International Version (NIV)

This applies whether we are talking about the love we have for a partner, a family member, or the love that we have for everyone, for if we want to be loved and cared about, then we should treat everyone with the love and care that we want from them, which this scripture defines.

1 Corinthians 16:14 - *"Do everything in love"*. New International Version (NIV)

As this scripture declares, love is not only an emotion, but a deliberate intentional act. When we are kind and caring to others, then we are treating them with love, and it applies to how we treat anyone that we interact with. It is intended to apply not just to marriage, but to how we treat everyone in our race. If we are ever going to come together through the use of *"Acceptance"*, then we need to show everyone in our race love by infusing love for our fellow human beings into everything that we do. The type of love that is mentioned in **1 Corinthians 13:4-7**.

Proverbs 10:12 - *"Hatred stirs up conflict, but love covers over all wrongs"*. New International Version (NIV)

If we are to bring our race together, then we need to treat everyone with love, no matter how much we may not like the way that they live their lives, and no matter if they have done something wrong to us in the past.   If we treat everyone with hatred, and we do not show them love, then it will only cause strife amongst us, and we will never be able to come together.   We need to allow the power of love to bring us all together, and let it cover *"all wrongs"*.

1 John 3:18 - *"Dear children, **let us not love with words or speech but with actions** and in truth"*. New International Version (NIV)

If we are to bring our race together in peace and love, then we need to show it through our actions towards each other, instead of only talking about it.

Ephesians 4:2 - *"**Be completely humble and gentle; be patient,** bearing with one another in love"*. New International Version (NIV)

If we are ever to come together with peace and love for each other, then we need to be *"gentle"* and *"patient"* with each other, instead of confrontational and hateful.

Forgiving Others

Luke 6:37 - *"**Do not judge,** and you will not be judged.   **Do not condemn,** and you will not be condemned.   **Forgive,** and you will be forgiven"*. New International Version (NIV)

If we are ever going to come together, then we are going to need to stop condemning and judging each other and start the healing process by forgiving each other.   If all we do is condemn and judge each other, then we will never come together in peace and love.

Luke 6:27 - *"But to you who are listening I say: **Love your enemies, do good to those who hate you.** "*. New International

A Visit to the City in the Light

Version (NIV)

If we want forgiveness and love from others, then we need to love and forgive others. This includes those who we consider our enemies. It is through forgiveness and love that we will be able to achieve true unity, and with that we will finally be able to come together. That includes doing good to others, especially those who might hate us. It will set the example for others to follow.

Matthew 5:44 - *"But I tell you, **love your enemies and pray for those who persecute you."***. New International Version (NIV)

If we are ever going to come together through utilizing *"Acceptance"*, then we need to stop fighting with those who persecute us and set the example by praying for those who persecute us for the way that we believe and live our lives. We need to stop letting those who hate us win by giving them what they want (by doing things like letting them know that we are hurt by what they say, and by giving them the attention that they want, through things like giving them *'likes'* and *'shares'*). Instead, we need to triumph over their hate by letting them know that we truly forgive them, and that we are praying for them in a way that lets them know that they will not win. We need to let them know that they are not hurting us, and that we really forgive them for their hate against us. In that way not only will they not win, but our love will triumph over them in a way that will give us the victory over their hate.

James 5:16 - *"Therefore **confess your sins to each other and pray for each other so that you may be healed. The prayer of a righteous person is powerful and effective."***. New International Version (NIV)

If we are going to come together, then we need to be able to

408

forgive each other by praying for each other and truly forgiving each other so that our hurt will be healed.   It will start the healing process between all of us so that we can finally come together in peace and love.

1 John 4:11 - *"Dear friends, since God so loved us, **we also ought to love one another."**. New International Version (NIV)*

If we want to be loved by others, and be forgiven for our actions, then we should be willing to ***"love one another"***, especially if we want to bring our race together in peace and love through *"Acceptance"*.

Being a Good Person

Isaiah 1:17 - *"Learn to do right; seek justice.   **Defend the oppressed.   Take up the cause of the fatherless; plead the case of the widow."**. New International Version (NIV)*

If we want to better our race through the example of who we are as a good person, then we need to show it through our actions of good towards others, especially towards those who need it the most. Therefore, we should always try and be there for everyone who needs it the most, like people who are homeless or who are trying to survive on a small salary.

James 1:19 - *"My dear brothers and sisters, take note of this: **Everyone should be quick to listen, slow to speak and slow to become angry."**. New International Version (NIV)*

If we want to stop all the hatred in our world, then we should care enough about each other to show each other that we care, by doing things like being good listeners to others, instead of just caring about our own selves when we talk to others. In addition, we should not be so easily angered when dealing with others. In that way, we will show others that we really do care about them and respect them, instead of showing them that we only care about ourselves. That can make a world of difference in their lives, and in our lives as well.

1 Peter 4:8 - *"Above all, **love each other deeply**, because **love covers over a multitude of sins.**"*. New International Version (NIV)

By showing each other that we have love (as defined in **1 Corinthians 13:4-7**) for all our brothers and sisters in our race, then we will all be able to come together, because love truly can unite us and bring us forgiveness from everyone for our past actions. Past actions should not define who we are. Our future actions should define who we are. We can be forgiven by others for our past actions if we are willing to change ourselves into the good person that we want others to see us as, and we are willing to forgive others for their past actions.

Proverbs 15:1 - *"**A gentle answer turns away wrath**, but **a harsh word stirs up anger.**"*. New International Version (NIV)

If we want to heal our world and stop all the hate that exists between so many of us, then we should set the example by not being confrontational towards others through our words.

Philippians 2:3-4 - *(3) "Do nothing out of selfish ambition or vain conceit. Rather, **in humility value others above yourselves**, (4) not looking to your own interests but each of you to the interests of the others.*"*. New International Version (NIV)

If we want to start the healing process where all the hate between us in our race is concerned, then we should start by not thinking that, or acting like, we are better than anyone else. When we think that we are better others, then our egos can get in the way of bringing us all together. We are all the same race, and the only thing that should be the determining factor, when deciding if anyone is better than anyone else, is the type of person that we are, and how much we really care about each other. Not what we do for a living, the color of our skin, or any other superficial reason. Therefore, when we interact with anyone in our race, we should put their interests ahead of our own. That way they will see that we truly do care about them, and in return, they will want to care about us as well.

Doing Good Deeds

Matthew 5:16 - *"In the same way, **let your light shine before others, that they may see your good deeds** and glorify your Father in heaven. "*. New International Version (NIV)

If we want to bring everyone together through being good to others, and doing good things for others, then we should set the example by truly being good to others always. That way they can see, through our actions, that the way to bring us all together is by being good to each other.

Galatians 6:9 - *"**Let us not become weary in doing good**, for at the proper time **we will reap a harvest if we do not give up. "***. New International Version (NIV)

As I said, bringing us all together will not happen overnight. However, if we truly do want to bring everyone together in peace and love, then we need to start being good to each other now, and we must not give up.   After a time, we will achieve our goal of total world peace through love and *"Acceptance"* if we do not become weary of trying.

Titus 3:14 - *"**Our people must learn to devote themselves to doing what is good**, in order **to provide for urgent needs** and **not live unproductive lives**."*. New International Version (NIV)

Again, we need to accept the responsibility to do good things for our brothers and sisters in our race in order to show everyone that through *"Acceptance"* we can come together in peace.   If we devote ourselves to doing good, like *"Acceptance"* dictates we do, then we can make it a reality.   It will keep us from living **"unproductive lives"** as well, because if we devote ourselves to doing good for our entire race, like what happens when we work a job that helps us to keep our race operating, then we will be able to advance into a better tomorrow for all of us.

1 Timothy 6:18 - *"Command them to do good, to be rich in good deeds, and **to be generous and willing to share**."*. New International Version (NIV)

Again, *"Acceptance"* dictates that, among other things, we should always care about each other by doing good deeds for each other, like being **"generous and willing to share"** what we have with those who need it (like with those who are trying to survive on a small salary by doing things like giving them tips).

Hebrews 13:16 - *"And **do not forget to do good and to share with others**, for with such sacrifices God is pleased."*. New International Version (NIV)

If we want to bring our race together through love and caring

412

for each other, then we should be willing to do good works for everyone, especially for those who need our good deeds the most. In this way, we can truly help everyone who is in need, like when I spoke about helping those who do not make much money at their job by giving them things like tips.   When we share what we have with others who are less fortunate, or who are struggling just trying to make ends meet, then we start bringing us all together through love by practicing *"Acceptance"*.

Love can bring us all together if we show that we truly do care about each other by helping each other every chance we get. Always try and show that you care about others by sharing what you have (even if all you are sharing with someone is your time), because it can make a difference.

<u>Conquering Fear</u>

John 14:27 - *"Peace I leave with you; my peace I give you.   I do not give to you as the world gives.   **Do not let your hearts be troubled and do not be afraid.**"*. New International Version (NIV)

In order to promote the philosophy of *"Acceptance"*, and to be the first to try and place it into action the world over, it will take courage.   The courage of all of us who will be the forerunners of teaching everyone about *"Acceptance"*.   There will be many who will not want us to all come together and work as one.   They will have their own agendas, and their own reasons, for not wanting all of us to come together and accomplish things like making education as cheap as possible for everyone (especially for everyone who we identify as having high intelligence levels), and like making sure that religious freedom is a right for everyone, and all the other things that I have discussed in this book.   Therefore, it will take true courage to make these things a reality, but if we are not afraid, and we do not waiver in our conviction to make our world a better place for all of us, then we can achieve anything that we set our minds to, including making *"Acceptance"* a worldwide reality.

Joshua 1:9 - *"Have I not commanded you?* ***Be strong and courageous****. Do not be afraid; do not be discouraged, for **the LORD your God will be with you wherever you go.***"*. New International Version (NIV)

      As I have stated, I was given the message of *"Acceptance"* to spread to the world, and this message is also spoken of in the Bible as well, and I have tried to show these things in this book. As such, I believe that God will be with all of us who follow this plan (whether we believe in him or not), and he will be with everyone who teaches the plan of *"Acceptance"*. Therefore, we should not be discouraged if this philosophy takes a while to spread and take effect. Instead, we should be steadfast in our conviction to make it happen. We should *"be strong and courageous"* in bringing our world together with peace and love through *"Acceptance"*.

2 Timothy 1:7 - *"For the Spirit God gave us **does not make us timid**, but **gives us power, love and self-discipline.***"*. New International Version (NIV)

      As I have previously stated, since I learned that the plan of *"Acceptance"* is also spoken of in the Bible, I truly believe that God has given me, and us, the *"power, love, and self-discipline"* to do what is necessary to spread this plan to everyone. It can happen, and it can work if we refuse to be *"timid"* in the teaching of it to everyone in the world.

Deuteronomy 31:6 - *"**Be strong and courageous**. **Do not be afraid or terrified because of them**, for the LORD you God goes*

with you; he will never leave you nor forsake you. ". New
International Version (NIV)

As I said earlier, I believe that there will be those who will
not want us all to come together with love and compassion for each
other through *"Acceptance"*, and they will have their own agendas
for not wanting peace and love to bring us together.   They will try
and stop us from spreading the message of *"Acceptance"*, including
ridiculing us, and even ridiculing this book for that matter.
However, as this passage states, we should be strong and courageous
and not afraid of them, because this is the plan that I was given to
spread to our world, and that is spoken of in the Bible.   As such,
God will be with everyone who puts this plan into action, whether
we are believers or non-believers.

Isaiah 41:13 - *"For I am the LORD your God who takes hold of
your right hand and says to you, **Do not fear; I will help you** "*. New
International Version (NIV)

Again, I really believe that God will be with all of us who
puts the plan of *"Acceptance"* into action.   He will not only be with
us, but he will do things to help us spread this plan to the world as
well.   Therefore, we should not be afraid when we are teaching the
philosophy of *"Acceptance"* to the world.

Teaching Others the Philosophy of Acceptance

Matthew 28:19-20 - *(19)* *"Therefore **go and make disciples of all
nations**, baptizing them in the name of the Father and of the Son
and of the Holy Spirit, **(20) and teaching them to obey everything I
have commanded you**.   And surely I am with you always, to the
very end of the age. "*. New International Version (NIV)

A Visit to the City in the Light

As I said, this is the plan that I was given to spread to the world, and more importantly, it is also the plan that God speaks of in the Bible. *"Acceptance"* tells us to come together in love and compassion, and as such, we should spread this plan to all corners of our world in order to bring us all together. Therefore, we should be comforted in the fact that, as this passage states, God will be there with all of us who spreads this plan.

Luke 6:40 - *"The student is not above the teacher, but **everyone who is fully trained will be like their teacher.**"*. New International Version (NIV)

This goes along with what I was saying when I said that we should not look at others like we are better than them, or like they are better than us, and this is especially true where teaching *"Acceptance"* is concerned. We should not treat others like they are beneath us or above us when we are teaching them this plan, or even when they are teaching us something about *"Acceptance"*. Rather, we should treat everyone like they are equal to us.

Romans 15:4 - *"For everything that was written in the past **was written to teach us, so that** through the endurance taught in the Scriptures and the encouragement they provide **we might have hope.**"*. New International Version (NIV)

As the plan of *"Acceptance"* is also included in the Bible, I believe that this plan truly does give us hope for a better tomorrow if we show, through our actions, that we have the fortitude and endurance to see it through by teaching it to everyone, just as it was taught to us. Teaching this philosophy and plan should give us hope. Hope for our race, our world, and for a better tomorrow.

1 Corinthians 15:58 - *"Therefore, my dear brothers and sisters,* *stand firm.   **Let nothing move you.**   Always give yourselves fully to the work of the Lord, because you know that **your labor in the Lord is not in vain.**"*. New International Version (NIV)

I really believe that, if we are steadfast in teaching the plan of *"Acceptance"*, and we do not let anything move us from teaching this plan, then our labor will not be in vain.   If we keep teaching it to everyone, then it will eventually take hold, and when that happens, then our world will become a very wonderful place to live in indeed.

Philippians 4:9 - *"**What you have learned** or received or heard from me, or seen in me - **put it into practice.**   And the God of peace will be with you."*. New International Version (NIV)

I wanted to end the scripture in this chapter with this one passage, because I believe that it pretty much sums up *"Acceptance"* and how, if we just follow this plan, and *"**put it into practice**"* in our own personal lives, then God will be with us all, for he truly is the God of peace, as this plan shows.

Now, I would like to present you with a couple of challenges, one that I mentioned before, and a new one as well. They are as follows.   First, as I stated before, we all have our own personal lives, and we have our own personal worlds that we live in, and I truly do accept you all for that.   Therefore, I would like to, again, first challenge you to seek out additional scripture that applies more specifically to your own personal lives and *"Acceptance"*. Then, as you do find scripture that applies more directly with you, I want you to write down why that piece of scripture applies directly to you, and your life, on a sticky note that is attached to your copy of the Bible, or even just in a diary with the piece of scripture written next to it.   That way you can look at it whenever you need some

417

A Visit to the City in the Light

inspiration.   Then, as far as the second challenge is concerned, I want you to try, every single day, to talk to someone about the philosophy of *"Acceptance"*.   Try to teach someone about the plan, because it is when we start spreading this plan that it will start taking effect.   In addition, I want you to try, every day, to talk to other people about coming up with ideas to solve our race's problems, because when we do that, then we are putting *"Acceptance"* into action, which is what we all need to do in order to bring us together to solve our problems as one.

Take care, and may you all receive love, mutual respect, compassion, caring, and understanding.......through *"Acceptance"*.

Chapter Fifteen
The Entire Journey

Well, as promised, here is the whole story of what happened when I crossed over and went to the City in the Light. My journey was multi-fold, because when I went through the light and reached the other side, I really saw, and talked to, four different people there. The man that I am convinced was an angel, and three other people, family members who took me different places. To start, the day unfolded like this.

I was having a really bad day when I had my heart attack. I had been pushing myself, trying to do too much, and because of my disability, I had gained some weight. So, I already had a lot of risk factors working against me. When I had finished doing what I needed to do downtown, I was already starting to feel *'funny'*, but I thought that it was because I was hungry, so on the way home I stopped and picked up some food. When I got home, I ate my dinner, and then I sat down at my computer. Suddenly, it felt like it was getting harder and harder to breathe, like my chest was being squeezed, and so I went from my computer to the couch, trying to relax but I was not able to. So, I grabbed the phone and called 911, because at that point I knew that I was in trouble. Since I live alone, I just sat there on the couch, praying that the ambulance would arrive when suddenly I started to feel an intense tingling. I remember leaning forward, trying to see if it would help, but when I did, it made the pain worse. I remember trying to stand up, however, when I did, the tingling became so intense that I blacked out.

The next thing that I remember I was flying through what appeared to be a tunnel made of white blinding light, and then I

A Visit to the City in the Light

found myself standing on a piece of solid ground, and I was looking at the entrance to what appeared to be a magnificent city. The city was beautiful. It shimmered with blue and white and gold colors, almost like there were no real edges to any of the buildings, or at least I could not see any sharp edges because of the way that the buildings radiated and glowed. It was at that point that I saw the man standing in front of me. He had short, wavy, white hair, and he seemed to have an aura about him, making him appear to almost glow. He was smiling at me, and I could really *'feel'* his smile, which kind of shocked me because I have never felt a smile before. I felt his though.

He looked at me, and he said, *"Be careful, don't fall."*, in a very calm, soothing, and in a weird way echoing, voice. I believe that he said that because he saw that I was a little unsteady. You see, I walk with a cane, and it surprised me when I realized that I did not need it to stand. Then he said, *"There are some people that want to see you."*. At that point I realized that I could see something other than the buildings in the city. I saw that there were shapes, sort of shadowy silhouettes, of what appeared to be many people, and they were approaching me, coming from the city. I thought that I recognized some of them, but I was not sure. As the shadows approached me, they started to come into sharper view, and I realized that they were staring at me, and I could hear something that sounded like slight murmuring. I could not make out exactly what they were saying, but they sounded almost excited, like they were curious to see me. To try and put it into perspective, I felt like the new exhibit at a zoo, sort of like I was the baby animal that everyone wants to see.

It was at that point that three figures started coming towards me, sort of walking through the shadows of the other people, and when they came near to me, I saw that there were two young men

420

and a young woman.   They saw my confusion as to who they were, and so one of the young men said, *"Don't you recognize us, kid?"*. I just stood there, stunned, when he said, *"Maybe this will help."*. At that point they started to change, to grow older as I stared at them, and when they were done, to my amazement I knew instantly that standing in front of me was my Dad, my Uncle Albert, and of course, my Grandma.

"Dad?", I asked.   He smiled at me and said, *"Yeah, kid, it's me."*.

"You remember us little (name)?", Grandma asked.   I looked at her, and then at my Dad and asked, *"Is this real?"*. Uncle Albert said, *"We're here, just like you."*.

Then Dad said, *"We've been watching you.   You done what I told you to do.   I'm proud of you kid.   You done good."*.

"Are you angels?", I asked.   Dad replied, *"No, we're not angels.   They watch over us."*.

"No favorites here.", Uncle Albert said.

"We're all the same.", Grandma added.   Then Dad said, *"Come on, kid, let's go for a drive."*

"Yeah, let's have some fun.", Uncle Albert said.

Do you know how it looks when you spin around in a circle, and everything sort of goes by real fast, so that you can tell that there are things there, but you cannot make them out because they are flying by so fast?   Well, that is what it looked like to me, but it only lasted for about a second, and then I found myself driving my

A Visit to the City in the Light

truck with my dad sitting next to me. In addition, I recognized the road that we were traveling down. It was a country road that was close to the house that I grew up in, which is just outside of my hometown. At this point I told my dad, *"I'm thinking about changing churches."*. I think that I said that because I have been disillusioned by the actions of the leader of my individual meeting house, and I have been thinking that maybe I need to go to a new church.

Dad replied, *"Well, you got to do what you think is best."*. This surprised me because my dad was a staunch Roman Catholic, and he always wanted me to be a Catholic when he was alive. Then, from the back seat, Grandma said, *"Look for the one with her in it."*, and she pointed out the window.

At this point it was like time slowed, because I was able to look out of my window and, passing by very slowly, I saw who she was pointing to. By the side of the road there was a girl in a summer dress that was blue and had white shapes on it, and the shapes looked like flowers, or maybe birds. She also had a summer hat on that had a big brim that looked to be made of straw, and it had a band around the hat that looked like a ribbon. She was also wearing white high heels that were conservative in height (they appeared to be only about 1 inch tall). She also had hair that was kind of strawberry blond, and it was mostly straight, but kind of wavy on the edges as well, and it flowed down to just above the middle of her back. I could not tell what her face looked like because she was bent over, tending to some flowers that were planted beside the road, and her back was to me. There was one thing that I noticed, though, and it was the fact that, even though she was on the side of the road, I could hear her humming a tune. It was a happy, joyous tune, like she was very content with what she was doing. I felt peaceful when I looked at her, like she made my

422

heart feel lighter just from hearing the tune that she was humming.

"Who is she?", I asked. *"Someone very special."*, Dad
replied. Then Grandma said, *"She's a good one (name). You're a
good one too."*.

"She sounds happy.", I said.

Uncle Albert said, *"She is. She likes tending to them
flowers."*.

*"It makes her happy. You've got to be happy with what you
do."*, Dad said.

Then Dad said, *"I want to show you something kid."*. After
he said this, everything started spinning again, and almost instantly,
we were at the top of a dam that I used to fish off when I was a
child.

"Why are we here?", I asked. Dad said, *"That's why."*, and
he nodded his head, gesturing down to where the water should be. I
held the railing and looked over. The water was gone, and instead,
what I saw were ever changing scenes of chaos and horror. I had
gone fishing off this small dam many times, because it was not too
high, and I would catch fish by the basket full here. This time,
however, when I looked off the edge, I saw something completely
different, and it shocked me. There was fire everywhere, and inside
the swirling flames were shifting scenes of absolute horror and
mayhem. I saw people fighting each other, killing each other in a
multitude of ways. There was screaming, and shouting, and people
crying out in pain.

I looked over at my dad, wanting to ask him what this was,

but it was like I could not speak.   It was like I was in shock because of what I was witnessing.   He did not say anything at first, but then he said, *"Bad stuff."*.

I said, *"What is this?"*.

Dad looked at me and he said, *"Isn't it obvious?"*.

Then, looking back down at the chaos, Dad said, *"I wish that I could help you kid.   I wish that I could be there to protect you, but I can't."*.

"Protect me from what?", I asked, but all he did was continue to stare down at the chaos.

Then Dad said, *"Too much hating."*.

Uncle Albert said, *"Rules."*.   I looked at him and asked, *"Rules?"*.   He replied, *"Got to have rules.   Got to follow them."*

"Otherwise, it's this.", dad said.

Then uncle Albert said, *"Got to stop."*

At this point I returned my gaze to the scenes of horror that were happening down below, and it was at that point that I saw it. The most horrifying thing that I have ever seen in my entire life.   In the fire was the scene of a little girl, about 9 or 10, and she had a look of terror on her face.   It looked like someone had her by the arm, and it sounded like she was pleading *"Nooooo! Nooooo!"*, and then she started screaming *"Owie! Owie!"* over and over again as someone dragged her away, and her cries rose in crescendo until they turned into a scream of complete hysterics as the scene started

424

to shift once again.   As it shifted, though, I could still hear her screaming and wailing as if she were being torn apart.   It was too much for me to bear, and I felt myself wanting to jump over the railing to save her, but before I could, I felt my grandma reach over and put her arm around mine, and then she put her other hand on mine and started to pat it, like she did when I was a little boy to comfort me.   When she did this, everything shifted again, and this time I found myself sitting in the stands of the high school that I attended, watching a football game at night.

I turned to my dad and, still shaking from what I saw and heard, I asked him, *"Is she going to be ok?"*, but dad just stared at the game.

"Nothing's set.", Uncle Albert said.

Then my grandma said, *"Look at the game, little (name)."*. I turned my attention to the game, and when I did, I noticed a few things.   The first thing that I noticed was that the two teams seemed to be playing in a spotlight, where you could see them while everything around them seemed to be in darkness.   I also noticed that the two teams were wearing the same uniforms.   Then I noticed that there was no scoreboard, coaches, referees, or cheerleaders.   As a matter of fact, there were no other people in the stands except for the four of us.   Then I saw that, every time one side made a good play, everyone on both teams celebrated.   Like when the offense would make a good play, even the defense congratulated the player who made the play or scored.   Or when the defense would make a good play, everyone celebrated and congratulated each other. There was no fighting or arguing.   Everyone just seemed to be having a good time playing together.

I looked at Dad and asked, *"Who's winning?"*

425

A Visit to the City in the Light

"Does it matter?", he replied.

"They know the secret.", Grandma said.   *"The secret?"*, I asked, but she did not reply.

Then Dad said, *"Look at them playing together.   They sure work good together, don't they kid?"*.   I turned back to the game, trying to figure out what he was talking about when he said, *"They got a good plan.   Works every time."*

"What plan?", I asked.

Grandma said softly, *"For happiness.   For life."*

Then Dad said, *"Kid, you need to be strong."*.

"Why?" I asked him, but he did not respond.

Uncle Albert said, *"Listen to your dad."*

"Do what he tells you to, little (name).", Grandma added.

It was at this point that I noticed that the spotlight seemed to be getting smaller and smaller around the players, and the sounds that they were making seemed to be getting fainter.   Then dad said, *"It's getting dark, kid.   Time to go."*.   When he said this everything seemed to be enveloped in darkness, and when the light came back, I found myself back in front of the City.

Me and my dad had a wonderful relationship while he was alive, and I remember feeling like I was a little kid again, like nothing could ever hurt me as long as he was there with me.   I felt like I never wanted to leave, like I just wanted to stay there forever.

A Journey There.......and Back Again with a Message of Hope

I looked at him and said, *"Can I stay?"*.

"You got a lot of work to do kid, and we've got to go.", Dad replied.

Grandma smiled at me just like she used to do when I was a child and said, *"We'll be here, little (name)."*.

"We'll be with you. Keeping an eye on you.", Uncle Albert added.

"We'll see each other again.", dad said. After he said that, Uncle Albert and Grandma smiled at me, and then retreated into the shadows once more.

Then, as I looked back to my dad, he pointed to the man who I originally saw standing at the gateway to the city, and he said, *"There's someone over there that wants to talk to you. Listen to him. Do what he says."*. Then my dad turned around and started to walk back into the shadows. I literally felt tears begin to fill my eyes, and I felt sad. I said, *"Bye dad."*. When I said this, he turned back to me and smiled the way that he always did when I was a kid and he was proud of me, and then he disappeared back into the shadows.

Walking back over to where the man was, I felt sad, because I really have missed my dad ever since he passed away, and it was like feeling that loss all over again. I looked at the man and said, *"I'm not ready."*. I do not know if I said that because I was not ready to leave my dad, or if I said it because I was not ready to enter the city. All I know for a fact is that I said it. This caused pause in the man, however, after pausing for a second, he smiled at me again, and he said, *"Of course you are not ready. It's not your time."*.

427

A Visit to the City in the Light

At that point he came close to me and touched my forehead, and when he did, everything was enveloped in a bright light again, and I found myself back home.

When I returned, the first thing that I heard were the paramedics banging on my door. I remember saying, *"It's unlocked."* in a faint voice. As they came in, I heard one of them say, *"I'm getting the paddles."*, meaning the defibrillator paddles to start my heart again. It was at that point that I looked up at him and said, *"I'm not dead yet!"*. When I did this, he got a shocked and surprised look on his face, like he was thinking *'Are you kidding me?!?'*, and he stopped what he was doing and just stared at me for a moment in disbelief. Then, after checking my vitals, the other paramedics got the stretcher and put me on a board, and then they loaded me into the ambulance. They put a Nitroglycerin Pill under my tongue, and then they started working on me. They gave me an IV and rechecked my vitals. At one point the paramedic in the back of the ambulance said, *"Hey, welcome back! Look, even your color is returning!"*. It was at that point that they explained to me that I was completely pale when they entered my home and found me, and they were convinced that I was gone, but then they were relieved when I said something (and slightly more than shocked. I mean, I wish I had been able to take a picture of their faces when I said that I was not dead yet. It was priceless), and now they felt better because the color was returning to my face and skin. The thing that I noticed the most was the fact that, even though I had gone through this traumatic experience, I was completely calm, even before they gave me the Nitroglycerin Pill and the IV fluids. I am convinced that the reason I was so calm was because of what I saw and experienced. I know what awaits me now, and I am no longer afraid of dying.

Later at the hospital, I was not concerned when they told me that I needed to have bypass surgery, and that I ran the risk of having another heart attack at any time if I left the hospital. Even though they told me this I just felt that I would be ok, like all the other times that I should have died but did not. After all, I had been given a mission to complete, and I was more excited about what I needed to do than I was worried about what the doctors were saying might happen to me. I could not wait to get started and get this book written so that I could share the message with everyone in our world.

I have heard of many people having what is called a *'Near Death Experience'* in the past, but I was always skeptical, wondering if it really was possible to visit Heaven and then return, but not anymore. It is easy for people to question something that has not happened to them, especially something like this, and I understand that completely. All I can tell you, though, is this. I am convinced that what I experienced was real. I am convinced to the point where I no longer fear death, because I know what is waiting for me when I do die (not to mention the fact that I know what it feels like to die as well, so that no longer scares me either).

I also know that I am not alone in this experience. Like I said, there are people all over the world who have reported having an experience like I did. I look at it like this. I do not know you on a personal level, so I do not know your life or even what you did today. Now, you know what you ate for breakfast (or lunch, or dinner) today, but since I was not there with you, I do not know what you had (or even if you ate at all). Therefore, I do not know, for definite, what you ate. You do know, though, because you were there, and you experienced it. It is just like what happened to me. I know that what I experienced was real, but you do not, because you were not there with me, so I understand why it is difficult for people to believe that something like this happened to me.

A Visit to the City in the Light

      This is why I said that one of the toughest things to do is to be a Christian, because it requires that you believe with a heart that operates on pure faith alone. Faith in the fact that God is real, faith in the fact that our Lord and Savior Jesus Christ was real and that he was here on Earth (and that he was empowered by God to perform miracles), and faith in the fact that what happened in the Bible really happened. Even as a Christian, though, having faith that what happened to me truly happened is hard, and I get that. I just hope that everyone concentrates on the message when reading this book, because it is a good plan to finally bring our race together as one.

      There is one more thing that I would like to add again, and that is this. Is this the end? Is reading this book all that we need to do? No, and I would like to reiterate why. You see, God, in his infinite wisdom, knows that a lot of times we read a book, or hear a message, and then we just forget about it and go back to our lives. That won't be enough this time, though. Not if we truly want to follow his message and enact the change in our lives that will be required to help all of us in these troubled times. Not this time. What will be required this time is that we will all need to truly do something to make this message a reality. If we truly want to see this message become a reality worldwide then we will need to make it happen, and the only way to do that is to start living our lives according to the message contained in the Bible, the one that this book talks about.......the message of love, forgiveness, and most importantly, acceptance. I will be doing my best to do my part.......will you be willing to help me? Now, let me be clear about something. To repeat, I know that it will not be easy, and that it will definitely not happen overnight. However, I do know that if we all, for once, just give it a sincere try, and follow God's message that is contained in the Bible, the message that I talk about in this book.......then we can succeed, and the change that we will see happen in our lives, and in our world, will be glorious to see indeed, because the change that we will see will be based on the power of God's love, the love that he has for all of us.

Anyway, that is it. The entire journey. Again, it is my hope that this book will inspire you to put its message into practice, because I truly do believe that it can help to bring peace to our world. God loves us all, even if we do not believe in him, and I am convinced that this is why I was entrusted to bring this message to everyone, so that we can finally have the chance to stop all the violence, and the freedom to do so as well. May you all be accepted in the way that you live your life, and in everything that you do.

Endnotes

[1] . . Tina Peng. (2015). 'I'm a public defender. It's impossible for me to do a good job representing my clients.' "The Washington Post". (online opinion). 3 September.

[2] . . Kathleen M. Dillon. (1987). 'False Sexual Abuse Allegations: Causes and Concerns'. "Social Work". (Volume 32, Issue 6). 1 January.

Yamini Pustake Bhalerao. (2019). 'Fake Molestation Cases: When Women Become Impediment In Justice'. "Shethepeople". (online edition). 29 January.

Jennifer Gonnerman. (2017). 'Has Daryl Kelly spent twenty years in prison for a crime that never happened?' "The New Yorker". (online edition). 14 December.

Maurice Possley. (2012). 'Tony Hall. Other Texas Child Sex Abuse Cases'. "The National Registry of Exonerations". (online edition). 18 October.

Doug Linder. (2003). 'The McMartin Preschool Abuse Trial: A Commentary'. "University of Missouri-Kansas City School of Law". (online edition).

Meredith Maran. (2010). 'Meredith Maran: Did my father really abuse me?'. "The Guardian". (online edition). 8 October.

[3] . . Karlyn Borysenko. (2020). 'The Dark Side of #MeToo: What Happens When Men Are Falsely Accused'. "Forbes". (online edition). 12 February.

David Hench. (2010). 'Back Cove assault a hoax'. "Portland Press Herald". (online edition). 21 July.

Families Advocating for Campus Equality. facecampusequality.org

Eugene J. Kanin, Ph.D. (1994). 'False Rape Allegations'. "Archives of Sexual Behavior, Vol. 23, No. 1".

Lynn Vincent. (2019). 'False convictions, ruined lives'. "World Magazine" (online edition). 14 March.

[4] . . Monte Whaley. (2011). 'Sentencing disparities in child-sex-assault cases point to double standard'. "The Denver Post". (online edition). 20 August.

Stephanie S. Reidlinger. 'Bad Bad Teacher!: How Judicial Lenience, Cultural Ignorance, and Media Hype Have Inevitably Lead to Lighter Sentences, Underreporting and Glamorization of Female Sex Offenders'. "Regent University". (online document).

Bianca Buono, Katie Wilcox. (2019). 'Is there equal justice for teachers found guilty of sexual misconduct with a student?'. "12 News Investigations". (online edition). 9 September.

Jennifer L. Howell, Patrick M. Egan, Traci A Giuliano & Braden D. Ackley. (2011). 'The Reverse Double Standard in Perceptions of Student-Teacher Sexual Relationships: The Role of Gender, Initiation, and Power'. "The Journal of Social Psychology, 151:2, 180-200, DOI: 10.1080/00224540903510837.

[5] . . Amanda Devlin. (2017). 'Twisted Liar Caged, 'Attention-seeking' woman cost taxpayers £900,000 after falsely accusing 15 men of rape after lies exposed'. "The Sun".

(UK Online Edition).   25 August.

[6] . . Daniel Tepfer.   (2018).   'Yovino sentenced to 1 year in false rape case'.   "Ctpost".   (online edition).   24 August.

[7] . . Sam Wolfson.   (2018).   'The free-love cult that terrorized America - and became Netflix's latest must-watch'.   "The Guardian".   (online edition).   7 April.

[8] . . Harmeet Kaur.   (2019).   'Country band Confederate Railroad says it won't change it's name'.   "CNN Entertainment".   (online edition).   1 August.

[9] . . Allyson Chiu.   (2019).   'It snuck up on us: Scientists stunned by 'city killer' asteroid that just missed Earth'.   "The Washington Post".   (Morning Mix - online edition).   26 July.

[10] . . Matthew Green.   (2017).   'CHART: How Many Soldiers Died in Each U.S. War?'.   "KQED".   (The Lowdown - online edition).   25 May.

[11] . . Chris Gardner, Seth Abramovitch.   (2019).   'Jordan Peele on Making Movies After 'Us': "I Don't See Myself Casting a White Dude As the Lead"'.   "The Hollywood Reporter".   (online edition).   26 March.

[12] . . Herman Wong, Lindsey Bever.   (2017).   'I hope Trump is assassinated: A Missouri lawmaker faces mounting calls to resign after Facebook comment'.   "The Washington Post".   (online edition) 18 August.

[13] . . U.S. Attorney's Office, District of Nevada.   (2016).   'British Man Who Was Arrested At Trump Rally Sentenced On Weapon And Disruption Charges'.   "The United States

Attorney's Office, District of Nevada". (online report).   13 December.

[14] . . David Mack. (2017). 'Kathy Griffin Says She Went "Way Too Far" With Beheaded Donald Trump Photo'. "BuzzFeed News". (online edition).   31 May.

[15] . . Reid Nakamura. (2017). '7 People Defending Kathy Griffin After Decapitated Trump Photo Shoot (Photos)'. "The Wrap". (online edition).   1 June.

[16] . . Carrie Wittmer. (2018). 'Roseanne Barr is defending an episode of 'Roseanne' that people are calling Islamophobic'. "Business Insider". (online edition).   9 May.

[17] . . Geoff Edgers. (2019). 'Roseanne Barr just can't shut up'. "The Washington Post". (online edition).   21 March.

[18] . . Lilah Burke. (2020). 'Whose Space?'. "Inside Higher Ed". (online edition).   14 February.

All the Bible Passages from Chapter 11 on:

Bible Study Tools. biblestudytools.com/niv

[19] . . Alfred Konuwa. (2020). 'Stardom Wrestler Hana Kimura Dead At 22 Amid Cyberbullying'. "Forbes". (online edition).   23 May.

[20] . . I was going to put the exact sites that you could find the pornography videos on, but then I decided that, in the spirit of "Acceptance", I did not want to promote these videos. If you do a search on pornography video sites, though, you will find them.

[21] . . Hannah Ritchie. (2019). 'How many people die and how many are born each year?'. "Our World in Data". (online edition). 11 September.

[22] . . United States Nuclear Regulatory Commission. 'Backgrounder on Radioactive Waste'. (Fact Sheets).

[23] . . Melanie Flynn. (2019). 'Trophy hunting - can it really be justified by 'conservation benefits'?'. "The Conversation". (online edition). 10 October.

[24] . . History.com Editors. (2010 - updated 2018). 'Civilian Conservation Corps.' (online edition). 11 May - updated 17 October.

[25] . . United States Census Bureau. census.gov . (quick facts sheet).

[26] . . DW News Top Stories. (2019). 'Germany's crime rate fell to lowest level in decades in 2018'. (online edition). 4 February.

[27] . . # Kashyap Vyas. (2020). 'Bamboo as a Replacement to Steel'. "Interesting Engineering". (online edition). 11 January.

www.ingramcontent.com/pod-product-compliance
Lightning Source LLC
Chambersburg PA
CBHW072336090426
42741CB00012B/2810